CANADA BEFORE TELEVISION

Canada before Television

Radio, Taste, and the Struggle for Cultural Democracy

LEN KUFFERT

McGill-Queen's University Press
Montreal & Kingston • London • Chicago

ISBN 978-0-7735-4809-1 (cloth)
ISBN 978-0-7735-4810-7 (paper)
ISBN 978-0-7735-9980-2 (ePDF)
ISBN 978-0-7735-9981-9 (ePUB)

Legal deposit fourth quarter 2016
Bibliothèque nationale du Québec

Printed in Canada on acid-free paper that is 100% ancient forest free
(100% post-consumer recycled), processed chlorine free

McGill-Queen's University Press acknowledges the support of the Canada
Council for the Arts for our publishing program. We also acknowledge the
financial support of the Government of Canada through the Canada Book
Fund for our publishing activities.

Library and Archives Canada Cataloguing in Publication

Kuffert, L. B. (Leonard B.), author
    Canada before television: radio, taste, and the struggle for cultural democracy/
Len Kuffert.

    Includes bibliographical references and index.
    Issued in print and electronic formats.
    ISBN 978-0-7735-4809-1 (cloth). – ISBN 978-0-7735-4810-7 (paperback). –
ISBN 978-0-7735-9980-2 (ePDF). – ISBN 978-0-7735-9981-9 (ePUB)

    1. Radio broadcasting – Canada – History. 2. Radio broadcasting – Social
aspects – Canada. 3. Radio broadcasting policy – Canada – History. 4. Public
radio – Social aspects – Canada. 5. Radio audiences – Canada. 6. Radio
programs – Canada – Rating – History. I. Title.

HE8699.C2K87 2016   384.540971   C2016-903921-8
                                               C2016-903922-6

This book was typeset by Marquis Interscript in 10.5/13 Sabon.

Contents

Acknowledgments

Writing a book is, for the most part, a solitary activity, but I happily acknowledge a number of debts. I extend thanks to the University of Manitoba History Department, to colleagues, and to the department heads (Mary Kinnear, Mark Gabbert, and Tina Chen), all of whom have been patient with this project's long gestation. The University of Manitoba and the Social Sciences and Humanities Research Council of Canada have funded research trips and assistance. The Kaufman-Silverberg Library in Winnipeg has been a quiet writing spot. Everyone at Villa I Tatti made a modernist as welcome as could be. As usual, archivists have been crucial collaborators: I thank Els Boonen at the BBC Written Archives Centre, a rotating cast at Library and Archives Canada who were continually required to do more with less, Harry Miller at the Wisconsin Historical Society, and the late Jessica Lambert Riddell for letting me read the papers of her father, R.S. Lambert. For their assistance putting physical and virtual stacks of research materials in order, thanks to research assistants Greg Di Cresce, Alanna MacIsaac, Heather Pitcher, Jessica Storoschuk, and Krista Walters. Andrea Smorang prepared the bibliography.

Even if they helped me a long time ago, or didn't notice they were helping, various colleagues, students, and non-historians have provided commentary on bits of the book, shared their own manuscripts (thanks, Simon), bounced ideas around, listened, invited me to departmental colloquia, or otherwise pushed the enterprise forward. Thanks to Jim Baughman, Anna Bensted, Jeff Brison, Lori Brown, David Carr, Nancy Christie, Debra Rae Cohen, Darin Currie, Filippo De Vivo, Michel Ducharme, Chris Dummitt, Ilaria Favretto, Giovanna Franci, Barry Ferguson, Gerry Friesen,

Michael Gauvreau, David Goodman, David Hendy, Cecelia Hewlett, Michele Hilmes, Derek Hum, Russ Johnston, Kate Lacey, Christie Macdonald, Bob McDonald, David McDonald, Anne MacLennan, Anthony McNicholas, Gary Miedema, Jorge Nállim, Derek Neal, Susan Neylan, Siân Nicholas, Scott Palmer, Simon Potter, Elena Razlogova, Michael Rocke, Phil St John, Maria Scott, Josh Skaller, Greg Smith, Susan Smulyan, Sadeesh Srinathan, Nick Terpstra, Paul Thomas, Erik Thomson, Mary Vipond, David Watt, Jeff Webb, Johannes Wolfart, and the late Shona Kelly Wray. Students in my Canadian cultural history, historical methods, and history of broadcasting seminars were invaluable, if sometimes sleepy, sounding boards. Jonathan Crago at McGill-Queen's University Press and the Press's anonymous readers have made this a more focused and balanced work. Joanne Richardson straightened a great deal out as copy editor.

Thanks to my mother, Darlene, and parents-in-law, Doug and Olive Cossar, for their continuing confidence and support. My father Leo didn't live to see this work finished but continued to inspire it. Much love and gratitude to Roisin Cossar for all that she is and all that she does to make my life the one I want to live. This "overdue book" is for our intensely loved children, Anna and Eamon, with the wish that they'll always have more enlightening and entertaining reading material at hand. In a true cultural democracy, they will.

LBK, Winnipeg, 2015

Abbreviations

ABC	Australian Broadcasting Corporation
BBC	British Broadcasting Corporation
BBG	Board of Broadcast Governors
CAB	Canadian Association of Broadcasters
CBC	Canadian Broadcasting Corporation
CBS	Columbia Broadcasting System
CNR	Canadian National Railways
CPR	Canadian Pacific Railway
CRBC	Canadian Radio Broadcasting Commission
CRL	Canadian Radio League
FCC	Federal Communications Commission
FRC	Federal Radio Commission
LAC	Library and Archives Canada
NAB	National Association of Broadcasters
NBC	National Broadcasting Company
NCEC	National Council of Education of Canada
RCA	Radio Corporation of America
TSO	Toronto Symphony Orchestra
UBC	University of British Columbia

CANADA BEFORE TELEVISION

When I was in public school I had a very dear friend whose mother was a hypnotist. She used to tell me the most amazing stories of the things her mother could do to people. In the same breath she used to tell me about a little machine her father made which could pick up music and conversation right out of the air – no wires like the telephone – right out of the air. And I can remember thinking her father must be almost as queer as her mother – until I learned that the machine was a radio – that other people had them – and it was something more or less respectable.

Marjorie McEnaney, "E.A. Corbett –
Views on Radio," 1951, LAC,
Marjorie McEnaney Papers, vol. 1

"Fashioned as We Go Along"

Within a handful of years after the First World War, broadcasters around the world transformed radio technology from a hobby and shipboard lifeline into an unstoppable medium of mass communication. Radio programs became public squares, theatres, and concert venues for listeners, who could tune in by the thousand or by themselves. Decades later, well after its moment as the flag-bearer for broadcasting, radio continues to cheat its long-prophesied death, and its history intersects with a wide range of other human stories, collective and individual. As one of those individuals, it's fair to say that radio transformed my youth, bringing voices and music from people unlikely to visit our village in the Saskatchewan parkland. Country music, Top 40, local swap shows, farm reports, and obituaries dominated the daytime. Distant American powerhouses and a faint Canadian Broadcasting Corporation (CBC) FM signal rewarded the night listener with odd accents, sports not played on ice, religious testimony, and music beyond the margins of "popularity."[1] And then there was the world of shortwave. Around the same time – to have blurted this out as a teenager would have guaranteed a pummelling – I became fascinated with how people evaluate their cultural environments and how they indicate preferences. *Taste* – our sense of what is or isn't pleasing or appropriate for us or for others – is a thorny subject because we behave as though these choices and alignments signify much about our inner selves. What we like is only part of the picture. We – listeners, viewers, *consumers* – hardly ever recognize that much of what we can choose from is pre-selected. Taste labels like "baroque," "redneck," or "modern" are a useful form of shorthand, categorizing what we can own, use, or experience, but few of those categories are of our own making. In practical terms, the categories we create for ourselves boil down to "for me" or "not for me," and we have long subscribed to a similarly dualistic view of how cultural outlets (including broadcasters) serve the audiences they cultivate. Legend has it that one faction believes that what it considers to be best is best for everyone and that this faction wants those works or experiences to be celebrated and reproduced so that everyone can come to appreciate them. Others defend the notion that people simply like what they like and that giving people what they like is an honest day's work. If you listen closely, you may hear sociologists yawning or others invoking Matthew Arnold or Raymond Williams, just two of many who have weighed in on questions of preference and cultural value.[2]

While my long-held fascination isn't novel, applying it to the study of Canada's broadcasting history seems especially worthwhile at a moment when much older preconceptions about broadcasting, taste, and the popular will continue to drive the conversation about what sort of system best suits a place like Canada. By uniting here to take a historical view of programming during broadcasting's earliest years, we have nothing to lose but our suppositions.

So, this is a history of what people living and working in a particular place and time said and did about broadcasting and radio programs. In the chapters that follow, I argue that in anglophone Canada, before television came to dominate, public broadcasters worked to realize a democratic vision of broadcasting, a vision in which programs appealing to mainstream tastes remained prominent but no listeners were "left behind." The riddles of which kinds of programs people liked and how listeners could be engaged by radio inspired a variety of solutions based on assumptions about listeners' habits and dispositions. Different ways of making radio programming reflected sharp differences of opinion about radio's purpose and about the world outside the listening parlour. All of this took place against the backdrop of domestic and international conditions and relationships, with contemporary values and a perpetual challenge to the public broadcasting model also informing broadcasters' ideals and actions. Operating within a mixed public/private system, CBC staff were often delighted or frustrated by programming that drew big audiences, but they sought to expand listeners' access to unfamiliar programs, not to constrain listeners' choices. Although they didn't believe that the commercial radio market presented a faithful picture of listeners' desires, they neither denied its existence nor sought to erase it. While commercial broadcasters understandably spent much less time and effort pursuing that sort of vision, they were nonetheless active in producing and promoting their programs and steadfastly represented what became the more orthodox way of making radio in North America. They insisted that listener preferences – listener agency in a dynamic industry – drove their programming choices. Regardless of who made them, radio programs deserve our attention because they were as malleable and historically contingent as anything else, and they could be made to serve almost any purpose. Whether undertaken for riches or righteousness, broadcasting quickly transcended its own novelty, drawing on established worldviews and tastes, and, in their different ways, broadcasters maintained the age-old conviction that most people would follow where they were led.

CENTRAL QUESTIONS, FOCAL POINTS, AND RADIO'S IMPACT

English-speaking Canada, from broadcasting's genesis in the early 1920s through to the mid-1950s,[3] was a society changing rapidly along with the broadcasting industry. By about 1956, television had taken root in most urban areas, radio programs that were going to migrate to the newer medium had done so, and a second Royal Commission on broadcasting was revving up.[4] Over a little more than a generation, radio grew up in plain public view, leaving behind evidence that encourages historians to engage with questions like: How did broadcasters allow for audience tastes as shows were planned, produced, and scheduled? Did influences from elsewhere make much difference? Why were certain programs thought to be in "good taste" or "bad taste," and how were these regulated? How did differing notions of "what the public wants" relate to programming strategies and choices? We can generate some answers to these questions even though the earliest one-third of this period is not well represented in the written record and even though privately owned stations did not tend to make their operational files accessible to the contemporary public, let alone preserve them systematically for any of us decades later. This has not prevented some useful work from being done on individual commercial stations and personalities.[5] Still, much of the evidence available comes from the later 1920s onward and blooms mightily with the creation of the CBC in 1936, thanks to the corporation's habit of keeping bits of paper, its two decades as Canada's broadcast regulator, and its tendency to exchange ideas and programs with other pack-rat broadcasting entities. As a consequence, the main themes and episodes here reflect what people at the CBC overheard, responded to, considered noteworthy, wrote, said, or did. This is probably fitting as the CBC was the institution at the centre of broadcasting's development and still draws its share of praise and disapproval.

While Canadian broadcasters and station owners came disproportionately from middle-class, white, European, or British origins, not everyone who enters or influences this story was an English-speaking Canadian. Some spoke other languages (usually French) and others lived elsewhere or identified with different places (usually the United States or various parts of the British Commonwealth). Some were silent initially and contributed later on, some spoke up early, never to be heard again. Not all of them addressed taste explicitly when they spoke or wrote about broadcasting, and some might not have intended to address it, even implicitly. You might say all of this is heading in a familiar direction: historian stakes out an interest in the activities of people who did a limited set of things, often in subtle and interconnected ways. So much for the grand narrative. Yet those same limits can help us to understand how a particular historical setting affected broadcasting and was in turn affected by it. We can address the work of program-making in general terms, even as we examine it in a narrower context.

Broadcasting inaugurated a new kind of social space in the 1920s, one in which the exchange of ideas was not always one-way or instant, and in which those making programs did not have a clear sense of what broadcasting would be like in ten years or even ten months. As educator Martyn Estall reminded Canadians in 1945: "technical change does not of itself determine the social purpose it is put to."[6] Seventy years later, we need reminding that programs, and the acts of producing and consuming them, were ways of working out what broadcasting was supposed to do as well as tracing contemporary thought or action. Listeners or viewers can take programs at face value or engage more critically with what makes it to air, but all of the ways programming can affect audiences reflect the larger environment into which they are sent. Media use, as Susanne Eichner argues, is "socially integrated," but the media also "leave their lanes, they don't disappear entirely when we switch off."[7] Even more elegantly, Paddy Scannell writes that the broadcast media in modern societies "disclose the everyday historicality of the world every day."[8] In the case of Canadian radio, broadcasters' efforts to fill schedules with enjoyable, enlightening, or informative programming were efforts to understand, adjust to, or even subtly alter the social and cultural environments into which programs were sent. Though we now have more ways to deliver programs, the tasks of broadcasting remain the same: alleviating boredom and ignorance, giving listeners or viewers a break or a challenge, and representing the world both as it is and as we might have it. The historical example of early Canadian radio programming is in this way both rooted in the past and relevant to our own contemporary surroundings, regardless of which medium we now attend to the most and how many stations, channels, sites, or services are offered.

While radio broadcasts were created for public consumption, most of the exchanges that went into their making happened between networks, station managers, producers, advertising agencies, and performers. Decisions about what should go on the air most frequently involved estimating listeners' appetite for one sort of program or another and creating and arranging programs to suit the vague demands of prevailing cultural norms or the rhythms of daily life. If, as the saying roughly goes, "there's no accounting for taste," how and why did a variety of people in the broadcasting field spend time, money, and effort trying to do exactly that? For some, there was profit to be made providing entertaining shows for listeners. For others, radio was where the recurring questions of *which* programs should be created and *how* they should be created were the priority. While broadcasters certainly lumped listeners together into audiences to justify the effort and expense of making programs of one sort or another, listeners also occasionally spoke up about what they heard. In 1956, with radio by then squarely in television's spreading shadow, a listener wrote to the CBC's Frank Willis, noting the pains that the corporation had taken to swim against the radio industry's tide for twenty years and admitting that the CBC's programming had changed his leisure life. The retired railway worker put the problem of taste in terms of familiarity and variety, evoking our tastes in food to drive home his point: "People like the best thing they know, no matter whether its [sic] a book or a beef-steak. The people who choose the poorest quality almost certainly never had much of a shot at anything else."[9] Giving them "a shot at anything else" meant making programs for someone other than the audiences already groomed to listen.

Although we have the benefit of (blurry) hindsight, historians are not the only ones able to recognize the power of broadcast music or advertisements to shape local, national, or international cultures. Nor are we alone in recognizing that the whole process could be ponderously slow and often unpredictable. It was plain that broadcasting was an evolving industry, and the consequences of what went on the air might not be immediately felt. One group, accused of promoting cultural "uplift" (and almost always pleading guilty), sought to broaden the range of programming available, knowing its programs would never capture huge audiences. Yet, for this group, capturing huge audiences was never the point. Gladstone Murray, the first general manager of the CBC, was a member of this group, though hardly its patron and hardly a saint. Having worked in press and public relations since the Great War, he harboured strong instincts about broadcasting's role. "To attempt to give the public what it wants by dishing up trash," he said, "is a fundamental fallacy long ago exploded in the experience of both radio and the press. The highest measure of success is achieved by appreciation, not by depreciation. Public taste is fashioned as we go along."[10] By "we," Murray meant *everyone* – listeners, broadcasters, performers – even critics like the American Deems Taylor, who acknowledged that, without a variety of programs, some of which listeners might not like, broadcasting would never reach its long-term potential.[11] Its potential was cultural democracy, a state outside *the* state and our customary political alignments, a state in which people stood a chance of hearing programs that they genuinely enjoyed, not just those they tolerated.

THE BASICS: PUBLIC, PRIVATE/COMMERCIAL, AND PUBLIC SERVICE

Throughout this book, I make frequent references to two modes of control over broadcasting, modes that influenced programming philosophies and choices. Here, and throughout the following chapters, I relate these modes to broadcasting fundamentals, which will be familiar to students of broadcasting history. For some readers, however, much of what I have to say about the ways broadcasting works will probably clash with what someone told you in a pub or on an internet forum, so saying it now should be well justified. The two modes are: (1) *public*, whereby broadcasters choose what you hear and charge you for the privilege and (2) *private* or *commercial*, whereby broadcasters choose what you hear and charge you for the privilege. Let's try that again, because there are definitely better ways of distinguishing these. A commercial or private broadcaster is an individual or group operating a station or stations. These operators make a profit by selling airtime above cost to others wishing to broadcast or, more often, by selling (again above cost) the opportunity to sponsor programs or advertise during programs that the station, network, or some third party produces. Profit depends on how large an audience can be drawn to a program because without programs that promise to have general appeal, broadcasters cannot "sell the audience" ahead of time to advertisers who want to reach consumers. In the late 1920s, a National Broadcasting Company (NBC) executive warned a Toronto advertising agent that this was a delicate business, noting "'tuning out' is so easy that it is safe to say that Radio comes into the home only upon invitation, and that no program is listened to unless the listener has interest and appreciation already aroused."[12] Commercial broadcasting, on both radio and television, has provided memorable, innovative, controversial, and edifying programming. On the other side of the fence, public broadcasters do not operate as for-profit enterprises, even though they need revenue to continue broadcasting. Such revenue comes from donations or bequests (the most likely sources in the United States), from taxation or licence fees (most prevalent in Europe and in Canada/Commonwealth both now and formerly), and from advertising (Canadian and much other public television, and some radio programs). This usually means public broadcasters do not need to pay *as much* immediate attention to the likelihood of a program becoming a "hit" and can set their schedules with a freer hand, sometimes producing shows that would attract few (if any) advertisers.[13] Public broadcasting, on both radio and television, has provided memorable, innovative, controversial, and edifying programming.

In the early days of broadcasting, commercial radio people looked to the models of print advertising and theatre production – proven methods for booking talent and making money – to guess what might appeal to listeners. Margaret McFadden's reading of early American broadcasting, that "producers turned to familiar popular performers and writers from vaudeville, musical comedy, and films,"[14] applies just as well to Canada, where even performers in small centres found their careers (if not their finances) boosted by broadcasting opportunities. Because they were drawing on what "sold" before the advent of radio, commercial broadcasters came to be confident in the marketplace of listener choice – almost fatalistic in their belief that whichever programs became "popular" were the right ones to make. They were the providers of entertainment and diversion for listeners beset by other obligations, and the matchmakers helping weary consumers spend their money more wisely on sponsors' products. On the other hand, public broadcasting's advocates considered radio too influential to cede entirely to their commercial counterparts. CBC personnel did not deny that they played a role in choosing or shaping what went on the air or that they thought some programs better than others. They wanted listeners to know that choices existed, and that it was impossible to avoid curation, no matter which audiences broadcasters wanted to reach. There were only so many pages in a magazine, so many movie screens, so many clear frequencies, and so many hours in a day. They, too, were guessing at what listeners would appreciate.

Public broadcasting can sometimes be conflated with *public service broadcasting*, with the misleading implication that only public broadcasters are capable of providing a service to the public. This is not strictly the case as both commercial and public broadcasters serve listeners who receive some benefit (entertainment, information, companionship) from their programming.[15] Public broadcasting is primarily a method of delivering programs, and public service broadcasting is an act that can be performed by any broadcaster who so chooses. Historically, commercial broadcasters have defined only a small portion of their output, usually airtime for which they are not paid, as public service. Public broadcasters, however, have tended to view their entire schedules as in the public service because even if some of their broadcasts generated advertising revenue, this revenue was ploughed back into serving the public by improving facilities, hiring more staff, or more often by creating or acquiring, and then emitting, a more ambitious slate of programming. The most relevant differences between public and private usually lay in each model's attitude towards minority or marginal tastes and the level of attention each paid to the ongoing impact of programming. Private broadcasters dependent on advertising astutely saw it as imprudent business practice to tinker with a successful machine by experimenting with new sorts of programming, so they rarely did that. Public broadcasters fretted often about listeners and what to give them, sometimes painting commercial broadcasters as villains for pursuing profits by making presumptions about audience desires or needs. Each type of broadcaster claimed it had the interests of listeners in mind and strove to do right by these people who trusted "the radio" – a home appliance as much as it was a succession of programs – to entertain them. Yet, as we have suspected in fields like literature for some time, listener preferences and audience bonds were difficult to pin down.[16]

Although it has often been accused of "ramming culture down people's throats," the public broadcasting model does not inherently restrict choice. Indeed, it runs counter to the commercial tendency to create only programs that advertisers will underwrite. In their own ways, both the public and the commercial models of broadcasting can be said to reflect listeners' preferences, and both fail to give listeners enough options. As a listener, it is difficult to sympathize wholly with either model. Private broadcasters claimed to be serving the public by tailoring their output to suit what most people had previously tuned in to hear. On the surface, this approach made perfect sense. Why not make programs to appeal to the largest group of listeners? Wasn't strict attention to audience ratings the way to ensure that you were giving the biggest part of the audience what it wanted? Public broadcasters countered: How would a broadcaster know that its programming was what the majority of people wanted? Do people tune in to a program because they like it, because it is on the air, or because it is all they have been exposed to in the past? What about taste minorities? While online services have lately made great strides in delivering content on demand to individuals based on their previously consumed music, talk, or video choices, a *broadcast* service able to predict individual listeners' moment-to-moment desires and deliver the appropriate content was, and remains, impossible to offer. Economist Joel Waldfogel deftly sums up the problem of individual tastes in a market setting, noting: "my preferences alone do not determine what's available to me."[17]

In Canada, Parliament put public broadcasters in charge of regulating the industry in the early 1930s. The public side got an early boost from radio licence fees, but, in the long term, it did not fare so well in the rhetorical battle over why it came to occupy a position of some authority. In North America, commercial broadcasting became the "normal" or "natural" mode, while the CBC was sometimes described as a "government monopoly." This was a thorough (and probably wilful) misunderstanding of public broadcasting's role and function, but it was quite handy for those hoping to convince Canadians that they were best served by private stations. More recently, even in Europe, where it has been more central to listeners' and viewers' experience, some regard public broadcasting as some-how an unnatural or special state of operation.[18] During radio's hey-day, public broadcasters sometimes trained the lens of legitimacy on private broadcasting, challenging commercial operators' motives and methods. This happens only rarely now. While differences in broad-casting style or purpose make for a more dramatic story, with more easily identifiable antagonists (effete "socialists" versus philistine broadcasting "barons"), the contrast between the commercial and public approaches should not be overdrawn to the point at which it bankrupts our understanding of broadcasting's fluidity or the accom-modations made in order to further the industry as a whole.

BROADCASTING AND (CANADIAN) HISTORY

British broadcasting historian Asa Briggs writes that "to try to write the history of broadcasting in the twentieth century is in a sense to try to write the history of everything else." However convenient or daunting this formulation seems, in order to focus on programming and taste, this book heeds Ian McKay's advice to "abandon ... syn-thesis as an unattainable goal" and offers neither a comprehensive soup-to-nuts history of Canadian radio nor a close study of particu-lar programs on the air.[19] While broadcasters consistently cited lis-teners as the reason programs were made, they fell well short of gathering sizable samples of listener opinion on particular programs or on the output of whole stations or networks. Consequently, the evidence available is largely from the production side, so extended commentary here on listener reaction would be tenuously informed as well as tentative. There is, however, a case to be made for taking on a Briggs-like burden in that programming needs to be considered as part of a larger "ecology," as part of its environment. In order to have my discussions of such topics as music and programming regu-lations make sense, it is necessary to describe the conditions under which broadcasters operated – for instance, the mixed character of the Canadian broadcasting system and the continual and powerful presence of American programming. I remind readers of such conditions in each chapter because, to take those two examples, the public-private contest plays into much that is done in the name of the audience, and everyone (yes, everyone) compared programs wafting in over the border to the output of Canadian stations. Those were not Canadian radio broadcasting's only important historical features.

Though debates about programming remain relevant to the more crowded media sphere today, and long-term comparisons might be in order, radio – more particularly radio in the era before television arrived for most Canadians – is the focus here. Peter Lewis notes correctly that radio has for a long time held a "relatively powerless cultural position compared to television,"[20] but this was not always the case. Radio as a technology enabled instant broadcast communication, and historians need to continue treating it as a distinct space with its own problems and possibilities, not simply as a competitor for newspapers and magazines or as the herald of television. To look (figuratively) at television here would add little. Like radio in its infancy, TV in the 1950s was a new medium but a *differently captivating* one. It also cost a great deal more to produce, and this was an abiding obstacle for smaller local broadcasters. Remember them? I barely do, as so many have been swallowed up by larger media concerns, never to re-emerge. Most relevantly for this study, however, the question of how broadcasters and listeners, performers and regulators, dealt with taste in broadcast programs had already been under consideration for years during radio's period of "solitary grandeur,"[21] and this question could not be "un-asked" in order to be "re-asked" when TV came along. Most categories of programming that existed on radio shifted to TV, and hence it would be difficult to suggest that entirely new *patterns* of accounting for listener tastes arose with television. Michele Hilmes says it better: "Attention turned to the new visual and aural medium, which hit the ground running not only with the industrial structure, textual forms, and audience formations inspired by radio but also with the accumulating weight of sociological study and critical concern."[22]

Nor should we be dissuaded from studying the actions or interpreting the motives of people who made radio programs instead of felling trees or fighting wars. Cultural history is real history, and it permeates other fields, just as they permeate cultural history. Perhaps this was what Briggs was getting at. Jackson Lears writes in his history of American advertising that "what seem like ephemeral changes in visual fashion turn out, on closer inspection[,] to be struggles over ways of being in the world."[23] The same idea is no less applicable to fashions and philosophies in what could be heard but not seen. We see, more often in historical work about other places, some examples of how early broadcasting fit into the broader and more complex historical picture. David Cardiff, to take just one example, though ostensibly studying how programming was financed, shows how British broadcasting drew together "a range of cultural forms" like music, drama, and commentary that had previously been thought of as distinct from each other.[24] Sure, we want to know how the bills were paid, but the cultural repercussions of running a station or network are also there to be observed. Histories that ignore, or understate, how immersed broadcasting was in its own times can lead us to likewise understate its relevance as both a venue for political and social discourse and as a weapon in the great and small battles over what we expect of individuals or even nations.

Keeping the interplay between programs and their "surroundings" in mind, how can we most sensitively write about the history of radio in Canada? Despite robust interest in the medium in the United States and elsewhere, the number of academic historians and students pursuing research on Canadian radio has remained small. In the 1960s, the first historians of broadcasting in Canada did a good job of outlining, from the perspective of power politics and money, why and how we came to have the system we do.[25] Those early surveys celebrated the CBC's centrality in a mature broadcasting industry and sought to explain or justify its hybrid character as the outcome of a series of negotiations between established interests and the cultural vision of a few well-connected dreamers. In a country where histories of colonial, and later federal or provincial, initiatives (fishing, fur trading, railway building, "medicaring") have cast the state as an agent of sustenance and stability, just telling the story of how broadcasting came to play a similar binding role seemed definitive, and the idea that there wasn't much more to add may have intimidated other historians for a while. Openings for revision and reconsideration nonetheless existed, and historians, along with committed amateurs, exploited them. Private stations occupied the margins of the early narratives, and a pair of commercial broadcasting veterans memorably set about rectifying this injustice through memoir.[26] Policy, broadcasting technology, and the public versus private broadcasting contest received more attention, and we also heard about some of the dynamic personalities whose presence on air or behind the scenes pushed Canadian radio forward.[27] Beginning in the 1980s, embarking from the established political economy narrative, students of broadcasting history showed us not only how early broadcasters were neither as noble nor as grasping as our stereotypes of them indicate but also how to position the history of broadcasting in Canada as being in dialogue with broadcasting, media, and cultural histories elsewhere. While it was hardly the "gold rush" we associate with writing a number of long-ignored people back into Canada's history, topics like music programming, commemorative broadcasts, and the social utility of radio got some of the attention they had been lacking.[28] At the head of that pack, the best monograph studies treating radio in Canada are both now more than twenty years old, but they remain pillars because they introduced us to a more inclusive story, one in which it was previously difficult to recognize human beings.[29] More recently, my Manitoba colleague Gerry Friesen, in *Citizens and Nation*, argues that Canada's ordinary and unsung humans shared a "history built on communication and culture" in which radio played an important role.[30] Despite such moves towards balance and a holistic view of broadcasting as a vehicle for social (and national) cohesion, we still know little about how the structure and culture of broadcasting in Canada affected what listeners got over the radio.

So, instead of treating governments and businesses as the only historical agents, I offer a history of radio broadcasting in Canada, but this story emerges from the apparently prosaic exchanges over things like what sort of radio programming to make. Programming was certainly symbolic, for instance carrying the burden of Empire as it brought Canadians word-pictures of Royal Tours,[31] but broadcasting's "harder" links with capital and the state have remained relevant. To discuss programming without reference to these elements of the story would be to deprive ourselves of important figurative and materialist perspectives. However, we can study programming as the foremost "product" of broadcasters' and performers' imaginations without denying or dismantling the existing historiography. The evidence I present here shows that we can trace how radio came to be seen as an instrument for what Marc Raboy calls "communication in the public good" and that ideas about what made for good radio involved much conjecture about listeners, their desires, and their communal aspirations.[32] This conjecture revealed conflicts over taste in programming and what serving listeners meant.

CULTURAL DEMOCRACY AND THE RESISTIBLE LURE
OF NATIONALISM

The "cultural democracy" in this book's title refers to an environment in which minority or marginal cultures need not fear being silenced or ignored, even if they implicitly or explicitly stand opposed to or apart from mainstream or "popular" practices. In a cultural democracy, no elections take place to seat a cultural parliament tasked with protecting or promoting the various forms and permutations of culture that people can appreciate or to which they can gain access. Cultural democrats might even act alone or in small groups, independent from the state itself but needing public support to mount exhibitions, make films, or broadcast programming. For broadcasters in particular, practising cultural democracy requires paying attention to what sorts of programming are in danger of being left out and requires that those programs be afforded a place in the schedule, even if not a prominent one. Cultural democrats acknowledge that raw numbers like ratings and audience estimates can indicate what audiences will put up with, but raw numbers matter little to cultural democrats because they are acutely aware that what is raw can generally be "cooked." To use an electoral analogy, cultural democracy looks more like proportional representation than like our more familiar first-past-the-post system. In a cultural democracy, winners (or leaders) do not take all.

While cultural democracy may also suggest a kind of loose system in which popular preferences are free to emerge, the nature of broadcasting as a costly pursuit carried on through a limited number of channels demands that broadcasters either assume control over what gets broadcast or risk losing their investments and wasting their efforts. Because of the expense involved in making programs and the accompanying tendency of broadcasters to make only modest innovations based on the perceived public appetite for shows already aired, there is no level playing field on which programs stand or fall on their own merits. These factors favour larger broadcasting organizations. Control over broadcasting can be achieved through political or economic means. Repressive governments can place strict controls on both public and commercial broadcasting, just as big advertisers and near-monopolies can steer entire networks. In either of those scenarios, the results will be predictably undemocratic if one or more audiences are "written off" as unrepresentative or unworthy of attention. A common belief about broadcasting in

North America, even as the industry developed, was that it was already democratic by virtue of arising inside a nominally democratic political environment. Things were not so simple. Tailoring broadcast programming to serve the largest possible audiences is nominally democratic in the sense that it strives to serve an imagined majority, but chasing this illusory group erodes cultural democracy as effectively as does trying to "civilize" listeners by depriving them of programs they might genuinely enjoy.

While we can't assume that listeners passively consumed broadcasts and were therefore utterly at the mercy of broadcasters' aesthetic or ideological projects, we should note once again that those on the production side controlled the supply of programming. Just as broadcasters worked hard to satisfy listeners' apparent appetites by aiming for the "popular," so attempts to diversify programming were attempts to let listeners find the sort of programming that satisfied them. Canada thus provided a good historical example of the contest between two powerful impulses, both of which claimed to be democratic in their essence. In Marc Raboy's view, a national broadcasting policy emerged in which both commercial broadcasters and the public system played negative roles, resulting in a series of "missed opportunities" to realize "alternatives to both state and market conceptions of a 'mass' public, alternatives that could be the basis for democratic uses of broadcasting and communications."[33] To Raboy's list of missed opportunities we can add the opportunity to serve Indigenous listeners, who were an ignored minority long before broadcasting began. Despite such stumblings, even those whose main goal was representing Canada as a unified entity benefitted from a mixed broadcasting system that, paradoxically, promoted a kind of cultural democracy by broadcasting hit shows *and* by defending commercially marginalized (usually Canadian) programming.

While it's hardly a revelation that such hopeful nationalists intended the CBC to be the "voice of Canada on the air" even before the CBC came into being, and that they wanted broadcasting to boost a "nascent national self-consciousness,"[34] Canada was not alone in this regard. Eager boosters in various countries seemed to agree with English public relations pioneer Stephen Tallents' declaration: "No civilized country can to-day afford either to neglect the projection of its national personality or to resign its projection to others."[35] We see nationalism at work more clearly, perhaps, in the promotion of national art traditions through museums and such physically "inhabitable" institutions.[36] Unlike museums, radio programs had to be remade weekly or even daily, and they relied, for at least some of their appeal, on listeners' remembrance of pleasures past. The "romantic nationalist vision" and what the CBC's Charles Jennings calls "a sense of mission" were never concealed from listeners or CBC staff whose works were part of the project.[37] In contrast, private broadcasters in Canada, according to BBC "spies" in the later 1940s, "denied that they had any obligation to use the medium in any way to promote a national consciousness."[38]

At the same time, British and American influences on Canadian broadcasting complicated the way programs were made in Canada. Hilmes makes a strong case for viewing those two broadcasting systems not as representatives of nation-states but, rather, as in dialogue with each other. It would be a stretch to say that Canadian radio people participated decisively and consistently in that conversation, but it was a conversation they could not help overhearing, and it was a conversation that incorporated itself into the way that Canadian radio related to American and British broadcasters and programming. Attempting to trace how significant such influences were and following the debate over whether radio should lead public tastes or follow them lifts a corner of the mantle thrown over Canadian broadcasting by a fascination with political economy and a tendency to view broadcasting's development primarily through the lens of nationalism.[39] By now, we understand pretty well that bringing radio to a place like Canada required considerable faith, negotiation, and, not least, a conviction that the future of the nation as culturally distinct hung in the balance. We see progress in recent work, such as Marco Adria's, which frames radio (and other media) as technologies having varied repercussions for national identity.[40] Power and the nation are undoubtedly useful frameworks for the study of history, yet these cannot be the only frameworks for understanding an industry whose most readily appreciable outputs were art forms such as music, drama, and commentary. While nationalism remains a constant presence in Canada's broadcasting history, and must figure centrally in any broad surveys of the system's development, here it is set largely aside in favour of tackling questions about taste in programming and how broadcasters created it.

TASTE

Examining taste in programming is a way of approaching "bigger" topics, both within the history of broadcasting and beyond it.

Scholars of media, frequently operating under the umbrella of cultural studies and exploring contemporary trends, emphasize taste distinctions. Divisions between "pop" media and more earnest forms of programming provide ready structures as we seek to clarify how societies and subcultures consolidated themselves and changed over time.[41] Radio examples feature among such projects. Hilmes's work on the Anglo-American broadcasting relationship shows that, although the relationship was complex, broadcasters behaved as though their respective nations could be almost effortlessly defined or even strengthened through broadcasting certain *sorts* of programs.[42] Robert McChesney continually addresses democracy and its connection to broadcasting – but from the angle of civil liberties and political pressure applied by commercial interests to take control of American radio. He identifies "popular" radio in the United States as an exercise in deference to power elites and as a failure of civic will to do the "right thing," and similar failures have been noted in Canada. Kate Lacey contends that some broadcasters hoped to discover what the most "radiogenic" sorts of programming were, and hoped (often naively) to "grip" listeners with these productions. Elena Razlogova argues that the American public played a prominent role in shaping programming through its suggestions and complaints.[43] I would add, echoing studies of varying scope, that programming itself was a contested space and that not all listeners were passive.[44] Taken together, works like these show us that congresses and parliaments may have been places for the disposition of power, but the air was a place for the disposition of meaning and a more subtle exercise of power. For this reason, what went on the air mattered, and perceptions of public taste helped broadcasters build their schedules.

The concept of "taste" itself, including aesthetic evaluation and categorization, has a long and complex history, often linked in the modern period with Immanuel Kant and with later participants in the debate over aesthetics.[45] Nineteenth-century innovations, from cheaper textiles to the march of literacy, bled into the twentieth century and exposed larger swathes of Western and non-Western people to both tangible and intangible goods to be adored, rejected, or tolerated. Notions of worthy and unworthy pursuits flourished in the Victorian age and in the long recovery from it.[46] In 1950, the Royal Bank of Canada's *Monthly Letter* quoted John Ruskin's pithy definition of taste: "the instinctive and instant preferring of one material object to another without any obvious reason."[47] Confining taste to household objects would never do when there were broadcasts and films to consider, let alone plays and concerts. Thanks largely to sociologists interested in taste as a mode of social differentiation, a number of studies enrich our understanding of how and why people choose/consume particular goods, services, or artistic creations. While class is one of the more obvious factors intersecting with taste, we should acknowledge that even such factors as where one lived might affect tastes, especially when we are discussing taste in radio programming, which required a clear signal for enjoyment. Political culture also mattered, as Jukka Gronow's work on taste and the consumption of luxury goods in the Soviet Union makes clear.[48] Other historians and scholars in sociology, anthropology, philosophy, cultural studies, and literature have waded in to help us think about high and low culture, the implications of aesthetic choices, prejudices and their subtle spread, canons, rebellion, status anxiety, and what Richard Ohmann calls "the simultaneous exploitation and creation of taste."[49]

Tastes in radio programming shifted just as did tastes in clothing and could be shaped thanks to the novelty of the medium and to the intimate appeal of the broadcast voice. Tastes for certain types of programming could only be created and maintained if those programs were made in the first place, and if they continued to be made. Because the number of stations and the often prohibitive cost of broadcasting limited opportunities to exert this level of control over listeners' expectations for radio, a sort of magical thinking surrounded the radio industry in its earliest phases. As an instrument for allowing the mass audience to hear the same music, radio play, actuality broadcast, or election speech simultaneously, broadcasting's potential to shape the experiences of listeners and even to homogenize their preferences was unprecedented and duly noted. This sense of broadcast power seemed strong but covert ("hegemonic" in Antonio Gramsci's formulation of that idea) because audiences did not have to be forced to tune in, and those given to ruminating on the significance of radio believed that the stakes (the development of listeners' aesthetic judgment, their social consciences, their attachment to democratic principles) were easily high enough to justify coordinated action. All of this is to say: listening was usually fun and compelling, and it didn't seem too likely to listeners that their minds and habits might be changed over the radio. One pamphlet on broadcasting from the mid-1950s looked back (and forward) to acknowledge that radio and TV were "potentially as influential as atomic energy."[50] Of course, *who* could or should broadcast emerged as one of the central points of contention, but without ignoring the question of the structure of the broadcasting system, my focus here remains fixed upon *what* could or should be broadcast and *how*. The material that some in radio found disturbing or in oversupply nonetheless had its appeal, no matter how reliant that material's reception might have been on advertisers' largesse or the promotional work of station managers, advertisers, and programming staff. Eager audiences existed for dance music and jazz, just as they did in smaller numbers for symphonies or folk music. Several radio people noted that listeners could easily have stopped listening if they had not in some way appreciated the programming on the air. They did not tune in to *Amos 'n' Andy* as a novel way of protesting its racist premise or, as a BBC official wryly put it in 1934: "People do not buy gramophone records in order to demonstrate to their friends their dislike of crooning."[51]

Sociologist Pierre Bourdieu's seminal work, *Distinction*, shows that class (as determined by how and for whom someone laboured or by the productive resources she or he owned or controlled) could exert a strong influence upon taste, as expressed through consumption or veneration of particular goods or experiences. Since that study emerged in the late 1970s, its influence has been considerable, and some scholars argue that people have become further inundated with opportunities and demands to exhibit their tastes.[52] Radio stations were (and are) owned by individuals, companies, or even governments with sufficient capital to set up and run them. The managers and staff who controlled the day-to-day operations of these stations (or the networks to which they were affiliated) most frequently came from the educated middle and upper classes. Aspirational program planning drew heavily upon middle-class cultural expectations or moralities because, as Nathan Godfried argues, the middle classes were "the presumed demographic, economic, and psychological core of the city."[53] Whiteness, too, was assumed, and racial difference could be exploited on the air.[54] Rural listeners received attention as well but were a consistently shrinking group by the early twentieth century. The women for whom a series of CBC talks on art were "designed especially" in 1945 were also a distinct target group.[55] Although the positions (class, education, gender, race, ethnicity, etc.) of listeners and of the individuals working in public and private broadcasting surely conditioned their attitudes towards radio as well as their tastes, programming decisions and listening choices did not flow exclusively from these positions. If broadcasters wanted to gather mass audiences, they were wisest to create and broadcast programs with broad appeal. Though program creators may have had a vision of things as they should be, that vision bumped up against audience preference (or perceived audience preference) pretty much all the time, and both private and public broadcasters heeded such cues in making and planning programs.

As the archives in places like Ottawa, Reading, and Madison yielded their bounty, it became clear that some of the best evidence we have about the Canadian radio scene comes out of the formal and informal links forged, broken, or refashioned between Canadian broadcasters and "foreign" broadcasting companies or authorities. The chapters here address themes that cropped up most prominently or consistently, and they do not attempt to deal at length with all types of programming (such as news, sport, or drama). I have published a separate article on talks but sometimes refer to talks here and there in the pages that follow,[56] usually when addressing daytime programming. Deciding which chapters should come earliest was difficult because each one touches upon or reveals something germane to the structure or story of early Canadian radio, and, consequently, each could stake a claim to coming before the others. However, each chapter builds upon the themes I explore earlier in the book. I chose to discuss the intimacy of radio earliest in order to highlight broadcasting authorities' conviction that broadcasting was a powerful instrument for shaping listeners' lives. Playing off the intimate "power of broadcasting," chapters on the influence of American and British broadcasting follow, placed next to each other to better contrast them and to situate Canadian approaches to programming as both related to and distinct from these models. What could Canadian authorities do to mitigate the impact of British and American broadcast power? They could make rules, and a chapter on regulation follows to illustrate the attention paid to certain types of programming as threatening to existing values. A chapter on music, the single most common type of programming on the air and one that broadcasters were especially keen to "get right," comes next. Finally, a discussion of cultural democracy brings us back to the questions of caring about and knowing about what listeners hoped to hear. In several places throughout, I allude to one type of program in the middle of discussing an entirely different idea. For example, a mention of "thriller" programs crops up during the chapter on intimacy. I hope that readers will benefit from these forays and cross-references. The chapter on intimacy is a slightly expanded and more-than-slightly rethought version of my 2009 article in *Media History*. A section within chapter 4 is much abridged from another article that appeared in 2010 in the *Canadian Historical Review*.

Research for *Canada before Television* took place over a period of about six years. During that time, my interpretation of what was going on for Canadian broadcasters and listeners during radio's "golden age" changed considerably. While my research indicated that private and public broadcasting were each indispensible in serving listeners, and that a continued or even strengthened role for public broadcasting would be advisable regardless of the number of channels available, this interpretation was not already in place. I knew before I began that the proponents of public and commercial broadcasting were each adamant that their way would serve listeners best. I expected to find flag-wavers, profit-takers, uplifters, and utopians, and they appeared, though not always where expected. In the CBC, I expected to find an easily traced caricature of public service broadcasting: earnest highbrows eager to reproduce the values of Canada's elites and contemptuous of the average listener. That expectation was not met, and the various ways it went unmet compelled me to tell a story that may look different from some of the others we've seen. Canada's broadcasting history is relevant beyond its borders because early Canadian radio was a special case, a system that involved both private and public broadcasters operating next door to the richest and most dynamic radio marketplace in the world. While political intrigue, money, and influence certainly coloured the early history of radio broadcasting in Canada, this history should also be considered an extended *experiment* addressing the question of what broadcasting was supposed to do for (and with) the listening public. The experimental result in a nutshell: public broadcasting (operating alongside a commercial system and regulating it) and commercial broadcasting (operating alongside a public system and influencing it) made the earliest phase of Canada's broadcasting history more diverse and, hence, more open and responsive to more listeners. The CBC, usually painted as an unapologetic nationalist/elitist enterprise, was more significantly a bashful combatant in the struggle for cultural democracy.

In my previous book, *A Great Duty*, I argue that responses to mass culture and modern life in mid-twentieth-century Canada could not be considered the domain of any single political tradition or neatly definable group. As much as our instinctive selves might like to slap labels (socialist, fascist, etc.) on ideas that do not appeal to us, my hope is that readers will not consider *Canada before Television* a tract for or against particular modes of broadcasting but, rather, a history of the way radio could reflect old prejudices and new possibilities at the same time. *Canada before Television* gives further space to a couple of themes touched upon briefly in *A Great Duty* – what the public wants and cultural democracy – because it is at least partly a call to recognize how manufactured and fragile consensus and the idea of a unified public have been. I have also tried to make this one a more lively read because I hope people who aren't academics pick it up. Although I've presented these arguments and variations on them at conferences and public lectures (receiving much helpful advice), and consulted with a number of colleagues and friends while putting all of this together, any errors of fact or faulty interpretations are mine.

NOTE ON SPELLING, PUNCTUATION, AND RELATED MATTERS

Canadian broadcasters used both the British "programme" and the American "program" to mean: a discrete broadcast or episode (e.g., the *HMS Pinafore* programme last Monday), a recurring show or series (the *Woodhouse & Hawkins* program), or an entire schedule or network (the BBC's Third Programme). My entirely unempirical finding is that they favoured "programme" by a healthy margin, but "program" appears to be the approved Canadian spelling these days. So, unless I am directly quoting a source, I use "program" for the purposes listed above as well as to mean a plan or system for achieving a particular goal. Although there seemed to be a gradual, but unsurprising, shift in Canadian sources from British spellings towards their American variants, all quotations are left alone. I also follow convention for broadcasting organizations, which is to refer to "the" CBC but to omit the article for entities like NBC or CBS.

1

"Telling Me and No One Else": Intimacy

A silence there, expectant, meaning,
And then a voice clear-pitched and tense;
A million hearers, forward-leaning,
Were in the thrall of eloquence.

A pause, a hush, a wonder growing;
A prophet's vision understood;
In that strange spell of his bestowing,
They dreamed, with him, of Brotherhood.[1]

On Dominion Day 1927, the still rapidly growing Canadian radio audience could have tuned to a nationwide transmission marking the Diamond Jubilee of Confederation, a celebratory broadcast that was itself celebrated as a feat of engineering. The booklet commemorating the occasion opened with the verse above but ploughed almost immediately into a list of broadcast committee members and technical details regarding sending the sounds of carillon and choirs to radio sets far and wide. The booklet also reported that Prime Minister William Lyon Mackenzie King, broadcasting from the Canadian National Exhibition in Toronto some weeks later, declared that listeners had become

for the time being, a single assemblage, swayed by a common emotion, within the sound of a single voice. Thus has modern science for the first time realized in the great nation-State of modern days that condition which existed in the little city-States of ancient times and which was considered by the wisdom of the ancients as indispensible to free and democratic government – that all the citizens should be able to hear for themselves the living voice.

King went on to suggest that the Jubilee broadcast was just the first of many occasions when Canadians would be "brought together" for their mutual benefit, their "unity and soul" nobly expressed.[2] If radio could occasionally make a temporary city-state, a "cradle of democracy," out of the vastness of Canada, what might it accomplish on a smaller scale, in the lives of individuals who listened every day? In the day-to-day practice of creating programs, a figurative "bringing together" was not always the desired effect. As King recognized, listeners rarely assembled in groups larger than a family. Even the family unit seemed like a crowd to broadcasters who, in several telling instances, envisioned the solitary listener in silent communion with a speaker who was simultaneously far away and "present." For program makers, the idea that a program reached its audience of thousands or millions via thousands or millions of cozy but separate experiences could be both exhilarating and burdensome. This idea, that broadcasting could intimately affect listeners one at a time in their homes, made a difference to the way programs were made.

Before about 1920, while the technical capability to broadcast had existed for more than a generation, neither production facilities (transmitters with broadcasting studios to accommodate performers) nor listening infrastructure (numerous inexpensive receiving sets in homes) were in place. Two-way or "point-to-point" communication, the earlier and more immediately practical application of radio waves, was used first for wireless telegraphy and later for voice transmissions. Before the advent of "one-to-many" broadcasting in the years immediately following the First World War, people not keen to engage in what was called wireless or radio "telephony" did not need radio sets. Broadcasting was, as Mary Vipond calls it, "a technology in search of an industry" because no one had completely worked out what a broadcasting service might do or who might benefit from it,[3] financially or otherwise. Jean Seaton dubs broadcasting a "social invention, not a technical one."[4] This reminds us of the human dimension, but we also need to recall the technical limitations, especially when considering how few broadcasting outlets there were and how that fact affected broadcasting's reputation as a potential instrument of civilization. Beginning in 1919, but taking off more rapidly during the couple of years following, stations offered limited service to small local audiences of set owners (usually hobbyists whose set ownership pre-dated the broadcast era), and word of the broadcasts spread. Some of the more powerful stations were backed by radio manufacturers seeking simply to spur sales of their sets. Other early broadcasters in Canada included local institutions like newspapers, railways, churches, and universities.[5] With music providing most of the content, broadcasting activity soared during the 1920s, offering listeners within range of the first transmissions a captivating new experience and, later, adding the signal power to reach further afield. In less than a decade, the primary "traffic pattern" in wireless communication had shifted dramatically to become one-way, one-to-many. Amateurs, who used to be nearly alone in vying to make the most distant two-way contacts and making small talk with their "conquests," had been joined on the air and eclipsed by broadcasters seeking to build audiences. *Contacts* gave way to *programs*, occasions during which listeners no longer responsible for keeping up their end of a conversation could be engaged by music, news, talks, or drama. As radio programming became less personal, it became more intimate.

HIGH ANXIETIES AND THE INFANT INDUSTRY

During the past thirty years or so, historians have paid some attention to the idea of intimacy and how it shaped radio. Lesley Johnson, in her work on early Australian broadcasting, argues that cultivation of a familiar voice style and treating listeners as "eavesdroppers rather than audience" won approval for private stations while the public broadcaster failed to make the same adjustment.[6] Discussions of broadcasting in North America have rightly highlighted radio's ability to eliminate distance and isolation as this change was an important contributor to its ongoing cultural, social, and economic impact.[7] Historians of radio as a new technology have differed in their interpretations of these developments. For example, radio could be the cure for rural estrangement from a modern and dynamic world,[8] even as "the very technology that expanded the possibilities of public communication carried with it reminders of individual isolation."[9] Music became one of radio's most reliable passkeys into the home, and the singing style of the crooners and old-time bands made broadcast music seem more personal.[10] The home still harboured its own divisions (e.g., age, gender), and potential listeners did not always rush to embrace the new arrival.[11] Yet, innovations like Franklin Roosevelt's "Fireside Chats," among other broadcasts, allowed for the construction of a space in which the mass of listeners defined themselves as inhabiting – sometimes simultaneously – homes, neighbourhoods, cities, or the nation.[12] Similarly, the idea of "home" helped define private space, but electronic communication had long been blurring the boundaries between home and away.[13]

It would be untenable to argue that Canadian radio was any more or less intimate than radio in other places. For example, Australian authorities were wary of "the supremacy of its power" to influence listeners.[14] However, in Canada, public broadcasters' anxieties about radio and actions related to programming strategy sometimes grew out of an abiding fear of the medium's persuasive clout and a pessimistic view of listeners' ability to resist. Spoken word broadcasts in Canada, like the folksy but short-lived "Mr Sage" partisan political dramas, proved to be persuasive enough during the 1935 federal election to prompt decisive action restricting political broadcasts and to hasten the creation of the CBC as a regulatory body.[15] Such interpretations of the early radio environment made Canada a distinctive example of the sort of cultural dynamic that historians in the United States, the United Kingdom, and elsewhere in the English-speaking world have only lately stopped treating as incidental to the development of broadcasting. If we are to fully appreciate how broadcasting developed in any of these places, the historical relationship between its form (*how* it came to listeners) and its content (*what* there was for them to listen to) needs to be considered.

During radio's period of growth and consolidation, listeners, critics, and broadcasters in Canada – public broadcasters particularly – perceived a special kind of trust or bond between broadcaster and listener. Radio was a transformative new communications medium, but, more significantly, it was a new social mode. We are familiar, most famously via Marshall McLuhan's work, with the idea that various methods of communicating work differently because they "extend" particular human senses.[16] Radio extended human hearing, and so it differed markedly from the press, which remained the authoritative medium at the local and national levels. Broadcasting encountered logistical barriers, just as the press had done. Both programs and newspapers had to be delivered somehow, and it required capital to operate a station or a printing press. However, radio's disembodied voices commanded a different kind of reverence, even when listeners were invited to talk back.[17] Disembodied voices had been emanating from phonographs for a few decades, so by 1920 it was easier for listeners to attribute the sounds produced to the cylinder or disc; the needle was "reading" the bumps on the recording, or, as Lisa Gitelman suggests, the recordings were present, like "morsels" to be consumed.[18] But when radio came along, without a phonograph in the room, how did people explain such voices? The voice of God from the burning bush? Voices or signals from departed spirits at a séance? One's own inner monologue?[19] Radio was like those intimate forms of communication in having no wires or discs, no apparent physical origin.

So, it was not terribly surprising that, soon after broadcasting emerged in the 1920s, observers marvelled at its ability to conquer distances in an instant, permeate walls and transfix listeners. Distances had already been conquered by the telegraph and telephone, but the first of these was never a *household* fixture, and the second had not yet become commonplace beyond the more urbanized areas of the continent. Broadcasts, however, reached anyone with a receiving set. They offered programming in which people willing to buy receiving sets took an interest, even though decent sets did not become widely affordable in Canada until after 1930.[20] Radio seemed to be at once a force of culture and of nature, a human-made conduit that relied for its appeal on little more than the instinct to be fascinated. Part of the appeal for more remote Canadian listeners was also the abrupt end radio put to their social isolation. In the early 1920s, one convert declared:

I am in a log shack in Canada's northland. Only yesterday to be out here was to be out of the world. But no longer. The radiophone has changed all that. Remember where I am and then you can realize how "homey" it is to hear a motherly voice carefully describing in detail just how to make the pie crust more flaky.[21]

John Peters's work on communication, especially his compact detour through "radioland," shows how momentous it was for listeners to encounter the idea that a speaker on the radio seemed somehow to occupy space near them.[22] Equating the broadcast voice with a personal presence – even a presence that might be selling pastry shortening – animated and complicated radio's early years. As they did elsewhere, listeners, producers, performers, and critics in Canada frequently noted the paradox of mass communication feeling like personal or small group conversation. This perception of intimacy affected their listening, production, and performance as well as their discussion of broadcasting and its future. "I think of homes," said vocalist Joyce Hahn when asked about her conception of the audience, "and depending on the hour, of what the people in them are doing."[23]

The cultural stakes seemed high, especially for those working in Canada's public broadcasting system, because, just like newspapers, magazines, or motion pictures, radio could bring harm or improvement on a mass scale. As critic Graham McInnes recognizes: "It is one of the dangers of radio – that sounding shadow of unseen voices that enters our rooms from the ends of the earth – that its very intimacy heightens its drama and its reality. It can sweep the uncritical off their feet, as Orson Welles did with his invasion from Mars, and it's the duty of a public service broadcaster to see that his audience is not so swept."[24] Unlike the other media dominant in the early part of the twentieth century, radio was live and its output could "put new windows in our homes."[25] Radio did not have to be brought there anew each day or consumed elsewhere in a purpose-built facility, and so broadcasting enjoyed the advantages of "its intimacy and its ubiquity,"[26] especially over "cold print."[27] These advantages had already been exploited elsewhere under authoritarian governments, and the absence of such regimes in North America did little to calm fears that listeners' minds and passions could be vulnerable to milder sorts of manipulation. To some, radio was an "instrument of democracy."[28] Its future loomed as glorious or horrific, depending on how broadcasters proceeded. As we will see in chapter 4, for about two decades, the CBC claimed the regulatory authority it had been granted over all broadcasters in Canada by referring to "the nature of broadcasting" and its "particularly intimate and direct appeal" as compelling reasons to keep a watchful eye on programs that could be considered obscene or offensive.[29] Even though the new medium's power to shape tastes, habits, and opinions may not have been greater than that of print or film, and McInnes reminded his listeners of "radio's special handicap: its thin-ness, its appeal to the ear alone,"[30] the perception that it could cast some sort of spell over listeners bred concern about broadcasting's potential, as one American radio executive put it, to "serve good – or evil – ends."[31]

In Canada, this concern was never articulated in class terms as clearly as it was in Britain.[32] Despite appealing to a set-owning public characterized as having both professional/bourgeois and working-class minorities but made up largely of a "great middle class,"[33] the norms reinforced by the CBC and its predecessor the Canadian

Radio Broadcasting Commission (CRBC) were broadly those of the educated Canadian elite. While these norms functioned as yardsticks against which various kinds of programming could be measured, broadcasters operating under both the public and the private models found it difficult to fathom the average listener's specific likes and dislikes. They nonetheless had a spirited go at supposing what these might be. Commercial broadcasters tried to guess what the mass audience wanted so that the audiences for each program in planning or production could be identified, and even quantified, for advertisers. Innovation in commercial programming consisted of variations on shows already proven to be acceptable to the vast middle of the pack or the adaptation of newspaper features such as advice columns. Exceptions to this pattern, like the CNR's *Romance of Canada* series of dramatized talks, were all the more notable.[34] Public broadcasters came to consider the broader listening audience to be, as James Scott notes in his study of large-scale social experiments, people without "the particular, situated, and contextual attributes that one would expect of any population and that we, as a matter of course, always attribute to elites."[35] In other words, "popular" tastes might seem less genuine or relevant to the public broadcaster because they shifted rapidly, appearing less rooted and more prone to influence or fads. The mainstream audience could look fickle, and, as American radio pioneer Lee DeForest warned the Canadian Radio League, although broadcasting "seemed destined when public interest in its etheric voice was first aroused to prove itself an Evangel of irresistible power,"[36] it could, if poorly managed, just as easily become a wasteland. The situation seemed all the more precarious because Canada's radio scene was distinctive, at least in North America. It was neither British Broadcasting Corporation-style monopoly nor US-style "open" market. In Canada, the two styles co-existed, with the CBC responsible for regulating a chaotic and underdeveloped new medium. In this context, the "civilizing" mission of public service broadcasting embodied in the CBC after 1936 meant that the perceived intimacy of radio became another reason for, at times, exerting strong control over programming on Canada's public and private stations.

AN INTIMATE INSTRUMENT

One attractive feature of having radio in Canada was that the voices of one's radio "neighbours" could visit even when the nearest actual neighbours were well beyond shouting distance. Unlike the more densely populated regions of the United States and Great Britain, in Canada radio continued to be trumpeted as a way for settlers to keep in touch with "civilization" through the later 1930s, when activist Nellie McClung, among others, portrayed it as "one of life's equalizers," bridging the gap "between the sod shanty and the home on the avenue."[37] In 1924, nearer the beginning of the radio era, Canadian National Railways (CNR) vice-president W.D. Robb saw the intimacy of radio as a way of keeping the western settler sane and productive. He supposed that as soon as radio – particularly the CNR's programs – reached Canadians, especially in the west, the listener's surroundings would be figuratively transformed. With radio on the trains and in the air, he claimed, "the longest evening no longer palls."[38] A year later, though still a good two years before the CNR network was operating fully, one of Robb's employees added that settlers no longer had to go to the city because, via radio, "the city comes to them."[39] Austin Weir, director of radio for the CNR radio system during the early 1930s, reported that a listener in New Zealand had written to station CNRV Vancouver, referring to its signal as if to a person, even a lover: "'Your speech was exceptionally clear,' writes Mr. Thomson, who adds 'it was not necessary to use headphones either to pick you up or to hold you.'"[40] Even in the late 1940s, with radio already more than a quarter century old in Canada, critic Thomas Archer still enthusiastically compared broadcasting to the railroad as a national achievement, yet one with a personal dimension: "Think of it. Broadcasting permits a man living in Quebec City to speak to a man in Vancouver as if he were visiting him in his very house."[41] With the advent of broadcasting, the ability to travel the breadth of the country in a few days had been replaced or augmented as a cohesive force by the ability to have a simultaneous radio experience. The regional differences that had divided Canadians looked less insurmountable.

When CBC general manager Gladstone Murray declared in 1937 that "the message of broadcasting is received at the fireside in the relatively unguarded atmosphere of the home, reaching young and old alike,"[42] he was commenting on the ability of radio to *seem* like personalized speech and to *act* as persuasive speech, simulating the effect of regular conversation. Producers spoke of their shows entering homes, being invited in, visiting. "What a miracle it is that music should thus be brought, by invisible means, into our homes,"[43] exclaimed one of the CBC's own brochures, doing nothing to demystify the mechanics of broadcasting but acknowledging home as the place where people listened. Despite the horrors of war and the tendency of technological advances to be put to destructive uses, programs created to suit the listener at home were viewed as therapeutic. Veterans' Land Act director Gordon Murchison emphasized this in his remarks during a 1945 Metropolitan Opera broadcast, noting: "There is one place where new inventions can only add to an age-old charm. That is the charm of the family circle and of the home."[44] The family hearth was a frequently mentioned site of contact, evidence that broadcasting, rather than sweeping away all before it, was best understood as grafted onto existing social rituals. The opposing idea, which Wayne and Shuster put most plainly when they noted that their shows could bring "fourteen million Canadians together in one great living room,"[45] seemed mind-boggling. Small worked. In 1931, the CNR network trumpeted its symphonic offerings for the upcoming season, adding: "We hope that the practice which became so general of forming little family and social groups on Sunday afternoon to listen to this concert will become even more widespread."[46] In his first broadcast address, CBC Board of Governors chair Leonard Brockington greeted listeners and placed himself, at least figuratively, in an unfamiliar position just inside the threshold of their domestic space: "I would like to thank each one of you for granting me the hospitality of your house, into which, guided by a sense of duty, I enter with somewhat reluctant feet."[47] Charlotte Whitton, social welfare activist and later mayor of Ottawa, expressed her concerns about radio's ability to change family life by comparing it to films and the press, over which parents could exercise more control. "The radio," Whitton noted, "enters the home as freely as the air which the family breathes. Under these circumstances, the responsibility of control of what goes on that air is a much graver and more far-reaching one." She urged her CBC friend Gladstone Murray to "keep before the public at all times the fact that the radio is ultimately as intimate as the life about the hearthstone in the average family."[48]

After the Second World War, despite improvements in receiving technology, expansion in the number of programs and more audience research, portrayal of broadcasting as a *presence* continued. Broadcasting's ability to reach into homes, cars, or public spaces was by then familiar, yet the social responsibilities of a person with a physical body still encumbered it. Although broadcasting was a public form of address, radio people, listeners, and critics often thought of radio in terms of a person entering intimate space – usually denoted as the family fireside – a "person" who must nonetheless behave as though he or she were among "ordinary decent company."[49] In 1946, on the eve of the corporation's tenth anniversary, CBC chairman Davidson Dunton addressed listeners, declaring: "Radio, with all its vastness, is an intimate friend. It comes to talk to you, or play to you, in your living room." In asking "What do you expect of this friend?"[50] Dunton distilled for his audience a question radio people on both sides of the public/private broadcasting divide had long been trying to answer. While listeners' responses to such a question might vary, evidence from the period before television's arrival in Canada indicates that public broadcasters and their opponents were still fighting this public/private battle at the same time as they were wrestling with the question of just how public or private radio could be. Public broadcasters took the idea of radio-in-personal-space seriously by avoiding distasteful topics or maintaining room in the schedule for soothing music or temperate talks. Their sense of what should be broadcast was thus predicated on an understanding of radio as more than background noise or advertising revenue generator. To an extent, critical opinion backed this cautious stance. *Saturday Night* editor B.K. Sandwell advocated protecting religious belief from what he considered radio's unfair threat on the grounds that "radio is not a suitable mechanism for disturbing the faith of anybody."[51] Though his metaphors were entertainingly mixed, Graham McInnes left no doubt as to the continuing influence of radio and where this influence would be felt most keenly: "For radio to be radio it must come into your home, and once there, like the Arab who let the camel put his nose into the tent, it compels you to follow its serpent voice."[52] Except for the highly publicized and lavishly produced shows during which they, too, ran advertisements and collected needed revenue, public broadcasters left the jobs of juke box and advertising vehicle to the commercial stations.

Listeners, too, remarked upon the ability of radio to mimic human contact, especially the sort of human contact associated with the home, small audiences, or cozy venues. Quiz shows resembled parlour games, occasions of confidence-building for listeners who could, in their own homes, be comfortable matching wits with the quizmasters.[53] Publicity material for *Find Your Fortune*, hosted by Monty

Hall in 1948, seemed to have the spatial and social contradictions of broadcasting down pat, inviting listeners to "meet the talented Ogilvie Parrot right in your own living room and laugh with Canadians coast-to-coast."[54] Radio made it possible to be at home, yet among a crowd. Talks, small-cast dramas, variety shows like *The Happy Gang*, or simple stories tended to bring performers into "personal" contact with the listener. Occasionally, listeners described being transported by a broadcast. Albert Whittaker of White's Lake, Nova Scotia, commended the CBC for its broadcasts of the 1951 Royal Tour, mentioning W.E.S. Briggs's announcing, which "gave his description of the occasion being covered a coating of intimacy which made one feel that he [the listener] was there in person."[55]

The illusion of presence conveyed by the broadcast voice made broadcasting memorable and convincing in a way that print was not, and, according to a high-ranking clergyman who had his flock in mind, it should be heavily censored because it could have "an extraordinary influence on the mentality of people."[56] This influence was, however, no guarantee that the voice reflected the thoughts of the speaker. One editorial asserted that the opposite was most often true: "the majority of them speak to the microphone through a distorting mask of dignity or learning or heartiness or modernity – whichever public face they choose to wear to hide their poor, fragile souls from the world."[57] The way forward was to recognize and exploit certain types of programming, like storytelling, that could complement the illusion of presence rather than raising doubts about the speaker's sincerity or the listener's economic or psychological safety. A measured challenge to apathy, the experimental CBC series *Sob Sisters* aimed to "disarm the listener. He thinks he is the only one left sobbing at the receiving set – while big broadcasts, built to make a play for his emotions, leave him unmoved."[58] To maintain the goodwill of listeners, the broadcaster must always be "invited," and the ideal, according to Graham McInnes, would be for broadcasters to operate "without making you feel that your privacy has been invaded."[59] Also in the late 1940s, Ted Allan, who would later pen *Lies My Father Told Me* and who had worked for a while as a pulp novelist, became a folk-tale teller on the CBC and received a fan letter from a young listener who appreciated "that you tell it in a way that makes me think you're telling me and no one else."[60]

The person "in" the radio need not be mortal or solitary. Radio could be a kind of spirit guide, marshalling its aggregation of voices in the service of the listener's imagination. In the *Canadian National Railways Magazine* for October 1925, Clara V. Barton's poem, "The Romance of Radio," testified to how magical the simple act of listening in had become:

> Beauty comes from far-off places
> On my alien hearth to dwell
> Looses here her winged sandals,
> Varying endlessly her spell;
>
> Radio, opening wide my portals,
> Leads the starry guest within
> And I find each room grown spacious
> Where her starry feet have been.[61]

Thanks to radio, listeners could be put in touch with events, ideas, or personalities they were unlikely to encounter in any other way. It was a boon to "folks in lonely places on the Prairies, in Northern areas and on the sea coasts,"[62] and it could keep the "nation awake at night eager and breathless while Nova Scotia draegermen dig for three men trapped in a gold mine."[63] As General Manager Murray reminded CBC announcers covering the 1939 Royal Tour: "Your microphones will be in fact the first magic carpet in Canada's history."[64] What was magical for some seemed miraculous or at least providential to others. Winston Curry, host of the long-running *Sweet Hour of Prayer*, included this bit of verse on the show's letterhead:

> If radio's slim fingers
> Can reach through the air
> Then why should we doubt
> That God hears our prayer?[65]

Curry appealed to the audience to think about – and believe in or know – God in the same way they believed in or knew radio. This presupposed a familiarity not only with radio but also with the metaphor of being reached by it, a metaphor instinctively accepted by 1950 when the Canadian Catholic Conference voiced its fears about the arrival of television, predicting that TV would "penetrate with a vividness far surpassing that of radio into the intimacy of more and more of our homes."[66]

INTIMACY IN ACTION

The interpretation of radio as an intimate instrument led to action – specifically to attempts to control the tone and temper of programming heard on public and private airwaves. Probably the most influential such interpreter and agent of control in Canada was Gladstone Murray, who has already been mentioned but who warrants a proper introduction. Murray left his home in British Columbia to take up a Rhodes Scholarship and stayed away to fight in the Great War. He served as director of publicity, director of information publications, and ultimately as assistant controller (programmes) with the BBC from 1926 until 1936, when he returned to Canada to head up the newly created CBC. While working at the BBC under Sir John Reith, he imbibed the message of broadcasting as public service,[67] which implied a profound listener trust in broadcasters. Having kept up with events in the struggle over which sort of broadcasting model would dominate in Canada, he was seconded there in 1933 to report on the efforts of the Canadian Radio Broadcasting Commission. In his 1933 report, it was clear that Murray had already partially worked out what would become a boilerplate response to questions about program content and why it mattered. "The intimate character of the broadcasting medium," he writes, "involving the acceptance of its message at the fireside, implies a special responsibility to avoid sensational and disturbing communications."[68] Once he took over as CBC general manager in 1936, Murray began his first talk with:

> Good evening Ladies and Gentlemen – or of course I should say good evening Listener, because a broadcast of this kind is best as an intimate, even if one-sided, conversation between two individuals; in the aggregate many people may listen, at least to begin with, nevertheless the link is between you and me as individuals.

During his time at the CBC, and even after his ignominious exit in 1942, Murray and those influenced by his approach to broadcasting would repeat the lesson he alludes to later in the same talk: "This medium of radio properly used is full of friendliness. Impersonality is foreign to it."[69]

In the simplest cases, intimacy became the reason for not airing certain programs or considering certain subjects for mention, even in a public service capacity. Among the "sensational and disturbing communications" Murray feared was the subject of venereal disease. The VD taboo lasted until after the Second World War on US radio,[70] and it was only broken during wartime on Canadian airwaves when National Health and military officials insisted that the risks be publicized.[71] Before the wartime change of heart, Canadian listeners were mostly spared the gory, but potentially vital, details thanks to Murray's standard response to suggestions that the CBC open up and educate the public. "Certain subjects," he wrote, "while meriting discussion elsewhere in the public interest are not necessarily suitable for this intimate medium."[72] The corporation, empowered to regulate the activities of private broadcasters, exercised considerable power over program content, citing its responsibility to judge which programs were suitable. As the CBC was finalizing its regulations in the fall of 1937, Murray managed to alter the final draft of Regulation 7, regarding what was admissible for broadcast. The phrase that became "this *intimate* medium" had existed in previous drafts as late as September 1937 as "this *public* medium."[73] Murray's elision of these two terms points to the paradoxical notion of a kind of "public intimacy,"[74] which became licence to exert control over the making and distribution of programs. Murray had also worried that Austin Weir, one of the veterans who came over eventually from the CRBC, was "too subservient to women members of his staff" and that this might hamper Weir's ability to make rational decisions about programming over the intimate medium.[75]

Murray's successor as CBC general manager, J.S. Thomson, changed nothing. According to Thomson's pronouncement on Canadian broadcast advertising standards, the "distinctive character of radio" meant that tasteful and permissible ads were those "in line with the finest standards of home life."[76] Station Relations Manager J.R. Radford, having jumped from private radio to the CBC, likewise adopted a cautious strategy in reviewing commercial announcements for sponsored programs. He reassured colleague Donald Manson that advertisers would understand, probably after multiple mandated revisions of the same ad script, that "the intimate broadcast medium presupposes a restraint unnecessary in the written word."[77] For instance, though the practice of mentioning prices for goods was common in print advertising, regulations differed for broadcast ads, which were not to provide commercial advantage by repeating price data, especially when prices targeted the supposedly impressionable soap opera audience – that is, women. Understanding and exploiting the likelihood that women would be the majority of daytime listeners had led to a pronounced gendering of "hobby" radio (male) and then daytime programs (female) in the United States during the 1920s.[78] This latter innovation had spread to Canada with little delay and was only rarely remarked upon.[79] Unable, and disinclined, to force the wholesale removal of soap opera style programs from commercial stations, CBC policy moved to restrict the scope of what advertisers were allowed to say to this audience. The reason for the regulation had to be couched in benign terms, and intimacy served this purpose well: "Mention of price, unless handled with the utmost discrimination, would tend to lower Canadian broadcasting standards, and would encourage radio advertising practices unsuitable to the unguarded atmosphere of the listening fireside."[80] The simple solution to the question of price mention was not to allow it, and the CBC only relaxed this policy on an experimental basis in 1948.[81]

More serious than price mention, potentially, was the threat of exposing women to programs that could shock them. For purposes of identifying this sensitive group of listeners, the CBC used the same term advertisers used to refer to their potential customers: the "housewife."[82] Just as the soap opera audience was assumed to be made up of adult females, the housewife label denoted a woman in the home, most likely without husband and children present, listening to the radio while busy with domestic work. This was an important distinction in that her listening would be solitary, away from the "hearth" atmosphere in which family groups usually encountered radio, and, as one American study of soap operas suggests: "the listener hears the voice of a familiar character as often perhaps as the voice of an intimate friend."[83] Even though housewives' actual lives may have been fraught with poverty, physical or alcohol abuse, or health problems, the broadcasting authorities at the CBC did not favour allowing those realities to be dramatized in commercial or unsponsored programming, handling them only via the less sensational format of the talk.[84] While some attention fell on the possibility of women forming listening groups and perhaps tackling meatier subjects together,[85] in constructing policy, the CBC defaulted to the image of the innocent housewife, unlikely to be familiar with or interested in the seamier side of life and, as in the United Kingdom, perhaps even eager to recapture prewar domesticity.[86] As CBC programming executives discussed the season's new crop of programs available to both private stations and the CBC in 1945, one of the opinions offered on

American star Eddie Cantor's show was that it "borders on the objectionable side of burlesque."[87] This intrusion of a male-oriented presentation style, even though the program was intended to air in the evenings, contributed to the CBC's decision not to sell time on its network to sponsors interested in underwriting Cantor.[88]

Programming people also fretted about the competition presented by American shows. The American networks had seemed to grasp effortlessly that, once they had been granted an audience in the home, the way consecutive programs related to one another mattered. For the CBC, which offered both sustaining (unsponsored) and sponsored programming, this also became an important lesson. The need to find hospitality for the CBC's own output frequently meant bowing to "popular" tastes and riding into the home on the coat-tails of big-budget American shows. In 1944, the corporation's Commercial Division reported that it had again booked US shows like *Kraft Music Hall*, *Bob Hope*, and *Information Please!*, noting that "sponsored programmes with their internationally known artists could not be excluded from the Corporation's networks unless Canadians are prepared to see the audience drift to American stations."[89] The relationships between programs mattered not only for retaining listeners over the course of an evening and not only for the purpose of developing Canadian talent but also because careful consideration of these relationships would spare listeners an unwelcome change of mood. Reporting to the CBC Board of Governors in 1952, Programme Division boasted about its insertion of *Musical Comedy Time* into the Sunday evening schedule, which contained several American programs, as "a good instance of programme planning; it serves as a welcome transition from the more serious *Sunday Evening Hour* and the classical music of *Little Symphonies* to the drama, light or serious, of *Stage 52*."[90]

News, another type of "serious" programming, presented another example of accounting for the broadcast voice's intimacy and potential influence. News was to be read in a manner that was "intimate without being undignified."[91] The CBC created its own news bureau in 1941, and staff noted the effect that newsreader Lorne Greene had on listeners: "The uproar over the portentious [*sic*] way that he read the news and his deep sonorous voice made [Director of Programming Ernest] Bush[nell] realize what a sensitive and intimate instrument radio was."[92] Wire services, newspapers, radio news departments, and, during the war, the Wartime Information Board, filtered the news so that the most disturbing reports did not invade the home.[93] Nonetheless, after the war, Claris Silcox of the United Church of Canada worried that sensitive people were at risk if censorship failed and the listener heard an unvarnished newscast: "if he is a God-fearing man and eager to fulfil all his human responsibilities, he will only suffer mental confusion if world-shattering news break upon his innocence."[94] Again, we see the assumption that the Canadian listener lived in an isolated way and that broadcasting might provide an unmediated dose of what was happening in more lively locales. The CBC strove, even before it created its own news bureau, to follow the example of western Canadian news announcer Earle Kelly, who maintained that the "news broadcast should be in the nature of a family fireside conversation." Kelly wrote:

> In pre-radio days, the farmer's son went to the nearest town on some routine business, and returned to regale the family with the latest bits of news. A news broadcast should, with obvious reservations as to grammar, take a similar form … I come in contact with hundreds of people who do not get a newspaper for weeks at a stretch. Invariably, they prefer the method I quote, which I have used for years. Even in the cities, judges, professional and business men prefer it also, as it is in the form of simple language they themselves use in the family council.[95]

When the CBC inaugurated its news service in 1941, Murray emphasized that the same care taken in producing talks would be used in creating news bulletins, adding that news staff had been chosen "for their experience and judgment in handling news, their enterprise, their fairness, and their feeling for radio."[96]

Murray's "feeling for radio" meant a sense of what to say and how to behave in personal conversation. CBC Talks staff, from which some news people had been drawn, had to provide advice to prospective speakers, a group including academics, experts, journalists, and even politicians, people likely to have some idea of what to do when addressing the public. In 1938, CBC Talks transcribed and circulated with approval an article by the BBC Talks Department's Christopher Salmon on "Talks Presentation." Salmon's main principles, which covered addressing the individual and the differences between speaking and writing, rated special emphasis.[97] In 1942, the Talks Department prepared its own briefing sheets for radio neophytes. Among the wisdom imparted: "There is no 'radio audience.' There are a number of 'radio audiences.'" The average size of these audiences was "four or five," and they were "informal groups, made up of people sitting at ease in the living room, or eating in the dining room – or kitchen – or playing Chinese Checkers in the parlour."[98] Building upon this theme in 1943, Talks reminded *Canadian Roundup* announcers: "it's not a public speech – your audience is in ones and twos."[99] In 1944, Talks staff suggested an "intimate approach," warning that "radio listeners dislike being addressed in their homes as if they were a public meeting. ... A public speaker has to raise his voice; he must be heard by people in the back rows. The microphone will carry a whisper across a continent."[100]

A whisper was usually enough, and a style of delivery that further enhanced the sense of intimacy worked on radio at least partially because it did not resemble stage technique. Playwright and occasional speaker John Coulter collaborated with artist Ivor Lewis on a 1937 broadcast, and they sought the effect of "overheard conversation," or the "airing of emergent notions,"[101] rather than a polished piece. Late in wartime, CBC supervisor of broadcast language W.H. Brodie reminded announcing staff that the phrase "Ladies and gentlemen" should be eliminated because "radio addresses itself directly to the individual." He continued: "[And]do not say 'we are now to hear,' but use the second person 'you are now to hear.'"[102] At war's end, Ernest Bushnell noted that listeners, like producers, had become more sophisticated in recognizing that the conventions of the circus and stage need not apply to radio. He told an audience of potential radio staffers at Queen's University that broadcasting had changed the entertainment landscape for good: "noise, fanfares, drum-rolls and the raised voice have their effect on a crowd, but their impact may be quite different on the individual listener or the small family group that forms the normal radio audience."[103] Little more than two months after Hitler's death, Bushnell offered a hopeful vision of postwar broadcasting in which, thanks to the examples set by operations like the BBC and the CBC, demagogues would have little power over small groups of listeners or the individual.

In the estimation of program producers, the "normal" radio audience wanted speakers who could use the intimate medium to make them forget about radio and perceive the personal qualities of the speaker during these periods of "mental contact."[104] After his discussion with director Tyrone Guthrie, himself an experienced producer of radio plays for the BBC, about how to produce radio drama depicting historical events, journalist John McCulloch concluded: "The voice is not so important as the personality it suggests. And personality is conveyed through the mike by inflexion and intelligence. It's very subtle, but the invisible audience is seldom fooled."[105] By the late 1930s, the audience also knew as well as Canadian radio people that greener pastures existed in the United States for the most talented microphone personalities. To slow the flow of talent to the United States, Edgar Stone of the CBC's Commercial Department advocated a workshop for Canadian radio actors still working in Canada, many of whom could not leave other employment for more intensive training. He suggested concentrating specifically on "acting to a microphone versus acting to an audience" and "creating a sincere characterization under the intimacy of a microphone."[106]

Production values could also affect the sense of intimacy conveyed with the broadcast and bring to light the differences between print and broadcast media. Good studios and studio technique, especially of the sort employed on American thrillers like *Inner Sanctum*, made these programs more dangerous in Bushnell's opinion: "listening to them on the air is quite likely to be much more detrimental than reading them because of the thoroughly realistic manner in which they are produced."[107] Breaking the spell was as much of a problem. Extraneous or ill-timed announcements, such as those coming over on a recording from the Edinburgh Festival, irked critic Constance McKay, who noted that, "through some extraordinary lapse of taste[,] ... a luscious Scottish voice ... with a quiver of emotion ... robbed us in Canada of the thrill of hearing the music in our living-rooms."[108] Likewise, the press representative of the CPR in New York wrote to NBC to complain about an announcer whose "cannonading voice" broke the spell during a program intended to convince American tourists to come north.[109] Performers and producers alike wanted to be prepared for the honour of speaking to the audience, no matter what the age group. Ottawa children's broadcaster Norman Cole told a magazine reporter: "I spend hours polishing up the details, for nothing sloppy is allowed to reach the children, as I realize the tremendous influence of the radio. I may be making or marring that priceless possession – 'character' – and so I really work in fear, lest I should harm and not bless some unknown, unseen little one."[110]

Cole's admission that he worked in fear suggests that at least some radio people in Canada had made a commitment to take great care as they made and monitored programs for the young audience. They could hardly do otherwise as they became ever more attuned to the idea that programs could inhabit listeners' imaginations even when they were not listening. However, the concern surrounding the issue of broadcasting's impact on the young mind was more complex and was rooted in uncertainty about the extent to which radio could be held responsible for problems within the home. An early postwar study conducted by the CBC and the National Committee for Mental Hygiene acknowledged that "thriller" programs should be investigated because they appealed to children identified in schools as delinquents and because they were "the poorer programmes, juvenile and unrealistic in character, relying on noise, action and supernatural powers and making no intellectual demands on the listener." The "troublesome" child, particularly boys between the ages of ten and sixteen, figured prominently, yet the investigators refused to indict radio. They placed a greater burden on the nation's parents: "Delinquency, Dr. Hincks points out, is 'caused' by a multitude of factors, with home conditions and atmosphere heading the list. If these are good, neither movies, comics nor radio 'thrillers' can distort the boy's development."[111] Following this curious logic, girls apparently possessed the critical faculties to withstand these distorting influences but would surely grow into women who warranted protection from programming that targeted their suddenly vulnerable minds.

Despite this expert recognition that radio alone could not transform a child into a criminal, radio in the home could certainly contribute to its "atmosphere," and, short of removing the set, radio was the only medium parents could not reliably restrict through the denial of pocket money, which worked well for movies or comic books. Even in the early 1930s, cautionary tales emerged in which parents saw the language of the street making its way inside the home thanks to radio, which, in this case, played the role of vulgar guest:

"Why is it that I should not say that, Mamma? I just heard it over the radio," said the boy.

I had to explain that one must not repeat what is said over the radio, more than what is said in the street. I gave him examples. On which he answered a little surprised:

"But why should they be permitted to say that over the radio if it is bad and common, as you say?"

"And there you are," concluded the mother who was telling me about this episode, "this shows how radio undoes the work we are doing in our efforts to teach our children to speak properly. The only thing left would be to shut off the instrument if these kinds of programs continue."[112]

In the later 1930s, the CBC recognized that, instead of shutting out "certain 'blood and thunder' commercial children's programmes," it could compete with them, and, on one occasion, it commissioned a series of programs on "safety" to be written by the Children's Programme adviser to the National Broadcasting Company.[113] By the latter stages of the war, programming presented in an intimate story-telling style, like *Just Mary* and *The Land of Supposing*, came to dominate the CBC's Trans-Canada Network output for children, with thriller/detective shows remaining on private stations and the CBC-supervised, commercially oriented Dominion chain.[114] The Trans-Canada Network remained the CBC's banner service, and its schedule had to reflect the notion that commercial thrillers, whatever their lasting effects, must be plainly balanced by gentler programming on the CBC or parents might choose to leave the radio silent, which, for everyone in the broadcasting industry, absolutely would not do.

Most examples of what we might call the "uses of intimacy" by those making, listening to, and commenting upon radio employed a sense of the listener as valuable, impressionable, or eager to be entertained. One of broadcasting's jobs was to become or to remain part of the listener's daily life by respecting daily invitations into the home, however fleeting these were. During the Royal Tour of 1951, W.H. Brodie kept CBC announcers on a short leash, warning those charged with describing their Royal Highnesses' activities to think constantly about the individual listener: "it is suggested that our observers might make a good psychological approach to their problems by thinking in terms of those who may have none but the vaguest idea of what Halifax, Calgary, Victoria or Hamilton may look like, or of what they stand for or what people do there."[115] In other words, the announcer was to help the listener enjoy the pageant of the Royal Visit without requiring study or preparation, as if tidying up for a lazy but fastidious houseguest. In keeping with the tone of polite conversation, announcers were to stay quiet on the subject of the King's poor health and the prospect of Princess Elizabeth's succession.[116] Even producers of sponsored programs put great stock in the intimacy developed with an audience. Frank Flint, producer of the drama series *John and Judy*, defended his decision not to publicize the identities of his show's performers. "Our sponsor believes," he told the CBC *Times*, "that as soon as a listener sees the actual person behind the voice of the character in the story, his ability to see himself in the role is destroyed. It lowers his horizon for vicarious living to face him with the reality of an actual person or place."[117]

Person and place mattered, or rather personality and place mattered, as broadcasting helped Canadian listeners to live vicariously by introducing them to personalities and places often well outside their usual ambit. The "magic carpet" called radio worked because it allowed listeners to be introduced to these foreign voices and places on what seemed like their own terms, in their own homes. Sponsors and networks, performers and producers made the programs, and most learned that care must be taken in the making. St John's-based critic Jean Pratt praised shows and announcers that struck the right tone, and he cautioned speakers against "the lilting, sugary tones adopted by some readers of 'commercials.'"[118] The intimate medium required extensive rehearsals, regulation, and restraint. As one editorial about announcers becoming *too* intimate warned:

> When anyone swallows the mike and lets us hear his private mind in its vanity, frivolity, deadly earnestness or bad temper he is in danger of becoming a popular favourite. I say danger, because being natural to microphone is a shortlived business. How many favourites have won all hearts by being natural and spontaneous and then lost the way of it until we heard them impersonating themselves and doing the job worse than a good mimic?[119]

Accordingly, it was best for broadcasters to cultivate affable but polite radio personalities who used broadcasting's intimacy – the double illusion of presence and exclusive conversation – to be the standard-bearers for the network, the sponsor, new tastes, or even a sense of national cohesion.

Though British social researchers Hilda Jennings and Winifred Gill found that youth did not pay as much attention to the radio as did their parents and grandparents,[120] and that therefore the listening public could be divided into a number of distinct groups, programming staff and advertisers in every broadcasting nation had to assume that, if the set was switched on, active listening could be taking place and that at least one such group might be offended or disturbed by programming. As Douglas Craig notes: "broadcasters paid rhetorical homage to the sovereign listener as the most powerful arbiter of the new culture of abundance. That power was privately exercised, and all the more powerful for that."[121] Judgments made in private did not excuse broadcasters from the burden of curation, they just approached that burden in differing ways. All broadcasters had an unremitting desire to know how hospitably their programs could expect to be received in the listener's parlour, but public broadcasters in Canada faced an additional, self-created obstacle. Their custodial desire to protect listeners without compromising the potential of broadcasting for social and cultural "improvement" irrevocably coloured the radio experience. Those in the best position to effect such changes, working in a field that was at least partially governed by the cold realities of ratings and budgets, nonetheless relied upon a powerful illusion to justify their efforts.

2

"The Only Other People Who Exist": American Programming

While the intimate appeal of broadcasting remained an intangible factor for Canadian listeners, the nation just across the border could be visited in person. Its radio programming could, intangibly, be appreciated and feared. Time has done nothing to weaken or erode either of these connections. Canadians still make their visits and continue to live in an economic and cultural environment dominated by the United States. Especially since the Second World War, prime ministers and presidents alike have reaffirmed the obvious compatibilities between anglophone Canada and the United States. Sharing a continent and some legacies from the same imperial power made alliances like the North Atlantic Treaty Organization and commercial arrangements like the North American Free Trade Agreement seem all but inevitable. Today, the "longest undefended border" in the world is not a militarized space, a site of continuous territorial wrangling, or a fence for preventing the movement of people or goods, yet much *monitoring* goes on. We can speak, broadly, of good will and peaceful co-existence.[1] Still, without even taking into account the regional or linguistic variations inside each country, it is plain that historical inequalities, divergent development patterns, and numerous other differences make it impossible to speak of a uniform North American way of life or culture.[2] Despite the friendly appearances, in the realm of communications and media, friction, anxiety, and discomfort have frequently accompanied Canadian-American relations, and some of the oldest axes (e.g., foreign ownership, Canadian content, advertising revenues) continue to be ground decades after they were forged.[3] While all of this suggests an intricate saga with plenty of implications for current and future policy debates, the purpose here is to discuss American programming's role in Canada during radio's reign as the dominant broadcast medium.

Even when we exclude works that are chiefly descriptive or intended to be read by fans of particular shows, historical writing about American radio and radio programming – as experienced by Americans – is still ample. In the last twenty-five years or so, historians of broadcasting in the United States have built on the sociological tradition of radio research, and the work of pioneer broadcast historian Erik Barnouw,[4] venturing into some previously darkened corners of networks', stations', and performers' pasts. Following the first of Susan Douglas's survey histories in the late 1980s, but especially since Robert McChesney's 1993 work on the doomed depression-era movement against commercial control of US broadcasting, studies of such varied topics as radio's connections to race, religion, regulation, consumer affairs, intimacy, independent stations, public broadcasting, network culture, and democracy have been steadily emerging.[5] Historians of broadcasting in Canada and elsewhere have acknowledged American dominance of the airwaves but have tended to focus on instances in which American programming was an unwelcome external force.[6] In Canada, American programs provided both encouraging and disappointing examples of the fare that could emerge under a commercial system blessed with a much larger potential audience. By 1931, "Pro Radio Publico" had already awarded American broadcasters the contract to supply programming north of the border because s/he was not certain "where or how in Canada, the following programmes [could] be duplicated: Roxy's Sunday afternoon hour; General Electric Orchestra in charge of Damrosch; ... to say nothing of Amos and Andy, etc., etc."[7] Novelist Hugh Garner weighed in retrospectively, and narrowly on the side of American shows' entertainment value, noting in the mid-1950s that "some of the early programs may have been corny by today's sophisticated standards, but they kept us from cutting paper dolls out of relief vouchers."[8]

Some of the negative attention directed at American programs undoubtedly arose because they came from "outside" and frustrated nationalists' hopes that broadcasting would help boost a sense of Canadian cohesion. Broadcasters rarely modified shows from the United States to suit the tastes or dispositions of their Canadian listeners, so radio joined the movies as another "window" on the United States of America, albeit a narrow one, omitting much of Americans' daily experience in favour of presenting welcome diversions.[9] Bart Beaty argues, at least for the postwar period, that the "struggle to make Canada a civilized nation ... rested on a reactivation of the perceived antagonism between Canadian morality and American licentiousness."[10] Supporters of public broadcasting wanted to differentiate between American and Canadian programming, but they charted a decidedly different course from those who sought to shut out crime comics. First, they recognized that the fundamental difference between print and radio – broadcasts could not be physically contained – would make prohibition of American programming impossible. In 1935, public broadcasting advocate Graham Spry acknowledged: "The listeners of both nations tune in upon the same programmes. WEAF and WABC are as much a part of the Canadian home as of the American. The North American evening begins with Amos 'n Andy and ends with jazz. Frequencies know no frontiers. In terms of radio, the homes of North America lie along Broadway."[11] As Arthur Phelps, a frequent speaker on the CBC, put it during the war: "We breathe American air."[12] Second, although portraying American programming as too commercially driven or sometimes distasteful helped Canadian public broadcasters define what they could or should do, they could not pretend that most listeners were appalled at what they got from the United States. Late in the 1920s, one radio engineer suggested that roaming the dial led Canadian listeners to admire their continental neighbours: "The owners of more powerful sets can get out [i.e., receive signals from outside Canada] at any time, and generally ignore Canadian Broadcasts completely, an unfortunate condition of affairs tending to accentuate the readiness found among untravelled Canadians, and especially among those who read only news from American sources, to say in tones of awestruck reverence 'They are wonderful people.'"[13] Scholars from Canada and elsewhere have done much to explore nationalism as it related directly and indirectly to the field of broadcasting,[14] but this should not dissuade us from examining aesthetic or moral responses to the *kinds* of programming produced in the United States. When we set aside the nationalist imperative, a more compelling question emerges: Even as broadcasters in Canada were creating material that was supposed to compete with American programming, how and why was American programming so regularly invoked?

A glib answer might be: "because it was there." Actually, this is a decent start, as long as we take the next step. With so many programs floating over the border "free of charge," some of Canadians' listening time was bound to be taken up by material that American networks and stations had created for domestic consumption, just as Canadians and others had become smitten with Hollywood films.[15] Even casual listening bred familiarity with "Vaudeville, variety, and other light entertainment as provided by the American chains."[16] Having heard enough examples of each, a member of the Canadian Authors' Association considered US and UK programming featuring women commentators to be vastly superior to the "preachy" variety of female-targeted efforts on Canadian air.[17] Familiarity left traces that can help us understand what Canadian listeners might have heard in American programming and how Canadian broadcasters positioned their own shows as a result. Without the economic advantages enjoyed by the American broadcasters, who were recognized early on as "too stout a foe to fight,"[18] Canadian private and public broadcasters each operated within a "continental framework" in which even news programming was affected by cross-border market pressures, despite differences between the American and Canadian broadcasting systems.[19] Entertainment value usually guided the tuning hand of the listener, and to most listeners, the national origins of a program mattered little. Over time, public broadcasters even began to worry that it would be difficult to determine what Canadian audiences thought of a program once they had caught wind of its reception/"popularity" in the United States. In 1947, when the CBC was considering a block of arts programming to run one night a week, touting any connection to the BBC's avant-garde Third Programme was considered bad strategy because there had been "considerable criticism of this BBC effort in the US, and Canadian listeners are susceptible to American reaction."[20] Without actively trying to disrupt the Canadian broadcasting industry, American shows still dominated it to the extent that, by 1955, with television reaching second-tier Canadian cities, historian Arthur Lower held out little hope that Canadians could keep American TV in check. Systemic resistance would be a monumental task, akin to building a transcontinental railway, and Lower suggests that the public will seemed absent:

There is no surplus of nationalism in Canada. And there is no surplus of taste, our taste being still that of the backwoodsman, heavy and undiscriminating. Hence the average Canadian has no objection to outside influences. Having no standards of his own, he is overborne by those of other people. And for the average man, the Americans are the only other people who exist.[21]

The CBC, although it had been charged in 1936 with the task of producing and promoting Canadian programs, admitted that US imports went a long way towards providing listeners in Canada with "remarkably rich radio fare,"[22] and, by welcoming private TV stations, declined to implement Lower's protectionist advice. Indeed, as Anne MacLennan shows, the CBC itself was a conduit for American programming.[23] Of the CBC's options, this practice was the more culturally democratic one. The corporation broadcast some American material to meet public demand for these well-known shows and to earn revenue, but it also competed with the big American networks, at times by offering an entirely different style of program. As consumers and producers, Canadian listeners and broadcasters had standards of their own, yet these standards were powerfully conditioned by exposure to American radio and were often expressed in terms of American shows portrayed as magnificent, awful, magical, or trashy, depending on who was doing the portraying. Although it would serve us well to remind ourselves, as does David Goodman, that American broadcasters produced a raft of educational, forum, and public participation programs,[24] several of which inspired Canadian imitations or variations, we should also bear in mind that, for most observers, that sort of program was not the type leaping to mind when American programming came up in conversation. In answering the question of why American programming attracted so much attention in Canada, this chapter looks at two main themes: (1) how listeners and radio people interpreted the strain of *commercialism* running through American radio and (2) how they viewed the *content* of American broadcasts.

ONE CONTINENT, TWO REALITIES

The *type* of broadcasting system that evolved in each place distinguished Canadian from American radio. Commercial broadcasters sewed up the American market during the 1920s, and they masterfully fought off attempts to break their grip on the industry.[25] From the late 1920s, regulation of these broadcasters, punctuated by the creation of the Federal Communications Commission (FCC) in 1934 and an early postwar attempt to make broadcast licence holders more accountable for their programming, largely amounted to cursory oversight of signal strength and monitoring programming for defamatory or illegal content.[26] Except for the inconvenient truths that it took up-front capital to equip a station, then more capital and a measure of patience to secure an open frequency, and still more operating revenue to produce and promote the programming, the broadcasting industry was a "free" market, leveraging the United States' relatively concentrated population centres to sell everything from soap to nuts.[27] The distances between profitable radio markets in Canada – "more than a day's bicycle ride," as one NBC staffer reckoned the Winnipeg-Calgary gap – gave American broadcasters pause.[28] Owing in part to commercial reluctance to carry the costs of a network in Canada,[29] the battles fought between 1929 and 1932 over private versus public control tilted in favour of viewing broadcasting as a public utility, and a kind of compromise was reached, with a broadcasting authority put in charge of building a national network and of regulating the private stations.[30]

These authorities – first the Canadian Radio Broadcasting Commission (1932–36) and then its successor, the CBC – were to make sure that Canadians living at a distance from the larger radio markets would have service and to offer, even in the larger communities, programs that were sometimes different from the most famous American ones broadcast at the same times.[31] To these ends, a yearly licence fee on radio receivers went towards building a chain of public stations and production centres. These public outlets radiated as much regional or national programming as they could, also sending this programming to private stations upon (frequent) request. Private stations chased local advertising revenue and produced sponsored shows, like CKNX's successful *Barn Dance*, as often as possible.[32] All the while, American broadcasters continued to produce shows for sponsors, and these came across the border, where they were rebroadcast by the private stations or picked up by the public broadcaster as a way of bringing well-produced material to Canadians.[33] As for sustaining broadcasts (unsponsored programs), commercial stations understandably tended to avoid them and shrewdly welcomed the CBC's interest in providing programming that was virtually useless as an advertising vehicle.[34] A BBC report on the North American situation put it best: "private stations in Canada are much the same as those in the States, except that they resent the authority which the CBC has over them while they tend to leave to the CBC the job of

she liked to be rescheduled so it would not conflict with her American Thursday night favourites.[41] In an anti-CBC piece, H.H. Stallsworthy of *Canadian Business* declared that the CBC could not match the appeal of American programs, also implying that they should leave the relaying of these programs to private stations.[42]

Not surprisingly, top American performers became household names in Canada. Orville Shugg, in charge of rural broadcasts for the newly operational CBC, had even seen local newspapers fuelling this familiarity, thanks to the American networks' well-oiled promotional machinery. "On a full page devoted to radio," he noted, "there is not a single word of Canadian radio publicity except the regular programme schedules. There is, however, a quarter-page layout devoted to the pictures of American radio stars. Two columns of colourful copy deal with CBS and NBC personalities." Even if Canadian output were to improve dramatically or be granted equal space in the press, Shugg thought it likely that rural listeners, set in their ways, would stick with familiar American shows.[43] Vancouver's *Western Canada Radio News* also featured American acts prominently, with some coverage of the Canadian scene and BBC output. Its extensive schedules reflected what was available to listeners in the city, but most of the featured stories in the paper were about American shows.[44] This sort of radio environment was not one in which home-grown talent was likely to be widely heard or acquire a dedicated following, or one in which writers could make a living in Canada, at least without another job for support.[45] In addition, the talent budgets for top American programs were about ten times those of top Canadian ones by the early postwar period,[46] and Canadian performers had long been affected by the problem of "imported American network radio shows and transcribed shows which can be brought in and broadcast for a mere fraction of the cost of a Canadian show."[47]

COMMERCE AND CULTURE

The prosperous and powerful American networks could reach the bulk of Canada's population, and some defenders of public broadcasting, even before it became a reality in Canada, cited the potential for American dominance. Testimony before the Royal Commission on Radio Broadcasting in 1929 warned that commercial control of radio in the United States was irrevocable and that the rapid growth of the US broadcasting industry affected Canada to the extent that "we [were] surfeited with United States material in every way."[48] This trend in programming did not abate, and what seemed to be a notable development in the later 1920s simply became the norm. Visiting BBC observers spoke of a Canadian audience habituated to tuning in even the marginal stuff from the US networks, of a more selective audience for whom "entertainment which might be called American in type is definitely not wanted," and of a rampant American materialism that, surprisingly, had not affected Canada as much as it had the United States.[49] With numerous American programs as a fixed part of the Canadian radio landscape by the 1930s, it fell to Canadian broadcasters to cope. James S. Thomson, interim general manager of the CBC in 1942–43, equated a strong national network with national dignity. "We know very well we have to associate with the United States of America," he told a meeting of CBC station managers, "but let us be in command of the situation."[50] By "command," Thomson meant reaping financial benefits for the CBC by carrying American programs and monitoring private stations so that they imported only material that was acceptable for reasons of content. These were ambitious goals, but, as the war dragged on, the CBC could not wean itself from commercial revenue, and its regional programming chiefs did not consider upsetting relations with the American networks to be a wise course.[51]

It is tempting to view the relationship between the commercial and public varieties of broadcasting in Canada as absolutely antagonistic, but that was hardly the case. Several senior CBC staff, such as Austin Weir, Ernest Bushnell, Augustin Frigon, Horace Stovin, and Donald Manson, had participated in the development of Canadian broadcasting as producers, teachers, private operators, or administrators in the pre-broadcast era as well as during the 1920s when there was no public broadcasting authority present.[52] For the most part, they maintained cordial relationships with colleagues who remained on the private side once the CRBC and the CBC came along. Private stations, especially in remote areas, often held true monopolies (i.e., they were the only station in town), yet carried sustaining programs some of the time. In a business in which local advertising paid the bills, taking American programming via the CBC-supervised Dominion network, a chain of mostly private stations carrying a greater proportion of sponsored American shows than the corporation's flagship Trans-Canada Network, allowed these smaller stations to offer shows that local listeners might otherwise seek out on distant stations and to keep listeners "in the path" of local ads.[53] Frigon, who succeeded Thomson as CBC general manager, admitted that the CBC was "bound to do commercial broadcasting" in fulfilment of its *obligations* to the listener:

> The Canadian public has the *right* to expect that our networks carry the best type of commercial programmes broadcast in America. We may refuse and we do refuse to carry certain types which, in our estimation, are not suitable to Canadian taste, but there are many others which have such an appeal to the public and are so well within and above acceptable standard that they must be accepted.[54]

For Frigon, who had warmed over time to the idea of broadcasting as public service, advertising was necessary when it accompanied the best programs. On CBC air, commercial programs *of any origin* never exceeded 20 percent of broadcast time but drew the bulk of listeners.[55] CBC Board of Governors chair Leonard Brockington presented American commercial programs as central to the building of a Canadian system: "Today, a few, specially selected for their value as entertainment, come into your homes throughout the land, through your Canadian stations. For that privilege they contribute to the funds necessary for the construction and maintenance of YOUR stations and the improvement of YOUR programmes."[56] Though some wondered if the advertising revenues actually justified the importation of programs,[57] this approach persisted well after the CBC's wartime growth spurt. "If the Canadian national networks did not carry some of the popular American shows," ran the logic in a CBC statement from 1949, "many Canadians would form strong habits of listening to American stations rather than to Canadian networks."[58]

Recognition of this dependency on American programs did not hamper the inclination to cast some of these programs as too market-driven or as only part of the Canadian listener's diet.[59] Even H.G. (Bud) Walker, who after 1944 ran the Dominion Network, did not advocate the promotion of programs beyond listing them in newspaper radio schedules. Even though the "popularity" of American programming spurred the CBC to create the Dominion Network as a successor to the practice of sending these shows out on a more ad hoc basis and, ultimately, allowed the Dominion to put out shows of its own like *Juke Box Jury*, modelled on an American program,[60]

Walker did not want to do everything in the American style. "All out 'commercial' promotion as exemplified by the flashy but effective campaigns of the American networks," he wrote, "is not to be desired. Our national system of broadcasting calls for an approach some-what more dignified and conservative."[61] He had listened to a great deal of American radio, understood the position of his underfunded employer, and could only echo opinions that had been voiced already in the late 1920s. A witness testifying in 1929 before the Royal Commission on Radio Broadcasting condemned the American sys-tem as dominated by selling and concluded that "there has not been a marked tendency to give the listeners-in anything more than that which will hold their attention in between periods of advertising."[62] Artist Lawren Harris deplored American commercial programs that had been "super-streamlined to a slick caffeine insidiousness."[63] Such readings of the American style travelled well as BBC staff also recognized that there were two distinct broadcasting cultures in English-speaking North America. BBC producer Derek Bridson lamented the BBC's chances of selling many of its productions to American networks thanks to the entrenched commercial system, complaining to colleagues: "Great Britain's radio relationship with the United States calls for the highest form of radio sales talk, and has to cope with the deepest form of sales resistance."[64] Some, like writer Ted Allan, had no trouble with the commercial orientation of radio but wanted it always to serve art. Pitching his talents to a friend in the advertising business, he wrote: "Either they get an ass-licking servile Charlie McCarthy who'll voice anything they write, or they'll get someone like me. It may scare them, but let them know what they're in for, if they hire me, because *then* if they do, we can have a wonderful program – and they can sell Ronson's."[65]

Despite awards for some of the CBC's output, and positive reviews of CBC productions by high-profile radio critics like the *New York Times'* Jack Gould,[66] US networks took few programs from Canada. In 1945, American entertainment bible *Variety* quoted Canadian "showmen" as suggesting that an American at the helm of the CBC could cure the corporation's well-known mediocrity. Commercial broadcasting had become North America's "natural order," and its cure for bland was to push further into for-profit territory. CBC Programme Department supervisor Charles Jennings reacted bitterly, assuming that the "showmen" were really "time salesmen, and not broadcasters," calling them "Radio Quislings."[67] The CBC came to view the US commercial system as not only the defining aspect of American broadcasting but also its sole foundation because it was so difficult to control advertisers[68] – and virtually impossible to control American-produced shows.[69] The CBC's Roy Dunlop, in his 1938 "Report from Hollywood," described with distaste the "intense commercialisation of almost every note of music and every spoken word. No sooner is a good idea born in the minds of some of those American producers than they are immediately seeking a sponsor." When he described some representative Canadian programs to his hosts at NBC and CBS, Dunlop found that, "for the most part[,] they liked the ideas and as soon as that was established, the inevitable question was, 'could it be sponsored, what would it sell and how would it go commercially.'" Dunlop then reflected upon how Canadian radio differed from its American counterpart:

It may be old-fashioned but I cannot reconcile myself to the thought that radio is most suited to commercial purposes. We in Canada, I think, have the better ideas that radio's chief purpose is to entertain and to educate and that in many instances a commercial sponsor not only detracts from the real value of the programme but entirely spoils its finer purpose.[70]

Besides discounting the views of private broadcasters as somehow un-Canadian, Dunlop was also looking down the wrong end of the telescope. In North America, commercialization was the established way to do radio, and pursuing a "finer purpose" was the innovation. Newspapers and magazines had long taken advertising, and, for most North Americans, its extension into radio, while possibly annoying in that it took up listening time, was not a complete departure. Newspapers eager to protect their business complained that the CBC failed to reduce the amount of advertising broadcast via Canadian stations.[71] Bud Walker had fallen victim to the same sort of error in calling Canadian radio more "conservative." If anything, American commercial broadcasters and their Canadian cousins were the conservative lot, clinging to a proven method of making radio pay. Advertisers in Canada had already built up viable client lists by 1929, despite lacking a commercial network to establish national links between particular products and programs.[72] In 1931, the CPR's John Murray Gibbon declared that women read newspapers and magazines for the department store flyers and that men, who were "absorbed in business," found print ads fascinating, warning that if "anyone on this side of the Atlantic sets out to eliminate advertising from the air, he would deprive more than half the population of what they want, so as to provide intellectual solace for few."[73] In this environment, it was the public service model that sought to change the game. Some Canadians wanted more ads if it meant that the sponsored Canadian programs would be improved, but companies were not always bold enough to underwrite the sort of programming (e.g., symphonic music) considered desirable by the arbiters of taste.[74] As a listener from Victoria put it: "it is of small consolation that we have little advertising on our national network when so many of the offerings are so mediocre that I cannot conceive of an aggressive industrial company sponsoring them."[75]

Though Canadian public broadcasting pioneers like Ned Corbett advocated a distinctive Canadian system of broadcasting to fill a tall order and "regulate advertising content, combat American influence, develop Canadian talent and pay the line costs to bring good programs to the scattered settlements of our Canadian community,"[76] they valued the *mode of making choices* about broadcasting as much as they worried about the national origin of the programs. As Leonard Brockington notes:

It is true that the programmes originate in the United States. So do many of our best sustaining programmes ... We belong, willy nilly, to the North American continent and North American civilization ... I really think it is an exaggeration to suggest that our national consciousness is going to be blurred by the fact that the International President of the Woodmen of the World, Mr. Charles McCarthy, is heard once a week on Canadian stations and that through the same medium you may now listen for Eight and one half hours out of Ninety-eight on Canadian stations to programmes that many of you welcomed from American stations in the past.[77]

The pressing errand for defenders of public service broadcasting remained protecting the Canadian broadcasting system so that it could offer distinctive content some of the time. One economical way to protect the status quo was through the cautionary tale. Public broadcasters often confided in Americans supportive of public radio and educational broadcasting and, like their allies in the United States, warned of a coming crisis.[78] Graham Spry, one of the architects of Canada's public radio system, addressed an audience in Columbus, Ohio, portraying Canadians as at a crossroads: "The Canadian people," he said, "have the opportunity to save their broadcasting from the intense commercialism and ruthless capitalism which seems to me to be the characteristic of the North American situation."[79]

As the 1930s unfolded and a war came and went, it was clear that the commercial model would only accumulate more capital – cultural and monetary – and that public broadcasters in Canada would, for a long time, have to be "modest in everything."[80] In 1933, the CRBC was eager, for reasons of "patriotism and publicity," to cooperate with an NBC plan for a thirteen-part series entitled "Canada Calling," but from the Canadian perspective, the biggest obstacle was cost,[81] and this sunk the project. In 1938, the CBC's liaison with the BBC noted that not having the resources of the American networks meant an even greater reliance on American programming: "If we had the money we would put in a trans-Atlantic beam telephone service [to get programs from the BBC], but this is out of the question just now. In fact, owing to lack of money, we cannot fill the forty-five minutes we are losing from BBC each day with Canadian programmes. We are having to replace BBC programmes with NBC."[82] Perhaps more embarrassing was the occasion when CBC general manager Gladstone Murray resorted to asking his former cronies at the BBC to pamper a Canadian millionaire visiting London:

> I have had to work hard on him to get the American complex
> dampened down – he is a pal of [NBC president David] Sarnoff's.
> But he is coming round nicely to public service broadcasting ...
> It is however of rather special importance in the scheme of things
> that a little fuss be made of him at [BBC's Broadcasting House].
> The lads at Radio City spread themselves last November.[83]

Operating in straitened circumstances meant that if the CBC wanted to prevent American commercial programs from crowding out other types of material it would have to do what it could to regulate the activities of Canadian private stations more strictly. Even earlier, the CRBC sounded menacing in its attempts to have American shows limit the advertising on their broadcasts via private stations in Canada,[84] but these threats did little to curb the behaviour. In the case of Sunday advertising, the threats prompted NBC officials to consider pulling their programs on that day of the week, but the CRBC backed down.[85] Compared to the money to be made in serving the US market, the American networks viewed potential Canadian revenues as gravy and, hence, as expendable if they proved inconvenient. Their commercial superiority was plain, as was the appeal of their programming. "To attempt a comparison of American and Canadian programs," writes Merrill Denison, a transplanted Canadian in New York, "is manifestly unfair. One might as well hope for definite conclusions to emerge from a debate on the relative merits of dinghy sailing and yacht racing. Not only is there not the money or talent in Canada, but talented Canadians are continually being wooed away from their own country to add their abilities to the American world of entertainment."[86] This version of events had held true for Denison's own career, and even though opinion would always be divided about the extent of the talent drain to the United States, it was clear where most of the money and/or power lay.[87]

CONTRASTING STYLES

One way for Canadian broadcasting authorities to exercise some control within the Canadian system was to question the ads or the format of the shows being imported. Some American imports strayed outside of the commercial arrangements already approved by the CBC, with "Stars such as Crosby, Hope and others giving free plugs to concerns which make gifts to them[,] or perhaps concerns in which the Stars may be financially interested."[88] Nor did Canadian technical staff know exactly how long the ads were going to run. The solution, for some CBC officials, was to reject certain programs as unsuitable for rebroadcast in Canada, and this was often done on the grounds of the import's transgressing a taste boundary.[89] When the axe fell on a sponsored program that the CBC itself carried, there was revenue to be made up. The decision to stop carrying Jack Benny on Sundays in 1944 was not taken lightly because it raised the questions of what would replace Benny and which sponsorships to allow. The cancellation itself appeared to happen because some of Benny's sponsors had created commercials that were not, in CBC-speak, "acceptable for Sunday advertising."[90] The occasion of American programs actually being prohibited, however, was rare, and the problem of finding high-quality replacements dogged program planners into the 1950s.[91] For most Canadians, reacquainting themselves with Benny simply meant tuning him in from an American station.

This, too, made the CBC reluctant to enforce its regulations too strictly because prohibiting an American program would only affect Canadians living outside the range of American stations, the very group that public broadcasters had vowed to serve equitably.

What the offending programs actually did was important as well. Giveaway and contest programs, also demonized in the United States as "subtle genuflections to Luck, the lazy man's idolatrous religion,"[92] were a prime example of how the perceived excesses of the commercial system could work against the importation of American material. Even though the BBC's J.B. Clark observed a trend away from offering "prizes of fantastic value (houses, cars, jobs, etc.)" on US programs by 1948, he still reported that Canadian stations expressed interest in the format as an advertising vehicle.[93] When a western CBC affiliate began a show resembling an American giveaway program, a listener questioned the value of listening to someone else's winning a fabulous prize: "There is no entertainment value in this programme for listeners," she wrote, "it is a cheap imitation of American 'stunts.' It is definitely not worthy of the CBC, which was never set up to amuse a small studio audience in Toronto." We know about this listener's letter because CBC executives quoted it approvingly as they fretted about how tacky it looked when sponsored programs on the Dominion Network would grant the privilege of being heard nationally for the price of "six pocket lighters or a few bottles of toilet water."[94] In the wake of the war, Roy Dunlop suggested that American broadcasters were starting to move away from aggressive commercials, and he linked this to "a strong and very general feeling in American radio today that commercial radio must clean house." He noted that men coming back from overseas had been hearing the "top-flight commercial programmes, with the advertising carefully cut out" and would not "react favourably to commercial sponsors who insist[ed] on shoving their wares down their throats in the guise of 'entertainment' ... Good-taste and good will [would] be the basic insignia of commercial radio in the United States – and this [would] follow in Canada as well."[95] If we go by what Canadians continued to say about American program standards, Dunlop's predicted housecleaning did not happen. For Canadians during radio's heyday, certain types of American programming provided powerful examples of what to avoid.

Whether their families had been in North America for generations or were newly arrived, people living in Canada were familiar with the United States' reputation as a more modern, exciting, if not more dangerous, destination. Graham Spry got a report from Kathleen Pratley, a member of the Canadian Radio League who was trying to explain why recent immigrants were not clamouring to pay their radio licence fees. Pratley characterized these people as

> foreigners who really do not care for Canada or its Government, many of whom would rather be living in [the] States if they only had the chance. They would willingly pay from one to five hundred dollars if anyone can smuggle them over the boarder into the USA but they would fight against a $3 tax to help our Government. To them Canada is a stepping off place for their future home where laws are not so strict, and if one cannot get work, at least they can get into some kind of racket with greater chances of getting away with it. The poor things do not know that they are giving up the substance for the shadow. I think they get more happiness out of the USA programs showing the life of the underworld, as we get it each week but especially Thursday from WXYZ at 9.30 and 10 WJR.[96]

Pratley wrote in the spring of 1931, not knowing that by fall of that year a thriller called *The Shadow* would exist on American airwaves, engaging millions of listeners by playing upon their fears. The crucial impression remained that, to Pratley, Canada was a place where, as the League had discovered, successes were hard won. In her estimation, the United States was a chaotic radio amusement park with a tendency towards dramatizing its excesses. For listeners seeking diversion, American shows were just the ticket. By comparison, Canadian programming seemed either derivative or dull. As American radio critic Robert Landry said of the CBC in 1946: "Choice evening time is turned over to broadcasts on a par with a church basement rally or in celebration of something strongly resembling a hobby."[97] Given the perceived differences in programming styles, it was not surprising that the contrast drawn between American broadcasting as a kind of radio carnival and the Canadian public broadcasting ideal of a radio Chautauqua would focus on certain kinds of programming and radio practice.

One often-exploited theme was the unalloyed showmanship of the big networks. "You just had to sit back and listen," wrote critic Thomas Archer of a program paying tribute to baseball great Babe Ruth, "It was delivered to you on a platter."[98] Canadian radio people could not deny the appeal of the most highly rated US programs, but they took pride in the more temperate range of Canadian productions and/or the quality of programming possible without a "star system."[99] As J.S. Thomson said during wartime:

> The whole North American continent rocks with laughter at the quips and sallies of Charlie McCarthy, Fibber McGee and Molly, Jack Benny and at the amusing adventures of the Aldrich Family. In Canada we have our own modest contribution to program material which is devoted entirely to popular amusement –
> I mean such features as the "Happy Gang," the "Allan Young" show, "John and Judy," and "Penny's Diary."[100]

Canadian performers could *amuse* audiences, but quips and sallies did not seem to be their strong suit. Considered susceptible to American radio comedy, but still identifiable as subjects of the British Empire, Canadian listeners were supposed to be hungry for "programmes that 'put over' England or English humour, to the exclusion of American 'wisecracks.'"[101] In 1951, Max Ferguson, creator of the long-running *Rawhide* character on CBC, applied for a bursary to study radio production at the BBC: "because I realize I have a lot to learn about 'showmanship' and yet cannot bring myself to copy the frenzied American technique of heavy-handed and contrived 'gags' thrust down the listener's throat in the name of humour."[102]

The sense that American programs tended not to take the audience seriously was a difficult one to fathom. The Canadian Association of Broadcasters (CAB), representing private stations, had told Canadians for years that American commercial programs had been "giving the public what it wanted" and that the Americans had long been conducting extensive listener research to determine which shows captured the most listeners. In addition, the CAB contended after the war that to attempt to limit the importation of American programming would be to condone "the erection of the cultural 'iron curtain' between our two lands."[103] But this was already an old refrain. As a long-time friend of Graham Spry complained in 1931, the prospects for educational broadcasting were bleak in Canada because "as soon as you put something on the air which the listener does not want to hear, or is not interested in, he will immediately switch the dial to another station, and I am quite sure that American stations will continue to cater to public demand."[104] In contrast to this notion of the listener ultimately favouring the best in programming, the belief that a kind of Gresham's Law was operating[105] – that is, that "bad" programming was driving out "good" – enjoyed a long life in Canada, and, among radio people advocating a balanced programming strategy, "American" became shorthand for lowbrow. When the head of the CBC's British Columbia Regional Advisory Council wanted to complain about the quality of the music hall programs being taken from BBC, he hauled out the big guns, calling the music hall stuff worse than the average American program.[106] In 1945, CBC regulators prohibited Eddie Cantor's program on private stations because, as the corporation's Austin Weir noted: "[It seemed to be] a series of buildups for rather low comedy wisecracks, a good many of which are definitely questionable, in our opinion. Whenever an attractive female appears, this type of alleged humour is stressed, not only by Eddie Cantor but by the Mad Russian and sometimes by other male guests."[107] Weir's colleague Harry Boyle supported the prohibition, adding that Cantor's show was bound to cause trouble no matter where it was broadcast in Canada, simply because Cantor had, in Boyle's words, a "voice with a leer."[108] The CAB responded by pointing out that, in its estimation, high ratings were a direct indicator of public satisfaction, and Cantor's "excommunication" was an example of the sort of attitude that would drive even more listeners to American stations.[109]

The Canadian broadcasting system's hybrid public-private status had always implied that "the CBC attitude is to achieve a happy mean between the impersonal serenity of the BBC and the breathless enthusiasm of some of our American friends."[110] American broadcasters' practice of putting out a higher proportion of fifteen-minute shows, timed to the second,[111] meant that some material could get cut out of a program, which struck the CBC's Hugh Morrison as "artistic butchery" when he heard it on an American broadcast carried in Canada by CFRB Toronto.[112] Canadian defenders of public service broadcasting could claim that this frantic pace had been adopted to sell more sponsorships, to hold listeners on a station they knew would be featuring something else before too long, or to wring novelty out of the unusual. In 1934, NBC wanted to broadcast the CRBC's unscripted, loosely timed *Northern Messenger* program as a one-off because it could "prove a highly entertaining fifteen minutes or half hour." The CRBC turned down the request on the grounds of intimacy because the program consisted of "personal messages to residents of the Arctic region."[113]

Canadian affiliates of American networks (like the Columbia outlet CFRB) came in for particular criticism when imported programs
were not considered "worthy of Canadians."[114] However, it bears
repeating that such programs could be heard fairly easily over the
American stations themselves. In early 1939, a performer outraged
with a CBC regulation prohibiting him from doing an astrology
show pointed to identical programs coming in unhindered from the
United States. His proposed solution, of course, was to head off the
competition by letting Canadians have home-grown astrology programs because to maintain the regulation would be to pretend that
American radio signals could not invade Canada.[115] The CBC's regulators could also be guilty of ambivalence regarding their role as
radio dieticians. During the war, the CBC's manager of Station
Relations in Quebec, in charge of making sure private stations
adhered to broadcast regulations, asked that an American show be
allowed over Canadian stations, chiefly because the American networks had no trouble with it. Eight years later, the same staff member argued that one way the CBC could be "intelligently different"
was by not allowing Bovril's bull or cow to "moo through the microphone of any network or private station ... even if the American
networks do."[116]

Even though the reputation of American programming as tightly
integrated with the advertising game was sometimes exaggerated for
effect, the basic contours of the North American system were well
mapped. A BBC representative visiting the United States called the
American networks "superbly expert in light entertainment and
showmanship" but summed up the rest of their output as "enrag-
ing," noting that "bogus cowboys entertain the children, and partisan commentators instruct those anxious to hear the news. They
have several good symphony concerts – trotted out repeatedly like a
stage army whenever the quality of programs is questioned."[117]
Early on in the war, long-time CBC staffer Austin Weir returned a
script to a Scottish friend, advising him it was too short for Canadian
radio and that, if he wanted to have such stuff broadcast, then he
should write a whole series. "The place where the big money is made
here in script writing," noted Weir, "is in doing more or less sloppy
love or family serials, and this is confined to a few individuals in the
States, but they are doing extremely well."[118] In 1949, CBC announcer
John Fisher found it encouraging that Canadian listeners, "following
a dull radio talk without soap opera inducements, would sit down

and jam our switchboard with calls."[119] In *The Chartered Libertine*, Ralph Allen's early 1950s novel about the broadcasting scene in Canada, the formula for success in broadcasting is an American formula, and even a hard-headed champion of commercial broadcasting can recite it: "movies about cowboys, plays about private detectives, programmes of recorded love songs, funny sayings by comedians, and serials about unhappy ladies."[120]

Such patterns were thought to do more than eat up listeners' time: they were supposed to be distracting listeners who might be better citizens if not for their radio choices. According to a 1937 letter from the wonderfully named J. Strathallan D. Nation, the most spectacular American programs had probably throttled informed political discourse in the United States and were likely to do so in Canada: "Shall 'Blues Singers,' Eddie Cantors, or even Jessica Dragonettes ... drive from the air the fullest possible discussion of public questions? Cannot the gluttons for jazz tune into Buffalo, Detroit, or some other station in the land of High Pressure Salemanship, if they are devoid of a sense of public duty which should make them want to hear the points at issue exhaustively discussed before casting their votes?"[121] And it was not only adults who were being affected. During its hearings, the Aird Commission heard from the secretary of a Fredericton service club that:

> We get nothing in this community but American programmes. Our womanhood who are teaching the young to prattle are being outdone by the ideas of the radio, because the children are listening to that hour after hour. We have not the powerful stations to keep out American stations and all the stuff that comes to us ... has a tendency to sap the loyalty of the children ... [i]f we have a better class of Canadian programme it will go a long way to prevent so much coming from south of the 49th parallel.[122]

Just before the war, some listeners in Montreal were dismayed when the CBC decided, on the grounds of taste, to prohibit some local programs that had been sponsored by local brewing interests. They complained: "Good programs, featuring excellent artists ... and not too much advertizing are all too scarce; and yet you would remove these and allow the general public, including children and adolescents, to fill their minds with the extraordinary *muck* we get over the air from other, particularly outside programs."[123]

During the early stages of the Second World War, especially before the Japanese attack on Pearl Harbor, the impression that American radio operated outside Canada's moral neighbourhood was even stronger than it was later. The war had affected Canadian programming but (except for war news) did little to peacetime American schedules. In November 1939, as CBC programming personnel were gearing up to deliver programs for and about the Canadian troops already overseas, Gladstone Murray wrote as follows to one of his BBC colleagues: "Our astonishing American cousins (N.B.C. vintage) are carrying Boche troops singing the 'Ave Maria' at Xmas!!"[124] J.S. Thomson noted in early 1941 that even the British United Press news service had "recently taken to giving spicy items about Hollywood stars." He continued: "and I think it is producing rather a feeling of disgust among most sensible people."[125] American stations still carried such items, but those stations were, as always, beyond the control of Canadian broadcasting regulators and tastemakers. It might be best, CBC's news chief Dan McArthur suggested, for the corporation to stop trying to police childrens' programming on the private or American stations and let parents take responsibility.[126]

If we use Thomson's definition, Canadian listeners must not have been "sensible." They were well-disposed towards American programming, as it generally attracted large audiences at the expense of local or CBC programs broadcast at the same times.[127] More representative of the public broadcaster's attitude towards American (or American-style) programming was the CBC's Ira Dilworth, who affirmed that the most famous American shows were probably a fair representation of what a majority of the listening public liked.[128] Canadian listeners got these American shows, but from the CBC they also got *Talking to the Stars,* a Dominion Network feature that let winning contestants, true to the show's title, talk to Hollywood stars.[129] Even when requesting programs from the BBC, CBC programming staff asked for some American-style gossip shows and fewer programs like the wartime morale-booster *Workers' Playtime,* which they did not consider suitable for Canadian listeners accustomed to more dynamic American offerings.[130] Indeed, there had long been strategic reasons for featuring American programming on the CBC. In the words of a 1949 document describing the Canadian radio scene as the most varied and stimulating environment for the listener: "Many listeners attracted by famous names on commercial programs from the United States remain tuned in to hear other types of programs which might not normally come to their attention. Radio tastes of listeners are often broadened in this manner, and the listener receives increased benefits and entertainment from his radio."[131] A year earlier, a survey of listeners indicated that 44 percent thought the amount of US programming was fine as it was and that 19 percent wanted more of it. Only 8 percent were in favour of "discontinuing US programming on Canadian stations, with soaps and crime shows the main target, followed by Benny, Skelton, Hope, quiz shows, *Amos 'n' Andy*, jazz, popular, Hill-billy music, *Life with Luigi*, silly short plays."[132]

This minority, however, tended to be, like some BBC Radio 4 listeners discussed by David Hendy, a vocal bunch, good at attracting attention.[133] In the catalogue of complaints, American jazz was a common theme, and an Aird Commission witness found it to be ubiquitous in Canada.[134] A couple of years later, a Calgary clergyman suggested that his own program had been successful in counteracting the spell of American jazz:

> South of us the waves are heavily laden with foot-music. All the
> kitchen utensils are called into play, with a honk or two of the old
> automobile squeeze-horn for good measure. The radio vibrates
> with such agitation that the family album on top of it jumps
> to the floor in an excess of indignation. People generally were
> becoming convinced that radio-tastes had been permanently
> cemented to this type of programme. Of late this has been abun-
> dantly disproved, and the *Vesper Hour* has been an important
> witness in the trial of that vagrant, familiarly known as Jazz!
> Today he is on parole, bound over to keep the peace, and not
> so apt to strut around as if he owned the world![135]

However, Reverend Luxton clearly had not contained the monster, as a listener wrote in 1938: "I thought the CBC was meant to lift listeners' taste. If so, you have failed miserably. From morning to night you pour out the disgusting decadent Yankee jazz eating at the moral fibre of our people."[136] Though it was difficult to deny that jazz was an indigenous American form of music, it is equally difficult to tell if such livid listeners were more upset by the music itself, its roots in the black community, or its importation from the United States.

Public broadcasting authorities could not, and would not, simply acquiesce to such portrayals of what was on the radio. They recognized the financial and structural limitations under which Canadian broadcasting operated and knew that if the most "popular" programs ceased to be carried over Canadian stations, listeners in Canada who were capable of tuning in to American stations would do so. American programming had made significant contributions to the radio art, but for the purposes of creating programs and developing Canadian public radio, broadcasters emphasized what they considered to be the troubling aspects of the American system, primarily its for-profit structure and its tendency to recognize and exploit commercially successful formats. Canadian attempts to shape programming in Canada relied upon American programming as a revenue source and as a lure to expose more people to Canadian-produced programs outside the commercial model. Early on, whenever a disorganized Canadian radio service made up of private stations and a timidly run CRBC tried to compete with the big-budget, big-talent, fast-moving American commercial programs, the encounter ended badly for the former. Tariffs could not be levied to protect the nascent Canadian broadcasting industry because the product in question had no physical form. The observant Malcolm Frost of the BBC laid his hand right on the problem: "with the lack of necessary experience and facilities, and with the limited amount of talent available north of the border, their programmes appear of second-rate quality to every listener who is able to tune in with ease direct to the stations of the [NBC] and the [CBS]."[137] Public broadcasters admitted that American programs had brought listeners much enjoyment, but, at the same time, they subscribed to the belief that "commercial radio leaves almost untouched many of the most desirable elements of public service exploited by the BBC and other non-commercial organisations."[138] Canadian public broadcasters sought to do what the Americans seemed to be only dabbling at – to present a broader range of programming as entertainment. Arthur Phelps, who strongly supported the CBC's experimental *Wednesday Night* slate of programs begun in 1947, believed that the word "entertainment" had been degraded. "We, the listeners," he said,

> have helped to degrade it. Surely there is entertainment in a
> Fibber McGee and Molly, or a Charlie McCarthy program; enter-
> tainment in lively music, in "easy" music, if you like; entertain-
> ment in spook or crime, or love drama at their levels. But just as
> surely ... there is entertainment in good and informed discussion,

3

"The Dark Radio Cloud Over Here": British Affiliation

Programs tumbling out of the American radio cornucopia may have attracted more attention, but the British Broadcasting Corporation was also a familiar presence on and around the Canadian airwaves from the later 1920s into the television era.[1] Built (almost single-handedly) by John Reith to educate, inform, and entertain (in that order), the BBC also sent programs, expertise, and, on occasion, staff members across the Atlantic to nourish broadcasting in the "senior dominion." Into the mid-1950s, through two decades of an uneasy détente between supporters of commercial and public broadcasting in Canada, and despite the CBC's wartime and postwar growth, the BBC kept its Canadian representative (and auxiliary staff) in place. Given Canada's colonial past and its own history of internal colonization, we might suppose its early broadcasting history would be marked by utter subordination to the BBC, an acknowledged authority identifying itself with empire and the imposition of order in "uncivilized" spaces like radio. Radio's early career would also seem to fit the standard narrative in which Canadians, "always trying to sit on two chairs – a feat never without danger!,"[2] displayed both an affinity for British tradition and an attraction to American show-manship.[3] Yet, despite an undeniably close connection from the early 1930s onward, no dominant pattern of deference, antagonism, servility, or dysfunction characterized the connection between British and Canadian broadcasting. At times the British way looked marvellous and worthy of imitation, and at others it seemed unsuited to Canadian broadcasting. Direct British aid certainly spurred the establishment of public broadcasting in Canada, but Canada's public broadcaster did not consistently behave as though it wanted to build a Reithian Jerusalem in what BBC observers sometimes found a mean, unpleasant land. The only consistent elements were the BBC's watchfulness, and its sympathy for the advancement of public service broadcasting in Canada.

Canadian public broadcasters thought it unwise to challenge the dominant pattern in North America, either by producing shows that could at best be pale imitations of American material or by refusing to grant US programs their audience among lovers of what had emerged as "mainstream" entertainment. Private broadcasters in Canada served local listeners and carried shows produced in talent-rich larger markets, with the public broadcasting body driven by its own proclaimed principles and revenue needs to air both sustaining programs and commercial hits. This incongruous set of accommodations was a by-product of living next to a radio dynamo and recognizing that, given Canada's population, a British-inspired broadcasting-as-public-utility strategy was the most likely foundation both for an enduring network reaching into the hinterlands and for ensuring greater variety in programming. Although the financial and regulatory clout of the state helped create and maintain a basic national service, broadcasting in Canada did not become a system like the British one, in which only the BBC was authorized to operate stations. Broadcasters in Canada did, however, look to the United Kingdom for examples of what might be done at home as well as recognize which types of British programming would not travel well. As the CBC's own publicity put it: "Canada, aware of British tradition and background, was interested in what the BBC had worked out. There were many things to be learned from the experience of other countries, in developing a plan that would best meet Canadian conditions."[4] While honing its own approach, the CBC both accepted some of the BBC's plentiful advice and used shortwaved and "econo-priced" recorded BBC programs to round out its schedule. With five (later six) time zones to cover, and onerous wire transmission costs, programming that was affordable, entertaining, or educational sometimes meant BBC programming, but it did not mean that the BBC was somehow reincarnated in Canada. The job of accounting for Canadian listeners' varied tastes would make sure of that.

The relationship between British and Canadian broadcasting during radio's age of growth and dominance primarily involved the BBC and the CBC, and this account of how radio people in English-speaking Canada used BBC programs, experience, and assistance is primarily about this relationship. Through the twenty years or so covered here, members of staff in both organizations worked at strengthening public service broadcasting in Canada, and working out what listeners in Canada might appreciate differently from those in the United Kingdom was part of that task. Over the same period, these different (and diverging) cultural contexts made for some friction between these allies as the CBC necessarily adopted programming strategies adapted to its domestic circumstances. Though they may seem like straightforward indications of like-mindedness, instances of cooperation and mutual accommodation between the BBC and the CBC also remind us that the making of programs depended on the interplay of traditional ties, local conditions, and an evolving approach to serving listeners.

What did cooperation and mutual accommodation look like? As the bodies chartered and empowered to oversee broadcasting in their respective jurisdictions, the BBC and the CBC were bound to create some form of working relationship, just as each of them needed to extend a hand of courtesy to the American networks. The Empire/Commonwealth bond, strengthened during the war in no small way by radio,[5] might have been enough to justify a collegial atmosphere, but a shared commitment to the ideal of public service broadcasting and a strong sense of its fragility in Canada prompted a level of familiarity beyond what either organization required to fulfill its mandate as a national broadcaster. This deeper entanglement, impossible to quantify but there to see in memos and programming files, often radiated warmth and commiseration. The BBC's Gilbert Harding, in an early postwar report from Canada, made it plain he was pulling for the CBC. He distributed blame and praise, despairing that this CBC employee was not performing well and lauding that one as evidence the whole enterprise would eventually be a first-rate outfit. He summed up by declaring: "there are all kinds of slits in the dark radio cloud over here through which one can see the near-silver lining."[6] A few months later, his colleague Michael Barkway warned that the BBC needed to work harder at appearing neutral in Canada because the American networks and the private broadcasters in Canada were especially attuned to any sign of "tyranny" on the part of the BBC.[7] Barkway's warning stands out because it was so rare amid the avowals that a much more important common task remained. In both organizations, policy and program makers casually embraced the sentiment Harding had betrayed: the problems and prospects of the CBC are the problems and prospects of public service broadcasting in North America, and the CBC does not have to face them alone.

This solidarity had two features. First, and perhaps more obvious, as the senior broadcasting authority in the Empire/Commonwealth, the BBC aided and encouraged the CBC in a variety of ways. When and how the CBC chose to accept this aid and encouragement had an impact on programming. Second – less obvious but no less important in relation to programming – CBC people expected the BBC's staff would be their allies in bringing a variety of programs to listeners. Crucially, they expected this alliance to transcend mere courtesy because it was based on a kind of *intramural* obligation, each organization committed to spend licence revenue wholly on providing programming, with nothing held back as profit margin. It was no great leap for CBC staff to avail themselves of the BBC's experience in making programs for a variety of listeners or to think they could send programming back to Britain in return. The BBC directed its Empire Service explicitly at places like Canada, and perhaps even more explicitly at Canadians ambivalent towards the emotional or practical utilities of empire. But the relationship was not only about empire consciousness and cohesion, it was about making programs.

STRUCTURES AND SIMILARITIES

In addition to the body of work on the broadcasting histories of individual countries, we have two fairly recent monographs on the connections between broadcasting efforts in the United Kingdom and among other English-speaking peoples: Michele Hilmes' *Network Nations* and Simon Potter's *Broadcasting Empire*.[8] By reading broadcasting's past as one that both engaged and transcended questions of nation and empire, these works join a few others in helping us to see how broadcasting organizations understood broadcast media and how they tried, with varying rates of success, to harness these powerful modes of communication.[9] On a more practical level, Potter and Hilmes also treat the overall development of broadcasting in a variety of places, making it easier to dig deeper into concepts like taste. Hilmes reminds us that the histories of cultural institutions whose chief products could travel anywhere in the world instantly are best handled by recognizing when borders mattered and when they did not. The British-American broadcasting axis she describes may not have been composed of people holding similar views on broadcasting's purpose, but Hilmes warns against pencilling in conflict when the evidence points to a generally friendly and artistically fruitful exchange, a "circuit of continuous influence."[10] Harmonizing with Hilmes's call for a transnational perspective, Potter argues that "the interactions of the BBC with a range of other organisations, across the empire's internal boundaries ... shaped the audiences available for BBC programmes overseas, and how those audiences responded to what they heard and saw." Even though he concludes that "public broadcasting was, in the end, simply not sufficient to the task of reinforcing Britannic identities in the dominions at a time of imperial decline,"[11] Potter's employment of "integration" and "disintegration," along with the concurrent "continuities" and "challenges" in the postwar period, suggest how entangled the BBC and broadcasting organizations in the dominions could become.

The present study is concerned only with the radio era, and this chapter pursues the theme of integration further by focusing on the *affiliation* between the BBC and the CBC and what it meant for programming. "Affiliation" is not a term normally used to refer to the relationship between broadcasters operating in different nations, partly because cross-border affiliations were relatively rare and perhaps because of the connotations of power imbalance the term carries. However, it is used here for precisely this latter reason. Affiliation seems to be the best way of describing the form of BBC-CBC interaction, in which one organization (the CBC) was the affiliate, the weaker partner, grateful for support but not especially keen to express this gratitude publicly. As the senior institution, having contributed mightily to the conditions necessary for affiliation by supporting the genesis of public broadcasting in Canada, the BBC influenced the CBC's operations by example and continuous contact. Programming, when it moved between the two, most often moved from the BBC to the CBC. Like stations affiliated to the CBC or American networks, the CBC developed its own philosophies of serving Canadian listeners. Yet these ideas emerged in the context of the kind of bond Jock Given calls "complex and shifting," through which "young institutions of broadcasting, like the nation states that crafted them, explored different kinds of relationships, complementing, co-operating and competing with each other."[12]

While broadcasting in North America (especially in the United States) was bursting forth in the early 1920s, adding stations at a

prodigious rate, British broadcasting had a more circumspect beginning, partly thanks to unflattering reports about American programming, and partly because post-First World War security regulations
in the United Kingdom all but precluded the sort of boom in amateur
radio that had helped clear a path for broadcasting in North
America.[13] In 1922, British radio interests formed a private con-
glomerate, the British Broadcasting *Company*, preventing a monopoly controlled by the dominant set manufacturer Marconi but
creating a multi-headed entity allowing Marconi and other set makers to cash in anyway, and drawing this first "BBC" into the business
of making programs.[14] By 1926, concern over reproducing the
"chaos" apparent in the United States had nudged the company out
of existence in favour of the British Broadcasting *Corporation* of
popular and historical legend.[15] This new BBC debuted as a tightly
controlled public entity that focused its efforts on programming.
Jean Seaton's sketch of John Reith's considerable influence illustrates
his dour spirit well, despite her well-founded, but counter-factual,
supposition that "many of the features of broadcasting which are
taken for granted today would certainly be absent" if the BBC's "first
director had been a career civil servant, a banker, or a Bloomsbury
intellectual."[16] By the early 1930s, a time of anxiety, indigence, and
adjustment for Canadian broadcasters, the BBC was in a position to
inaugurate its Empire Service[17] – and to evangelize public service
broadcasting in the dominions and colonies.[18] In most accounts cen-
tred on Canada, the period leading up to the creation of the CBC is
one in which the BBC kept a close eye on the Canadian situation,
standing in the wings to prompt supporters of the public option during Canadian broadcasting's most "improvisational" phase. Austin
Weir, on hand for some of the crucial moments, portrays the BBC as
a helpful re-broadcaster of momentous occasions like canal openings, generous with its engineering help, and a provider of expert
witnesses to appear before parliamentary committees.[19] The resulting alliance was based not only on the desire to project "closer imperial connections" over the radio,[20] but on the BBC's astute reading of
Canadian public broadcasters' chronically disadvantaged position.

Late in 1936, ex-BBC executive Gladstone Murray returned to
Canada to run the CBC and maintained ties with some former colleagues, further formalizing some of the earlier connections between
the BBC and Canadian public broadcasting.[21] The Royal Tour of
1939 stoked the embers of imperial connection in Canada, and

broadcasting historians have rightly pounced on broadcast coverage of the tour as a rich source.[22] Wartime brought a tighter integration between the two corporations, especially while the United States remained officially neutral. Like the BBC,[23] the CBC came into its own during the Second World War, becoming a broadcasting authority – though perhaps not meeting the rosiest expectations of early public broadcasting advocates – and assembling the Dominion Network to offer more listeners a wider variety of programming options. During the Second World War, both corporations found themselves at the service of their nations' respective war and information ministries, and even clumsy propaganda like *Canada Carries On* found favour at the BBC.[24] After the war, a larger, more vigorous CBC began to exercise the power it had and eventually became, as Marc Raboy has called it, the "only institutional power in Canadian broadcasting."[25] Relations with the BBC remained familiar, even familial, but coloured by such factors as postwar trade imbalances, the further recession of empire, and, after television's arrival, by the CBC's newly expressed desire to participate in showing less developed Commonwealth nations how broadcasting was done.[26] The objective here is not to recount the history of both broadcasting institutions but, rather, to examine how the visions and experiences of people working in and through those institutions prompted them to modify and amplify their understandings of what broadcasting should be doing.

COVERT ACTIVISM

It is tempting to treat the time before the CBC's arrival in 1936 as a kind of "anteroom" to the spacious "suite" occupied by a more robust and prolific broadcasting organization. Although the years before 1936 were no less important, temptation wins out. The two eras were distinct because of the BBC's role in demonstrating that the Canadian Radio Broadcasting Commission needed replacement but, more important, because the earlier period introduced some of the main themes that would affect how the BBC and the CBC interacted over the longer term as public entities in charge of broadcasting. There is also a disparity in evidence. Mary Vipond notes that, "although the perception may be an artifact of archiving choices made in the 1960s, it does not appear that the CRBC held formal meetings on program policies, and there is no evidence that any of the principals, including Charlesworth, consulted with programming executives at the BBC or the American networks."[27] Perhaps the CRBC did not practise consistent documentation of its programming policy or the material did not survive in Canada, but the BBC archives contain some significant evidence of contact worth mentioning here. The problem remains that, in comparison with the CBC period, the commission era was both shorter and more obscure to us.

Keeping in mind the public service mandates the BBC and the CRBC/CBC adopted for themselves as national network carriers, it is easier to see why these organizations employed broadcasting strategies and practices that seemed similar, especially to public broadcasting's detractors. In contrast, private broadcasters' participation in the international program trade tended to be directed towards piping in shows already proven successful in the United States. And why not? Those programs paid the bills, and private broadcasters were most effective at serving local audiences with amateur hours, ads, and local announcements, thanks to regulations that prohibited them from forming networks and thanks to the cost of making more elaborate programming.[28] Despite a broad congruence of outlook between public broadcasting bodies, BBC methods were not easily transferable to Canadian radio. Still, the BBC's longer experience in the field and Britain's dominant position in Canada's colonial and imperial past suggested a cooperative relationship from which the CBC needed to emerge if it was ever to dismiss charges that it took its cues from London. Not everyone wanted it to emerge. Part of the Canadian listenership wanted the CBC to strengthen those waning associations. Others saw the BBC's programs and Canadian imitations of them (when those occurred) as sought-after islands in the ocean of American programming available via Canadian and US stations. Still another group hated the BBC because it was a public broadcaster and so, for it, incompatible with the spirit of Anglo-American free enterprise. Plainly, the discussion of broadcasting reflected some of the preoccupations floating around English-speaking Canada, some of which were only incidentally related to broadcasting itself. In such surroundings, the BBC and the CBC had their moments of harmony and discord over programming. To make better sense of those moments, we should spend some time in the anteroom.

Even (and perhaps especially) before the creation of the CBC, the unsettled state of Canadian broadcasting drew British attention. Canada's broadcasting history commenced with private, and a few educational, stations starting up from the early 1920s, and came to include the ambitious but rudimentary CNR and CPR networks. Adding the time it took to conduct the Royal Commission on Radio Broadcasting (the Aird Commission) and the ensuing debate over control of radio, the future of broadcasting was discussed on and off, inside and outside official channels, for over a decade. During that time, the BBC had no institutional counterpart in Canada. This did not preclude contact between the British authority and those invested, in one form or another, in Canadian broadcasting. Supporters of public service broadcasting had become used to looking to the BBC as an example by the time the CRBC came into being in 1932, and the new institution helped focus British concern. While Britain and Canada seemed to be growing apart during the early 1930s, BBC interest in the CRBC, then struggling to become a national broadcaster worthy of the name, only deepened the sense of detachment. In spite of a near sundering of ties, timely interventions on the part of BBC personnel helped nudge the CBC into being as a *North American* broadcasting organization – not a miniature BBC, though arguably inspired by it.[29] The advent of the CBC settled the question of public broadcasting's survival, but that development hardly marked the end of an intricate connection.

Before there were any public broadcasting outlets in Canada, the BBC had an impact, in practical terms, as a resource for public broadcasting advocates and, more abstractly, as a fixed point towards which some wished to travel and others did not. Listeners, broadcasters, and others curious about broadcasting's future considered themselves well aware of what the BBC was and the sort of programming it offered. By the mid-1920s, the BBC's radio infrastructure had been developed to the point at which, even though his broadcast from CNRA Moncton – offering "solace to the landless men of Britain in the manless land of Canada" – was meant to be heard across the Atlantic, CNR vice-president W.D. Robb presumed that many British listeners would be tuned in as usual to their own domestic programs.[30] The CNR radio division, the first Canadian broadcasting organization to attempt running a nationwide network, sought help from the BBC in 1930, and its trust was rewarded by an effort to send the right person as a dramatic program advisor. The BBC valued the reputation it had already established in Canada, knowing whoever they sent would "go out to Canada with, as it were, the cachet of the BBC upon him and upon his work."[31] When the CNR's Austin Weir hired a programme assistant in 1929, he looked to Edinburgh native Esme Moonie, who, in addition to being well connected in Women's Institute circles, had broadcast for the BBC – a clear signal to Canadians that she could be trusted to create programming "on a high plane" anywhere.[32] When the time came for the CNR to wind up its radio operations and hand them over to the CRBC in 1932, Weir angled for a job with the commission, boasting that, along with being able to play well with American networks and with performers, "Canadian National ha[d] been the only Canadian Broadcaster heretofore enjoying the full confidence of the British Broadcasting Corporation."[33]

Before the handover was even considered a possibility, Canadians debated what sort of broadcasting system would most faithfully serve the public. The status quo for more than a decade was an industry made up of privately run stations, some owned by newspapers, some by radio manufacturers, the railways, and other institutions or stakeholders. Those who owned or operated commercial stations in the late 1920s held the position that the public was already being well served. People kept tuning in and buying more sets, and sponsors were willing to underwrite the production of more elaborate and expensive programs. To the "free enterprise" camp, this growth was both sustainable and suited to audience appetites, and an industry driven by profit appeared to be the prescription for Canada's broadcasting future. The Aird Commission, however, heard nationalist/imperialist witnesses calling for intervention in favour of the imperial connection: "since we cannot resist the influence of the Republic to the south, a determined effort should be made to augment it by making closer contact with British culture through this medium."[34] Commissioners also heard some words of warning about BBC programming, which, one witness timidly suggested, could "occasionally suffer from occasional overweighting of heavier programmes which a great many people are not yet prepared to hail with continuous delight."[35] To supporters of commercial broadcasting, the BBC, not officially a party to the hearings, nonetheless served as a proxy for state oversight or involvement in the industry. The commission's final report put the commercial status quo in jeopardy by recommending that broadcasting be nationalized in a manner more similar to the British arrangement than to any other nation's.[36] This recommendation set up a clearer division between the competing models because, by 1932, thanks to relayed programs and to the

CNR's selective adoption of BBC studio design and program presentation elements,[37] Canadian listeners had encountered British broadcasting and Canadian broadcasting in the British mode. Supporters of public or private broadcasting for Canada could, with help from sympathetic journalists in Canada and the United States,[38] remind others what they were not supposed to like about the opposing style. Beginning just over a year after the Aird Commission delivered its recommendations, the Canadian Radio League (CRL) led the campaign to secure a nationalized system for Canada, a campaign that some citizens joined and some prominent Canadians supported but that commercial radio interests opposed.[39]

The debate intensified in 1931 with R.W. Ashcroft's call to leave Canadian radio as it was. Ashcroft managed the NBC-affiliated CKGW in Toronto, "Canada's Cheerio station," and was quick to frame the question in stark political terms, contending: "In Great Britain, where the Government maintains a monopoly, broadcasting is a lamentable failure, from the standpoint of a large majority of the audience. The slogan of the British Broadcasting Corporation might well be: 'The public be damned!'"[40] Another strident response to the CRL's activism came the same year from J. Murray Gibbon of the CPR's publicity wing. Gibbon began his condemnation of the CRL on reliable ground, by identifying it with the BBC. Amid his concerns that the adoption of public broadcasting would force talented Canadian performers to seek work in the United States, Gibbon supposed that a "BBC or Continental European" system would not be suited to the "North American mentality." He repeated Ashcroft's false contention that the BBC was a "government monopoly" and warned Canadians that, if such a creature were to come to Canada, variety in programming would suffer.[41] In his heated response, Graham Spry dismissed Gibbon's call for a privately run network of stations and defended the BBC as a testament to the "economy and efficiency of a publicly-owned company."[42]

The BBC had been named in this tug-of-war over Canadian broadcasting because it was already a well-known example of public service broadcasting and was certain to trigger reactions of approval or outrage. Regardless of one's orientation towards broadcasting's role in shaping the lives of individuals or communities, the distant corporation, despite having no *official* status in Canada, carried symbolic weight. Its Canadian critics liked to suggest that it was interested not in entertainment but in regimentation, and they made comparisons between virtuous Continental radio operators and the BBC. As one of these sceptics noted: "a business organisation is always ready to cater to public taste and has always done so more successfully than any bureaucracy."[43] From the other side of the fence, CRL members suggested that a "bureaucracy" like the BBC could be a beacon because, to them, it was simply an "organization of experts trained in making up programmes."[44]

Advocates of a wide-open radio industry found themselves answering to a new regulator when R.B. Bennett's Conservative government established the CRBC as Canada's broadcasting authority in 1932. This development dashed the wildest dreams of everyone involved in the post-Aird Commission mudslinging – Ashcroft, Gibbon, *and* the CRL – but everyone also came away with some positive news. The details of this process, and the ensuing political battles, have been covered exhaustively in historical writing about Canadian broadcasting.[45] For the purpose of interpreting these developments in the light of programming, it is most important to note that, despite legislation empowering the CRBC to take over the private stations, those stations continued to operate independently of the commission. Their economic clout, in the political climate of the Great Depression, resulted in a hybrid system.[46] The CRBC, with a tiny budget relative to the expectations placed on it, and a slate of commissioners ill-suited to managing a fledgling broadcasting institution, was nonetheless a single public broadcasting organization. After a considerable time in the wilderness, public broadcasting in Canada had an address and could receive callers in a more formal fashion. The BBC was a frequent (though not always welcome) guest, especially while the CRBC was struggling to do work for which it was woefully under-funded. The programs the CRBC selected to import, while not British enough for some, were not typical of local or American network-produced fare either.[47] Add to this the practice (deplored by the BBC) of American networks dumping recordings of their unsponsored material onto the radio marketplaces in the dominions, and we can see how charged the environment was. Private station operators and representatives of American networks characterized the few BBC Empire Service programs coming to Canada after 1932 as typical of BBC output, a development that concerned BBC reps who considered these shows to be their second-best offerings.[48] One of the CRBC's commissioners, Colonel W.A. Steel, knew there was a demand for British programming but resented BBC control over which programs would be sent to Canada, and he issued a hollow threat to look to France and Italy as more suitable partners.[49]

Merely by existing and growing for a decade, the BBC set a standard that was plainly above what had been (or could be) accomplished by a public broadcasting outlet in depression-era Canada. The *Montreal Herald*'s editors lamented the CRBC's inability to meet such a standard, adding that the Canadian public was misguided if it believed "the Radio Commission was going to banish all advertising from the air, shift it back to the newspapers where it belong[ed], and give music, laughter, and intellectual edification the right of way."[50] Despite some posturing on the part of the CRBC about knowing best what sort of programming Canadian listeners would appreciate,[51] it was too new to the game, and too poor to resist the temptation of asking for some help from the BBC. On one occasion, the request was for: "a special half hour programme daily, at a time when the reception is good in this country, of such a nature that we could afford to pay the artists' charges for recording. This need not be your very highest class artists, provided it was a typical British programme."[52] Requests like this one, which required sharp correction from the BBC on several points of international copyright law,[53] convinced the BBC that its experience was a resource to be drawn upon. Canadians knew this, too. For instance, inside and outside of provincial education departments, Canadians believed that there was much ground to be made up before they could match the BBC's record in the field of educational broadcasting.[54] Even late in the CRBC's lifespan, input from educational program staff at the BBC remained highly valued in Canada. When Major Frederick Ney of the National Council of Education of Canada (NCEC) heard that the BBC's R.S. Lambert could not attend its conference, he wrote: "This is a year of blows! ... I had counted on Lambert upholding Adult Education, which after all, in recreational form, is the very essence of BBC, and what we need so badly in Canada."[55]

Likewise, with respect to "recreational" programs, where the need to cater to audience tastes rather than to a set curriculum determined what went on the air, the CRBC occupied a difficult position. As the body in charge of transforming Canadian broadcasting from a jumble of independent operators and commercial interests into a national system, the commission needed to come out of the gate providing shows comparable with everything else available in North America. But on a continent where much of the population believed that commercial radio entertainment came to them for free and perhaps even considered it quaint to knowingly pay a fee towards the cost of programming,[56] doing a good job on inadequate revenue was unlikely. The CRBC did not produce spectacular results, fuelling suspicions that publicly controlled radio should not have been tried at all. Newly knighted Toronto Symphony conductor Sir Ernest MacMillan noted that even "a national radio board which seeks to uphold the principle of quality first" would not be immune to political deals and regional gripes, and would be "bound to be vigorously attacked by those whom they pass over."[57] The BBC did not have such existential worries. As the established broadcaster at the centre of the Commonwealth, able to corral much of the talent in Britain and to implement its strategy centrally from London, the BBC looked – and was – considerably more self-assured than the CRBC. Privately, BBC officials remarked that "Dominion and colonial listeners [were] less sophisticated than those at home."[58] Real or imagined, this gap did not absolve the CRBC from having to find ways to grow up quickly, and one obvious approach was to establish and maintain a cordial working relationship with the BBC. However, as Mary Vipond explains, the CRBC failed to do this, and it took direct analysis and action from the BBC to bring about changes that would enable such a relationship to be possible later, under the CBC.[59]

Despite the tremors rumbling through the Empire after the First World War, with the dominions taking on more international responsibilities and legal ties to Britain loosening via the Statute of Westminster in 1931, some Canadian listeners believed that the BBC could offer them worthwhile radio. When the CRBC announced the arrangement to pick up shortwaved Empire Service programs and record them for rebroadcast, the news was viewed favourably, even though listeners tended to prefer live performances.[60] This was a symbiotic "push-pull" in which the BBC created programming so that Canadians (and others in the Empire) could "imagine themselves as part of a global Britannic community,"[61] and at least some Canadians asked to hear from Britain not only about current events and concerns but also about artistic matters. Knowing that the BBC had already broadcast some Shakespeare, John Craig of Winnipeg's Little Theatre wrote to BBC Drama's Val Gielgud to have some practical questions answered and to ask for scripts. Besides showing us that Shakespeare had claimed a spot on the second Sunday of every month on the BBC's domestic schedule,[62] Gielgud's helpful but casual reply showed that he *expected* to be fulfilling this role, supplying guidance to a would-be broadcaster "out there" in a place that had not quite worked out how radio should be done.

The selective adaptation of some British broadcasting standards and practices was a tricky proposition, but one eased by Gladstone Murray's visit to Canada in 1933, early in the CRBC's mandate, as the guest of Prime Minister Bennett. At that time, Murray was still working for the BBC and had already come to Canada in 1932 to testify before a parliamentary broadcasting committee. He had turned down the top job at the CRBC after his first visit,[63] and he had returned to offer the commission a kind of manual advocating several strategies that smacked of BBC practice adapted to Canada, along with some other strategies that broke the mould entirely.[64] Publicly, he warned that the "idea of direct State management in addition to State control should be eliminated with the minimum of delay," but in confidence to NBC's Merlin Aylesworth, Murray mentioned that a combined effort among private stations, in which the CRBC could become like the original British Broadcasting Company, would be desirable.[65] This was a lesson lifted from his interpretation of the BBC's experience, and it was relevant in a Canadian radio environment in which opponents of public broadcasting had already raised the spectre of a national broadcaster as the mouthpiece for the incumbent government. In his operational vision for the commission, radio announcing was to be "an opportunity to set a new standard for the North American Continent" but without "imposing a uniform dialect," one of the BBC's most-caricatured features. Still, Murray hoped announcers in Canada could develop a BBC-like "sense of repose which is not as evident as it should be either in Canada or the United States."[66] Musical productions were to be the single largest component of the programming schedule, and Murray counselled the CRBC to create a music department centralized like the BBC's but without (for the moment) a dedicated symphony orchestra, and he recommended a more tolerant attitude towards dance music.[67] At the same time, Murray was busy arranging for BBC programming to be picked up by the Canadian arm of Marconi and passed on to private stations because the CRBC was either not equipped or not motivated to act as the BBC's distribution agent.[68]

Given the commission's unfamiliarity with the job at hand, Murray's nudges seemed justified. After this initial phase of involvement, which also included the first of Malcolm Frost's visits, BBC officials seemed to take a greater interest in the CRBC's fortunes, keeping up something well short of a vigil but clearly giving Canada more than the occasional glance. The BBC monitored listener correspondence for its Empire Service broadcasts into what it called the "Canadian Zone," concluding: "Dance music and Vaudeville entertainment, provided it is essentially English in character, is obviously enjoyed."[69] Through 1934 and 1935, the BBC had a reasonably clear picture of the whole North American broadcasting industry. It wished to exchange and sell programs to American stations and networks, and maintained its North American office in New York for that purpose, but was unable to guide the US radio market.[70] In contrast, the internal doings at the CRBC were something it could monitor and influence, thanks to the Commonwealth connection, a common role as national public broadcasters, and well-timed visits. On his return from a visit early in 1934, Frost brought, along with some unflattering portraits of the commissioners, news that two of them, Hector Charlesworth and Col Steel, were relaxing the CRBC's limits on advertising to suit their friends at NBC and CBS.[71] This seemed like a small rebellion against the BBC practice of banning ads entirely but was most revealing because of the extent to which it set wheels in motion at the BBC itself. Within a couple of weeks, there ensued further speculation about Charlesworth favouring friends at Marconi over his natural allies at the BBC and a letter/edict signed by Director-General Reith laying out how programming was to be beamed to Canada.[72] Later the same year, BBC Empire Service director C.G. Graves asked permission to go to a conference in Chicago and also to check on Canada because, in his words, "there may be a certain need to umpire relations which are at present none too good."[73]

Presuming that one could simply swoop in and act as an umpire suggested that, at best, the BBC considered the CRBC a troubled organization that would welcome the input and,[74] at worst, a ward that need not be consulted in advance of action. Nor was this ambiguous connection between the two organizations easy to hide. In 1935, NBC tried to discourage the commission from carrying some Mutual network programming by informing Steel that the BBC only dealt with NBC and CBS, hoping he would be cowed by the prospect of BBC disapproval.[75] The connection was less ambiguous to Gladstone Murray, who nonetheless remained keen to avoid the appearance of BBC interference in Canadian radio. On two occasions in 1935, he wrote to the CRL's Alan Plaunt expressing his fear that Canadians would think the BBC too heavy-handed in its dealings with the commission. The first time he noted that "any suggestion of an English racket would be fatal!"[76] The second time he elaborated on his own delicate role ("I work a lone hand on this advisedly") and admitted that not all Canadians would view British involvement in a favourable light: "It will be difficult, at best, to combat the suggestion that UK interests + particularly the BBC are trying to get hold of Canadian radio. It is in fact a great ambition of my worthy boss Sir John Reith to have a satellite system. Needless to say this is madhouse doctrine."[77]

Other BBC employees did a more effective job than Murray when it came to influencing the overhaul of the Canadian broadcasting system in 1935–36. Felix Greene, who would later become BBC controller of programming, paid a timely visit to Canada late in 1935, when "a general unrest was very apparent in all those connected with broadcasting."[78] He advised certain changes to Canadian broadcasting in a memorandum, which he thought Liberal minister of marine C.D. Howe followed quite closely when plans were laid for the CBC.[79] Greene condemned the CRBC operation in early 1936 as "dreadfully slip-shod" and confessed that the commission's inauspicious first attempt at public broadcasting in Canada was "almost enough to make one lose patience and give up any attempt at helping them."[80] There remained the danger of having such help appear as though the BBC were imposing its will, and here Greene's fears surpassed Murray's. Aware of appearances, Greene categorically ruled out sending anyone else to persuade Canadian officials of public broadcasting's virtues,[81] preferring to hold quieter meetings that were more easily interpreted as relating to the BBC's routine interests in North America. At any rate, Greene knew that wholesale adoption of the BBC style would be extremely difficult given the entrenched positions of private stations, Canada's sparse population, and the ubiquity of American programs. In 1936, a joint plea from advertisers and private broadcasters portrayed public broadcasting as heavy-handed, British listeners as disadvantaged (or brainwashed), and Canadian listeners as independent, noting "what perhaps may be the greatest difference of all, between Great Britain and Canada – a difference of psychology. If the British listener will willingly consent to being deprived of the right to choose his own programmes, his attitude provides a marked contrast with what we would expect from

Canadian listeners."[82] American broadcasters familiar with what Greene was doing in Canada supposed that some Canadians took a dim view of BBC involvement, but they seemed more concerned with who would head the new Canadian radio authority than with the remote possibility that the whole system, including private stations and American affiliates, would be nationalized.[83]

Under the CBC, the avenues of influence were widened and improved, and modes of interaction characteristic of an affiliate relationship appeared more plainly. These were: mimicry or adaptation of BBC practices; a mutual effort to make sure BBC programming could be heard via public and private stations; BBC observation of Canadian broadcasting; advice about programs and how to make them; and, finally, a mutual desire to make these interactions incidental to the BBC's normal operations and the consolidation of public service broadcasting in Canada. With the arrival of the CBC, the free flow of information and expertise between public service broadcasters did not constitute collusion to deny listeners programs they might have wanted to hear. On the contrary, much of the exchange had to do with ensuring that listeners' various tastes were adequately served.

A JUNIOR PARTNER?

As far as listeners were concerned, the CBC began functioning (i.e., producing programs) in early November 1936, with Murray as general manager, and the mixed public-private system remaining in place as a "special peculiarity" of Canadian broadcasting. Few listeners knew, and undoubtedly even fewer cared, that Murray's return home was connected to politics within the BBC as well as to politics in Canada, owing much to lobbying on his behalf by the CRL, especially Alan Plaunt.[84] Murray's ouster in 1942, after an inquiry into his sloppy expense account management, showed that there was much more to the ongoing relationship than Murray as a lynchpin. Once the new public broadcasting organization was established, the BBC had no urgent reason to team up with Canadian public broadcasting advocates in the same way it had when the overall composition of the Canadian system was still unsettled. After the fall of 1936, programming served as the main link, and for the BBC this meant associating more openly with the CBC, the chief producer and procurer of programs for Canadian radio. The structure of the CBC's departments and directors only loosely reproduced the complex and stratified structure of the BBC because the number of staff the CBC could afford was so much smaller, and the cost of serving the various regions of Canada prevented outright imitation. However, once it commenced operations, it cost the CBC little to present itself as having achieved a BBC-like status at home or to tout other kinds of connections between the two organizations. For Gladstone Murray and others who had worked in both places, these were sometimes personal connections. One of Murray's early broadcasts ginned up publicity for a slate of imported holiday shows from the BBC and NBC, but he made sure to mention that a former colleague would be arranging the BBC material to his specifications.[85]

Murray suggested that, in the new CBC era, Canadians had improved access to one of the world's most respected programming sources and that there would be more to come. He supposed that listeners would be generally enthusiastic to get British programs and to hear UK news. Even by the BBC's estimation, the CBC usually did a decent job of getting these programs on the air from the outset and reassured the BBC that there was a "definite demand" for them.[86] Still, bumping up the amount of BBC material carried over the CBC to two hours per day in 1938 was a risky strategy that might have backfired without patience or without confidence in the ineffable appeal of British culture to at least a large minority of Canadians. R.T. Bowman, a Canadian Murray had lured back from the BBC, told a BBC associate: "at first people in Canada found these broadcasts strange but in the last two or three months we have noticed an ever increasing interest and appreciation among our listeners."[87] Despite the wide range of positive and negative responses to individual programs or genres, this overall pattern of interest in or reverence for particular portions of the BBC's output held up well into the postwar period.[88]

As we might expect, broadcasting staff and listeners themselves supposed that an appreciable number of Canadians would (or should) want to have access to programming from the British Isles. The BBC voice, especially when reading the news in wartime, meant authority, and this attribute could not be simulated in North America.[89] By virtue of its monopoly and decisions about what to broadcast, the BBC successfully cultivated the impression that it represented Britain at home and across the Empire/Commonwealth. Gilbert Harding, looking back after the war on his time in Canada, spoke of feeling like he could never quite live up to the importance

Canadians "seemed determined to attach to a man from the BBC."[90] If Canadians seemed determined to venerate people like Harding, it was at least partly because Reith's BBC had shown determination to label itself foremost as a broadcaster of quality programming, and this label stuck long after Reith's departure. Michele Hilmes argues that, especially in the 1920s and 1930s, this label and the accompanying characterization of American commercial broadcasting as chaotic but "popular" were each used to achieve the goal of preserving the status quo in the United Kingdom and the United States.[91] Although such dualisms invariably reveal themselves to be constructed to serve particular interests, they worked, and they worked outside of the United Kingdom and the United States. As the CBC spread its wings, gaps in available programming did not seem troubling to listeners like Toronto doctor Harold Clark, who confessed to Gladstone Murray: "I am glad we have the short wave and can hook up with England and enjoy the quality of things over there."[92] Others maintained that programming suitable for British listeners would be suitable for Canadian listeners and that it was the CBC's duty to uphold standards based on those current in the "Old Country."[93]

Such enthusiasm was more than simply an uncritical attraction to the BBC and its programs. A disposition towards British habits, events, or symbols that predated and transcended radio emerged as both consumers and producers of programming essentialized the British approach to broadcasting and categorized BBC-made shows and those treating British themes as good bets to succeed with Canadian audiences. Of the multitude of programs he had ready for the CBC, Darby Coats of CKY in Winnipeg only raised the corporation's interest in one, a children's talk for George VI's coronation.[94] As well as ceremony, atmosphere and an appeal to emotion were important. Graham Spry made occasional prewar broadcasts from London, and a listener in Victoria encouraged him to continue these, adding: "'Just to think of hearing about the jasmine on the Embankment away out here. It makes the British Empire all one,' say the old ladies."[95] Listeners in British Columbia could be relied upon to ask for more BBC programming, regardless of sometimes poor signal quality and the quality of the programming itself.[96] Even after a war that showed how vital Canada had become as a military and economic force in its own right, the expectation remained that Britain still had a great deal to offer Canada and Canadian listeners, given the central role the British peoples had played in shaping Western civilization since the eighteenth century.[97] Britons were assumed to be steeped in this tradition. As Esme Moonie had done before the creation of the CRBC, Gerald Pratley was able to get work at the CBC soon after arriving in Canada in the mid-1940s as a young Englishman with little radio experience. His film review style borrowed heavily from the British literary review style and from the BBC film criticism the CBC was eager to get.[98] Born in England, raised in Canada, Max Ferguson felt drawn back when he had the opportunity to take a leave from the CBC to study production techniques at the BBC, where he hoped that he could imbibe more of "the maturing influence of the English system on our own."[99]

In addition to the appreciation of British achievements inside and outside broadcasting, a climate of mutual surveillance and mostly one-way advice settled in around the two public broadcasting authorities, indicating that the BBC took a keen interest in the CBC's career and that most at the CBC welcomed, or expected to have, regular and sympathetic contact with their British counterparts. As Gladstone Murray closed in on his first anniversary as the CBC's general manager, the BBC's monitoring of his mental state (not healthy) and his drinking (scarcely restrained) occurred both before and after Murray requested help from his former colleagues.[100] BBC staff despaired when the CBC seemed inept or fractious (i.e., frequently) and cheered when it seemed to be acquitting itself well.[101] The BBC also kept hopeful tabs on CBC Board of Governors' chair Davidson Dunton after the war, when he took an active role in shaping programming policy, lauding his "clear conception of what the CBC ought to be and of the subordinate and local role the private stations ought to play."[102] This trio of examples does not indicate that the BBC was a disengaged former ally in the victorious struggle to establish public broadcasting in the Dominion but, rather, speaks to an ongoing affiliation. To the BBC, Canada was, like other dominions, a friendly destination for programming, where listeners were not supposed to be suspicious of British fare. At the CBC, this meant being able to selectively borrow or adapt BBC policies or practices and, most important, maintaining a continuous and usually frank dialogue with the BBC about programming.

In terms of policies related to what went out over the air, the CBC recognized that the BBC had set the tone for broadcasting in the United Kingdom, obviously through its position as the sole domestic outlet but also via broadcasting guidelines that, for years following the Reith era, upheld an artificially dignified brand of radio discourse (as opposed to an artificially folksy one) and took a learned approach to broadcast language. Confidence in the BBC's reputation as a paragon of tasteful radio, or at least inoffensive middle-class radio,[103] spread beyond the confines of broadcasting institutions. In 1938, the London, Ontario, school board pointed to the BBC's contributions towards improving English usage and suggested that the CBC play a similar role in Canada.[104] Given its position as broadcast regulator in Canada, this seemed an obvious task for the CBC, and, in fact, it was already on the job. In 1937, W.H. "Steve" Brodie became supervisor of broadcast language and the following year compiled the *Handbook for Announcers*, modelled on the BBC's more comprehensive publications already a decade old.[105] Though Brodie seemed to pop up all over the CBC as the language policeman, and to recommend a distinctive CBC style for announcers, the corporation did not have to compile a complex code of practice. It issued revised editions of the *Handbook* in 1942 and 1946 but otherwise had free access to the BBC's material, making "good and constant use of these books."[106] It took until 1948 for the CBC to emulate the BBC's practice of putting out a weekly program magazine, the CBC *Times*, despite pressure to do so since at least 1940, mainly from ex-BBC staff member R.S. Lambert, who had run *The Listener* before coming to Canada.[107]

While some resistance to following patterns set by the BBC indicates that CBC staff were determined to steer their own course, it is more important to remember that the BBC example was *always there to be diverged from*. The affiliation between the BBC and the CBC did not oblige CBC personnel to work hard to get information about how the BBC made programs or decisions about programs, and it did not oblige BBC personnel to wonder for long about what the CBC was going to do next. One example of this measured coziness involved the CBC's negotiation of BBC Sunday broadcasting practice. Sunday, as Séan Street shows, was a battleground in Britain because, in its earliest days, the BBC's sombre Sabbath programming and restricted hours differentiated it sharply from continental broadcasters.[108] By the end of the war, some compromises had been made at the BBC, but the overall tone of Sunday programming was still subdued.[109] At this same moment, the CBC moved to loosen its grip, too. Sunday was not so contentious in Canada because Canadian and American programs were available throughout the day and lighter in tone. However, even as it aped the B B C tradition of recognizing that "a very large number of listeners regard Sunday as a sacred day" ideally free from "cares and intrusions,"[110] the C B C backed away from definite prohibitions, reserving the right to recommend that certain products be advertised at other times and remaining vigilant against scheduling highly rated programs at times that might interfere with church attendance.[111] The C B C had neither adopted the Victorian attitude that had for so long characterized the B B C approach nor had it neglected to mark Sunday as "special or exceptional" in the same way the day was set aside elsewhere.[112] There were certainly moments of supplication by C B C staff. In 1952, Robert Weaver's diffident fishing expedition for any planning material the B B C could supply on serial book readings and poetry programs was approvingly noted by the B B C's Canadian representative as evidence of "a very culture conscious C B C!"[113] A month earlier, C B C director of programme planning and production Ira Dilworth had pushed for more "staff listening" – that is, self-auditioning of shows already in production, not strictly because that practice was a B B C fixture but because he knew from ready access to B B C personnel the extent to which they employed it and how effective it had been for them.[114]

Occasionally, through formal exchanges and arranged visits, personnel from each organization spent time with their counterparts, learning new techniques, aiding in production, or observing the sort of programming being produced in a less familiar environment. More commonly, staff at the B B C and the C B C, despite working for what were supposed to be separate broadcasting entities, did not need to be seconded anywhere to share a mission that transcended institutional confines. When exchanges occurred, they generally involved Canadian radio people going to the B B C to learn, and B B C people going to Canada to learn what Canadian audiences might like to hear. Even as the C R B C was getting under way in 1932, the N C E C suggested a visit by Canadian radio students to the B B C as a potential boon to radio training in the Dominion,[115] where practically everyone who knew anything about broadcasting had learned as an employee of private stations or the C N R and C P R operations. The C R B C had neither the money nor the inclination to follow up on such suggestions. In the C B C era, formal exchange schemes fared better. Within a few months of signing on at the C B C, Gladstone Murray tried to interest N B C in a tripartite exchange that also involved the BBC, doubtless to bring in experienced producers from whom CBC staff could poach ideas.[116] The surprise in that instance was the inclusion of NBC, a wrinkle that probably led to the BBC's reluctance to go through with the idea. Murray pressed the BBC further in June of 1937, and, that fall in London, Alan Plaunt managed to extract a pledge from the BBC to "do our best to let Gladstone Murray borrow a suitable producer."[117] By 1939, the CBC could report that it had done a swap not only with the BBC but also with the Australian Broadcasting Corporation (ABC) – exchanges that inspired producers at the CBC to focus on making "characteristic features suitable for exchange."[118]

During wartime, it was understandably necessary for some CBC personnel to be away providing news coverage of war events, and the more leisurely type of exchanges had to be curtailed. Working closely with the BBC presented few problems for CBC staff because of previous exchanges and a common approach to broadcasting as a public service. Ernest Bushnell made a visit in 1940. His cohort of producers, announcers, and engineers were in the United Kingdom and later on the Continent for longer than he was, mainly for the purpose of producing war-related programming to send back home through the North American Service. When one of them, Bob Bowman, needed to spend less time in the company of his BBC counterparts, BBC assistant controller of overseas service R.A. Rendall was "anxious that the CBC should not as a consequence be put at any disadvantage as compared with the American broadcasting companies."[119] On a couple of occasions early in wartime, Rendall praised the level of cooperation, in 1942 reckoning that "relations between the BBC and the CBC [were] closer than the relations with any other Dominion broadcasting organisation." One of Bushnell's band in the Overseas Unit, Rooney Pelletier, stayed on to work for the BBC afterward.[120] Also, if CBC governor Howard Chase's version of events is true, CBC personnel managed while sheltering from the Blitz in London to hatch the idea for the successful BBC program *Front Line Family*, a serial that, when broadcast later in Canada, struck some listeners as too profane.[121] At home during the war, the CBC claimed to be still reaping the benefits of prewar producer exchanges and took pride in its discovery of acting talent despite lacking one characteristic of the larger British and American markets, a "stock" system whereby actors were under continuous contract.[122]

Resuming "normal" operations after the conflict was impossible. The CBC had not only grown a news department but also expanded its operations in every direction. Along with other Commonwealth broadcasting organizations, it participated in pilgrimages to the BBC made possible by the Imperial Relations Trust, bursaries that funded exactly the reverse of what Murray had been eager to establish a decade earlier. Instead of bringing knowledgeable outsiders to Canada, the trust took broadcasters to the BBC, where training and fellowship awaited.[123] With this arrangement in place, producers or performers connected to the CBC but not on a trust bursary, like composer/conductor Godfrey Ridout, were largely on their own if they came to the United Kingdom. Having not heard of Ridout, the BBC's overseas liaison officer declined to accommodate him with a broadcast opportunity.[124] Davidson Dunton arranged a tour of the BBC for Royal Commission on National Development in the Arts, Letters and Sciences member Father G.-H. Lévesque in 1949, when Lévesque was in England. Hoping a look at the BBC's operation would impress upon Lévesque a general idea of what the CBC wanted to do, Dunton confessed to George Barnes at the BBC: "We are a little afraid that the Commissioners may not have time to get a thorough grasp of all that is involved in broadcasting in this country.[125]. Other kinds of fact finding and cross-pollination required varying levels of contact. In 1950, CBC Drama's Andrew Allan noted that, in his field, Canada had long been plugged in to a theatrical world that included the BBC as a patron, and writers submitted scripts directly to the CBC or through their agents,[126] so visits and exchanges were not as vital to livening up a dramatic schedule. In addition to their less-taxing missions to observe how American television was made, CBC explorers went to the United Kingdom, and the CBC Board of Governors' 1948 statements on private TV echo some of the BBC's strong objections, which were instrumental in preserving its television monopoly until 1955.[127] When television was about to arrive in Canada, BBC veterans in the field perked up at news of the CBC's miserly reaction to the high prices charged for imported US programming. This was a chance, wrote the BBC's Canadian representative Tom Sloan, to "help them to realise just where their true friends are."[128] Friendship, with its peaks and valleys, happened in between official visits, in the day-to-day work of planning and producing broadcasts.

NEGOTIATED COOPERATION

The CBC's affiliation to the BBC comes through even more clearly when we examine how intensively they debated the sort of programming Canadian and (less frequently) British listeners would appreciate. With the CBC and commercial stations already carrying advertiser-friendly music, variety, and drama programs, these debates were predominantly about what Canadian audiences might like to hear *in addition* to the performers that advertising agencies and commercial stations had placed before the microphone. Without the listener research data upon which advertising-dependent stations and networks relied,[129] the BBC and the CBC wanted to know what either of them could supply that Canadian listeners might come to demand. Of course, finding the "right material" occupied all broadcasters everywhere,[130] but the task seemed a more fundamental one for public broadcasters committed to balancing their schedules. Late in 1935, before there was a CBC, and before he had been chosen to head its operations, Gladstone Murray was not above handing out advice. Though he did not want to "count the chickens prematurely," he wrote to his friend Alan Plaunt suggesting, among other things, that the new service should distinguish itself in North America by producing "features" in the BBC mode – that is, short pieces on people or places, with interviews and a light tone.[131] After he took over, Murray's view of programming was not as "wide angle" as we might suppose, in that he was likely to chime in on detailed discussions about what the CBC got via the North American Service. Around the time of the Battle of Britain, he nearly shut down talks production, favouring "inspirational" rather than "probing" talks, and taking up the slack with over four hours of BBC transcriptions per week.[132] This was not the "continuous reciprocity in programmes which we both desire" that Plaunt had mentioned to the BBC's G.M. Groves a couple of years earlier,[133] but it indicated how much the CBC looked to the BBC as a supplier of material that would not be criticized in Canada as amateurish or, in wartime, as subversive. For its part, the BBC had neglected to establish a "take-it-or-leave-it" tone early on and recognized that the CBC had become accustomed to asking for what the Empire Service's C.A.L. Cliffe called "special treatment" compared to the further-flung dominions. The CBC had also become accustomed to getting what it asked for, within reason. Fairness was admirable in principle but, in practice, it tended to be trumped by the BBC's desire to "do what [it could] to encourage wide distribution of programmes of British origin."[134]

As Simon Potter amply demonstrates in *Broadcasting Empire*, wide distribution remained the BBC's goal through wartime and beyond. The CBC's chief motivation for carrying BBC programs was to supplement its own sustaining output and the revenue-generating commercial shows it carried. At a minimum, each organization's aims were complementary, with the BBC getting wider distribution and the CBC staying within its operations budget. Greater significance lay in the programs themselves. Though programming had an exchange value or cost (e.g., twenty pounds for an hour),[135] within the affiliation between the BBC and the CBC it was less a commodity than a means of providing entertainment, enlightenment, and information, upholding the relationship between metropolis and dominion, and demonstrating the viability of public service broadcasting as a programming source. If Empire and North American Service transmissions sent in the middle of the night from London were relayed immediately, they went out against evening shows from American stations, hardly the ideal matchup for the BBC, the CBC, or potential listeners. If they were not directly relayed, these transmissions had to be recorded for later broadcast. As a rule, recorded programs did not fare well against live ones, but there was little that either organization could do to get around that particular impediment to growth in listenership. While the technical and financial limitations of broadcasting would remain outside their control, those planning and making programs at the BBC and CBC recognized that they could (and should) be opening new conversations about programming, and continuing older ones, within the BBC-CBC framework. This cooperative arrangement worked to fulfill different aspects of each corporation's mission, and, despite some definite instances of friction that required working through, obstacles to the sharing and movement of programs and ideas for making them were negligible. On the eve of war, Mary Grannan asked for scripts from the BBC's *Children's Hour* program because she intended to produce a "Young People's Hour" on the CBC. Unable to provide the scripts she needed, Overseas Service suggested a number of plays, and Grannan drew inspiration for stories and programs from them well into the television era.[136] A decade later, the CBC trumpeted a two-way flow of programming, noting that the BBC and CBC staff responsible for this flow were "in constant communication, sounding out programme 'appetites' of each other's broadcasting system."[137]

While Leonard Brockington acknowledged in 1938 that the CBC wanted to produce more of its own programming, the fact that programs came across the Atlantic or across the Canada-US border did not alarm him. As the chairman of the CBC's Board of Governors, he saw those programs as contributions to the maintenance of goodwill between "the peoples of the British Commonwealth, of Canada and the United States."[138] Representing the CBC in its infancy as a national broadcaster, he was not in a position to detect the extent to which the BBC and the CBC would become involved in reinforcing "each other's broadcasting system" through the selection of programming or to detect the work and worry behind the shows exchanged. This work involved more than Gladstone Murray's urging BBC colleagues to "let that hour come over snappy with transitions that will make the Yanks look like a bunch of pikers from the creek wayback."[139] It involved both parties reading the Canadian broadcasting scene with an eye to building audiences for CBC and BBC programs, a goal that would necessarily be accomplished at the expense of American goals. We must acknowledge the nationalist/imperialist motives embedded in any such effort but must not ignore the significant attention paid to what programs were: opportunities for listeners to listen, to listen elsewhere, or to leave the radio silent. In 1940, the BBC recognized the value of lighter Overseas Service programs in "holding a wide public in the face of hot competition."[140] Every listener staying with the programs available – directly by shortwave, relayed, or recorded – was another listener exposed to Britain, so it mattered what was on the air. Yet it was not quite as simple as the BBC's Geoff Bridson supposed in 1942 – that Britain "ha[d] only to present and express herself to be better understood and, accordingly, better appreciated."[141] In April 1943, Canadian listeners' "regrettably passive" response to *Radio Newsreel* and *Front Line Family* prompted the BBC's Laurence Gilliam to call for measures directed at "freshening Canadian interest in the BBC relationship." That the relationship could be considered "static" shows that the movement of programming was not its only object.[142] In other words, the BBC's previous interventions had helped create a climate in which keeping CBC programming dynamic was synonymous with defending public service broadcasting and in which the fluid cooperation of both organizations would continue to be required.

Fluidity marked the entire radio period, even though each broadcaster had different priorities and the exchanges between them were not always positive. Wartime talks like *Canada Calls from London* or *Britain Speaks* originated under the direction of CBC staff on duty in the United Kingdom,[143] and they played to presumed listener interest in wartime life at the centre of Empire. According to early wartime reactions, BBC-produced features along those lines were generally well regarded in Canada but only after some BBC nudges to try them.[144] Even though the BBC offered such programming to the CBC and private stations in Canada at the same cost, the CBC came to have the right of first refusal.[145] Other broadcasting operations in Canada, especially those few already taking American programming as affiliates, had the equipment to receive and record BBC transmissions. However, the CBC was the BBC's de facto agent because of the likelihood that the CBC would be the only customer for many of the broadcasts the BBC could send with sufficient audio quality (e.g., talks and features) and the ease with which private stations could get BBC programs from the CBC if they wanted them. When the BBC undertook to sell more recorded entertainment programs into the US market during the war, it was justifiably worried about the strength of the competition and vowed to deal only with broadcasters, not with advertising agencies or potential sponsors.[146] When it looked at the same possibility in Canada, attempts to set up a reliable distribution method for BBC programming through third parties like the Dominion Broadcasting Company foundered as on-again, off-again experiments for the better part of a decade.[147] BBC sources reported that they nonetheless managed to move their recorded programming in Canada after the war because of "CBC's shortage of programme funds" and the "extended contacts" of the BBC's Canadian office, which brought orders for individual programs from private stations.[148] Critic Thomas Archer offered a qualified appreciation of the recorded stuff available, noting: "[The BBC] have no commercial radio – no 'Whistlers,' no 'Suspenses' – they also seem to have no Fred Allens, Bergens, or Bing Crosbys. But in serious programs they do undoubtedly set an example to the world."[149] Sending more entertainment programming, however, became central to the BBC's North American strategy in the postwar period. Canadian representative Michael Barkway was gratified to see how much BBC material was available in Canada in 1948, and he reiterated some advice he had given a couple of years earlier: "In Canada, no amount of 'projectional' or educational programmes could do as much for British prestige as one entertainment programme with as great an appeal as the United States shows. To be superior about entertainment is to abandon the whole struggle."[150]

Despite this higher proportion of entertainment programming beamed to Canada from the BBC, the CBC did not rearrange its schedule to feature the imported material, and it certainly did not take all the BBC had to offer. Rather, it eventually settled into a pattern of airing these lighter musical programs somewhat haphazardly, in the late evening and in the morning on weekends, taking more care to schedule, for example, regional news tidbits from the United Kingdom[151] After the fall of 1947, Wednesday nights contained BBC programs on a regular basis, but Wednesday nights had been set aside in any event to feature programming differing from the usual weeknight output. The networks certainly worked closely together in setting up shows during the earliest months.[152] Given the high cost of producing the concerts and dramatic spectacles the CBC wanted for Wednesdays, some of this was bound to come as recordings from the BBC. The "BBC boom" in Canada was not dominated by highbrow stuff, and CBC producers' appetite for light entertainment frustrated BBC representatives, who were on the one hand happy with the increased interest from the CBC and at least one private station but, on the other, acknowledged that there was a certain amount of "sponging" going on.[153] With so much American material as competition, the BBC had to remind CBC programming people of what it could offer, despite frequent contact. Employing a record player supplied by the CBC, BBC staff in Toronto would invite CBC producers to their offices and let them audition the BBC's wares, a tactic that John Polwarth supposed would be unnecessary in Australia, where the ABC would just "use what they need."[154] Broadcasts of various Gilbert and Sullivan works in 1948 hit the spot for both parties in that the BBC considered these to constitute the sort of quality programming it should be sending, and the CBC considered these works suitable for the Dominion Network at a time when the privately owned Dominion stations were at their most irritable about the CBC's control over broadcasting regulations and programming.[155]

As the national broadcaster in charge of who could form networks and when, the CBC was in the strongest position to carry ceremonial and commemorative programming. When such occasions involved

the Royal Family, it became even more important that CBC procedure resembled BBC practice. In 1937, when an advertising agency
asked if the CBC would allow broadcasts of George VI's coronation
to be sponsored, the reply was that sponsorship would be "entirely
out of the question," a response fitting in well with the BBC line that
programming about the Coronation was as sacred "in its twentieth-
century way" as was the ceremony itself.[156] Preparations for the
Royal Tours of 1939 and 1951 demanded similar care, and the CBC
urged its personnel to hew to the BBC example, issuing warnings
against announcers' unpleasant tendencies to comment on aspects of
the tours that were not splendid or affirming.[157] The CBC was the
only operation that could field the people and equipment to cover
events like these, and private stations carried CBC broadcasts eagerly.
Still, the CBC's Augustin Frigon reminded Ernest Bushnell: "[It] happens too often that the private stations' owners substitute their
announcement to the CBC's identification which goes out with such
programmes. I suggest that you instruct your announcers to mention
the name of the Corporation in French and in English, as the case
may be, at proper intervals during the broadcasts. In this manner, we
shall not be foiled of the credit that belongs to us."[158] The BBC did
not face anything like the same competition, but Frigon's solution to
a Canadian problem erected an edifice of self-promotion that rose
only as high as needed, slightly above the modest foundation of BBC
sign-on and sign-off announcements. A final example of the CBC's
protecting its authority to package the public reception of such
events came at the other end of George VI's reign, when word went
out to CBC stations to cancel soap operas, use suitable (i.e., morose,
"serious") music, and, on the day of the funeral, to cancel all CBC
programming except for the service itself. Private stations left accom-
modations for the mourning period up to station managers.[159]

The BBC also understood the CBC's position in North America,
aware that, in terms of volume of programs and numbers of listeners, the CBC's output would, in all foreseeable futures, continue to
be overwhelmed by commercial competition. Laurence Gilliam
declared in 1943 that, despite some growth in program exchange
during wartime, "the voice of the BBC is still but a triangle in the
vast orchestra of American broadcasting."[160] Yet not all listeners
tuned reflexively to sponsored material. Gilliam's BBC colleague,
Canadian-born Seymour de Lotbinière, struck a note of optimism
later in the year when he noted that, "wherever [he had] been

amongst Anglo-Saxons" in Canada, listeners were still patient with
BBC programs because they had formed an impression of a "calm
and confident" BBC early in the war. He warned, however, that it
may not be long before listeners started to remember a BBC service
that also "idled its way through pauses and overruns and suffered its
announcers to drop their papers on the floor and gossip about their
summer holidays."[161] Creating programs along the lines of those
that had been successful at the BBC saved work for CBC producers,
and a fair portion of the working day at the BBC's Canadian outpost
involved seeing which programs or show/series ideas would be
transferrable. The rest of their job, more or less, involved using their
passkey to the CBC to find CBC-produced shows that could run on
one or more of the BBC services, in the hopes of redressing a severe
imbalance in program traffic.[162] Program reciprocity was meant to
foster a taste for programming that would package and present each
place for listeners who were living on another continent but still
within the wider bounds of the Commonwealth. While the BBC's
intentions in this regard were noble from the outset, with Felix
Greene asking for a fairly wide range of contributions from the
CBC,[163] in practice the imbalance persisted, much like it would in a
domestic affiliation. Sometimes circumstances such as scheduling
conflicts conspired against plans to get Canadian performers or
voices on the BBC. More commonly, eastward traffic was thwarted
by the BBC's anxiousness to take only programs that presented
either some novel aspect of Canadian life or programs that met their
literary standards. Stephen Leacock, for example, would be fine if
wearing his political economist's hat but not if he spoke in what BBC
staff called his "Frenzied Fiction style which ... would be embarrassing at the microphone."[164] When trying to arrange a talk on
Canadian landscape painting for the BBC's Third Programme,
Overseas Controller George Barnes emphasized: "The approach is
an aesthetic approach and not a national one; I know how difficult
this is, but, as you will know, the serious, aesthetic, critique of
Canadian landscape painting, devoid of Empire Marketing Board
phraseology, will interest the people who matter here, and that is the
purpose of the talk."[165] At other times when Canadian programs
were used, it became apparent that these were taken not as the main
event but to fill gaps. It did not help that some Canadians also
doubted the CBC's capacity to produce the sort of programming that
the BBC would want to give its listeners.[166]

LIMITED SOLIDARITY

Attempts to maintain a fluid exchange of programs and program planning information took place in the context of a common sensitivity to the odds against public broadcasting. As Michael Barkway put it in 1946: "The CBC are aware, as I am, that the supporters of commercial broadcasting on this side of the Atlantic are always trying to make capital out of the fact that many – or indeed a majority – of British listeners before the war listened to Radio Normandy or Radio Luxembourg in preference to the BBC."[167] Reports that listeners preferred light or dance music to anything else were hardly surprising, but such reports were invariably seized upon by those asserting that the BBC and the CBC, as public broadcasters, were government puppets wedded to an imperious style of making programs and ignoring the popular will.[168] Even some old BBC hands needed to be reminded that, unlike the ABC in Australia, the CBC catered to audiences for the biggest American commercial programs simply by broadcasting them.[169] Sometimes, BBC observers lumped those programs together uncritically and misrepresented them as having biased North American broadcasting against a more measured form of presentation. In 1948, J.B. Clark reported after a meeting including private station owners and managers in Canada that the BBC practice of quiet introductions to programs "strikes most Canadian radio men as lacking in vigor" and "in some cases led to a rejection in Canada of BBC transcriptions of some of the most popular (light entertainment) programmes in the UK, because it was feared that such presentation would not *compel* the audience to listen."[170] Despite such implications that the British style was too subtle for Canadian listeners, the CBC continued to cultivate the connection, identifying with the BBC as a fellow national broadcaster, and sometimes pressing, as it did in 1949, for listener research data from the BBC or inviting BBC personnel to make public pronouncements on the value of the CBC to Canada.[171] The following year, Davidson Dunton gave British readers an update on how public broadcasting was faring in Canada, describing the CBC's efforts in relation to the BBC's Home Service, and the Light and Third Programmes.[172] Though the BBC's Canadian representative had an overall impression of Canada in 1952 as "linked in spirit to a European ideal" and influenced by the United States, he also valued the mutual candour that led the CBC to share a continuous stream of impressions about what Canadian listeners might like as well as confidential plans to overhaul the corporation's management structure.[173] The inadvertent omission of the Canadian contribution to a Commonwealth program embarrassed the BBC in 1953, and the BBC's Cyril Conner worried needlessly how the CBC would react to the slight. Conner's worry was misplaced because, even though television had arrived in Canada (perhaps *because* it had arrived and strained radio budgets), the CBC continued to welcome BBC news, commentary, and recorded programs, including the surreal comedy of *The Goon Show*.[174] The flow of information continued quite informally, leading Conner to read the riot act to Gordon Winter, the BBC's Canadian representative, who was merely doing things the way they had been done for close to two decades. Conner wrote:

> I am wondering a little how it is that the CBC seem to be in a position to ask by name for individual reports. Such reports are sent to the BBC's Representatives in order to enable them to keep in touch with trends in public opinion and taste here, but it is assumed that they are not discussed with anyone outside the Corporation, even including such good friends as the CBC. Possibly this has not been clear to you.[175]

Possibly it has not been clear in this discussion of a complex and resilient relationship that the two organizations also experienced definite conflicts over how their affiliation should work. Those moments of disagreement work largely to reinforce our sense of each institution's overall connection to the other and also reveal a great deal about perceptions of what Canadians would like to hear on the radio. For reasons of convenience, quality, "Britishness," and budget, the public network frequently looked with favour on ready-made BBC programs but, for reasons of listener preference and balance, could only justify carrying those that promised to provide entertainment or intellectual value to listeners. The cruel economic realities of the North American broadcasting industry met the shifting aesthetic realities of what the public might like. Along with the countless affirmations of solidarity and friendship that passed between these broadcasting authorities, there were countless expressions of doubt and reservation about how suitable British programs were for Canadian listeners, a diminishing proportion of whom could be assumed to have dearly held family or sentimental connections to

Britain. The CBC's assessments of where BBC material fit into its programming needs were frank because the link between the organizations was not provisional or dependent on compatibility between personalities in management. An early, and arguably the most extreme, indication of cautionary thinking about British broadcasting as a model for the CBC came from – who else? – Gladstone Murray. In June of 1936, he privately condemned the BBC for various sins, not foreseeing that less than a year later, he would be begging his former colleagues for help coping in Canada. Of the BBC he was leaving, he wrote:

> Entertainment generally has suffered from amateur handling
> and from falling into the hands of cliques. But the chief defect of
> British broadcasting is its inhumanity and absence of friendliness.
> The organization of broadcasting has grown into a self-contained
> hierarchy completely self-satisfied and complacent, priding itself
> in freedom from control either by the listening public or by Parlia-
> ment. It has become the hunting ground for a super-careerist,
> afflicted by pronounced and growing megalomania. The organiza-
> tion is run on a mixture of terrorism and favoritism; there is no
> continuous policy, no stability, no confidence. The result is chronic
> unhappiness and malignant persecution. Much effort is unprofit-
> ably expended on intrigue. While the product undoubtedly has
> its merits, these are far below the potentiality of efficiency and
> rightmindedness.[176]

Such venom, arising largely from his social annoyance, contrasted sharply with Murray's public zeal, once at the CBC, to get shows from the BBC and to show Canadians that his former employer was a programming source as reliable as the American networks but more amenable to offering guidance in developing programs. Through the CBC's prewar days, when everyone at the CBC learned by close experience what they were up against in terms of operating costs and American programming, Murray softened his stance and owned up to pinching some desirable BBC traits: "The programme policy of the CBC is that of the BBC, adapted to Canadian requirements. There is the same refusal to underrate the public taste; there is the same constant endeavour to provide the best in all lines of entertainment and thought." At the same time, he was sure to note what he thought the Canadian public needed to hear and to affirm that the CBC's broadcasting authority had not fended off American incursion only to be absorbed by an even more distant, if traditionally familiar, power:

> On the other hand, there is necessarily a greater measure of freedom, flexibility, and elasticity, as required by the nature of the country and its mixed population. Talks, discussions, symposia, forums, and debates are wide open to all the main points of view, competently expressed. The range of entertainment on Sunday is wider than that allowed by the BBC. There is no censorship.[177]

This strategy of "we're just like the BBC, only different" proved useful. The CBC could host "media events" like the 1939 Royal Tour with plenty of creative borrowing from the BBC,[178] yet claim that its routine needs differed sharply from those of other dominions and that it needed some lighter programs from the BBC to fit in with the commercial fare it carried.[179]

During the CRBC era, it was already plain that differences between the public broadcasters in the United Kingdom and Canada arose out of their differing national contexts. In addition, a weak and sometimes spiteful commission prevented effective cooperation.[180] These contexts did not change appreciably after 1936, but the CBC's ability to admit that it shared broadly similar goals with the BBC made their differences of opinion much more about programming needs and less about control. Cranks, along with some more orthodox commentators, insisted that the BBC was somehow controlling the CBC, or infiltrating it,[181] and did not want to explore instances of disharmony between the two. Such instances were part of an extended conversation in which both the BBC and the CBC tried to understand audiences and what audiences wanted. Some elements in this conversation addressed types of programming, others addressed tone, content, and the all-important listener.

When the programming conversation turned less cordial, suppositions about what listeners would appreciate versus what they found alien or unsuitable loomed large. After about a year of operation, the CBC was forced to object to some of the humour coming across to North America on Transmission 4. Gladstone Murray told BBC Overseas personnel that listeners, especially in western Canada, did not welcome some of the more broad British humour, adding: "a joke about someone releasing a fixture off his torso in order to accommodate more fermented sugar" had "displeased the Bishop of Saskatchewan." J.B. Clark asked Murray to advise his staff to: "let us have a note of individual turns which in their opinion might have given some offence to the pure and delicate ears of Canadians."[182] Murray took the matter straight to John Reith a month later, admitting humour was a tricky proposition on the radio but declaring that "the more the BBC lives up to its reputation for high seriousness, the better it will be regarded in Canada and the better for broadcasting in general."[183] The subsequent discussion of Canadian tastes was more constructive, with BBC program people willing to get listener feedback from the CBC, yet more determined to press on with more of the same: "for listeners, if they hear our programmes regularly[,] will accustom themselves to the type of traditional British humour which we transmit to them."[184] Although the CBC's Bob Bowman observed this very phenomenon in action, as initially "strange" programs gathered "an ever increasing interest and appreciation," the CBC did not back down. It chose what to relay and could replace variety programs with other BBC material, which it asked for specifically.[185]

Listener approval was an elusive beast, and reports of a particular program's reception or audience appetite for a style could vary widely over time. Canadian listeners had been getting music hall programs from Britain before the advent of the CBC, and, in late 1936, the CRBC welcomed the main export, *Let's Go to the Music Hall*, as a "particular joy of 'Old Country' folk." The CBC was open to taking more of this material a year later, citing even imitations of music hall turns as "very popular."[186] Yet, while some of the big vaudeville acts had made a successful transition to radio long before, one radio journalist declared that music hall was different: "Canadian tastes simply do not run to the English type."[187] In wartime, further Canadian imitation of the music hall style did not play well when it involved comedians Al and Bob Harvey singing "smutty songs to get a laugh," and it appeared as though this sort of thing had fallen out of favour. However, before war's end, *Memory Music Hall* emerged on the CBC's Dominion Network. With an authentic English ex-pat emcee introducing recorded variety acts and toning down the ribaldry, the show enjoyed a run of several years through the early 1950s, even fooling some Canadians into thinking it was a BBC production.[188] Not every genre or sub-genre of programming followed exactly this path, but the fact that the CBC eventually hit upon a style of presenting music hall that held an audience while preserving many of the elements of the old theatre shows illustrates a broader idea. The simultaneous, multi-cornered, and often contentious discussions of programming by the CBC, BBC, private stations, critics, listeners, and performers owed a great deal to the BBC-CBC affiliation as a stable platform upon which program ideas could be initiated and refined.

In the course of sending and selling its programs to North American listeners and broadcasters, the BBC maintained a busy American operation and had occasional dealings with private stations in Canada, the ones hoping to secure a particular program not already distributed by the CBC itself or via the Dominion chain. The existence of a North American market for programs outside the BBC-CBC system meant that the BBC did not have to rely exclusively on the CBC for information on what sort of programming Canadian listeners might like, although the suggestions it received from private stations were invariably for material that could be sponsored. After leaving the CBC in 1942, Gladstone Murray almost immediately indulged his political orientation as a supporter of "free enterprise," throwing his lot in with another ex-private radio/ ex-CBC employee, Horace Stovin. At Stovin and Wright, Murray advised potential sponsors about broadcasting opportunities and was not shy about telling former BBC colleagues what his new clients might buy. He suggested that the BBC should have its announcers warn North American audiences about the accents they were about to hear and insisted that, in the name of entertainment: "[The BBC needs to send] low, fast comedy with wise-cracks, but keep it low. You know the sort of thing I mean." Stovin lobbied for significant alterations to British programs intended for North America, promoting the idea of using a Canadian voice so that listeners would "place more trust in one of their own and [be] less inclined to label the material as propaganda". The same suggestion had come earlier in the war from the other side of the political divide: "tell the BBC (if it is capable of being told anything)" that "the emasculated drone of the voice from London does more to undermine morale on this side of the ocean than all our own fifth columns."[189]

CBC programming staff had plenty to do managing the shows they created. Keeping the "emasculated drone" at bay while scheduling the sort of imported programs Canadians might embrace was yet another task. When the potential imports came from the BBC, *both* parties became involved in assessing how or if the program in question would be welcomed. Like any dialectical process, these readings could clash. In 1937, the BBC asked what would fly in Canada, and Murray came back with: "Military Band music, particularly Walton O'Donnell conducting the BBC Military band in 'straight' programmes ... voices of leaders of British thought and affairs ... Descriptions of home events and opinions ... Light music programmes: theatre Orchestra in 'middle-brow' numbers, arranged on a theme, with as 'British' a motif as possible." The CBC requested more of the same in 1938.[190] While the BBC was not averse to filling such a standing order over the Empire Service, the CBC's Charles Jennings lamented that these transmissions were "not at the happiest times and [that it was] difficult therefore for the programmes (as a general rule) to gain a loyal following". The BBC's Tony Rendall later wondered why Canadian listeners seemed ignorant of features programs, which went over well in Britain.[191] His sense of dismay that a BBC staple would be too unfamiliar for the CBC touched on the whole question of how receptive Canadian listeners could be to programming styles that were not North American. Having spent time in both Britain and Canada, Seymour de Lotbinière seemed to think in 1945 that listeners were justified in being "choosey," given the volume of programming available to them from Canadian and US sources. Reports like his reinforced the idea that Canadians were not exactly yearning for BBC programming above all else but would listen if program quality were high.[192]

The BBC had not stopped trying to sell programming to US stations, and it pursued this goal after the Second World War. This was an economic strategy. At the same time, supplying BBC productions to broadcasters in the dominions took on a new urgency. While visions of a reinvigorated Commonwealth connection may have buoyed spirits, the BBC also tried to defend itself and other commonwealth broadcasters against a tide of commercialism in the later 1940s and early 1950s.[193] BBC director-general William Haley had resolved that high-quality programming would be the corporation's exclusive stock in trade, and staff responsible for overseas broadcasts and sales took particularly to his metaphor of programs moving by "suction, and not pressure."[194] But to create demand, some attention to the customer was necessary. When the BBC suggested programs, the CBC said "no" frequently. In Canada, "the most competitive of all Empire markets (with the possible exception of Australia)," BBC representatives saw their efforts falling just short because, although the material might be of high quality, not all of it seemed exciting or relevant to CBC program staff trying to build an attractive and balanced schedule. More "popular" material was generally a safe bet, and Michael Barkway urged his BBC colleagues to "resist the temptation to weave elaborate webs of 'policy' and 'projection' and 'important series' [that would] make no more appeal to rebroadcasters [in Canada] than the similar plans of the CBC International Service make to the BBC domestic services."[195] Canadians did not need a steady stream of dance music or detective stories, but nor did they need to be forcibly reminded of Britain or given more "high culture" than the CBC already diligently supplied.

When it emerged, discord within the transatlantic affiliation flowed from the immutable fact that the primary purpose of each organization was serving its own listening public, and programs produced in one place would not always be considered a good fit for listeners in the other. The CBC recognized this more readily than did the BBC, which was committed to its secondary cause of reinforcing imperial relations and could only serve Canadian listeners in ways that furthered this cause. The CBC needed some BBC programming to achieve its programming goals but remained eager to be seen at home as an autonomous member of a partnership, not as a dependent or copycat service. Gilbert Harding dubbed this "the dreary old question of prestige," and CBC drama chief Andrew Allan remarked: "The BBC is doing an excellent job, but on well-worn paths. In Canada we have a chance to blaze new trails. This is still the country of adventure."[196] The arrangement did not operate smoothly when handling wartime or commercial broadcasting left little space for taking BBC output and virtually no time to make programs to go to Britain or when the BBC appeared to view its Toronto office as subordinate to the larger New York office.[197] Committed to public service broadcasting in a radio environment that made carrying out such a commitment an expensive and thankless proposition, CBC personnel had to work within the limitations of their environment, and their BBC counterparts were only too aware of those limitations: Gladstone Murray was jealous of the BBC's ability to suit two listener moods via two transmitters; Barkway saw the private stations as a mix of community-minded operators and mercenaries only nominally regulated by the CBC; Richard Lambert reminded the BBC it could not assume all Canadians had British roots or familiarity with British history; and the Canadian-born head of the

BBC's North American Service, Warren MacAlpine, reported that listeners, especially in the west, "dress, talk, and think as Americans, much more than I had thought was the case."[198]

Staring at such dark radio clouds would not make them go away. Even when the CBC was able to arrange a second network, it used private stations to carry the more highly rated programs. By the reckoning of Lord Simon, who surveyed the Canadian and American broadcasting industries in 1948, the CBC was doing well, under the circumstances, to uphold the banner of public service broadcasting.[199] Public broadcasters in Canada had managed to save Canadian listeners from "the never-ending repetitions of trifling programmes rendered by teashop fiddlers,"[200] but they had neither the power nor the resources of the BBC. Adrienne Scullion notes that the BBC is best thought of as the "paradigmatic cultural institution of the interwar period, a core producer at the very centre of the hegemonic practices of the contemporary state."[201] This was perhaps all well and good in Britain, but the CRBC and CBC had to inhabit some of the places listeners had been led by commercial broadcasters protecting a ten-year head start. Though listeners were not clamouring for it, trying to provide a BBC-like service in Canada, even if it was not all "serious" programming, did not constitute a betrayal of listeners' trust. Instead, it was an approach that CBC management could identify as "public service." It set at least some Canadian programming apart from the Continental mainstream and settled the nerves of listeners eager to stay in touch with British ways and doings. *Becoming* the BBC in Canada was impossible for the CBC, having been constrained politically from displacing the existing commercial stations and needing to do more than dabble in sponsored material. However, buoyed at crucial moments by an unorthodox affiliation with a self-appointed guardian of public service broadcasting and an international force in programming, public broadcasters in Canada became the face of an alternative kind of cultural democracy – in the market but not wholly of it.

4

"We Introduce Ourselves Almost by Force": Regulating Radio

From its inception, the broadcasting industry churned and grew quickly along with listeners' appetites for more programming. It was a kind of fantasy-world where radio stars lived and listeners eavesdropped. However, there was much going on inside that fantasy-world, where, every day, broadcasting needed real people to do real things like playing music, acting, selling ads, or planning programs. In their various ways, all of these people had a role in "producing" radio for listeners' consumption. Listeners held up their end of the bargain by listening and, advertisers hoped, by dutifully consuming sponsors' products or services. Sometimes listeners provided criticism those on the production side might heed. Broadcasting appeared to be simple: make programs, keep making them, and people will keep listening. Microphones and scripts could be touched; the experiences of listening or having a reaction to programs could not. Yet those experiences were no less real, especially when it came time to consider the potential long-term economic, cultural, or social implications of what went on the air. A radio show might end, but it did not become "dead" to listeners. Their tastes, beliefs, or habits could be affected by the programs they heard – exactly *how* was difficult to predict. This uncertainty did not absolve broadcast regulators from having to be decisive about what could be aired. Likewise, broadcasters purporting to serve the public needed to look beyond the broadcast itself, towards the way listeners might take programs and advertisements on board.

The tension between broadcaster responsibility and regulator oversight has been at the core of most debates about codes of conduct or programming regulations.[1] In the case of early Canadian radio, the fact that Canada's public broadcasting authorities, the Canadian Radio Broadcasting Commission and the Canadian Broadcasting Corporation, also served as broadcast regulators for more than twenty-five years further complicated matters. Competing ideas about who should determine what was allowed on the air and which programs were "in good taste" or "in bad taste" often threw the division between public and commercial broadcasters into sharper relief. However, when it came to policing what could be broadcast, private broadcasters did not seek an entirely unregulated industry, merely an industry not regulated by the CBC, which they viewed above all as a competitor. For their part, regulators were not out to sanitize radio. Although they were the final authority on broadcasting standards, CBC regulators allowed broadcasters to appeal deletions or modifications made to scripts,[2] often relaxing or loosely interpreting broadcasting regulations and frequently neglecting to enforce them. This was about as free as such a system could be in balancing the democratic desire to broadcast whatever producers or advertisers dreamt up with concern for disturbing listeners who may not have expected or appreciated what they got.

No matter how raggedly they were made, interpreted, or enforced, the existence of explicit rules created by a public body helped thrust the questions of public taste and tolerance into the open, where listeners, advertisers, station operators, and performers could contest rulings. When misleading speech or transgressive advertising appeared to threaten the public peace or the reputation of broadcasting as a source of wholesome entertainment or education, Parliament decided that centralized censorship of such material would be less dangerous or unsettling than the imagined outcomes of a radio free-for-all. In practice, fear of demagogues, charlatans, and others inciting social chaos, fleecing the gullible, or indiscriminately raising indelicate topics informed regulators' approach to program content. The points of contention and cooperation between CBC regulators and a range of hopeful broadcasters and advertisers included areas like patent medicines, "thriller" programs, and the occult, all of which required some sort of ruling or resolution and continuous vigilance. Carrying out their duties by prohibiting certain kinds of shows, recommending the alteration of scripts, or forbidding certain kinds of commercial speech left regulators open to accusations that they were imposing their own moralities, tastes, and interests on the entire listening public, which they were. The mistaken belief that the state itself was reaching deeply into radio also gained traction. Opponents of regulation thought a sharp reduction in rules would unchain the invisible hand of the market and so satisfy listeners. They did not recognize the fact that programs and advertisements would still be controlled if ad agencies, producers, and stations were allowed free rein. Without officially appointed regulators imposing their own moralities, tastes, and interests visibly on the whole broadcasting industry, a different set could be imposed behind the scenes through "a rigid catholicism of structure, in which there is one indisputable and arbitrary authority (the sponsor)."[3] Radio without rules would not be radio without rulers.

In an article on radio censorship, Mary Vipond shows that, during its tenure as regulator, the CRBC aligned itself with a dominant "liberal order" ideal according to which individual rights were sovereign, but this was tempered by the notion that free speech had limits.[4] The commission, like the Ministry of Marine's Radio Branch before it and the CBC after, used its powers to deny broadcasting time to speakers (e.g., the Jehovah's Witnesses) it considered detrimental to the existing order. CRBC chair Hector Charlesworth, who wore the hat of "chief censor," fiercely protected religious orthodoxy but allowed radical political speakers (e.g., Communist Party of Canada members) as long as they did not incite violence.[5] Using two rich examples, Vipond ties the CRBC's methods to Charlesworth's grudging preference for engaging in constructive dialogue over inviting Armageddon. She also sees her analysis as "an opening for further exploration" and, by positing that, for the liberal democracies of Europe and North America, "the function of free speech was essentially a political function,"[6] provides a jumping-off point. Because a public broadcasting institution created by Parliament regulated broadcasting in Canada, we cannot completely separate the motives for regulation or the act of censorship itself from the political wrangling (e.g., elections, appointment of ministers) that first enabled the public broadcaster to be created and then to assume some control over what could be broadcast. Here we set aside the question of free speech and "jump off" in the direction of regulations made to preserve decorum and to "protect" listeners against manipulation via "this intimate medium."[7] Regulators framed their rulings about programming in terms of aesthetic or listener protection measures, and these, even within the CBC, received less attention than did the more conventionally momentous regulations designed to prevent hate speech or unfair political utterances.[8] Political discourse on the air remains part of the history of broadcasting in Canada, but is treated here as a sidelight to the more particular process of using and challenging regulations to work out a code of "good taste."

REGULATING THE AIR

On paper, Canadian listeners had little opportunity to affect broadcasting rules, even though these rules had ostensibly been created with their well-being in mind. Broadcasting authorities did not have to publicize regulations beyond making them known to all station operators. The CBC and private stations informed advertising agencies about regulations that might affect planned or ongoing advertising campaigns. Ideally, programs created by agencies or stations were to be broadcast with potentially objectionable elements already removed by writers or producers familiar with the regulations. So, for listeners, regulated radio was simply supposed to be radio, and broadcasters would soon learn the ropes, banishing offensive material before it reached the air. Few observers were as optimistic as L.P. Teevens of the Ministry of Pensions and National Health, who mimicked the patent medicine ads he knew well when he joked: "No matter how heavy or coarse the growth may be, it can be permanently and painlessly removed through the use of a Department of Good Taste."[9] Changing the culture of commercial broadcasting was not a matter of putting up a few fences and keeping them mended. Private station operators and advertising agencies found their activities restricted for the sake of listeners, and they believed that some of these restrictions went too far. Rules made to protect listeners from unsavoury topics had their own curious logic but were not much different from the programming guidelines drawn up in the United States by the National Association of Broadcasters (NAB) or networks like NBC. In Canada, however, regulators were less comfortable with what they saw as the tendency of commercial speech to disregard conventions of conversation and to find its way into programming. Customer service did not seem to them to be always compatible with public service. They were also uncomfortable with programs that might threaten dominant belief systems, but they fretted even more about keeping radio as open as possible. The examples presented below address these themes and illustrate the difficulties created when entrenched social expectations and mores came under pressure from a still-expanding medium. Regulators bore the brunt of this pressure as they were the ones obliged to indicate what was considered appropriate at any given time. Program producers, at both public and private broadcasting outlets, merely had to adhere to the regulations and exercise their right to complain. And complaint could be surprisingly effective.

So far in this study, I've equated taste in programming with listener preferences or cultural values, factors that were themselves contingent upon countless categories or influences, from gender to signal strength. If some Canadian listeners could not or would not warm to British music hall, for example, I assume it was because their desire to experience that kind of variety show did not overcome their urge to listen to the available alternatives. If some liked *The Happy Gang*, those same listeners could probably be counted on to give similar programs a chance now and again. Broadcasters, especially on the commercial side, used listener data and ratings to estimate who was listening when, and they developed a rough sense of what else might draw equivalent or better audience numbers in the future.[10] Categories like variety, serials, light music, and so on made sense to program makers and advertising agencies who needed ways to package and sell particular audiences to potential sponsors. Programs could also be classified in a more binary fashion, as "in good taste" or "in bad taste" and, ideally, programming regulations indicated where the boundaries between these discrete categories stood. If regulations were to be effective, the definition and redefinition of these boundaries – the process of prescribing norms and deviations from norms – had to take place *before* listeners heard programs. Regulators, like program makers, employed the fallout from already-aired programming to aid their decisions, but their primary orientation was to the *future*, to acts of consumption that had not yet happened. So, by default, regulations targeted the sites of production: ad agencies, stations, and performers.

The impulse to prevent certain content reaching impressionable audiences did not emerge in response to radio's arrival. Already, in the nineteenth century, mass-produced books, magazines, and films all caused some form of alarm or scrutiny, and in Canada this scrutiny often came at the initiative of women's organizations.[11] Once radio joined these other mass media, its distinctive characteristics prompted a different kind of action. As noted in chapter 1, broadcasts most

own tastes in presuming what might minimize annoyance for listeners. In 1926, CNR president H.W. Thornton wanted to prevent radio from becoming an "atmospheric billboard" by supporting the "necessary and proper limitations" on sponsorship,[14] but radio was simply too new, too fragile. Without a viable broadcasting industry made up of sponsors, programs, and radio set sales driving each other, the Radio Branch would have little more to regulate than the sets in logging camps or on ships. By 1929, the CNR's prototype network, the growing number of stations, and a furor over religious broadcasting contributed to persuading Parliament that broadcasting warranted closer supervision.[15] In addition to addressing technical problems like allocating frequency space, the Aird Commission acknowledged the extent to which broadcasting mattered economically and culturally. Perhaps most important, the commission heard witnesses say it was time to stop thinking of broadcasting solely as analogous to flyers or billboards and to recognize that a code of practice needed to replace remedies applied only *after* a program or advertisement had caused offence. When he appeared before the Aird Commission, Cardinal Rouleau asked: "Would it not be advisable to establish a Committee for the purpose of examining or preparing programmes, leaving out entirely anything immoral or irreligious, banning anything aggressive against any group of citizens, or grotesque, and liable to debase our people?"[16] This was a broad set of demands, but when CRBC and CBC officials eventually came to examine program and advertising content, the criteria they adopted echoed Rouleau's.

Having a single regulatory body in charge of policing the frontiers of taste and allowable programming seemed incompatible with the subjective nature of the job, but to go without such a body was untenable given the scarcity of broadcast frequencies and the potentially limitless supply of special pleaders with enough money to buy airtime. Setting up a system for overseeing broadcast material was definitely not a Canadian innovation. For public monopolies like some European state broadcasters or the BBC, such oversight was designed to be handled internally, during a program's planning phase. In the United States, the Federal Radio Commission (FRC) was empowered, until its replacement in 1934 by the Federal Communications Commission (FCC), to set rules by which stations had to abide or face a wide range of disciplinary actions.[17] Setting aside their effectiveness or the zeal with which they were enforced, these measures had been in place in the United Kingdom and the United States since at least 1927, while Canada stumbled along without a similar authority until 1932. In 1930, a rumoured shake-up of broadcasting in Canada spurred a correspondent for the *Baltimore Sun* to predict that strong public control would put advertisers in their place and to portray a future Canadian broadcasting authority as tough on "bunk artists."[18] It was a vision that failed to materialize. When the newly created CRBC took charge of censorship and programming standards, it took charge of regulating stations that were by then several years more entrenched in terms of profitability, political pull, and programming experience. Charlesworth and his fellow commissioners could confidently take on the more clearly confrontational or abusive speakers, but the commission dithered, as the CBC would later, when it came to milder cases. Programs coming in from the United States and programs with advertising contracts already in force muddied the waters even further because responsibility for the scripts or general atmosphere of these shows did not rest entirely with the Canadian stations carrying them. Over the years, these uncertainties encouraged broadcasters to view regulation not simply as a matter of acceptance or rejection but of negotiation. When negotiating with regulators failed to produce the desired result, the affected broadcasters were typically not shy about appealing to their parliamentary representatives or the Canadian public. In this way, the flexible system in place during the radio era set the stage for the late 1950s handover of regulatory control from the CBC to the Board of Broadcast Governors (BBG), which, as Marc Raboy concludes, was "structured and staffed in such a way as to ensure that [private broadcasters'] interests would, at last, be served by a public agency."[19]

The ensuing BBG phase, during which Canada also gained a private television network, was not even a gleam in the eye of private broadcasters when the CRBC began its watch in 1932, vigilant lest "the 'excessive,' the irrational, the senseless" find their way onto the radio.[20] Early on, the commission received advice from Gladstone Murray on the maintenance of standards and censorship, two issues he viewed as related, but separate. He considered it most important to have a "measure of general public confidence" rather than a "rigid formula" when it came to determining what should be censored. Having common sense standards would make the censor's job as easy as possible. "In general," Murray noted, "nothing should be broadcast which might be expected reasonably to offend the susceptibilities of any considerable section of the listening public." Ultimately, he suggested that, in return for assuming power of "life and death" over broadcast content, the CRBC (or an authority that might succeed it) became a kind of character reference for any programs it allowed on air: "Although these programmes will be provided by outside commercial enterprise their acceptance by the Commission will impose responsibility for their appropriateness and bona fides."[21] Murray was not (yet) in charge of the day-to-day operations at Canada's public broadcaster, but he perceptively described the odd relationship between the CRBC and the more numerous private stations it subsidized.[22] Even though those stations would most likely be the creative source or conduit, any offensive material getting past regulators would damage broadcasting's overall reputation and undermine the commission's position as public safeguard. In addition to the cases Vipond cites, a couple other programs exemplified the extent to which more careful monitoring seemed necessary. One of these, a series of six radio dramas aired on the CRBC network prior to the 1935 federal election, no doubt contributed to the CRBC's end. The Conservative Party series, *Mr Sage*, rubbed a "considerable section of the listening public" the wrong way. These were mostly Liberal voters, whose victorious representatives in Parliament wasted little time in overhauling broadcasting and banning dramatized political announcements as well as mandating the allocation of free time for radio campaigning during election periods.[23]

The other case related more directly to the problem of listener preferences. In the waning months of the CRBC's short lifespan, an objectionable program on the NBC-affiliated station CRCT illustrated that leaving censorship to Charlesworth's discretion, or to the discretion of over-worked station staff, was unwise. Eddie Cantor's show, sponsored by Chase and Sanborn coffee, generated complaints from listeners stunned that they were not spared a "feast for the moron and the morbid." The listener who came up with that description acknowledged Cantor's was an American program but assumed that station staff would have some sort of knowledge of what they were relaying: "Having heard it yourselves," he reasoned, "you must surely have realized that it is hardly the thing to serve up to Canadians on a Sunday night." Other annoyed listeners complained to the commission, which, in their estimation should have been disciplining those responsible for producing and approving the program.[24] There seemed to be no primary motivation for listener complaint, despite

Cantor's track record for racy material and the inevitable potential for backlash against the Jewish part of his identity. It was clear that a web of trust had broken down. CRBC staff members were more anxious about controversial talks as well as unlikely to request program scripts in advance from broadcasters whose acts were classified as entertainment and, in the case of Cantor, supposedly "pre-vetted" by NBC. In the estimation of Graham Spry, by the mid-1930s, no longer evangelizing public broadcasting full time, the CRBC was not only "an instrument for subsidizing private enterprise" but had also "become a creature in some measure of the party in power, and its regulations, though not enforced, [were] a challenge to the freedom of the air" because they privileged commercial speech. Oddly enough, Spry cited Charlesworth's reluctance to prohibit communist speakers as evidence of lax enforcement. Speaking on the same occasion about the Cantor case, Radio League member Brooke Claxton suggested the coordination of standards with American networks to reduce the chances of offensive material going across the border.[25]

NEW AND IMPROVED

After its creation in the fall of 1936, the CBC took about a year to formulate its own regulations, circulating drafts internally for several months before finalizing the new code in November 1937. These rules were an operational interpretation of the Broadcasting Act, an attempt to set out the boundaries, indicated more broadly in the act, between acceptable and unacceptable material. During the draft phase, Murray anticipated that cleaning house would require the regional representatives of the CBC to be strict: "There is going to be a good deal of trouble about some of these regulations. We shall probably have to make examples of some stations – perhaps in the way of cancellation and suspension of licences."[26] Such measures were not necessary. Probably the most important thing to bear in mind about these new regulations was that they "faced outward" to address the programs created by private stations,[27] ad agencies, independent production houses, and broadcasters outside Canada. The regulations applied to CBC-produced programs as well, but the CBC's own programming staff was to take care of complying with the regulations during program planning and rehearsals. Little of this was ever satisfactorily explained to private station owners and staff, many of whom laboured under the impression that the CBC had drawn up the *Regulations for Broadcasting Stations Made under the Canadian Broadcasting Act, 1936,* solely to thwart private stations whenever possible. About a month after the new rules were in force, General Manager Murray made a feeble attempt to dissuade owners and managers from seeing the regulatory relationship as adversarial. He wrote to Phillip Morris, who managed CFPL in London, Ontario, emphasizing the intimacy of broadcasting and the role of private stations in upholding the regulations. He also asked Morris to make it clear over the air that any censorship or schedule changes arising from the regulations were not "at the direct instance of the CBC. For the most part there should be an identity of interest between the station and the CBC as it is bad for broadcasting generally to encourage the misconception that either the Act or the CBC is responsible for tyrannous censorship."[28] Asking station managers like Morris to view regulation in this way was a tall order. By 1937, most private stations were profitable enough to resent any broadcast bureaucracy hampering their operations, despite the leg up they had been given through the CRBC and the CBC's assumption of production costs and wire costs for the distribution of national programs.

Overall, under the CBC, regulation came to be framed as a public responsibility undertaken by the only public institution in the industry, a job entrusted to a body not dependent on the whims of sponsors for its continued existence. James S. Thomson, who became the CBC's caretaker general manager upon Murray's departure, was still a member of the corporation's Board of Governors when he congratulated the movies for having become *cinema* thanks to a self-imposed code of censorship. Radio, he claimed, lagged behind film and had been taken over by the commercial element, quite unlike newspapers and magazines: "Could we imagine any self-respecting journal handing over the writing of its matter to advertisers? Imagine the degeneracy of journalism if soap-vendors were to dictate the substance of magazines. Yet, this is the ignominious position into which radio production has fallen." Thomson's solution was to interest all broadcasters in North America in "the entire question of what function we want radio to fulfil." Following in the footsteps of the film industry, he suggested, "an aesthetic and moral code could be formulated. The vulgar exploitation of human cupidity could be eliminated. Offensive references to personal hygiene could be shut off. Sordid tales of betrayed affection might be banned." In Canada, the progression towards a healthier radio diet would involve sacrifices, and Thomson declared: "We have got beyond the pioneer stage. The private station must now take its place much more fully in a genuinely national policy. To accomplish this end is the role of the CBC."[29] When the opportunity arose in the spring of 1942 for the Canadian Association of Broadcasters to endorse the "desirability of raising the standards of broadcasting," it did.[30] No strings were attached to making such a pledge, and drastic changes to regulations affecting sponsored programs were unlikely, given the CBC's mild addiction to commercial revenue.

Viewed from outside, regulating program standards seemed to be the definition of a thankless task. Some observers, like radio journalist R.B. Tolbridge, concluded that the CBC had been insufficiently vigilant and too eager to make deals, neglecting to use its "full power to control the character of programs broadcast by private stations, including time and *content* of advertising." Tolbridge also argued that, instead of binding private stations to a good taste manifesto like Thomson's, the CBC's management and Board of Governors were merely consolidating commercial radio's hold on Canadian broadcasting by letting it carry on largely unhindered.[31] While this was a fairly accurate reading of the situation, Tolbridge ignored the fact that it remained difficult to police broadcast content during a war fought to protect, among other things, freedom of speech. The CBC's most effective strategy, its only strategy from the outset of its regulatory career, was to tackle messages or broadcast methods that threatened to disturb the individual listener in her home or challenge the beliefs of larger groups. Continually, and as far in advance of a program's scheduled air date as possible, regulators had to estimate the public's capacity to be offended and, still more difficult, to imagine how communities of potentially offended listeners might constitute themselves. Accordingly, the general trend in regulation involved creating a two-tiered hierarchy comprising acceptable and unacceptable programming. The first set of regulations in 1937 took the simplest path and named the kinds of programs (or elements within programs) to be prohibited. But those prohibitions were not arrived at in a vacuum by an omniscient force able to discern just what listeners could handle. Regulators had their own personalities, beliefs, and prejudices to contend with, as well as having to keep in mind the regulations in force elsewhere, and they had to deal with the questions that followed virtually any exercise of regulatory power against an artist, station, or sponsor.

As the reach of both CBC and private stations increased through the later 1930s and early 1940s, the original regulations underwent formal changes and spawned informal rulings or special dispensations on a case-by-case basis. These regulations were the sole restraint able to be applied to broadcast content before it was broadcast. As the CBC's Donald Manson explained: "If it was not for public laws, we would see some very queer handling of publicity."[32] With varying degrees of effectiveness, personnel in the CBC's station relations and commercial departments applied the general principles of listener protection and tasteful standards to the examples below. As the CBC was part of an operation with its own commercial arm, its regulators understood why other broadcasters viewed content regulation as obtrusive, but they believed those broadcasters could adapt over time, given clear indications of what was wrong with proposed material, or material already aired contrary to the rules. In 1943, program and administrative staff decided: "[It] would not be enough just to say that a programme was no good and unacceptable. It would be our responsibility to say in exactly what aspects it was not desirable and it would also be our responsibility to advise the advertiser in what ways it could be made acceptable."[33] In order for such conversations to take place, however, the CBC had to clarify for its own people just what sort of programming needed work. In addition to collectively thinking through why a program could be classified as an "outlaw," any staff member in a position to make a ruling or to interpret regulations to private broadcasters or ad agencies was reminded of the possible consequences of cancelling or disrupting a series.[34]

Owing to the tension between stewardship over broadcasting and the desire to keep serving listeners with a variety of programs, CBC regulators were almost guaranteed to displease someone each time they made a ruling. The BBC's Michael Barkway observed that they simultaneously had a reputation for inadequate enforcement and for secretive deliberations. He later noted that, while regulations were no doubt helpful in establishing a benchmark for broadcast content, private stations did the most they could "within the law," placing the moral responsibility on the custodian CBC.[35] Even the CBC's own programming staff struggled to find a balanced perspective on content regulation. Gerald Pratley told his audience he would like film censors to practise more judicious censorship on "cheap productions exploiting the rottenness and evils of sex and crime" but not on films like Alfred Hitchcock's *Rope*, which had been banned in Ontario.[36] Pratley was free to disparage that ruling, but his movie-going listeners could not see the film, and while controversial radio programs sometimes snuck out or wafted across borders, there was little chance the Hitchcock-deprived would happen upon an accidental screening. Aversions to certain kinds of programming also varied regionally, so issuing definite prohibitions against one sort of show might seem prudent in one part of the country but prudish in another.[37] Regulators were acutely aware of their position and wanted to reassure the public that they took the power entrusted to them seriously, viewing regulations as necessary intrusions. CBC Talks staffer Neil Morrison told an audience of psychologists that regulations were "designed to protect the interests of the listener and in so far as possible to guarantee fairness. I think everyone who has studied the question recognizes that freedom isn't absolute or unlimited, and that in the interests of freedom and of public welfare, there must be certain laws, such as the laws of libel and slander, defining what people may or may not say."[38] Without some form of oversight, this line of reasoning went, it would only be a matter of time and money before sleazy programming or extreme views dominated the public airwaves.

LOOKING OUTWARD AND INWARD

Broadcasting rules adopted in the United States were relevant to Canadian regulations, and vice versa, in that broadcasting organizations in both places had reciprocal knowledge of the broadcast standards in place across the border. Although regulators did not set up formal means to discuss or coordinate regulations, it remained easy to get copies of the CBC's latest regulations, FCC statutes, or NAB guidelines. Canadian broadcasters took an interest in US commerce secretary Herbert Hoover's efforts to impose some structure on the American broadcasting industry during the 1920s. Visitors from the United States occasionally offered first-hand accounts of an American government that had "delegated slight powers to a supine Commission, whose members tangled in technicalities meticulously allot higher frequencies, but ignore fundamentals."[39] Canadians learned that, in the United States, especially after the failure of the broadcast reform movement during the early 1930s, and even during the war, programming drew the most attention from regulators when it affected the interests of sponsors.[40] Given the FCC's limited authority, fear of lawsuits for lost business, copyright or patent infringement, defamation, and fear of Federal Trade Commission sanctions was a more effective way of keeping broadcasters within the rules.[41] Regardless of their motivation for regulating content, the American networks did so, and script departments were busy vetting the output of writers from all over. NBC estimated in 1937 that it rejected 15 to 25 percent of scripts for "poor taste."[42] While the CBC was finalizing its own regulations, it adopted parts of NBC's policy on products unacceptable for advertising, keeping these rules in place until at least the early 1950s.[43] CBC programming and commercial staff studied US network codes of practice and NAB bulletins to determine how these bodies handled sensitive topics, and they were on the lookout for any (infrequent) polling the American networks did regarding the tastes of Canadian consumers.[44] CBC and FCC regulators perhaps came closest in their approaches to content regulation during the postwar "Blue Book" era in the United States, a brief period in which commercial control came under close examination.[45]

With respect to regulation, the BBC's role in Canada was less significant than was the CBC's attention to American practices, for two reasons. First, the advertising messages accompanying American programs were the main source of work for Canadian regulators, and reviewing ad copy in light of broadcast regulations became one of their core tasks. British programming came without ads, and if recorded BBC programs were sponsored once they came to Canada, any oversight could be conducted via the CBC's own departments. Second, the BBC was itself not an organization constituted to regulate anything. It held a monopoly over radio broadcasting, but it did not have to make sure other "British" broadcasting enterprises, like Radio Luxembourg or Radio Normandy, measured up to broadcasting standards because those organizations were based on the European continent. However, the BBC sometimes dispensed advice about how to handle the rather more precarious Canadian broadcasting situation. As part of the consulting work he did prior to the CBC's formation, Felix Greene recommended to Canadian authorities that strict regulations on commercial programming would be as necessary as the revenue-generating commercial programs themselves.[46] As much to protect its own reputation as to avoid causing problems for the CBC, the BBC also imposed a kind of informal internal regulation on its own programs going to North America, aware of standards of taste there, and aware of Canadian regulations.[47]

To a much greater degree than either the American networks or the BBC, the organization most affected by Canadian radio regulations, materially interested in their interpretation, and able to do something about them – though it took at least fifteen years – was the Canadian Association of Broadcasters (CAB). This assembly of private station owners was a trade association, lobby group, and mutual benefit society. Members of the CAB correctly viewed the regulation of program content as an obstacle to their business model and hardly missed an opportunity to convince Canadians that the CBC and its predecessor had overstepped their bounds. The CAB contended that the CBC should not be the regulatory authority because it also put out programming, and it did not consider the CBC's regulatory role to be fully legitimate. As T.J. Allard, long-time CAB member and former president, recalled in the late 1970s: "broadcasting activities were governed by rulings from a department or tribunal which had the force of law, although not sanctioned by legislation or official regulation."[48] The CBC's *Regulations for Broadcasting Stations* were indeed official, but Allard and his colleagues at the CAB sought an "independent" regulator, not a public broadcaster whose rules were applied across the industry. The CAB longed for a system in which stations and networks regulated themselves, relying upon estimates of audience size and listener mail to decide where acceptable ended and unacceptable began. Well before any public broadcasters arrived on the scene, the CAB conceded there was "no doubt that advertising should be limited and subject to censorship during the evening hours," but it was far more occupied with the threat of outright nationalization posed by the Aird Report.[49] Members got a reprieve from that fate, but, under the CRBC, they still found rules stifling and detrimental to their bottom lines. While Gladstone Murray was consulting with him late in 1936 on the CBC's proposed regulations, Major W.C. Borrett of CHNS Halifax recalled his still recent experience dealing with the CRBC and complained of business lost when commercial scripts under regulatory review were "were never returned in time and sometimes not at all".[50]

Once the CBC enacted its regulations, the CAB strove publicly to demonstrate that its members could be trusted to follow them, but it continued to publicly question the basis on which the rules had been put in place. During the war, the association registered a subtle protest by presenting its own "Code of Ethics" as proof that its members would have served the public just as well without the CBC's rules.[51] Getting bolder as the war went on, CAB president Glen Bannerman played on wartime fatigue with regimentation to suggest that the CBC may be leading the Canadian radio community down the wrong road: "Is it the Road of Freedom of Expression; is it the road of community responsibility; of community strength and effort, or is it the road of state centralization with its bureaucracy and red tape?"[52] Some of the code words were there: private stations served the *individual*, living and working in *responsible communities*, while the CBC intended to sweep all of that away for the sake of *centralized control*. The CAB's faith in the entertainment and advertising industries to police themselves went hand in hand with its distrust of centralized or uniform regulation. When Eddie Cantor's show was cancelled in Canada (a second time) late in 1945 for its suggestive humour, the CAB's organ, the *Canadian Broadcaster*, put out a dismayed editorial quoting the sponsor's Canadian vice-president, who declared: "We know that our own parent company would not sponsor any program deleterious to the public interest. We doubt if the NBC would accept such a program. We question whether any program guilty of such charges would enjoy the high rating that the Cantor program enjoys in the United States."[53] Unable to appeal beyond the CBC to overturn such cancellations, the CAB wisely stepped up its public appeals, in which the CBC became "the Government's CBC" operating with "Crystal Set Laws" (See figure 4.1: "What's wrong with this pitcher?").[54] Fundamentally, the CAB did not view broadcasting as different from the press or film and asked: "[If] specific regulations have not been found necessary for other media of mass communication, therefore why is the general body of the law of the land not the safest guide also for radio?"[55]

HEALTH AND SAFETY

For regulators, the problem was that the law of the land, at least in civil cases, concerned relationships between individuals and organizations conducting specific business or personal affairs, and radio relationships were not always so plainly defined. The press operated under the common law, and publishers took care (usually) to exercise their freedom just enough so that anyone aggrieved by something in print could not sue for defamation. Parliament chose to treat radio

What's wrong   with this pitcher?

IN CANADIAN RADIO, ONE OF THE PLAYERS IS ALSO THE UMPIRE!

The Canadian Broadcasting Corporation competes with the independent (local) stations for both audience and business! AND it writes and enforces the regulations!

That's why the independent stations ask Parliament for an impartial regulatory board, one that will be SOLELY an umpire! This already exists in air and rail companies where both government and non-government operations are regulated by a non-operating, impartial board.

The independent stations want an umpire, but one who isn't in the game. If you think that's fair, write your Member of Parliament and tell him so!

> The Canadian Association of Broadcasters,
> Victory Building, Toronto.

Figure 4.1 "What's wrong with this pitcher?" leaflet, n.d. [1947], Library and Archives Canada, Records of the Canadian Broadcasting Corporation, vol. 988, file 4, Canadian Association of Broadcasters, 1947, 1955.

differently, giving the public broadcasting authorities a quasi-judicial role, because the broadcaster-listener relationship in radio differed from the relationships covered under existing laws. They chose a centrally administrated broadcasting code for an industry in which programs and advertisements came to stations from multiple sources, frequently unauditioned, and the reach of a program was not restricted by the size of a print run. Thus chosen, the CRBC and the CBC needed to curate the tone of broadcasts by estimating what community standards would tolerate, and by predicting if, or how, public safety might be affected by the unrestricted airing of programs touching on certain themes. Concern for public safety and public decency mingled as regulators had to evaluate broadcasts on personal health, references to illness, and the touting of proprietary remedies. Programs advising or recommending particular courses of action to those who were ill could potentially damage listeners' health, and even programs on the topic of illness or the normal functioning of the body could be considered in bad taste.

Radio's intimacy figured prominently among the motivations for regulating program material about health and illness, and taking a different perspective on a theme discussed in chapter 1 – intimacy – illustrates how. Although broadcasters had to consider their potential audiences listening *at home*, radio advertising begged listeners to consider products and their uses and, for a moment, sought to whisk listeners' imaginations away from home into a commercial space where commercial speech would sound less jarring. From a regulatory point of view, such abductions could not go unnoticed. Did the message suit the environment into which it was broadcast? Would program makers and advertisers ever acquire a sixth sense about tasteful programming? When he called for a rededication to upholding broadcast standards in 1942, J.S. Thomson remarked that the job of keeping an eye on advertising content was really a simple one: maintaining "canons of good taste that are in line with the finest standards of home life."[56] Regulators had to synthesize their own sense of the topics a polite guest in the home could raise and then rule accordingly. Such a guest could not address everyone as though they were perpetually ill, as advertisers were accused of doing once consumers started to spend freely again after the war.[57] The CBC reviewed program and advertising scripts, and reacted to complaints about ones already broadcast, with the ideal of tasteful conversation in mind. Regulators had to weigh the need for timely, useful information against the desire to eliminate potentially intrusive and unappealing messages, whether these messages came from sponsors or not.

Several considerations governed the way regulators engaged broadcasters and the public over health-related programming. If the program in question offered some form of public service by bringing a pressing issue to light, it was looked upon more favourably, but this was not a guarantee that it would go on the air. Quite early in the CBC's career as regulatory agency, a listener asked Murray why broadcasting had not yet been harnessed to combat ignorance about venereal disease. Murray replied that the subject was too delicate for radio, and, even though the regulations allowed officials some latitude, he was reluctant to err on the permissive side.[58] Regulation 13 required such programming to be approved two weeks in advance by officials at the Department of Pensions and National Health, and some of these officials had definite opinions regarding on-air restraint. The department's J.J. Heagarty, who handled a number of these consultations, recommended in 1939 that a proposed talk on VD should be stripped of words like "brothel" because "the radio audience is not confined to adults but comprises many children whose ears should not be offended by the use of such words or whose curiosity should not be aroused in regard to prostitution and all that applies thereto." A prospective speaker on the subject of colonic irrigation also ran afoul of Heagarty, who noted that he did not object to her use of the term "but to the impression that is conveyed" and advised the CBC to disallow her script. The CBC staff member handling this particular case told her she should try one of the private stations.[59] She would still have to undergo the same review process but would have more time to come up with a more decorous name for her calling, one that was suitable for a mixed audience of adults and children, women and men. Contrast this with NBC's commercial policy articulated in 1940, in which there were similar controls on laxative advertising but only for programs going out over the whole network, and script review was done internally.[60]

By the middle of the Second World War, referring health copy to the Department of Pensions and National Health involved sending about three thousand items for clearance every month, and the CBC considered itself a liaison between health authorities and advertisers, though it did not charge advertisers for the service. In addition to having "done away with broadcasts by 'health' cults," the practice of running copy through Ottawa allowed the CBC to boast: "The

Corporation protects the listener from false and misleading claims and exploitation. The Corporation also protects the private station manager, agency and advertiser as the element of probable, even though innocent, transgression of the law is removed."[61] Regulators even prohibited mention of ailments that "result from the neglect of personal hygiene,"[62] and they went through submitted material assiduously "to revise the copy in such a manner that extensive re-writing [would] be unnecessary."[63] While the CBC clearly presumed to decide what sort of material was appropriate for radio, this was hardly the action of a competitive enterprise hoping to hobble its commercial foes. Some of the most controversial topics were ones in which private broadcasters saw little to no worth, and they had little trouble complying with regulations. Descriptions of childbirth, for example, had their uses in the field of educational broadcasting, but in themselves were not entertainment, nor did they have advertising value. If a dramatic script involved childbirth, the CBC recom-mended handling these scenes "off mike" and reminded private sta-tions that ignoring this guideline could mean costly last-minute revisions.[64] When listeners were distressed, it was easier for them to write to the CBC and remark "if one has company in it is embarrass-ing to hear the characters discussing when and how the baby is to be born" than to figure out if a sponsor or some other third party was involved in a program's production.[65] As the broadcast regulator, the CBC often took flak for the state of broadcasting.

When commercial products were involved, however, the stakes were higher, and the opposing motives of advertisers and censors emerged more clearly. The CBC found itself in a difficult position as regulator because bans or bowdlerizations of broadcast material were only supposed to be necessary when standards of good taste had been violated, yet discussion of certain topics would be neces-sary in the public interest, even in advertisements. So, anyone hoping to sell remedies for ailments that affected pretty much any part of the human body had to navigate (with the CBC's help) a welter of guide-lines flowing out of the CBC's "good taste" policy. The word "laxa-tive" could only be used once per announcement, likewise "Athlete's Foot." If you had "soft, spongy, bleeding gums or gums that seem[ed] to shrink away from your teeth," you would not hear your problem described that way on the radio. "Boils" and "blackheads" became "blemishes," and references to "thick strangling mucus" were right out.[66] Neither CBC nor pensions and health officials wanted to deny advertisers access to airtime, but they did not think a graphic approach to advertising copy, with its accompanying sound effects, was entirely necessary. Even what we might see as straightforward or urgent public health messages had to meet standards set with the family audience in mind. In the case of a few proposed announcements by the Canadian Cancer Society, R.D. Whitmore from Pensions and Health left the particulars in the hands of the CBC's copy reviewers, but mused: "It is, from a point of view of good taste, unfortunate, that Cancer so often manifests itself in the female reproductive system, in the breast, and in the bowel." He also hoped that scheduling the amended announcements "at a proper time of the day" would allow them to be broadcast.[67] CBC programs about mental illness, like the early postwar *What's on Your Mind*, or the early-1950s *Man's Last Enemy – Himself* and *In Search of Ourselves*, largely avoided this sort of scrutiny.[68] Even though some of the neuroses described in those broadcasts could be unpleasant for listeners to contemplate, picturing mental illness did not seem as disturbing as picturing eruptions of the skin.

While a tasteful tone in the discussion of health and illness remained important to regulators, the main reason the CBC drew upon the expertise of authorities in the field was to protect listeners from misleading claims, false cures, or potentially harmful products. As American broadcasting regulators found out during the 1930s, the greatest danger of harm to consumers, and of collateral damage to the reputation of the industry, lurked in the patent medicine sector.[69] In 1935, Hector Charlesworth had proclaimed that those who had "largely employed quackery and the 'fear complex' as means for inducing the gullible to purchase and consume all manner of dangerous concoctions" had been driven from the temple.[70] His tendency to train the CRBC's regulatory energy on stamping out political and religious demagoguery perhaps contributed to his optimistic view of the matter. During the early CBC period, patent medicine advertising returned.[71] Much of the regulatory activity surrounding these nonprescription or "proprietary" medicines was restricted to a couple of years during wartime in which the CBC learned a great deal about the business, and advertisers learned how valuable they were to Canadian radio. For awhile, programs sponsored by patent medicine firms went out over what CBC called its "alternative" network – that is, private stations carrying the same programs simultaneously, with the CBC paying the wire charges.[72] Until nearly the end of 1942, the

CBC had no specified desk for clearing scripts and advertising copy. Staff would read what came to hand, and particularly thorny problems were passed on to the supervisor of Station Relations. After his eye-opening trip to the NBC and CBS continuity clearance departments in New York, Station Relations head Jack Radford recommended adopting such a desk. He noted that NBC and CBS employed their own script checkers because they were wary of listener or competitor complaints that could launch federal investigations: "The loss of an account through FTC action is a loss of money, effort and prestige, and it is encumbent [sic] upon the Continuity Acceptance Departments to safeguard their company's interests by skilfully guiding the sponsors with respect to commercial continuity and good taste."[73] Although the CBC did not face the same liabilities because it was not legally identified with the commercial programs it carried, the difference between the CBC's ad hoc arrangements and the US networks' zealous checking of scripts was plain. Advertisements for patent medicines and remedies started to attract attention from the CBC in the spring of 1942 and were shuffled off to the Dominion Network by late in 1944. In cases in which the CBC suspected an advertiser of making a false claim, it tended to trust the judgment of the medical officers at Pensions and Health. In one prominent case, that department took its consulting role quite seriously, urging the CBC to write to the American originators of the Jack Benny program after the comedian had touted the "pepping up" effect of Benzedrine, classified as a narcotic in the United Kingdom. Two Canadian soldiers nearly died attempting to get out of drill by taking the drug, which produced fever symptoms when taken to excess.[74]

In its vigilance over drug and patent medicine ads, the CBC was ostensibly on the lookout for *verbal* excesses – unverifiable claims made for products that could sway consumers without scientifically proving that the products had any effect. As J.S. Thomson affirmed: "Our listening public need to be protected from such shameless exploitation of their defencelessness."[75] In the regulators' estimation, the use of superlatives in advertising was not only untruthful, it offended the sensibilities of the listener and, thus, justified a more discerning and critical approach. Gladstone Murray, in his new post as director general of programmes late in 1942, had to placate one of the pensions and national health consultants after the accidental airing of an unaltered American commercial script over the CBC network, and he hoped that North America could become a place where the only exaggeration that is effective is that of understatement. When we come to consider the usage of commercial programmes originating in the United States the solution is not easy. It seems to me that if the problem of literal exaggeration is to be tackled in this connection it will have to be done on a wider front than appears to be contemplated by deleting the words "famous" and "wonderful" from the Chase and Sanborn commercial.[76]

CBC regulators operated on this wider front, where two distinctive broadcasting cultures clashed and where advertising powerhouse J. Walter Thompson tried to sell its programs to private stations as well as to a CBC network defining itself as the guardian of both the physical and the cultural welfare of Canadian listeners. J.R. Radford only succeeded in emphasizing this contrast by noting, sympathetically, that south of the border "such words as 'wonderful', 'famous' and 'magical' are not looked upon as misleading or false but are accepted as 'common usage' and the employment of such adjectives come under general sales appeal and actually cause no harm to the health of the nation."[77]

Radford's sympathies aside, words such as "magical" were not allowed on the CBC, and its personnel did their best to keep them off private airwaves as well. Sometimes, their task was much simpler than banning superlatives. In 1944, Radford wrote to one station manager: "I can say without any fear of contradiction that this PAZO PILE OINTMENT copy is the most revolting radio advertising material we have yet received in this office." The copy claimed that, thanks to PAZO's "perforated Pile Pipe," which lubricated "hardened, dried parts," swelling and bleeding would vanish.[78] Regulators rejected PAZO's campaign because it would not pass the "mixed company" test and because it mentioned a condition that might arise from personal neglect.[79] Initially, however, such material was subject to a double standard. One of the reasons prompting Radford to suggest the commitment of some staff to full-time continuity review was that, as late as 1942, CBC policy banned references to such vexing problems as "'under-arm odour,' 'stale sweat,' 'body odour – BO'" on CBC stations, while still allowing private stations to air them.[80] This situation changed relatively quickly, and bodies ceased to smell or ooze, at least on Canadian radio.

The process of ending the double standard began thanks to input from L.P. Teevens at Pensions and National Health. He compiled a sample of commercial scripts that did not make false claims but that were deemed to be in bad taste. Armed with this litany of offending references to infirmities or annoyances that were to be banished by using well-known remedies like Lydia Pinkham's Vegetable Compound or Carter's Little Liver Pills, the CBC began to pay more attention to patent medicines in particular.[81] Despite the fact that John Dunlop thought of Pensions and Health staff as "technicians and chemists without radio or advertising experience,"[82] his observations of American script censorship were employed by the CBC to turn what had been a somewhat haphazard, internally enforced policy into a more sophisticated system that applied to all stations. Dunlop's trip to New York preceded his supervisor Radford's by a few months, and he found the networks there willing to work with advertisers and the Food and Drug Administration to avoid offensive material. Dunlop not only advised that this be done in Canada as well but also that the CBC adopt a more "rigid" policy in order to justify the licence fee from which it drew part of its revenue. "The listener is not paying an annual fee to have advertisers tell him how 'sour and sunk' he may feel," wrote Dunlop, adding that broadcasts "are heard by the whole family in the drawing-room, and at the dinner table[,] and to have some of this distasteful advertising exuding from the radio set is inexcusable."[83] The assumption that the Canadian listening family actually *had* a drawing-room or assembled around the dinner table with regularity reflected an assumption that taste standards could be generalized from a middle-class norm to apply to all set owners. For the purpose of granting access to airtime in Canada, the CBC regulated for an archetypal family of listeners. Regard for this archetypal family was so high that Dunlop also recommended that copy be cleared before any contracts to broadcast were signed.[84] This was an inversion of the American practice, which applied script checking to the program and ad content of shows already "bought and booked" by sponsors.

The sort of ad copy that found favour with the CBC from early 1943 onward could best be characterized as the "institutional" announcement, often a simple mention of the sponsor's name, or a brief exhortation to try a product – assuming that the listener would be able to identify the ailment based on the product's name or other subtle cues in the announcement – rather than a more detailed description or dramatization of the product's qualities. Despite a shift towards institutional ads, listeners still found ways to be offended. Montreal architect C.R. Tetley wrote to the CBC Talks department complaining of CFCF's poor taste in running an ad that invited listeners to "be honest with themselves and think when they last took a laxative."[85] Before passing the complaint along to Station Relations, Tetley's correspondent at Talks, Neil Morrison, replied to Tetley agreeing that the ad was "in bad taste, particularly following immediately on a broadcast talk by the Archbishop of York."[86] Regardless of the class and religious implications of CFCF's scheduling choices, Tetley was most incensed by what he saw as a blatant disregard of broadcasting's position in the public sphere, wondering if the announcer would "make an announcement of this kind in the face of a room full of people, and just how long he would last in decent society if he did so."[87] Radio, a medium through which the anonymous voice could reach thousands or millions of listeners in their homes, was for him a sacred trust. Listeners' goodwill had been violated too often by advertisers who did not recognize that making a broadcast was subject to the conventions that went along with public speech.

By 1944, a system had evolved for dealing with advertisers reluctant to see how their copy could be considered in poor taste. CBC general manager Augustin Frigon evoked the theme of listener goodwill for one particularly concerned representative of the Young & Rubicam agency (a multinational with an office in Toronto) who was trying to schedule time for a show sponsored by Anacin. "You will understand," Frigon wrote, "that we are trying to avoid the type of statements which invariably find their way in[to] patent medicine continuities and which, in many cases, are not only annoying to listeners but quite unfair to the most serious firms."[88] Frigon considered Young & Rubicam to be the representatives of a "serious firm" and clearly expressed his distaste for the tone and content of the more aggressive or descriptive patent medicine ads. The problem with the Anacin program had arisen when the CBC rejected the show's bid for a schedule spot based on the style of ads to be broadcast. Even commercial manager Austin Weir, usually well disposed towards sponsored programs carrying decent advertising budgets, agreed that these locally produced spots imitating the Jack Benny-style American patent medicine ads (i.e., testimonials by the show's star or other performers) were "dangerous."[89] Further ammunition for the Anacin ban came when CBC staff noticed that Jack Kent Cooke, who had lately acquired a reputation as a maverick and somewhat mercenary broadcaster, had been enquiring about carrying patent medicine shows with testimonial ads on his Toronto station, CKEY.[90]

Regulators did not ignore the commercial welfare of the CBC, and they tended to give advertisers looking to book an entire season's worth of programming more opportunities to comply with regulations. At the same time as he was reminding colleagues about the danger of unrestrained advertising for proprietary cures, Weir noted: "some maintain that provided the sponsor is willing to produce a programme of the first order and has his continuities approved by the Department of Health (also that they are in good taste) the CBC has discharged its duty insofar as the public is concerned."[91] By 1944, with the tougher review policy in place, Augustin Frigon followed another suggestion from Weir and intervened to admit that it would be difficult to restrict long-time advertisers to institutional announcements if they believed that other firms were getting away with more.[92] The Anacin account was a good example of how commercially sensitive the topic had become for potential advertisers. The agency representing Anacin did not try to challenge the CBC's taste decisions but was critically aware of what strict enforcement of these decisions could mean to business. The agency ultimately got to Ernest Bushnell, who warned his superiors that imposing the rules could lead to significant consequences, namely: "Bayer Aspirin salesmen might not be adverse to commenting on the fact that CBC has banished Anacin from the air, leaving their listeners to draw whatever conclusions they like. I am afraid that in the eyes of druggists and other retailers the CBC might quite easily come to be considered a judge of the merits of the various patent medicines." Sensing a commercial and legal minefield ahead for the corporation, Bushnell proposed to shove patent medicine ads off the CBC entirely, allowing existing shows to remain on the air until the expiration of their contracts but leaving the private stations to broadcast material passed by Pensions and Health and vetted on the grounds of taste.[93] This "grandfather" arrangement would not release broadcasters from the restriction of allowing only a mention of the sponsor's name, so Bushnell could tell an audience at Vancouver's Canadian Club, with some justification, that it was "gratifying to learn that quite a number of broadcasting stations in the USA base their acceptance of certain kinds of advertising continuity on the standards set by the CBC."[94]

The accommodation of a "serious firm," while clearly informed by a concern for the corporation's budget and commercial welfare, was also inextricably linked to matters of taste in programming. The potential loss of listeners (and therefore advertising revenue) via the winding down of shows sponsored by patent medicine makers alarmed Frigon, who decided to keep the patent medicine programs on the CBC as well. He worried that audiences might retreat after the departure of advertisers like Anacin and the programs they funded, undermining all the work the CBC had put into its own sustaining programs.[95] If listeners were not enticed to listen for a whole evening, the CBC's goal of providing a wider variety of programming would be in jeopardy. Sustaining programs simply could not be as lavishly produced and could not afford the performers' salaries that sponsored ones could – especially those produced in the United States. The solution adopted was rooted in a hierarchical notion of which kind of show would suit which advertisers. Earlier in 1944, the CBC had established the Dominion Network, allowing more private stations to take some CBC programming and allowing the CBC to relay American and some British shows at a lower cost to stations otherwise unable to afford them. In late November 1944, taste and commerce found some accommodation with an arrangement to move patent medicine shows to the Dominion and to make advertisers pay for the whole network at once, a variation on the old arrangement by which the "alternative" network had been used before 1942. The first deal made along these lines involved Dodd's Medicine, and soon others followed.[96] Charles Jennings pressed those in charge of enforcing the rules to consider the "moral aspect of the business which is something a Corporation like ours cannot put to one side." He was concerned that his colleagues did not want to exercise the full authority they had been granted, and he believed that the whole situation arose from "our fears that we may be charged with discrimination."[97]

The CBC took on additional responsibility in running an "experiment" over which it would wield the same power it always had. Crucially, the Dominion Network was not the prestige vehicle that the Trans-Canada was for the CBC. Its composition – twenty-eight private stations led by one CBC station – would not reflect as poorly on the corporation if some programming or advertising on it were considered inferior to the material on the senior broadcasting service. According to Dominion Network manager Bud Walker, a double standard had been recreated.[98] His complaints had little effect. As Augustin Frigon told him: "The Canadian public has the right to request for the 'Quiz Kids' a Canadian network; it is our duty to make sure that such a program reaches us in a form acceptable to Canadians."[99] Only when the potential commercial impact of taste enforcement was made plain did the CBC relent yet still manage to distance its leading service from the too-intimate discussion of human decay and from dubious claims. Patent medicine ads stayed on the air, and the experiment was soon formalized as policy because,[100] without the money coming in from programs like the comedy, musical, and variety shows patent medicine makers (and most other sponsors) wanted to underwrite – shows many listeners tuned in to reliably – the CBC would be less capable of providing other kinds of programming.

THRILLS AND CHILLS

While regulators could claim that their interventions related to health or disease were justified as public safety measures and acts in defence of the broadcasting industry's status, the same could not be said for the regulation of material meant solely to entertain audiences. Still, that sector of broadcasting could hardly be left alone. Although they were in the minority, listeners and organizations gravely concerned about the subject matter and the execution of radio entertainment would continue to address their complaints to the national broad-casting authority, lamenting the tendency of advertisers to "cater to an average intelligence of that of a child of fourteen years of age."[101] By the 1930s, the colonization of radio by mysteries, detective sto-ries, and tales of the supernatural had raised questions about which sorts of broadcasts might be harmful. Just as they wondered about how adult broadcasters could relate to children appropriately over the air, parents and broadcasting authorities alike wondered about the effects rambunctious programs might have on children's speech and about their potential for over-stimulating young listeners. It is a question that has never gone away.[102] The belief that radio pos-sessed an unprecedented intimacy only increased such fears, yet broadcasting regulators had not created a system for classifying or controlling "thriller" programs. This did not stop them from becom-ing identified with such ill-defined phenomena as delinquency and a retreat from morality, just as pulp novels had been in the early post-war period.[103] As Annette Kuhn shows regarding film in 1930s Britain, movies likely to horrify children under sixteen were rated "H," and, although this rating was rarely bestowed between 1937 and the early 1950s,[104] the fact that horror-seeking youth could only succeed by eluding parents and deceiving cinema operators emphasized a fundamental difference in the way authorities could regulate film and radio. While the Hays Film Code in the United States and provincial film censorship in Canada brought some order, radio thrillers took what must have seemed like unfair advantage of the audience by airing exciting, improbable stories dealing with gruesome or eerie action. So formulaic had this type of program become on US commercial stations by the 1940s that professional and populist critiques of horror programs and "true crime" thrillers emerged.[105]

The programs became widely available in Canada as well and were "popular," according to private stations able to do a brisk trade in ads to accompany the shows. CFRB Toronto produced its own series, *Out of the Night*, for over a year.[106] The CBC even listed a thriller-type play as one of its programming highlights in 1940, but this play, Reby Edmond's *Murder at Mr Garcia's*, was most notable in the corporation's national schedule because there were so few others like it.[107] A report on the CBC's first five years of dramatic production explained the dearth of murder mysteries candidly: "As one of the inheritors of the great tradition of the British stage, radio as a public service has special responsibilities."[108] What the CBC itself produced did not encompass what Canadians heard. American and Canadian private stations supplied thriller and horror programs to a greater extent later in the wartime period. The CBC had not initially classified thrillers or horror programs as worthy of a ban, and it did not move to do so. The outcry over such programs originated outside the CBC. Although the CBC followed US studies on popular sorts of programming,[109] an internal memorandum from 1944 indicated that the corporation received "resolutions" on thrillers from various organizations from time to time and that enough of these had finally piled up to warrant a response.[110] According to Jack Radford, who appeared to be the CBC staff member most motivated to do something about thrillers, the relative success of the war effort in the latter half of 1944 had encouraged complaints about the type of programs available to Canadians. As the war wound down and peacetime routines resumed, panic about various media as potential contributors to social decline seemed to be one way for underemployed pleaders to recapture the urgency of their wartime commitments, and Radford argued that the state of homefront radio could and should be contemplated. He was especially concerned with children in wartime who were "deprived of normal parental supervision because of parental employment."[111] This was a veiled comment on the domestic changes wrought by war, and it showed that Radford either saw the corporation as the only broadcasting entity able to act in loco parentis or thought that parents had abdicated their roles as moral guides.

This did not mean that broadcasting authorities instantly acceded to calls to "clean up" the Canadian airwaves, but it did mean the issue had to be addressed publicly. General Manager Augustin Frigon acknowledged radio's special qualities and argued that, because these programs were wholly intended to entertain, the CBC could not simply wade in to set a precedent about such programs or to ban them outright. "We might be greatly embarrassed," he wrote,

> in having to ban well-known classics which, well produced, should not produce the effect which is condemned by educators and people interested in health, especially of the children. It is all very well to say that on the stage dramas frequently fall in the category of horror stories; but radio broadcasting is a different matter altogether. In the first case, people go out and pay to get their thriller and that indeed is their own business; in the latter we introduce ourselves almost by force into the minds of young and old and this calls for careful treatment, good judgment and a certain degree of dignity. We have already acted in many cases where we thought the very story of a script was detrimental to good morale.[112]

What Frigon calls "extreme cases where ultra sensationalism is evidently all that is aimed at" prompted action, but this action was of course limited to preventing Canadian stations from relaying the programs. Nothing could be done about cross-border signals. Within the CBC, Frigon's dissembling approach was about as officious as it got. It would be more difficult still to discuss a ban once it became known that the BBC also dabbled in thrillers, producing *Appointment with Fear* in 1944.[113] Complaints about thrillers and horror programs just as often led regulators to muse about the validity of any criteria for estimating the potential damage a broadcast might cause. Austin Weir wrote to Frigon early in 1945, certain that listeners alarmed about such programs were "not very sure just what they have in their minds," and counselled even less intervention than the prohibition on relaying certain episodes of sponsored series.[114]

Ernest Bushnell faced the issue of censorship frequently as director general of programmes and found it incredible that so much responsibility had been laid at the feet of the corporation. He suggested that, although he would classify "horror" programs as in bad taste, and thrillers as less objectionable, he found it difficult to differentiate between them, noting that the CBC would be "putting [itself] in an extremely difficult and vulnerable position if [it tried] to legislate generally in a field where it is most difficult to lay down specific programme definitions."[115] Like Weir, he wanted chronic complainers to draw a line somewhere. Even if such a line could be drawn, he argued, there could be no guaranteeing the effect produced by banning everything on one side of it: "Would you have us remove altogether from our schedule the sort of stories that you, and I, as boys read and revelled in? And I doubt if any of us can truthfully say that we confined our reading entirely to the classics." Setting aside Bushnell's implication that girls somehow possessed a magical resistance to thrillers, it is most significant to note that he wondered why radio should be pilloried while newspapers and periodicals continued to carry "the most lurid stories of crime and sex." Bushnell went on to suggest that listeners take their protests to the sponsors, who he believed would respond more readily to letters or even a boycott. Finally, he half joked that worried radio owners might lobby manufacturers to make sets incapable of receiving the American stations putting out a large proportion of horror and thriller programs.[116] Predictably, private station operators reacted in much the same way, even recommending in early 1945 that the CAB work with the CBC in studying the problem, and concluding: "until the complaining organizations checked on the effects of comic books and newspaper comic strips and other forms of thriller entertainment, it was unfair to pick on radio broadcasting."[117] The news department's Dan McArthur chimed in, suggesting that, regardless of what came of the excitement over thrillers, the corporation should not miss this opportunity to do (or appear to do) "some housecleaning" in its own schedule and thus bring pressure to bear on sponsors and private station operators. Then, no matter what these stations did to get rid of thrillers and horror programs, the responsibility would rest with the parents who permitted their children to listen.[118]

McArthur also suggested seeking expert help from outside the world of broadcasting to put the panic in perspective. First, however,

CBC regulators and other interested staff discussed the problem early in 1945 at their National Programme Conference and struck a committee to clarify their own policies on such programming.[119] Howard Chase, the departing chair of the CBC's Board of Governors, wanted to assure listeners or, as he called them, shareholders, that those in the CBC responsible for programming standards were up to the job. Chase responded to concerns about suspenseful, morbid, or horrifying programs by asking the public to inform the corporation when such programs aired and to be clear about the offence caused. Chase also suggested, as had Bushnell, that the line between horror and wholesome or edifying broadcasts was a thin one. To comfort those who might worry about the committee's boundaries, he noted that *Macbeth* could be classified as horror yet was taught in schools and a broadcast version was in the works. "I'm pretty sure your criticisms aren't directed against Shakespeare," he ventured, "but against lesser writers."[120] For more than a year, the committee gathered information, paying close attention to American programming studies, attempts to institute stricter program regulations through the FCC's "Blue Book" movement, and resolutions from a convenient test case in Los Angeles.[121] In May of 1946, the committee decided to initiate a listener survey designed to protect the corporation's position regardless of what the experts found, even though the mental health professionals designing the survey thought it would be difficult to divorce radio thrillers from the context of "newspapers, comics, movies, home and neighbourhood environment." As the records of this first survey planning meeting indicated: "Whether such a survey exonerated the thriller type of programme as a potential or active cause of delinquency or whether it was condemnatory of such programmes, the CBC would in either case be placed in a much sounder position in meeting criticism or in taking action to restrict or ban programmes of a certain type."[122]

The survey also seemed necessary because radio listening was, if not entirely displacing reading as a pastime, certainly cutting into it. According to Board of Governors chair Davidson Dunton, leaving room in the young listener's radio diet for a bit of "dessert" was little different from the indulgence the parents of previous generations had shown young readers. He declined to call the programs themselves harmful, especially because banning them would alienate a youthful audience hoping to escape its own daily grind as much as were adults. "It is no good putting on a children's program that will be switched off by young listeners," Dunton declared, and he returned to the theme of the thriller as a kind of ur-type: "Most of the great stories that young people have heard through the ages are packed with suspense and horror – Jack the Giant Killer, The Babes in the Wood, Hansel and Gretel, most of the great stories by Andersen and the Grimm Brothers, Treasure Island, Oliver Twist with Bill Sykes and Fagan – even the Old Testament stories of Daniel and the Lions, Joseph and his Brethren and so forth. Most children like and always have liked stories that 'make their flesh creep.'"[123] Dunton skated past one important difference between the stories he mentioned and the typical thriller of the mid-1940s. The stories he listed tended to be fantastic or set in remote locations and times, not a period and place familiar to listeners. Radio detective stories were set as contemporary dramas and featured violent or intense acts augmented by realistic sound effects. A large proportion of episodes in the popular American series *The Fat Man* had the word "murder" in their titles.[124] Recalling what Frigon called radio's forceful introduction to the home, one might be forgiven for thinking that the ground had shifted under the feet of regulators who, at least in relation to thrillers, were still thinking in terms of print.

When the results of the survey arrived and no conclusive links were found between programs and delinquency, the CBC eagerly released them, stating: "[They] should reassure parents who are worried because Junior sits glued to the radio listening to *Superman*, *The Shadow*, *The Green Hornet* or similar thrillers. It does not mean that he will become a gangster any more than reading *Uncle Wiggly* means he will turn into a rabbit. Forbidding such programmes will only frustrate him and tend to increase the possibility of his rejecting his parents' views in more important matters." Private broadcasters were not about to be let off the hook. The survey results indicated, at least to the CBC, that all broadcasters should eventually follow the pattern the corporation was trying to set to "refrain from broadcasting programmes of sub-standard literary merit which base their appeal only on cheap sensationalism." The CBC wanted it both ways – to avoid erecting a complex set of rules governing thrillers and horror programs while at the same time limiting the growth of the most obviously manipulative ones. To justify its call to inaction, it relied on the opposing notions of delinquency and normalcy to argue that most kids were equipped to shrug off potential ill effects: "As the child grows older thrillers lose their appeal, except for the delinquent boys who continue to enjoy them. The normal children show a steadily widening range of choices, with serious drama taking a high place and *Lux Radio Theatre* topping the list in popularity."[125] Mature listeners, the ones the CBC hoped to cultivate over time, may have exhibited a childhood infatuation with the thriller, but this, too, was destined to pass. Heavy-handed programming policy enacted for the sake of redeeming a likely unresponsive or ungrateful delinquent population seemed unwarranted.

Stations in Canada continued to carry these controversial programs, and a vocal minority of the public, drawn from a variety of backgrounds and beliefs, continued to attack these indefensible targets, craving the satisfaction that could only come with a complete ban.[126] As domestic life showed signs of returning to normal after the war, policing broadcasting's role in shaping the lives of a young generation that had known little but depression and war seemed like the worthiest of jobs. Yet the CBC's reluctance to shut down thriller and horror programs showed that this particular moral panic was not powerful enough to displace the corporation's dual ambitions: (1) to be an aesthetic leader by presenting programs that were of necessity challenging and *sometimes* thrilling or horrifying and (2) to allow listeners (or their parents) to switch off when the going got rough. NBC's 1947 decision to reschedule some of this programming to later in the day made sense to CBC regulators,[127] who recognized that broadcasting's impact would be blunted if programming became too safe or sterile, and the opportunity to bring listeners into contact with both innovative productions and adaptations from the literary and dramatic canons would be lost.[128] Implicit here is the belief that children would throw off the things of youth and embrace more sophisticated programming if they were first left to have their thrillers. Allowing listeners to complain about individual shows rather than enacting a rigid formula to exclude content would also help them, as the CBC's Ira Dilworth reasoned in 1952,[129] to recognize that life was complicated, requiring personal judgment and an awareness of one's own tastes.

CONJURING THE OCCULT

Regulators assumed that members of the Canadian public would not appreciate being reminded of their mortality or bodily functions and that an over-stimulated thriller audience would be a social blight.

They also had some definite opinions about more unusual topics. As I argue elsewhere,[130] shows featuring the "esoteric arts," "mystic sciences," or dispensing personal advice rated special attention. It is worth abridging that discussion here and tying it to the broader questions of taste and public service. In 1937, regulators came up with Regulation 7, which covered all controversial material, especially false advertising and attacks on individuals or groups, and enabled the arbitrary prohibition of content. One part of it, Regulation 7(j), prohibited broadcasts by anyone considered a "fortune teller, character analyst, crystal-gazer or the like" and banned broadcasts offering personal advice.[131] CBC regulators believed strongly that the audience for prophetic or advice programs – the one targeted when readings, amulets, or pamphlets were sold – would be the vulnerable, desperate, and gullible working-class listeners (women in particular) who normally patronized palmists or seers in person.[132] Sometimes those hoping to evade the regulation succeeded, but, as late as 1950, regulators still considered the "direct appeal of broadcasting" too powerful to grant to the "'psychic' or 'soothsayer' type."[133] Politicians, lawyers, broadcasters, advertising agents, sponsors, and listeners defended such programs, and, despite indications that listeners found even watered-down occult and advice programming enjoyable, the prohibition remained in place long after the CBC stopped vigorously enforcing it. It persisted because experience had shown listeners could be misled,[134] but it became difficult to justify during the early Cold War period, with more public and private stations operating and listeners being able and accustomed to tuning out programs they disliked. It ended with little fanfare in 1953, when the corporation drafted a new set of regulations.

Though the CBC did not use it as a basis for prosecution, in 1938, Gladstone Murray sought to justify Regulation 7(j) on legal grounds by noting that the Criminal Code of Canada indicted anyone who "pretends to exercise or use any kind of witchcraft, sorcery, enchantment or conjuration, or undertakes to tell fortunes, or pretends from his skill or knowledge in any occult or crafty science, to discover where or in what manner any goods or chattels supposed to have been stolen or lost may be found."[135] When the regulation was in force, the CBC could only slowly or temporarily excise offending programs from the air since regulators usually allowed existing sponsorship contracts to run out, and there was no standard way to punish stations that aired prohibited material. After receiving scripts station managers judged to be borderline, the CBC gave practitioners and advertisers a chance to redefine what they did to avoid the trouble of changing their acts significantly or, worse, losing the sponsor entirely.[136] Commercial revenue, time, effort, and industry prestige thus depended on how station managers and regulators classified programs. Despite the variety of practitioners seeking to stay on the air, only a few persisted. Appearing as "Astrolite" (an anagram of "Aristotle"), Carl Lewis of Toronto attempted for several years to convince CBC officials that astrology as he practised it was a science, a popular form of entertainment, and a boost to wartime morale. The CBC disliked dealing directly with the performers affected, possibly because of Lewis's frequent pleading letters,[137] and most of the others eventually learned that their days on radio were numbered. There were repeated appeals for more lenient interpretations and subtle changes to scripts in hopes of escaping the prohibited categories. The three most common guises adopted were those of the evangelist, the scientist, and the entertainer.

The public wanted prophecies, and disciplines like astrology and numerology were attractive to audiences and advertisers because of the implication that speakers had "irrational" knowledge of the supernatural. For regulators, science was best equipped to predict the future, and practitioners' potential ability to affect listeners' decisions rivalled the influence Western society had reserved for clergy and, more recently, for scientists and medical doctors. Diviners, psychics, and handwriting analysts could not claim scientific authority and settled for pitching their fields as ancestors of modern scientific inquiry or as pursuits bridging the gap between the sciences and the humanities. Despite the opinions of CBC's own legal staff and other legal experts, who could not affirm that practitioners were making "scientific" truth claims,[138] the CBC considered such links spurious at best. As Murray told cabinet minister C.D. Howe, another intercessor on Astrolite's behalf: "horoscope reading and like expressions are defined in all the recognized dictionaries as being pseudo sciences."[139] Since private station managers served as initial judges of the material, several revised scripts slipped through by paying lip service to science.[140] In the fall of 1938, Lewis/Astrolite's discussion of cosmic particles was cleared for broadcast on CFCF Montreal, and he mused in a subsequent show about how much astrology resembled medicine, adding that the astrologer's skill could come "only by experience, actual experience in casting astrological charts of thousands of human lives and pondering on the psychological reactions to cosmic impulses."[141] Within a couple of months, some astrologers were prepared to stage a radio debate on the scientific merits of their craft, an idea that Murray rejected.[142] Instead of accepting the proposal of a debate or granting broadcast permission to practitioners who had adopted pro-science rhetoric, the CBC insisted on reviewing all scripts that might fall under the regulation. D.W. Buchanan from the Talks Department confirmed in 1939 that debunking mystical beliefs remained the preferred course for public network programs, and, at the same time, the CBC restricted what could be broadcast by the private stations.[143]

Throughout the life of the prohibition, the rules prompted practitioners to create programs with a religious or scientific tone, but sponsors frequently backed away from such dry fare. The more mystical the shows and the more outrageous the predictions, the more saleable the programs became to sponsors looking to sell what the presumed listener (women, working-class people) might buy. During the mid-1930s, Ernest Butler ("Koram") worked as a seer. Under Regulation 7(j), he presented himself as an entertainer who never claimed "that [he] could find lost people, lost articles, [or] gave advice about Stocks or Shares, [or the] Wheat Market," and he promised that, once his contract at CFCN Calgary expired: "I am through as far as broadcasting in this country is concerned."[144] Koram, like Astrolite, was able to succeed for a time because he had a contract and because he used his radio program as a means of advertising his live shows.[145] His promise allowed him to lie low and to continue selling readings, but he returned. Broadcasting again at CFCN and elsewhere across the west as an astrologer early in 1939, Koram answered questions on the air for free; however, he sold readings for as much as correspondents offered, while claiming: "this is not a racket to fleece a gullible public."[146] A month later, the CBC informed CFCN that Koram was banned, and he bowed out of the business.[147] As genial and cooperative as Koram had been, CBC regulators feared that individuals' lives and financial fortunes might be ruined by the trust placed in radio seers or radio versions of the agony aunt. Jane Gray, the "Wise Little Lady of the Air," had been a radio numerologist since about 1931, but, after 7(j) arrived, she began to offer personal advice. Armed with an outdated letter of approval from Murray, she toured the west, arranging programs on private stations, advertising her cosmetics business, answering listeners' letters, and publicizing worthy local causes. In November of 1938, Gray wrote to Radio College, an institution set up to train personnel for the growing radio business, and told it that "many mothers of boys" sought career advice from her. She said her mail "could be of great commercial value to an organization such as [Radio College]" because she could steer these ambitious mothers, via "indirect inferences" during each broadcast, towards a course in radio engineering for their sons. "For this service", she wrote, "you would be required to pay for the radio time only which is fifty dollars per week." Gray had proposed a simple sponsorship deal, but the head of the school sent Gray's letter to the CBC, which smelled a "racket" and ordered a crackdown on advice programs. Between December 1938 and February 1939, Station Relations closed off Gray's opportunities to broadcast.[148]

Although CBC staff knew the regulation forced sponsors to choose from a smaller pool of talent and increased the likelihood that private stations would have to carry imported programming,[149] it took another type of business concern to nudge the corporation towards change. The CAB used 7(j) as leverage for its larger project, getting the CBC out of broadcast regulation, claiming that, under 7(j), certain programs prohibited by regulators were crucial to commercial broadcasters' ability to employ Canadians. CAB officials argued that entertainment was changing and that audiences were becoming more sophisticated – perhaps less mystified by broadcasting: "there is some question as to whether presenting a magician on television would not be an infraction of this regulation." The CAB also contended that the rule had been applied inequitably, suggesting: "the Regulation needs more careful wording and that it should be administered to all stations alike by [a] separate regulatory body."[150] The regulation seemed less relevant in the late 1940s and early 1950s, when most areas supported more than one radio station and the urgency of offering listeners some alternative to fortune tellers had abated. The second section of the regulation regarding personal advice could – especially later in the 1940s – be bent. Station Relations allowed quiz shows during those years under 7(j)(ii) because they were considered "genuine question and answer programs, where there is no suggestion of extraordinary powers."[151]

By January 1953, Regulation 7(j)(i) vanished, replaced by 5(g): "No station shall broadcast any program presenting a person who solves or purports to solve personal, moral or social problems or questions submitted by listeners or members of the public,"[152] which did not target fortune-telling style programs. The CAB found the change unsatisfactory, calling the amended rule "an attempt at thought control" that prevented even "religious broadcasting since a priest or clergyman is certainly a person who solves, or purports to solve, moral or social problems." In Cold War-era Canada, accusing the CBC of "decid[ing] for listeners what they shall or shall not hear in the field of ideas and philosophies" was effective as part of the CAB's broader campaign to associate the public broadcaster with censorship.[153] Within weeks, Davidson Dunton was reported to be "reconsidering" Regulation 5(g), and, by that summer, the handwriting analysts clamouring to inform the CBC of the scientific principles behind their work were appealing a rule no longer in force.[154] In 1957, the Royal Commission on Broadcasting recommended the dismantling of the Broadcast Regulations Division,[155] and, within a year, the Board of Broadcast Governors arrived to relieve the CBC of its regulatory duties.

The debate over astrology and advice-giving programs showed how careful a regulating authority had to be if it took its role seriously. Given the CBC's mission to preserve the ideals of public service and stewardship, broadcasts offering targeted readings or advice to people who provided real natal information or described real problems had to stop because broadcasting might not only entertain but also have an intimate and inappropriate emotional or financial role in listeners' lives. As if on cue, Jane Gray proposed dodgy business deals, and Astrolite's scripts suggested he had helped clients succeed at the racetrack, the Irish Sweepstakes, and even Toronto's infamous Stork Derby.[156] No matter how many listened, the CBC interpreted mass-distributed character analysis and the public forecasting of personal destinies as both more dangerous and less tasteful pursuits than the parlour games or fairground attractions from which they had sprung. Regulations like 7(j) *had* to be made if the CBC was to present itself as a public servant, even if it meant sometimes arbitrarily deciding what listeners should hear.

The responsibility of regulating and the act of broadcasting must have seemed thoroughly incompatible, even though they were not, in practise, all that different. In early Canadian radio, both these tasks fell to the public broadcasting authorities, who considered some material beyond the pale in both commercial and public settings – as detrimental to goodwill between advertiser and audience, and as a betrayal of broadcasting's invitation into the listener's home. Forced into making the rules, the CBC tried to protect listeners against the unintended consequences of thrillers or predatory commercial messages and to nudge program and ad makers towards an impossible ideal, an instinctive sense of tasteful programming that would prevent "broadcast-and-be-damned" moments. Unconvinced that controls were necessary, broadcasters whose livelihoods depended on attracting big audiences consistently and keeping advertisers friendly could not develop such instincts. Although enforcement was light – in 1956 historian Arthur Lower echoed DeForest's much earlier opinion of American enforcement, calling CBC regulators "supine"[157] – commercial broadcasters flew the righteous banner of opposition to a bureaucracy they considered inconvenient and out of touch with the desires and values of mainstream listeners. Broadcasting and regulation both required the manufacture of categories and divisions of taste and interest before a word, note, or testimonial could be aired. The corporation enforced its standards by envisioning and acknowledging public taste just as did private broadcasters and advertisers, but often applied a pessimistic or unflattering view of listeners' ability to listen for themselves. Rules became necessary because some broadcasters lacked the ability to listen *to* themselves as they entertained and sold. Regulators of broadcast content presumed the same familiarity with listeners' habits and inclinations as did other broadcasters: an assurance that they knew what the public deserved.

5

"Our Job Has Not Been Fully Done": Music

Regulations were decidedly less necessary when broadcasters simply wanted to give listeners some music. Broadcasters still paid considerable attention to their musical output, despite the drastically reduced odds that lawsuits or bans would result from sending out a half-hour of waltzes. Radio had proven a boon to musicians, especially in light of the limited opportunities for listeners to experience live performances. From the late nineteenth century through the First World War, most Canadian communities could not support more than a small music scene or had to be content with itinerant acts and talent displayed at family gatherings.[1] Eventually, commercial sheet music and recorded music supplemented the "play-it-yourself" variety. Then broadcasting arrived, rendering "the world's treasure house of music fully accessible to every man."[2] Making programs to suit the varied moods or preferences of listeners required decisive action. Broadcasters speculated about what the public wanted to hear, and they speculated most vigorously about music, the staple in almost everyone's radio diet. Broadcasters assumed supply needed to meet demand but disagreed over where the meeting should take place. Ratings data were far from comprehensive and did little to settle the disagreement.[3] Most broadcasters wanted to move to where audience tastes seemed to be, following the crowd. With part of the public's leisure time at their disposal, program makers shouldered considerable responsibility. Private broadcasters greeted this responsibility with brisk optimism, filling the air with broadly appealing shows certain to attract sponsors. Public broadcasters responded with anxious circumspection, wondering what else they could do to cram both diverting and diverse material through the same radio loudspeakers and into the same homes. Though Canadians may not have recognized it, the co-existence of optimism and anxiety made them some of the most fortunate listeners in the world, with access to a variety of programming unsurpassed elsewhere. Optimism helped build some local and national media empires. Anxiety begat more anxiety, a heap of reflection on what broadcasting meant to listeners and the larger society, and some novel programming. The CBC took on the job of nursemaid to musical subcultures, hoping to accommodate listeners they considered ill-served by mainstream programs, which included, paradoxically, much of what the CBC broadcast as part of its public service mandate. This was perhaps a clumsy acknowledgment of the aesthetic divisions spawned by everything from ethnic, class, or regional identity to generational differences, but it did not assume there was a typical listener, a majority for which the tried and true formats would be adequate.

Music programming delighted listeners when done well and exasperated them when done poorly, and listeners were not shy in expressing either opinion. Having brought performers onto imaginary stages in every home and made household names of musicians "drafted" into broadcast service, music programs became readily associated with a station or network's overall philosophy of broadcasting. Music was more than entertainment: it was at the same time part of a dynamic "entertainment industry" and the heir of a longer artistic tradition needing to adapt, or be adapted, to the requirements of broadcasting. Genres and themes in music could be approached as commodities to be shuffled around a broadcasting schedule, as tools for building a better society through leisure, or sometimes as unwelcome symbols of more pervasive social change.[4] Musical categories were absolutely central to programming and are likewise central in this chapter. Music illustrated how broadcasters curated their programs and how their curatorial attention simultaneously formed and responded to listeners' tastes. By examining music in early Canadian radio, we see most vividly where the public and commercial systems diverged in their conceptions of how broadcasting should happen and how audiences could be both created and served. Because public broadcasting institutions needed to develop and maintain longer-term programming policies and strategies, and this required systematic record keeping, much of the evidence we have comes via the CBC and, to a lesser extent, from the CRBC. However, we also hear from private stations and sometimes from ordinary citizens mainly because public broadcasters, mindful of being portrayed as out of touch with mainstream tastes, expended significant effort monitoring these outlets and gathering listeners' reactions to music programming, whatever its origins. Historians have not paid sufficient attention to such acts of interpretation in early Canadian broadcasting because the projection of a Canadian personality, a nonetheless important chore for the CRBC and especially for the CBC, overshadowed a less obvious form of nation building: the cultivation of listeners who were also seekers.

CATEGORIES AND FORMULAS

These days, we are used to music-oriented stations employing formats like country, pop, or classical, with some even serving sub-specialties. For a while now, we have called the trend towards specialization "narrowcasting" or, more hopefully, "knowing your audience." This practice had its most immediate mass culture ancestor in the marketing of phonograph records to identifiable groups based on characteristics like race or ethnicity.[5] Airing what one thinks listeners might want to hear has always been a guessing game – never more so than in broadcasting's earliest years when, even in larger towns or cities, there were only one or two local stations trying to hold the local audience, and the guesses mattered more. Local stations also had to compete with more powerful national and international networks unlikely to present programs catering to local tastes or mindful of local traditions. In that environment, to ask what sort of music to put on the radio meant asking: What sort of music could listeners appreciate without reaching for the dial to find something else or switching the set off? The people making musical programs found themselves in the same position as regulators: having to answer that question *before* programs were made, even though the most scientific way to get an answer was by presenting a wide range of programs, with no particular type of program given any special advantages, and waiting. For commercial broadcasters, that wasn't a very good business model. When the CBC regulated broadcasting or speculated about how much American material was enough, it had slightly more leeway to consider its programming decisions in light of what the longer-term implications for the listening public might be. In addition to treating music on the radio as an entertaining pastime, the CBC treated the various sorts of music available as indicators of cultural or social orientations or ambitions. Translation: broadcasters committed to the ideal of public service worried about music because they thought the assorted musical styles each stood for a way of life or might affect listeners in a particular way.

Responding in 1957 to the findings of Canada's second Royal Commission on Broadcasting, the CBC's Ray de Boer used his professional experience in the "pop" music market to blast the commercial stations then atop the ratings pile in Toronto:

> CKEY can be relied upon to program only that which is not likely to give offense to their "hit parade" audience. Consequently, they are limited to programming recordings of the most familiar tunes in the simplest arrangements. With this kind of programming policy, the Record Librarian only needs to follow the "Variety" and "Billboard" trend columns to fill up most of his schedule. The result is a succession of "Bandstand" programs offering an insipid mixture from the juke-box, past and present.[6]

The impressions contained in de Boer's rant would have been familiar to programming staff colleagues during the war and after, and, twenty years earlier, to his predecessors at the early CBC. Indeed, the tendency to interpret music this way pre-dated the CBC and even pre-dated broadcasting: witness the nineteenth-century regard for certain classical composers whose veneration could confirm the listener's gentility.[7] In the radio era, however, public broadcasters' reading of commercial broadcasting's structure and purpose reinforced their sense that they stood alone against the "juke-boxification" of radio music. Early Canadian radio listeners expected to hear musical programs, and at first those were largely what broadcasters could supply, given their budgets and limited sponsorships. Short, lively shows were familiar, and they were attractive at least partly because they resembled what audiences had been hearing in music halls or taverns. Radio also gained some listeners who had tired of their own recorded music at home, and, from the outset, music arranged in "concert" events proved effective at raising public interest in the new medium.[8] In 1933, Gladstone Murray, still at the BBC, called music the "main constituent of broadcasting," and with broadcasters still working to accelerate the symbiotic cycle of program and audience building through the 1930s, music continued to own radio schedules.[9] Like the process of producing any kind of program, the mulling-over of musical selections was a continuous one, with broadcasters attuned to trends and necessarily quick to judge how (or if) their output should be altered to increase audience and/or advertiser appeal. Largely via the CBC's attempts to satisfy itself that listeners were being served, we can see more clearly how listening patterns flowed from what commercial and public broadcasters did. When the latter tried to feed back into the system by introducing programming that acknowledged the role of the broadcaster in shaping listeners' radio experiences, it revealed still more of the "baggage" music carried.

Although the prewar, wartime, and postwar eras are tidy temporal divisions, these divisions have limited applicability when it comes to how those holding opposing notions of broadcasting's purpose handled musical programming throughout the whole "golden" age of radio. For-profit and non-profit broadcasters made few adjustments to their methods of producing programs. While producers, performers, listeners, and critics all considered the divisions between musical genres important, they expressed varying levels of concern about the *quality* of what was broadcast. Musicians appreciated the work, listeners liked getting entertainment without much effort, and there was no shortage of material to broadcast, but those who saw radio as a medium for improving listeners' musical tastes found an astonishing variety of ways to be disappointed. In the estimation of a Montreal musician (and listener) testifying before the Aird Commission, sublime music played badly or mangled by a poor signal was "one of the tragedies of art."[10] Almost from its inception, the CBC displayed a sensitivity to criticism of this sort directed at any Canadian broadcasts, even though the corporation itself was not responsible for the music on every station. Musical programming provoked such anxiety among public broadcasters because, as the mainstay of entertainment broadcasting, it stood to affect listeners' leisure time more than any other single type. For example, although the CBC considered what it might do about songs with suggestive lyrics, acknowledging a "responsibility to counter such tendencies or trends,"[11] these songs were already on the charts and were becoming more "popular" simply by virtue of being there and, thus, being heard more often. As Susan Douglas notes, this cycle of promotion succeeded in affecting tastes and the commercial bottom line: "song 'pluggers' could take the basic building blocks of a pop song, put them together, and convince broadcasters to keep playing the song, announcing it was a new hit until it became one."[12] The CBC could not argue directly with "popularity," yet it attempted to make programs whose reputations had not been artificially enhanced by charts and ratings. We can get a better sense of this process by exploring two themes: (1) the place of *categories* like dance, jazz, and "serious" music and (2) attempts to "improve" musical programming.

While acknowledging that "serious" music held a special place in twentieth-century Western culture is hardly a revelation, it is worth noting that the CBC saw its musical programming as the only reliable way to connect Canadians with something that promised to endure beyond the next edition of the pop charts. A potentially overwhelming supply of anodyne music that did little to prompt Canadians to consider their own circumstances (and even less to stir national feeling) drew the attention of CBC staff who directed some of their efforts towards carrying improving music for improvable listeners. In other words, staff members came to identify music with some educational or canonical value as part of a more worthy subset of radio entertainment and to see cultivating a taste for that sort of entertainment as part of the CBC's work as a national broadcaster. In trying to fulfill this self-imposed job description, they reflected further on the work that broadcast music did and constructed a programming strategy based on the idea that the music on the air could, for good or ill, affect listeners' lives. It mattered to CBC producers and managers that different kinds of listeners should have different kinds of music and that, on occasion, something unexpected might be broadcast in the name of exposing Canadians to the unfamiliar. They did not want indiscriminately scheduled programming to jar listeners and could not resist stirring up discussions regarding how some treated radio music as background accompaniment to other pursuits.[13] Instead of proceeding as though some level of background listening were inevitable, everyone connected with making programs had to presume that everyone with a radio set could be an active listener, able to enjoy the programming on offer, take offence at suggestive or graphic material, or be convinced by a sponsor's pitch. Otherwise, announcers, orchestras, and actors might as well have left their microphones off because broadcasting would not result in communication. The presumption of active listening made it possible for commercial stations to rent *x* thousand pairs of ears to advertisers and for CBC producers to imagine what their instructional and experimental programs might set in motion. One listener even suggested that making such ambitious programs would lead Canadians toward "realizing our potentialities – becoming an active rather than a passive nation."[14]

Studies of music broadcasting – and music in the age of broadcasting – note the multitude of tensions or divisions underlying what seemed to be the simple matter of transmitting shows to people eager to receive them. The great leap forward into broadcasting certainly did not *create* divisions over matters like morality or relative levels of education. Susan Douglas shows that, in the United States, such divisions affected broadcasting's construction as an activity even before it became a huge industry.[15] Likewise, Jody Berland demonstrates that Canadian broadcasting, music broadcasting in particular, resonates with the "contradictory political and social forces" that helped create it.[16] Particular historical moments, especially war, could sharply affect the uses to which broadcast music might be put as military goals eclipsed or altered civilian listening habits.[17] For all the novelty surrounding it at the outset, broadcasting took on many of the characteristics of the society into which it emerged. Musical categories already long in use survived well after radio became an important mode of communication and entertainment, often becoming linked with existing social distinctions like class.[18] Using some of these older categories, stations defined their own audiences by broadcasting music of various types and generally became more sure of their definitions over time. These choices about what to broadcast determined what listeners got, and what they could expect to get, whether the performances were live or not.[19] In their rush to produce programs acceptable to listeners and advertisers, broadcasters employed (and thereby reinforced) stereotypes, at the same time upholding useful prejudices, social structures, or identities and,[20] in one well-studied demographic corner, pegging rural listeners as likely to flock to country music.[21] Accounting in this way for musical listening habits allowed broadcasters, critics, and even listeners themselves to link musical tastes with such characteristics as intelligence and authenticity.[22] Whether those interpreting such signs were right or not remains secondary to the fact that such interpretations were made and that suppositions about listener preferences drove programming decisions. By putting programs on the air, broadcasters of every description engaged in the management of musical tastes. *How* they did so depended on their motivations for making musical programs.

For every broadcaster, from tiny station to complex network, getting and maintaining the interest of listeners remained a primary goal, and music helped immeasurably. In Canada from the later 1920s onward, but especially after radio sets became more affordable in the early 1930s and radio advertising's potential reach became apparent, the profitability of commercial stations confirmed for station owners that their programming choices were generating profit as intended. With little reason to reinvent a wheel that was already spinning money, private operators continued to play records (regulations against doing so had been relaxed in 1926) and book acts likely to appeal to most listeners. They also learned early on to use amateur hours to unearth more low-cost entertainers and to broadcast hotel orchestras as a cheap option for filling airtime.[23] In these fundamental ways, by providing the musical fare most listeners considered worthwhile, local commercial stations served their audiences. Still, venturing opinions about music on the radio became a common activity. At any given time, there was always too much or too little of one sort of music or another, and a raft of self-appointed experts pointing out what needed to be done helped define the roles of private and public broadcasters alike. All broadcasters could exert control over the music they aired, yet the pressure to improve musical programming came to bear on the *public* institutions, from without and within. Listeners frustrated with radio music or feeling deprived of what they might like to hear over any of Canada's broadcast outlets tended to complain to the CRBC or the CBC. In the unfolding conversation about music on the radio, with the participants often speaking past each other, blame for substandard material or praise for decent entertainment relied upon musical categories to describe programs, revealing some of the main preoccupations of broadcasters, critics, and listeners. No particular kind of music had proven so captivating that its worth could not be appraised in relation to the other kinds of music on the air or prevent observers of the radio scene from diagnosing the shortcomings and admirable qualities of its audience. In short, nothing was sacred. Although the CBC made no secret of the fact it wanted more Canadians to listen to classical or even semi-classical stuff, and was often accused of pushing "culture," it was most eager to ensure that listeners did not get too much of anything.

Jazz was one of the earliest musical categories rating widespread notice, and it is a good one to mention first because, later in radio's golden age, it took on a different role, symbolizing divisions between more than just younger and older listeners. An American creation, with origins in American urban centres with established or growing black populations, it appealed to broadcasters and younger listeners throughout North America and beyond, even though its appropriation by white musicians on the radio was often a "misguided and condescending dilution of the original art forms."[24] Its association with what some considered undesirable communities was one point of objection. A note to the Aird Commission suggested that jazz be barred: "The Government should not permit a crowd of idiots to broadcast negro music [musique pour les negres] and force us to listen to them ... [T]he musical element of the province of Quebec ... does not enjoy being bored by a lot of jazzy Jews picked up in New York or elsewhere, who compose programmes more or less droll, of certain Ontario firms, or of music and singing of a poor order."[25] The continuing appeal of jazz beyond the 1920s stemmed partially from its reputation as more casual than older forms of music, and its supporters urged the CBC to cut back on the "cursed symphonies and high brow talk jabber day in and day out. For heaven's sake give us more jazz and vaudeville." From the opposing camp, a listener who assumed that the CBC also selected the music for commercial stations berated Gladstone Murray, declaring: "Morning to night you pour out the disgusting decadent Yankee jazz eating at the moral fibre of our people."[26] Although jazz could include ragtime, swing, or almost anything that sounded improvisational, stations could not be justifiably accused of playing jazz, or anything else, morning to night. Still, how broadcasters accommodated the strong likelihood that stations pursuing bigger audiences would embrace more "light" music (including jazz) emphasized the stark differences between private and public broadcasters' priorities.

PLAYING (YOUR) FAVOURITES

In discussions surrounding music, the CRBC and the CBC responded continuously to the state of music broadcasting as they found it and as it evolved through depression, wartime, and beyond. Their responses were not limited to one style of music and, indeed, seemed to be part of an interminable round of diagnosis and prescription. But before the creation of the CRBC, as the above commentary on jazz suggests, listeners and others with a stake in the programs on the air did not keep their opinions about music to themselves. The

CNR radio service – "a phonograph for the entertainment of its guests" – promoted "a just balance between popular and serious music" through the engagement of musicians like the University of Toronto's Hart House String Quartette, an outfit that had already made a few local broadcasts.[27] One grand vision for the reinvigoration of Canada's youth through a more varied radio music diet believed that much damage had already been done by the late 1920s: "Ask any boy what instrument he would care to learn, given the opportunity, saxophone, banjo, ukulele, xylophone; all trick instruments not provided for in the classification of full orchestral works and only suitable for dance music."[28] Dance music, for some community leaders attempting to influence the future direction of radio via the Aird Commission, was little different from intrusive advertising.[29] "Catching up" to the American networks and the BBC meant moving away from nuisance radio and making room for more sedate or richly orchestrated material than that relied upon by individual stations. With Austin Weir at the programming helm, the CNR was the only broadcasting service reserving some schedule space for classical concerts from the metropoles of London or New York, bringing Canadian music lovers "of howsoever modest means" into a previously inaccessible fold.[30]

While program-creation budgets for the CNR and CPR chains, and individual stations, depended on the amount of revenue they could allocate to securing talent, they could bring in revenue through sponsorships or commercial connections. In the case of the CPR, more revenue could be generated through programs like its 1930 *Musical Crusaders*, a blatant promotion of CPR Mediterranean cruise packages that tapped into listeners' interest in biblical history and suggested that connoisseurs of fine music would be "transported" just like the show's fictitious host family.[31] For most families, even the ones able to afford radio sets, getting to see a musical concert was about as likely as that luxury cruise. Program makers saw the radio symphonies they provided as an adequate substitute for listeners prevented by distance or too little income from attending the real thing.[32] Bringing decent performances to the radio, however, was a source of some concern. One of Graham Spry's correspondents during the uncertain period before the CRBC's formation found himself in a quandary, having warned against putting out substandard broadcasts of "music of the highest grade" but hoping that broadcasters would keep trying to win over new listeners by striving for the "one superb performance" that could be "of infinitely greater value than one hundred mediocre ones."[33] It was difficult in a country like Canada to know what to do while the broadcasting industry was still developing. Spry's nemesis J. Murray Gibbon thought adopting a centralized music arrangement like the BBC's would invite corruption because "the number of politicians who ha[d] musical relatives [was] surprising." In response, Spry considered the opportunity presented by a centralized national system to be too good to pass up because it would enable both a national orchestra and a national theatre.[34]

Music remained vital as the mixed public/private system came into being. Spry, along with other supporters of public broadcasting, used the prospect of a permanent radio orchestra as a selling point in favour of creating what became the CRBC. While the CRBC was finding its feet, Gladstone Murray advised such an in-house system as well, partially driven by his aversion to paying unionized musicians for individual performances. He did not advise the commission to change musical programming on the radio overnight but valued the prestige of having a network orchestra able to manage complex works. Dance music, though plentiful over US stations, could not be left out of Murray's prescription as there were "several excellent dance bands which deserve to be broadcast under the auspices of the Commission."[35] The CRBC was already sifting through the musical possibilities for itself by the time Murray wrote. Symphony concerts and martial music from outfits like the Canadian Grenadier Guards band provided some of the earliest commission programming, but George Wade and His Corn Huskers drew the biggest outpouring of public approval in the spring of 1933.[36] Wade was a good bet from every angle. His band was Canadian, pleased many listeners, and had attracted sponsorships when it was on CFRB Toronto. Although other artists whose work did not have such obvious mass appeal may have been talented, they had to keep one eye on their live careers, and, as Austin Weir reported: "[They] generally have standards to which they must adhere if they are to maintain their reputation and make progress. They dare not be heard on the general run of commercial programs broadcast from night to night on local stations, and in Canada broadcasting is almost entirely a local matter."[37]

The new CRBC, in its humble and halting way, altered that pattern to knit localities together in the same way the CNR network had tried to a few years earlier. Programming for a national audience meant embracing a core public broadcasting strategy, as Weir did in both places until he was abruptly dismissed from the CRBC. He remembered inaugurating a series of symphonies for the CNR, and being

> told at that time that the public did not want symphonies – such music was too "highbrow" – only a few would listen – that it was not our function to educate the public but to give them what they wanted, forgetting that the public could not say what it wanted until it had heard it. We paid no attention to all this. We took care to give Canadians the best orchestra then in the country, under competent direction, in a superior studio, at an hour when we should get the maximum audience.[38]

Public broadcasters thus devoted resources and effort to what looked like an improvident errand, serving and shaping the tastes of what were, at times, small groups of listeners. Although chapter 6 deals with exactly this sort of serving and shaping, it is worth noting that, in the case of music, the CBC in particular kept a close watch on what listeners were getting, what they were asking for, and what could be delivered. This observation and speculation about music on the radio confirmed public broadcasters' suspicions about their private-sector counterparts and convinced them of the righteousness of their own cause.

Yet most listeners were not interested in righteousness, they were just eager to hear music. Again during the CRBC's first months, the Canadian gleanings from BBC Empire Service listener correspondence contained little criticism of recorded music and a range of opinion about favourite genres. Some rejected highbrow stuff, others despised dance music but adored music hall or "serious" material.[39] Providing attractive programs in what was already a fairly crowded space for broadcast music, with a number of inexpensive acts trying to break in,[40] would be difficult for the BBC, especially given CRBC commissioner Colonel W.A. Steel's tendency to relish listener complaints about Empire Service programming.[41] American shows blended more easily into the CRBC's lineup, and it was also easier for the commission to carry imports, like New York's Metropolitan Opera, even though these might not attract the biggest audiences. Add to this the problem of tighter Canadian copyright laws making some domestic productions more expensive even before the first note was sung, and the resulting tilt towards importing shows from the

United States, itself awash in musical programming, became even more pronounced.[42] Musical programs commanded much of the commission's schedule, and the CRBC trumpeted them in its print publicity, especially catch-all variety material like "Everybody's Music," a gay kaleidoscope of tunes and melodies – not "'highbrow,' not low, just everybody's choice."[43] Supporters of public broadcasting at the time believed, with justification, that commercial stations would rather book "old-time fiddlers, Hawaiian orchestras, Yodelling cowboys" and see a "good singer worked to death" than diversify the programs they offered.[44] Prairie stations in particular made a habit of bundling such talent together, as an employee at CKMO Vancouver reported:

When the Western hotels are running their Saturday night dances all we do is broadcast them under the caption "The Dance Band Parade" and believe me it is a parade. As a general rule we start at Winnipeg and for an uninterrupted one hour and thirty minutes all we hear is jazz bands from all the Western towns. Coming as they do from such places as Saskatoon, Regina, Edmonton etc. they are bound to be of the best. It is a wonder New York stands for the competition.[45]

Just before the CBC took over as Canada's public broadcaster in the fall of 1936, musical eminence Sir Ernest MacMillan condemned the CRBC for being unable to do much for the musical consciousness of a population spread too thinly to be served effectively on a limited budget and too close to the United States to be denied cross-border programming.[46] Within a few years, despite the persistence of the same density and location problems, the CBC's efforts would benefit from larger revenues, thanks to its limited commercial broadcasting and more sets in use. However, for the CRBC and the CBC alike, selecting music to put out over a nationwide network involved constant categorization and an attempt to represent the major categories in their schedules so that listeners could feel as though they were getting something for their licence fees. After 1936, the attitude of public broadcasters towards music did not change radically – they still saw it as the hub of broadcasting's entertainment function – but the CBC's capacity for classifying, analyzing, and undertaking its own program development far exceeded that of the commission. As part of the long process of working out what public broadcasting could do in Canada, trying to understand the role of music programming while accounting for listener moods by offering original material became one of the CBC's prime functions.

We find ourselves again having to address categories. Styles or families of music already delineated in the pre-broadcast era and carried through to the mid-1930s continued to affect how those responsible for musical programming at the CBC approached their jobs. Evaluating the lineup during the spring of 1937, programming personnel recognized music's prominence even while critically tearing some of their own offerings apart. Staff described the corporation's shows as good or mediocre examples of their kind, while offering constructive advice: *Choral Echoes* was "an excuse to put Saskatoon on the network," and *Atlantic Nocturne* should not be "referred to as a 'Prelude to sleep.'" These examples could perhaps be dismissed as ill-advised attempts to highlight regional talent, but the overall impression was of a schedule in need of immediate tending, a haphazard stream of musical programs without much thought given to the relationship between them.[47] Murray had already gone on record as opposing this kind of indiscipline, insisting: "[Even] if the programme is of dance music it should be so contrived and presented as to preserve the artistic unities and be a model of that kind of harmonious interpretation."[48] Hoping to set the right tone for the opening of a new regional transmitter in Ontario, he admitted that, while lighter music would always bulk largest in a broadcaster's output, such an occasion demanded "dance music with choral accompaniment instead of conventionalized crooning."[49] With the continued division of musical programming into older musical categories, public service broadcasting meant being noticeably selective and pursuing standards that, if upheld, would probably translate into fewer listeners. For example, choosing the musical programs for official exchanges with other networks before the Second World War saw the CBC recognizing it could not produce the sort of light stuff that public or private broadcasters in other countries would be keen to get. Early on, the CBC tended to bring in symphonic and classical material when exchanging programs, and even though the press did not always give it credit for pursuing such esoteric stuff, these tendencies contributed to the corporation's identification with "highbrow" types of music outside the mainstream.[50]

The Canadian Association of Broadcasters declared in 1950 that "any group of people has the right to say what is 'good' entertainment. Good music is the music you enjoy."[51] While the CAB's implication was clear – people know what they like and trying to give them something else tramples on their freedom of choice – the CBC's own actions were just as effective in creating an impression of the public broadcaster as unsatisfied with the status quo and willing to experiment. CAB members flattered themselves by assuming that the CBC sought to prevent listeners from enjoying the sort of entertainment commercial stations provided. During its first twenty years, the CBC did not play the role of aesthetic censor, instead articulating a different vision of musical stewardship simply by handling the day-to-day questions surrounding what the public network itself should broadcast. Reports and reflections on the radio music scene came from places like Winnipeg, where an aspiring performer and producer, who supposed his inability to play a ukulele or accordion had led to repeated rejections by the CRBC, greeted the CBC's arrival with hope.[52] A listener in Saskatchewan voiced his preference for an imported symphony hour over "trashy cowboy songs or swing music,"[53] and a journalist in British Columbia questioned the justification of licence fee increases without relief from either "a flood of the cheapest and squawkiest jazz" or "an inordinately lengthy siege of grand opera."[54] The particular targets mattered much less than did the dialogue about music to the CBC's overall approach, which distilled listener opinion and staff observations while employing a plainly hierarchical sense of what constituted suitable music to shape programming choices. We know far less about such deliberations going on at Canada's private stations, but we know station operators took pride in providing what they called "local or regional" service,[55] while the CBC's national English-language network (or networks after 1944) endeavoured to cover the whole country. Given this division of labour, private stations' musical output was undoubtedly a better reflection of local tastes than the CBC's or, rather, a better reflection of local stations' guesses about local tastes. No matter who was doing the broadcasting, some listeners were bound to be left out or alienated, and, at the CBC, addressing the concerns (expressed or imagined) of underserved audiences became a central theme in the making of musical programming.

Paying heed to musical categories and imagining how the musical entertainment offered to Canadians might be enriched were inextricable parts of the CBC's self-determined vocation. With music programming accounting for just over half of the CBC's broadcast time by 1941 (down from about 70 percent in 1936), and accounting for still more of private stations' output,[56] the corporation reckoned the potential influence of all these hours on Canadians' listening experience to be substantial. Commercial broadcasters could be counted upon to supply variety, dance, light, and even some of what the CBC categorized as "semi-classical" music,[57] but for-profit stations had little incentive to do anything else. Nor did CBC staff expect private broadcasters to take many artistic or financial risks.[58] While the CBC provided plenty of the same stuff found on private radio – over two-thirds of its musical programming in 1945 was "light," "dance," or "variety"[59] – its attention to how those programs were deployed was markedly different. The idea of balance figured largely: "Since there is so much music in the day's programme, those who plan it must be careful to preserve what is called 'programme balance.' It will not do to have two programmes of the same type of music follow one another. It will not do to spoil serious music by the juxtaposition of 'jazz'; and the same musical items must not appear too often."[60] On Sundays, Gladstone Murray contended, "good symphony" music should stand out.[61]

Plans, ideals, and prescriptions advocating balance or appropriate scheduling of musical material made up only part of the picture. Any attempts to tailor musical selections to more equitably represent the range of music available rested on CBC staff assumptions about the various musical categories already being broadcast on North American radio. In other words, broadcasters like Director of Programmes Ernest Bushnell, who thought radio had been responsible for getting more listeners interested in "good" music, brought his own musical sensibilities as a former singer and experienced radio hand to bear on the CBC's efforts to "keep just a little ahead of that change."[62] For Bushnell, "good" music was classical or semi-classical, although the broadcasting industry's sense of "good" expanded slightly to include "standards" or adult-oriented mainstream numbers after the Second World War.[63] The majority of music broadcast remained new, upbeat, and oriented towards younger listeners. "Swing," the danceable, energetic variation on jazz played most famously by the "big bands," claimed a prominent place during the later 1930s on private and public airwaves. Broadcast early in 1939, a debate on swing found its detractor, a Vancouver critic contemptuous of the form's physicality, eager to dismiss it as a fad driven by the "commercial side" of the music business and confident that youth would come to their senses. Swing's defenders, including bandleader

Percy Faith, countered that it was a valuable expression of the popular mood, an outgrowth of modern culture.[64] Swing became more entrenched during that same year, and Bushnell could instruct his staff to amend the CBC's schedules simply by remarking: "the troops would look for swing music rather than sing-songs in their Christmas Day entertainment."[65] Opinions about one type of music or another could be strongly held, but within broadcasting organizations, labels like swing, country, or symphonic music served as a kind of taste shorthand for what would please one among the many types of listener waiting to be entertained.

Sifting through these labels and employing them in the process of making programs was relatively straightforward for private stations, which had to select almost all of their musical programming to draw advertisers, and viewed public broadcasting as less sympathetic to popular tastes.[66] On commercial stations, musical labels could be attached to likely audiences, allowing, for instance, the teenage and young adult swing music audience to be "sold" to advertisers as likely customers for acne remedies. In 1939, an advertising agent representing Bright's Wines begged Gladstone Murray to lift a relatively new regulation prohibiting beer and wine advertising, suggesting that, if the ban went away, his client would be most likely to serve an adult audience by sponsoring classical music programming – everybody wins![67] For the CBC, musical categories could be both helpful and a source of insecurity, with broadcasters mostly relying on their experience and on their own tastes as they planned new programs. The CBC's Elizabeth Morrison displayed this uncertainty in her comments about the musical score to accompany the wartime public service program *Rubber Salvage*: "Good show. Somehow the music did not seem right. Can't tell why nor can I say what music goes with rubber."[68] The network welcomed the ad revenue it got for the few commercial shows it carried, and that part of the operation was scarcely distinguishable from private broadcasting. When the CBC allocated time for its unsponsored sustaining programs, it found, to no one's surprise, that the sorts of music attracting large audiences elsewhere also did well on the CBC,[69] indicating those choices met with broad approval from most listeners. In considering program balance, however, CBC programming staff paid close attention to musical categories that might be marginalized if boosting audience size were the only goal. For every effort to make one type of program, like the Dominion Network's *Juke Box Jury*, a showcase featuring chart-toppers and talk about "pop" performances, there needed to be a program like *Album of Familiar Music* to offer some counterpoint.[70]

BALANCING ACT AT THE CBC

The CBC arrived at such decisions about its musical programs and the relationships between them by interpreting thousands of bits of information, criticism, and conjecture about the music scene in Canada and beyond. Understanding the role of those programs in listeners' daily lives meant regularly evaluating the relative function of each type of entertainment. Critics' condemnations of pop tunes as something pressed out of the "Tin-Pan angel-food mould" were among the easier signals received and understood,[71] yet there was no suggestion of eliminating dance and light music from CBC schedules. As noted above, programs of that sort comprised a clear majority of all musical programming on the CBC, and the network continued to invent new ways of packaging "the hits of today and tomorrow," like *Kla-How-Ya, Tillicum!*, a Vancouver-produced show featuring well-known Canadian artists like Juliette, not, as the title suggested, the music of coastal First Nations.[72] Similarly, in 1950, the CBC promoted a battle of the bands between Toronto's King Edward Hotel orchestra and the Toronto Philharmonic, with most of the repertoire drawn from familiar tunes and only a couple of semi-classical pieces.[73] That sort of cross-category stunt played with the boundaries between the kinds of music available but did not require listeners to venture into territory very far from the familiar. Several of the variety programs on the CBC were American imports following similar guiding principles to suit sponsors, and when they took musical transcriptions from the BBC, the ones CBC programming staff demanded were likely to be light, "popular," and dance music, with shows like *Music for Romance* encountering little friction on their way into the schedule.[74] Programs like these held enough appeal that, by using them as the core of their musical output, the CBC and private broadcasters alike could be confident they would be satisfying, and thus serving, most Canadian listeners.

Providing mainstream material was clearly a public service, and the supply was plentiful. For the CBC, figuring out how to supplement mainstream material became the more pressing task. Martial music filled part of the bill during the war as Canadians enlisted or were drawn into service at home. Ernest Bushnell recommended one of these shows in particular to his immediate subordinates, noting: "the '[Musical] March Past' programme at 8.30 a.m. EST strikes the note." He also suggested that listening to it at work "may also have the desired effect of getting you to your desks at a somewhat earlier hour" and insisted that "fullblooded [*sic*] vigour must exude from *everything* we do."[75] Bushnell presumed that the tenor of programs mattered because some listeners sought more from broadcasting than entertaining companionship, and only the CBC could provide radio that had not seemed to disengage itself entirely from contemporary events. Private stations were technically capable of carrying more marches or more symphonies, but they could not afford to do so. On Friday evenings in the early 1950s, for example, the CBC could air *Songs of My People*, a program devoted to "traditional musical forms" from many lands,[76] but commercial broadcasting's range of possibilities during those valuable hours was severely limited. The CAB recognized this fundamental characteristic of the broadcasting industry and, when pressed to enumerate its contributions to public service, wisely chose to trumpet private broadcasters' efforts to discover local musical talent.[77]

The CBC provided its own listeners with a generous dollop of conventional "pop" fare, but the network's position as a public broadcaster relying on licence fees to meet its expenses allowed it to keep some critical distance from the music business. Like any other broadcasting operation, the CBC hired professional musicians, paid royalty fees, played records, and boosted the careers of the artists whose performances it broadcast. Yet, in comparison with commercial stations or the American networks, such activities were less tied up with the CBC's own purpose. They could run the Dominion Network's talent-seeking program *Opportunity Knocks*, which awarded its winners a short series of broadcasts on the full network, without having, in the future, to favour those artists over others representing a rival broadcaster or sponsor.[78] They could publicize new shows from other stations or networks, or promote talent incubated elsewhere without fear that such gestures would put their own future in jeopardy.[79] They could air the series *Speaking as a Listener* (1948) and *Critically Speaking* (intermittently 1949–57), over which critics offered their candid assessments of CBC programs and the tribulations of broadcasting in general. The CBC avoided dependency on a system whereby musicians, broadcasters, and advertisers effectively served as shills for each other. However, programming regulations did not extend to policing stations' musical choices, so the CBC could do nothing, for example, to address a critic's complaint that there were "far too many blues singers singing 'Daddy.'"[80] The CBC took such complaints into consideration, analyzing existing musical programming with a view to planning its own. This was a double burden: creating appealing programs in various musical categories while trying to work out how or why certain programs or types of music resonated with their audiences. Private stations did not concern themselves with this latter task, instead relying on program ratings and their own reckonings of what their primary audiences might like next, in aid of booking acts that would draw advertisers. Commercial broadcasters employed a simple, self-contained broadcasting strategy, and they were confident in their ability to put on a show for listeners rather than preoccupied by the concerns of making radio while striving to understand it.

It was sometimes difficult for public broadcasters to grasp the logic of musical programming, or at least to account for why audiences gravitated to shows or performers that seemed second-rate. Austin Weir told the story of an agent for the infamous Crazy Water Crystals company coming up to Toronto and looking for musical acts to put on CFRB, rejecting an experienced local group in favour of one that sang off-key. The incident obviously amused Weir, but it also puzzled him that the group "got a very large following."[81] The result did not tally with his expectation that the more professional, competent act would have greater appeal to the advertiser as its representative and to listeners as entertainment. For CBC staff who evaluated musical programs in this hierarchical fashion, it was easier to see merit in events like a performance by a two-thousand-voice Doukhobor choir celebrating Peter's Day at home in the BC interior. The choir would, presumably, be the best interpreters of its own traditional songs, and the event promised to "add to the national understanding" and be a musical "scoop," according to the Ottawa Programme Division employee who suggested carrying it.[82] The more solemn the occasion, the better. In 1950, the informality of the commercial "disk jockey" drew sharp criticism from General Supervisor of Programmes Charles Jennings, who had heard some CBC announcers starting to "ape" their commercial cousins by "indulging in all sorts of chit-chat and homey philosophies usually delivered in a confidential phony-friendly atmosphere."[83] To their credit, some at the CBC recognized that not all recorded music programs need be disparaged and that it mainly mattered how much freedom a host had to arrange a memorable and coherent slate of musical experiences for listeners.[84]

Some of the best examples of the corporation's approach to musical categories lay in efforts to comprehend what listeners expected and how they listened. For an organization almost congenitally reluctant to steer its programming strategy via ratings and other measures of audience size, the CBC's attention to changes in musical tastes, especially after the war, made it seem like an organization trying hard to read the minds of listeners. In these attempts to fathom how and why people listened to one type of show or another, the CBC nonetheless resorted to some of the same demographic divisions that ratings agencies used to lay a program's commercial utility bare for interested advertisers. Farmers, classical music lovers, and women were among the groups targeted for attention.[85] In one instance, CBC programming staff dug into a survey done for *Chatelaine* magazine to discover "what the average Canadian housewife likes to hear as she dusts and scrubs and bakes." Directly out of the survey came *Let's Have Music*, a daily show founded on the principle that "housewives want sentimental music as a background for their daily chores – the smooth ballad, light operatic favorites, semi-classics, and lilting music – 'the kind that makes you want to waltz while you work.'"[86] No gender stereotypes were harmed in the making of *Let's Have Music*, but the musical categories highlighted in the poll became the basis of the program. The CBC favoured qualitative clues about listener preferences, even the ones left indirectly through surveys done by other organizations, and had always considered listener mail an especially valuable resource. In the context of reporting to CBC chairman A.D. Dunton on mail and other forms of audience feedback, producer Harry Boyle told the story of another producer gathering programming intelligence even while hitch-hiking to his rural home. He was picked up by "two rather seedy looking characters in an old car" who were listening to a CBC music program, and their approval of it was noted.[87] The CBC's own investigations, into what sort of music would be popular in 1951 or the state of the romantic ballad, were concerned with "mood" and, generally, with which categories of music might be in the ascendant.[88]

The CBC's attention to musical categories indicated that, while broadcasting "in the moment" was essential to public service – that is, ongoing musical trends should be monitored and accounted for in everyday schedules – a longer-term purpose could likewise be served by looking at categories outside those most obviously catered to throughout the industry. With jazz "all over the dial,"[89] the CBC took up the cause of "serious jazz," pleasing some listeners who had been denied their pleasure, pushing others away, and pushing others towards a new experience. It was a move designed to give "wide scope for musicians to work out musical ideas apart from the so-called commercial arrangements of dance tunes."[90] Not long after the CBC took over as the public broadcasting authority in Canada, commercial broadcasters and advertisers quickly came to identify it with some of these outlying forms of music. In his own view, the agent for Bright's Wines mentioned earlier was doing the CBC a favour by freeing it up to broadcast sustaining classical shows. Musical categories provided a common vocabulary with which to talk about programming, a vocabulary that remained relatively fixed. While the CBC used this vocabulary of tastes to ensure it was broadcasting shows that appealed to most listeners over the short term, it also used it to reject the notion that categories defined audiences. In other words, tastes were mutable, and improving programming variety created opportunities for musical works to foster change in listening habits.

The task of "raising" public tastes presumed not only that music had intrinsic value but also that some could be rated "above" the more commonly heard stuff. Drawing upon their experience in categorizing musical programs, CBC producers appealed to commonly held notions of worthwhile music, notions emerging during the nineteenth century and nourished in the period before broadcasting, to identify directions in which listeners already well supplied with dance music might be enticed. Although every broadcaster chose its lineup without consulting listeners directly, broadcasters could not choose programs without considering musical trends or program ratings. Opponents of public broadcasting declared that only commercial stations put the customer first and implied that the CBC shared the BBC's prescriptive style.[91] Rather than bluntly suggesting that a slate of programs could bring on social or cultural "improvement," the CBC found it easier to present its efforts in the field of musical programming as efforts to introduce listeners to music they might not otherwise hear. Music that was "varied, substantial and stimulating" would undoubtedly challenge listeners but need not be packaged as programming for experts.[92] Building a "radio class-room" in which listeners could choose to educate themselves seemed preferable to pushing out hour after hour of programs aimed at audiences that, from the perspective of a commercial broadcaster, were nearly worthless.

Despite the central role light music occupied in radio schedules, public broadcasters saw ample room for other styles alongside it. Demonstrating broadcasting's ability to preserve the Western musical heritage often required unsponsored broadcasts of orchestral arrangements, a circumstance public broadcasting entities considered part of their calling. Just as the most famous bandleaders had become renowned in towns where they were never likely to play live, radio presentations of works created a century and more earlier could be well received, convincing Ernie Bushnell: "Broadcasting of the great symphony orchestras of this Continent has had a tremendous effect on the musical appetite of thousands of people. Evidence that this is so is confirmed by the fact that the recording companies are today selling thousands of discs each year of the works of the so-called 'great masters' whereas ten years ago the sale of these and similar recordings was practically nil." Bushnell also thought CBC programming people could take some credit for this resurgence of interest in the classics,[93] but none of them was under the illusion the tide had somehow turned decisively in the direction of reverent nostalgia. Instead, they sought to define the more "difficult" forms of music as currently relevant, as enduring artistic forces, and as genuine mood lifters, not just as entertainment.[94] A listener from Edmonton wrote her local CBC affiliate about hockey taking over the airwaves, complaining: "[There is] no food for the soul or anything glorious to remember in a hockey broadcast, only noise and information, whereas a symphony concert is a little bit of heaven on earth."[95] A music student in Toronto complimented the BBC on its light opera transcription series carried by the CBC, noting music's ability to relax the mind, and adding: "wherever Gilbert and Sullivan is sung and heard people are a lot happier and gayer."[96] Though his description would have fit most listeners at some point during the broadcast day, Leonard Brockington spoke of the desire to feel transported by music and to be united with those of a similar sensibility. He set the established classical canon apart from the mass market without hesitation, announcing: "all great artists and those who revere them are citizens of one city."[97]

Inspiring this sort of radio fellowship among converts like Brockington was hardly a chore. A more significant goal for the CBC was to help sceptical listeners to see the wisdom in leaving their sets tuned to musical programming that was simultaneously melodic and therapeutic. Byrne Hope Sanders, nearing the end of her time as director of the Consumer Branch of the Wartime Information Board, encouraged women already listening to another import, the Metropolitan Opera, to evangelize it to their friends who might not normally listen to such programs. She reminded her audience it was easy to attend to household tasks during intermissions and noted the opera's ability to "deal with the most fundamental emotions each one of us know in some form ... These mighty conflicts of emotion we listen to are woven around the stuff of life."[98] For an appreciable portion of set owners, hearing everyday conflicts set to music was not an attractive proposition, and most preferred to stick with lighter musical choices. Still, the CBC could not ignore responses to its programming that painted certain forms of music as transformative, inspirational, or suggestive of a human spirit engaged with the surrounding world. Such music could be soothing, especially during wartime setbacks, for which staff decided they should be ready: "two or three fine choral programmes should be 'disced' [recorded] and be ready for use, not necessarily immediately after such momentous announcements as event may make necessary, but within a period which would make it possible to give a real 'lift' to public spirits."[99] In times of crisis and calm, music could be a portal to the sort of individual or societal improvement that public service broadcasting's advocates had always considered possible. To reinforce this inclination, it took only the odd listener chiming in to say the singers in a broadcast of The Messiah were "not so much rendering Handel's music for us but just using their voices to enunciate something in which they believed."[100]

The CBC set out to introduce music, and sometimes entire musical categories, that appeared to be underrepresented elsewhere on the dial or had been enshrined in the Western musical tradition. It did so cautiously, especially wary of seeming superior to, or aloof from, its listeners. In 1937, W.H. Brodie issued a warning to CBC announcers not to be too precious or to decide for listeners how marvelous a piece of music might be.[101] Brodie wanted his announcers' foibles to stay out of the way of the music, but he did not advocate the BBC practice of keeping announcers anonymous. Ernest Bushnell also believed, after the better part of ten years handling programs at the CBC, that listeners would be put at ease by a low-key style of presentation. He viewed both faux-populism and the remote approach to presenting music as insincere and, therefore, as possible barriers to introducing new music successfully.[102] The idea of making listeners comfortable with unfamiliar music was also a common theme, and some programs identified as instructional included short lectures/primers to orient those treading new musical ground.[103] Primers and tips for listening were meant to ease the transition to active listening, and some thought their previous absence may have explained "why so many have been overcome by a sense of bewilderment on their first approach to music, and have remained convinced that 'this highbrow stuff' may be all right for some people, but not for them."[104]

The CBC frequently geared its introductory musical programming towards overcoming the sense that some categories of music excluded some categories of listener. To demystify his works, the CBC *Times* tried presenting Beethoven as a popular, versatile composer who sought in his own time to thrill audiences.[105] Such an approach was considered necessary because the CBC *Times* readership, while generally supportive of the CBC's overall function as a national network, included subscribers who were uncomfortable with too much cultural activism on the part of the corporation or who were looking primarily for information about upcoming programs. Program publicity staff were on the lookout for ways of reaching that sort of person, a hook to draw their interest without making the program being promoted seem too penitential or medicinal. As it did for older classical works, the CBC tried using a kind of "celebrity profile" to introduce unfamiliar contemporary music. The initial broadcast from an early wartime series on Canadian composers noted the playful side of Robert Farnon's musical life, where he cavorted with *The Happy Gang*, but reminded listeners that Farnon's "aim is serious composition."[106] A late wartime idea borrowed from the BBC featured "This Week's Composer" and targeted the early morning crowd.[107] As CBC musical director Geoffrey Waddington explained, the radio was just the place to bring people into contact with a variety of musical forms, even Canadian music.[108] Radio did not require them to invest in recordings, spend the time and money necessary to darken the door of the concert hall, or risk being seen attending a particular event. Robertson Davies suggested that, among those who followed music, or pretended to, "almost any assembly of strange sounds can command a few respectful hearings,"[109] but he was referring to a fairly rarified group in Canada during the radio era. Economically disadvantaged listeners, and even listeners in small cities like Davies' Peterborough, were usually unable to make it to established concert venues. By the later 1940s, they had come, like rural listeners, to "rely on radio for music education."[110]

The music program that best illustrates some of these ideas about listener instruction is *A Layman's History of Music*, a two-segment series broadcast in the fall of 1948 as part of the CBC's *Wednesday Night* program bloc, which features prominently in chapter 6. Music appreciation series were not new at the time. American composer Walter Damrosch had run his *Music Appreciation Hour* on NBC from 1928 through at least 1942, excited that radio had "swept away the barriers and admitted all the people to the charmed circle of music's devotees."[111] However, popularizers like Damrosch and Deems Taylor sometimes saw their work attacked, at one extreme, for its "soporific effect upon social consciousness."[112] The proportion of American airtime devoted to classical material varied, depending on who was doing the reckoning,[113] and regardless of how high the production values were, CBC programming staff could not rely on Canadian listeners' ability to pull in those signals. While the CBC aired familiar selections from the repertoire of "good" music on a regular basis, it did not put together a music appreciation series so much as give listeners piecemeal introductions to acclaimed works or composers. *A Layman's History of Music* was intended to appeal to the active listener for whom music had been a closed book. The CBC had never wanted to alienate listeners via musical programming, but it came to recognize more clearly after the war that the "finer" sorts of music had been cordoned off as objects of veneration. In the spring of 1948, in an article for *Good Housekeeping*, George Marek, the magazine's music editor (and a recording industry executive), used the image of estrangement to disparage the way classical music had been handled on US radio, arguing that, despite some efforts to treat it as music, American listeners still felt shut out by announcers who exalted its composers and conductors. The article did not prompt the CBC to produce *Layman's History* – it was reportedly a listener who wrote in asking for a "serious attempt to tell the origin and development of music" – but Brodie circulated Marek's piece and responded to it as a teaching moment for announcers and continuity writers.[114] Still, the CBC had in mind listeners of both genders who were, like the readers of *Good Housekeeping*, ostensibly interested in improving their physical and cultural surroundings.

The program itself tried to distill the musical history of several centuries, doling it out via narration and lavishly produced musical selections to listeners presumed to have a wide range of musical knowledge.[115] Some may have heard the music before but were unlikely to have understood it as part of a grand tradition or thought about it as connected to the period in which it originated. Others may have been considerably greener. As critic Eugene Kash put it: "in this catch-as-catch-can world of radio we may have caught a listener who was hearing the harpsichord for the first time."[116] Others chimed in to applaud and suggest shortcomings. "I would personally prefer to be talked up to than to be talked down to," said Graham McInnes after the first part of the series aired, referring to the script's tendency to tell listeners what to listen for in advance of the relevant piece's being played. He urged them to tune in for the second instalment, certain they would be surprised "how quickly those hours slide away on magic wings."[117] A correspondent on Vancouver Island saw *Layman's History* as evidence that "CBC seem[ed] to be successfully pulling radio out of the cultural garbage can in which so many Networks [were] endeavoring to bury it."[118] The series got some notice in the United States, where *Variety* mused that "perhaps only in a nationalized radio setup" could something like it be made, adding: "academic but sugar coated with humor, this series is an important milestone in the CBC's dissemination of 'culture.'"[119]

Characterized in that way, the series seemed sinister, like part of a conspiracy to remake the leisure time of Canadians according to some highbrow blueprint. Any such conspiracy carried out over the long term would have unravelled as the bills came due for productions on the same scale. *Layman's History* required five separate studio set-ups, the use of a pipe organ, and the cost of all the extra musicians and technical crew to get the live broadcasts out.[120] CBC general manager Augustin Frigon offered his reaction two days after the series aired, confirming that these were indeed meant to be music appreciation shows, not classical extravaganzas, and that he was disappointed in their execution. "I assume," he wrote to producer Harry Boyle, "that these two programmes were meant to educate the layman and that our job has not been fully done if we did not attract the interest of the listener who, although he may belong to the above-average intellectual level, may not be particularly interested in music." To become "interested" in music was to consider it not only an entertaining pastime but also as part of human history, like war or money. To expect listeners to make such a shift in five hours was ambitious. To expect to sense such a shift after two days or two years was futile. Still, Frigon went on to tell Boyle that

> the manuscript was read somewhat too fast and in a tone of voice which, at times, seemed to say "of course you all know this." Certain words and expressions should have been underlined in the reading, so that they could be easily understood and retained by persons not already familiar with the language. In other words, instead of a narrator we should have had a professor or more precisely a lecturer. I am afraid quite a number of persons must have missed a good deal of the value of the programme, and even may have turned to another programme for lack of comprehension of what we were trying to do.[121]

The thought of driving away the very listeners they were trying to reach was perhaps the most sobering one for Frigon, who nonetheless saw value in a didactic approach. After all, he thought success might be achieved through throwing more experts at the problem. For years, the CBC had been championing the category of classical music as a symbol of engaged listening, and the logical next step was to learn from *Layman's History*. Late summer of 1949 brought another attempt, along the lines of *Layman's History*, but with a stronger – or at least more carefully articulated – vision of its motivated listener. *Musical Pictures* was another music appreciation program "intended for the listener who has never been able to attach any particular significance, or meaning to music, despite a strong desire to appreciate it." It was not the last, and measures like Brodie's encouragement of translating foreign musical titles, a suggestion about translating operas, and "pushing" the gateway drug of Gilbert and Sullivan on the bustling streets of the Dominion Network also reflected a desire to meet listeners in the middle without abandoning relatively fixed ideas of what could pass for "good" or "serious" music.[122] Long gone from the CBC, Gladstone Murray wrote in about the latter series to proclaim that, in his circle, the "only true way to determine a Philistine or a bounder was on his attitude to G.

and S.!"[123] On the public and private airwaves, planning programs to suit any type of listener qualified as speculation, and at private stations it was profitable. At the CBC, however, producers' main concern was to imagine how radio fit into listeners' lives and to concoct programs to address those imaginings. They could hardly afford (in the budgetary sense) to produce *A Layman's History of Music* every week, but they could not afford (in terms of public service) to stop trying their hand on a smaller scale.

As a way of balancing programming, and especially as a way of giving a nod to regional artists or serving listeners with uncommon musical tastes, the CBC devoted a small fraction of its time to shows that might best be described as *experimental*. These were not instructional experiments, like *Layman's History*, but programs born of insight into how musical tastes were formed and could change. The more esoteric forms of music, already associated with smaller audiences in the pre-radio era, seemed even more threatened by the economics of broadcasting, which could find sponsorship for crooners and jug bands more readily than for symphonies or choirs. The CBC's patronage, for instance, made a difference to the Toronto Symphony Orchestra (TSO) in the early going, just as the patronage of contributors to its Sustaining Fund had done since the First World War. In the period before the CBC was able to use the orchestra regularly on national broadcasts, its president begged Murray to book it as often as possible, at one time convinced that conductor Ernest MacMillan would leave and the players would starve if more broadcasting opportunities did not materialize.[124] In the absence of sponsorship, the CBC offered literal sustenance to another cultural institution by making the TSO a part of its sustaining broadcasts and came through again within a couple of months by brokering a sponsorship deal.[125] Almost two decades later, the CBC put considerable effort into scoring and performing the music for its *Stage* series of dramas without expectation of commercial revenue or expecting much notice for the music as more than an accompaniment to each play.[126] Those examples, along with dozens of other sustaining programs in the intervening years, were themselves experiments, made even though a sponsor might never step in and intended primarily to present listeners with a more complete picture of the musical landscape.

By broadcasting only marquee concert events and a few sponsored shows, private stations ceded the territory of classical and some semi-classical music to the CBC as sustaining programming destined for a small audience. Unlike the Broadcasting Act's ordination of the CBC as the national network and private stations as local fixtures, this was a more organically arrived-at division of labour, one that meshed well with CBC's self-identification as a public service broadcaster and private stations' need to be paid for airtime. We see this division illustrated well in 1948, when CAB columnist Elda Hope gave reluctant, but high, praise to the CBC's *Musically Yours*, making sure she first mentioned that the show's host started his career at a private station, and noting only that the program could be heard "over Trans-Canada," without naming the CBC. Hope suggested that breaking through to the average listener was not something broadcasters out to entertain should be doing but admitted that Elwood Glover's handling of the show, which explicitly tried to introduce music of one sort to fans of another, "ha[d] spoonfed [her] to the place where [she] even enjoy[ed] concertos and symphonies."[127] "Spoonfeeding" meant eating one's cultural broccoli or taking a bitter remedy, the administering of which fell to the CBC. John Adaskin, who would later produce the talent search *Opportunity Knocks*, was in charge of CBC *Singers* in 1938, a show featuring professional talent but designed to "encourage choral singing of four to eight voices in the Canadian Home."[128] Just as encouraging choral singing at home required a project like CBC *Singers*, moving opera into living rooms required the formation of the CBC Opera Company in 1948, to transform operatic works from something originating in New York or Milan and "coming at" listeners to something Canadians were doing for themselves.[129] In 1945, the CBC released a small pressing of recorded works by Canadian composers aimed at international record societies and broadcasters. In 1949, boasting that "national radio ha[d] offered the most sought after concert hall" for these works, the CBC teamed up with RCA to bring out a similar line-up for domestic sale.[130]

Such ventures acknowledged that broadcasting and other forms of mass communication could not be viewed simply as supplements to a sublime live performance but, for most Canadians, would be their primary mode of contact with classical works or anything that did not fall into the light, dance, or otherwise sponsor-worthy categories. In other words, the CBC saw each of these radio experiments as perhaps its best and only opportunity to expose listeners who were set in their ways to less "popular" fare. Already a well-attended "shirt-sleeve" event, the "Proms" concert in Toronto made it onto the radio in 1937, one of the more obvious candidates for broadcast, but nonetheless a bold choice to air "serious" music without presenting it as an unnecessarily illustrious occasion.[131] Trolling for new listeners over the Dominion Network in 1948, as the CBC did with *British Concert Hall*, seemed like a risk, potentially antagonizing station owners who were hoping for something they could sell advertising time around. However, the BBC did not charge a premium for the rebroadcasting rights, and station owners, as usual, did not have to pay the line charges for taking the program. Coupled with the fact that, in the BBC's estimation, it was still difficult for the CBC, let alone individual Canadian stations, to produce material of the same quality, the BBC shows offered an excellent bargain.[132] Pat Paterson's *Musical Playroom* (Trans-Canada Network) and *Pat's Music Room* (Dominion) were perhaps the most middlebrow experiments the CBC rolled out. Paterson played classical selections but avoided discussing composers' lifespans or their musical educations: "Presumably they were all born, and all started studying sometime. Who cares when?" Treating classical works and performers as people, albeit talented ones, gave these shows a tone that was "a bit gossipy, in a light sort of way." Paterson did not specialize in classical music, as the CBC also had her presenting *Light and Lyrical*, "soapsud" music for domestic listening.[133]

In planning and producing a slate of musical shows that could be broadcast over the entire network, the CBC also faced the problem of accounting for regional variations in musical taste. In theory, private stations could do a decent job of this, but in practice they faced the obstacle of affording it. Sponsors could usually be found for "local originations," but the small advertising budgets for such broadcasts limited the calibre of talent to little beyond amateurs or rebroadcasts of performances already paid for by box office receipts. In 1943, one of the topics debated by CBC and CAB member stations was precisely how these stations could do more to reflect local preferences. The CBC's control over network hook-ups, as always, frustrated commercial broadcasters hoping to sell their programming, in imitation of American stations, outside the confines of their own signals.[134] For better or worse, the CBC operated the only national network, spending a large portion of its budget on the cost of transmitting programs over leased lines. When it sent less orthodox shows out to the whole network, it was difficult to predict which ones would be well received in which parts of the country. At the end of the Second World War, for example, a report from British

Columbia said listeners were responding well to "serious musical shows" and to singing from Quebec.[135] A few years later, in 1951, the CBC's Maritime representative wanted to see more programs originating in the various regions, even if this meant experimenting along the lines of hoedowns, local choirs, or a "National Sing-Song." By 1956, the CBC's regional production centres were able to produce both music and drama programs for national broadcast but only "in the advanced and challenging fields of drama and fine music,"[136] not daytime serials or the emerging genre of rock 'n roll.

The CBC also tended to "trust" classical music or other categories that did not obviously originate in mainstream radio. These forms of music were for the most part safely distant from what commercial stations viewed as their bread and butter, so the CBC could explore them without fear of duplicating service nationally or in a particular listening area. It even teamed up with J. Murray Gibbon, a long-time foe of public broadcasting but a champion of folk songs and tunes, to broadcast *Canadian Mosaic* and *Heritage of Song* by early in wartime.[137] After the war, folk ballads – "not to be confused with hill-billies" but "one of the lively arts" – found some airtime with shows like *Ed McCurdy Sings* and *Tales of the Minstrels*, designed to give listeners a dose of "authentic" popular singing. At times, however, CBC staff and managers exercised their judgment in not going ahead with folk programs that might not work on radio because the musicians' costumes would not be visible or the "inaccurate, out-of-tune singing and playing of native instruments" would be nakedly apparent.[138] A 1955 production of Mexican folk music was an innovation, but the BBC flatly turned it down as an exchange program because it was "highly academic."[139] Surprisingly, after its polarizing presence early in the radio era, jazz fared much better on the postwar CBC, where, via shows like *Jazz Unlimited*, it underwent a rehabilitation, or at least a kind of vivisection, in which the gin-joint bands were separated from "musicians like Ellington who [were] truly musicians and who play[ed] for people who [were] willing to sit and listen and think."[140] This was "real Jazz," not a favourite for most listeners but valuable for the CBC in the late 1940s and early 1950s because it was improvised, not run through Tin Pan Alley. Blues music received a similar treatment on *Blues for Friday*, which became *Starlight Moods*.[141] Only by broadcasting such programs more frequently or unceremoniously could the aura of exclusivity or edification surrounding less "popular" forms of music be dispelled. They could only become everyday music if they were heard every day.

The CBC's efforts did not alter the fact that every day on Canadian radio, even on the CBC's own stable of stations, there was more Glenn Miller than Beethoven. Staff at the corporation recognized that supplying listeners with Beethoven to the exclusion of what they already got (and that most appeared to like) would be neither welcome nor desirable. The various types of music existed before radio arrived, and classifying audiences using those same categories helped public broadcasters get a sense of which audiences were being well served and which were not. On commercial stations, the question of what to do about music was a less ambiguous one, and advertising agents' ability to convince sponsors that ready takers existed for dance, old-time, or jazz music gave those categories of music an advantage. Radio exposure brought familiarity, and familiarity assured more radio exposure. Outside that comfortable bubble, and despite some success for "pops" orchestras, the poor relations – for example, classical, folk, and modern music – remained on the margins. The CBC sought balance not by rushing towards these marginal musical categories in a frantic attempt to "counteract" all the other music programming out there but, rather, by trying to build programs that would forge links between the "great artists and those who revere them," even if the reverent had not yet declared their devotion. At times, this meant presenting opportunities to learn about music as opportunities for self-improvement; at others, it meant experimenting. Most of the time, it meant broadcasting the same stuff as commercial stations, as well as producing the musical comedies or shortened versions of well known compositions that might persuade listeners to hang around for more or to include a particular program in their regular listening habits.[142] Listeners needed actual programs if they were ever going to become a loyal audience, or even a casual one. Convinced that it was in the public interest to instil a kind of hunger for musical variety, public broadcasters wanted to create audiences for some of the musical subcultures spurned by a radio market that had already chosen which audiences were worth creating.

6

"Everywhere among All of Us":
Broadcasting and Cultural Democracy

Thanks in large "measure" to music programming, which could act as an invisible phonograph at home, broadcasting went from being a sensation during its first decade to an indispensible presence in anglophone Canada through the 1930s and into wartime. This was a society spread thinly and beset by its own regional divisions, as it had been before broadcasting's arrival. Canadians made time to listen daily and became even more prone to cross-border influences. Few recognized the importance of making the industry socially and culturally responsive and responsible to listeners regardless of their tastes. In the United Kingdom, the BBC played a vital role in raising interwar aesthetic standards and enabled people "to take an interest in things from which they had previously been excluded."[1] In contrast, Canada's radio output in the period before television took over yielded little conclusive evidence of changing listener habits, even if we assume that more hours of programming meant more varied schedules or more hours of the same material. Broadcasters could serve or alienate listeners by carrying unfamiliar programs. They could serve or alienate listeners by aiming for the biggest audiences. If listeners came away from the available programs better informed or acquainted with new forms of entertainment, those salutary outcomes did not seem to alter how broadcasters approached their jobs.

American programming may have posed the gravest threat to Canadian nationalists' hopes for cultural self-determination, but a simultaneous conflict over broadcasting's role in modern democratic societies did much to define how programming was made and reflected conflicting ideas about democracy itself. In the realm of programming, did democracy mean majority rule or did it mean providing something for listeners of various descriptions? Was it most democratic to broadcast all the time what the bulk of people were likely to accept as satisfactory or to supplement those mainstream programs with other material? Was radio supposed to be a mass medium or an intimate one? Were listeners (individually or collectively) at the centre of broadcasters' democratic visions or on the periphery? Commercial broadcasters considered the "majority" model superior because it indulged the human instincts to profit and be entertained and appeared to satisfy many listeners – residents of the imaginary "boardinghouse in which there is only one radio"[2] – without appearing to impose programming choices on anyone. Implicitly and explicitly, private broadcasters portrayed the CBC (and similar institutions) as in the business of denying pleasure. In response, public broadcasters in Canada acknowledged light entertainment's central place in any broadcasting schedule but offered, as had the BBC under John Reith, a wider-ranging and more aspirational menu of programs. Public broadcasters endangered their own reputations as public servants and cultural democrats by giving listeners more of an opportunity to work out for themselves what they liked, an invitation often mistaken for paternalism.[3] As David Hendy argued BBC Radio 1 needed to do during the 1960s, the CBC needed, for purposes of revenue and breadth, to "face both ways along the commercial–public-service divide."[4] The intention to broadcast, at least part of the time, programs of interest to Canadian listeners with minority tastes became more clearly visible after the Second World War, when the CBC uprooted its schedule one night of the week to make room for "cultural" programming. The corporation's frank acknowledgment of all broadcasters' curatorial role contrasted sharply with commercial operators' insistence that they simply perceived public desires and responded.

Efforts to enhance broadcasting's profitability and reach shaped programming during a period encompassing depression, war, and cold war, when democracy reigned as a compelling, but often shoddily-defined, ideal in North America. In order to harmonize with the democratic orthodoxy, broadcasters emphasized their function as faithful purveyors of entertainment and information and as conduits open to listeners to use as they pleased. Choosing and scheduling programs remained integral parts of broadcasting, and commercial broadcasters displayed a Panglossian confidence that they were already fielding the best of all possible schedules because more people tuned in.

On the public side, public service meant not only carrying programs for mass audiences much of the time but also forging ahead with avant-garde or middlebrow programs that were not highly rated. Whether the programs on Canadian stations originated in larger cities, smaller centres, or as imported commodities, whether broadcasters produced their own shows, let advertising agencies do it, or bought broadcast rights, radio's gatekeepers determined what listeners heard.[5] In the late 1940s, radio critic Graham McInnes praised some listeners for making a fuss about programming, noting that, while they were likely to find something to appreciate at some point during a broadcast day that had by then expanded to eighteen hours, "a radio audience – unless it listens and criticizes – has its creative work done for it. Because of the costs[,] it's imposed from on top or from outside by a select few."[6] As the ones doing the imposing, private and public outlets had different reasons for being in the industry and approached program making in distinct ways. Still, both these "denominations" in broadcasting's broader church claimed to be making programs for the benefit of listeners. These approaches are illustrated in this chapter by an examination of some ideas (or ideals) fought over on the battlefields of program preference and supply, namely: (1) the commercial broadcasters' powerful talisman, "giving the public what it wants" (i.e., big audiences meant popular desires were being met, and proven programming formulas maintained those audiences); and (2) public broadcasters' commitments to serving "minority" audiences and to program variety, founded on the belief that public service meant giving everyone some enjoyment from their radio sets.

WHAT THE PUBLIC WANTS

In the fall of 1934, the American radio magazine RADEX asked its Canadian readers to vote for their preferred form of broadcasting and to reflect upon how radio was being managed by the broadcasting commission. RADEX reported that just under 55 percent of the 4,554 respondents favoured a "commercial system with advertising," with the rest, still a significant minority, supporting a "governmental system with a tax."[7] These labels, "commercial" and "governmental," ignored subsidies the CRBC paid to private operators for transmitting national network programs and mistook the commission's responsibility to Parliament for its being an institution that was controlled by the government of the day. For broadcasters, listeners, and historians of broadcasting alike, it has been easier to notice monopolies operating in the public sector than in the private.[8] At any rate, the report charged that the radio licence fee, or "tax," had been misspent and that some listeners wanted it to go towards worthy causes like eliminating signal interference. In the area of programming, one RADEX reader found the commission's programming choices vexing: "The CRC [sic] has only one idea of what its public wants and they always guess wrong. In other words the US system pleases all of the people some of the time but the Canadian system pleases very few of the people, very little of the time."[9] This correspondent, like any of her/his contemporaries, had no way of knowing how pleased "all" the people were or of conveying what "some" time meant, but painting CRBC programming as aimed at a tiny audience apart from the "public" introduced a resilient falsehood to discussions of how radio should be done: that public broadcasters were somehow sheltered from cultural market forces, unable or unwilling to detect or serve the mass public's desires.

Another fiction proved similarly resilient. This was the notion that, before they could make a profit, commercial broadcasters had laboured to secure regular listeners by offering the programming listeners liked. As the CAB put it: "Commercialism does not proceed [sic] public interest. It follows it."[10] In this formulation, commercial operations had to "give the public what it wanted" to gain audience loyalty or their enterprises would collapse. Fortunately for station operators, few listeners recognized that any such financial collapse was more likely to result from poor program ratings and the accompanying *loss of advertisers* than from poor program *quality*.[11] That is, to keep advertising revenue flowing, broadcasters only had to keep listeners from switching stations (assuming another was in range) and did not need to provide precisely what each listener most wanted at a given moment, an impossible task in any case. "Good enough" was good enough, and selecting the *type* of program to be broadcast often played second fiddle to identifying an audience that would draw sponsors. Before advertising agencies had gained much experience integrating radio with their campaigns, agencies serving Canadian clients sought American know-how in the field. One agent asked a bigger US-based outfit for advice, scarcely bothered by what sort of program would eventually be made, and understandably most concerned with delivering the promised audience: "Should our client make his program a musical hour at 10 p.m. or should he broadcast hints to housewives on preparing dainty meals at 3 p.m.? How can we best check 'listener' interest? etc. etc. These are some of the things we are trying to decide."[12] Agencies and production companies made sound business decisions often enough, and after a few years of getting by on revenue from indirect advertising (sponsorship announcements at both ends of the show), direct advertising (portions or "spots" of airtime devoted to sales talk) came along as well.[13] Canadian commercial stations reaped the rewards, making or importing more shows advertisers wanted to back, reinforcing the beliefs that even the limited audience data available revealed "what the public wants" and that they used "probably the most nearly foolproof method of pleasing the majority of the listeners."[14]

Seeing ratings data as a kind of perpetual election to determine listener-approved programs made some sense. After all, the programs most people spent their time and battery life on had drawing power, and ratings agencies tracked which ones their sample groups tuned into most often. As Ned Corbett, a pioneer in educational broadcasting, admitted: "There are a great many people, to my surprise, who enjoy soap operas. I do not know how they can, but a number of them do, otherwise they would not be listened to."[15] Looking at the proportions of sets tuned to various programs available in the Toronto market in 1941, socialist researcher Philip Spencer confirmed a significant gap in listenership numbers that had always been there. "If anyone is feeding the illusion that the public really prefers 'high-toned' programs even though given low-tone ones," he wrote, "these figures should dispel it." He presented data showing commercial, often American, programming with a several-fold advantage in audience size over CBC offerings. The numbers did not lie about how many had their sets tuned to soap operas or dance music. Spencer then had a flash of insight but just as quickly dismissed it as futile given the way broadcasting tended to work: "Whether sponsors supply types of programs according to the demand, or whether public preferences become attuned to the supply available, is an insoluble problem. But in any case, the public likes what it gets from commercial sponsors, and commercial sponsors know how to dish it out." The "chicken-and-egg" problem of what the public wants – does it get what it likes or come to like what it gets? – was secondary for Spencer, who wanted socialists to be heard in a broadcasting culture that had capitalism baked in.

Ultimately, he advised that his comrades adopt some commercial program techniques,[16] acknowledging that people usually had their radios tuned to highly rated and conveniently scheduled shows. He did not interpret high ratings as the result of hype and savvy distribution arrangements. Bolder critics of the commercial model did.

Commercial broadcasters inside and outside Canada kept insisting that high ratings proved commercial radio's ability to cater to public desires, and their narrative prevailed. It was the same sort of narrative (the best-selling product meets all consumer desires) that attended the marketing of Bibles more than a hundred years earlier.[17] The narrative prevailed in the broadcast era to such an extent that, by the early 1990s, even academics who might otherwise be scrupulously careful in defining ideas like "cultural populism" could write that "chart music and television programming, for instance, are much more firmly grounded, for good commercial reasons, in the tastes and preferences of ordinary people,"[18] as though broadcasters themselves had nothing to do with shaping those tastes and preferences. One alternative view held that, by wartime, listeners had been "reduced to voting on a limited number of existing programs, whereas earlier they could shape radio shows' conception and meanings,"[19] and another suggested that "shows presented what producers perceived to be the mainstream values of the nation's consumers, namely the white middle class."[20] In 1931, when Canadian commercial operators dominated the field and hoped to keep it that way, CKGW Toronto station manager R.W. Ashcroft declared that "the objective, one that could be most easily achieved and measured, should be to 'please *most* of the people, *most* of the time'" (emphasis in original). He assumed competition would provide enough variety to satisfy most listeners and ignored the fact that advertisers were chasing the same big audience. Spending money to encourage Canadian talent was ill-advised, in Ashcroft's estimation, because most listeners would seek out the higher-rated shows from the United States, and advertising dollars would follow, enriching Canadian stations that hopped on the bandwagon.[21] Mary Vipond outlined the advantages for these private stations of remaining independent and being able to tap into American programming in the early 1930s. South of the border, NBC's success during that period testified to the earning power of grooming acts and broadcasting their performances widely. Yet the network itself insisted, even though it competed with Columbia (CBS) in the field of "prestige" programming, that the public was really in control.[22] Elena Razlogova argues that, in the United States, listeners enjoyed a kind of golden age *within* radio's golden age. Following an initial phase during which listeners had much more influence on commercial stations, this power waned as broadcasting became a bigger business. Popular participation in radio then took the less potent form of plaintive letters to broadcasters who had stopped collaborating with listeners in favour of surveying them.[23] Industry in service of the listener was a compelling interpretation of the business, and it was one that transcended international borders. In an environment in which sales became a proxy for consumer preference, competition between private stations had, according to one Canadian station owner, improved program standards that, earlier in the 1920s, were "far inferior to those broadcast now."[24] Fielding a program that sounded professional and attracted hordes of listeners required paying for the sort of talent that would appeal to most people. While it is tempting to attribute the CRBC's anemic schedule to the commission's efforts to present a variety of entertainment and to broadcast Canadian acts, Canadian Marconi's J.H. Thompson summed up the CRBC's woes by suggesting that "one cannot make bricks out of straw; not enough money was voted to make a decent showing."[25]

Presumably the establishment of a more securely funded new entity, the CBC, would address the problem of getting and keeping radio talent. Even after the CBC had been running for a couple of years and could pay for better acts, one of Austin Weir's friends in advertising told him that "numbers that only the classes could appreciate" were not "what the public wanted." What radio should be doing, R.E. Messer advised, is sticking close to what radio had been doing: "the poor old masses, the farmer, the stenographer, the city clerk, Mamma and the older kids want something they can 'get,' it doesn't have to be swing or dance music, but numbers with color, some dash, and a bit of hokom, something they have heard before."[26] The paradox of commercial broadcasters following the crowd of listeners to a place that only the stations themselves could have led eluded Weir's helpful friend, and he was hardly alone. The CAB, in the months before the CBC took to the air, teamed up with the Association of Canadian Advertisers to sneer at the BBC model even while unwittingly admitting that broadcasters governed what the listener got: "It is only natural that the British listeners would be relatively well satisfied with whatever standard of programme quality the state might be willing or able to set up for them. Conceivably the British programmes might be of fairly low entertainment value, and still be quite attractive to a listener who had never heard anything better."[27]

In defending their programming style as giving the public what it wants, commercial broadcasters held two interdependent positions: (1) we are "popular" because we aim to serve the most people; and (2) we must be serving the public well because the shows we carry have the most listeners. It's worth reiterating that private stations' representatives suggested their stations would soon be defunct if they did not cater to listeners' desires and that commercial revenue could only start flowing once a station had captured a regular audience. This Horatio Alger story had them offering programs as a kind of loss leader to satisfy the tastes of most people, building up their reputations and thus attracting advertisers.[28] Over time, however, those programs became the standard fare, enabling broadcasting entrepreneurs to profit by making radio for majorities they were continually creating and selling to advertisers. Sometimes, as Alex Russo shows in his study of radio on transit buses, those audiences were practically captives and actively resentful of having their time monopolized.[29] Aside from such isolated pockets of resistance, increasingly sophisticated ratings systems provided greater assurance that listener desires could be predicted, a situation that *Variety* radio editor Robert Landry referred to as the "stranglehold" of popularity surveys.[30] Robert Dunbar, working in Vancouver's radio market in the early postwar period, suggested that experimentation had become less likely over time because "radio thinks purely in terms of percentages."[31] Aspiring radio writers like William Brewer felt this more keenly, complaining of undue interference in commercial broadcasting, where, "lest in his untractable creative process, the writer should produce a script that is dramatically honest, and sound from the standpoint of literature, he is provided against his will with a staff of highly-paid advisors who are instructed to make sure he gives the public what they want (as demonstrated by nation-wide polls)." A reply to Brewer scoffed at the notion that commercial stations should sabotage their own operations, which were built on "selling as much as possible to as many possible."[32] Questions directed to private and CBC announcers, bandleaders, and producers in 1951 about the upcoming year's musical "mood" revealed that the industry rode quantifiable trends for as long as audience interest could be maintained. "Success" went undefined, but it was most easily measured in sales of records and sheet music, a business driven not only by the perennial appeal of waltzes but augmented by the latest dance, ballad, and novelty material. Radio provided instant and plentiful exposure, and record companies and music publishers had program directors to thank.[33] Confronting the reality of a fast-paced radio market, poet Earle Birney asked: "Do works presented to the public represent the best that has been thought and written; or are they selected to cater to what the public taste is thought to be, so that the project will not lose money?"[34]

Proponents of the idea that commercial broadcasting would provide what the public wanted found it useful to argue that broadcasting authorities like the BBC and the CBC were not only unnecessary but coercive and dictatorial, actively *denying* the public what it wanted. Before the advent of a public broadcasting presence in Canada, the BBC's fastidious control over its programming was a well-known image with which to conjure, an image that its director general, John Reith, had only burnished by suggesting: "he who prides himself on giving what he thinks the public wants is often creating a fictitious demand for lower standards which he himself will then satisfy."[35] Such hauteur could be set against the ethic of a supposedly more humble private system, a system as "fully alive to the wishes and needs of their listeners as any Governmental body might be."[36] To some North Americans, the BBC gave the public "Not What It Wants But What the BBC Thinks It Should Have,"[37] Even after the war, the BBC's representative in Canada, Michael Barkway, noted that commercial broadcasting's supporters in North America were "always trying to make capital" by recalling that, before 1939, the BBC had been less popular than Continental stations.[38] Commercial broadcasting accounted more easily for a variety of opinions, at least according to an NBC spokesman who credited American broadcasters with presenting "as many points of view ... as can be made articulate" and championing public engagement through programs like *Town Meeting of the Air*.[39] By contrast, national public broadcasters in charge of some or all broadcasting activities in a given place faced charges of monopoly control or restraining the medium. Sometimes, public broadcasters sabotaged their own cause, as an Australian did by declaring: "*what the public wants and has always wanted is to be taught what to want. The Public has a wavering mind which responds readily to those who* have stronger minds than its own."[40] It was more difficult for commercial broadcasters to admit that they were just as surely teaching listeners what to expect and appreciate.

The Canadian Association of Broadcasters strove to differentiate its members from the CBC throughout the 1940s and early 1950s by trumpeting the quality of sponsored programming and insisting that "radio imposes no price of admission."[41] Even during wartime, the CAB's public relations department urged association members to be on friendly terms with their members of Parliament and to remind listeners that commercial stations brought them entertainment "without cost or obligation" while "fighting for the survival of private enterprise."[42] Perhaps its boldest stroke was its contention that CAB members should be "permitted and encouraged to make money so as to develop those beneficial services and to remain free of subsidization from any source whatever."[43] In the CAB's view, the licence fees sustaining the CBC were subsidies, but advertising dollars were nothing of the kind. The public relations campaign worked well, if slowly, nudging Parliament towards establishing a separate regulatory agency by the later 1950s. Marc Raboy, along with Robert McChesney in the United States, argues that, going back to radio's days as the dominant medium, private interests have consistently been able to reconfigure broadcasting. While, arguably, Raboy's work is less polemical than McChesney's, he nonetheless notes that, through the 1980s, the Canadian broadcasting industry and its "arm's-length" regulators had: "followed the path of diminishing attention to public interest in favour of increasing regard to market considerations. In the process, it has contributed to redefining 'the public' in consumer terms."[44] Mark Rothenbuhler later stated it more plainly, seeing commercial broadcasting as part of "a culture produced and distributed by collaborative work among the employees and contractors of large business organizations whose interest is profit."[45]

Such readings of the situation relied upon a half-century of cultural/political criticism and seem anything but fresh now. Back in 1942, commercial broadcasters felt affronted and threatened by the authority vested in the CBC and worked to get their version of events into public view. The CAB proudly claimed that sponsored programming enjoyed more than a threefold advantage in listenership compared to sustaining shows on the CBC and that any corporation officials suggesting that "the entertainment element is out of place on the airwaves" were deluding themselves.[46] In 1943, pioneering commercial station CFRB Toronto broadcast a dramatized discussion about the radio business, equating "public monopoly" with unnamed systems in Europe "in which some high handed official sits in his office and dictates just what people shall listen to – whether they like it or not."[47] Although the only monopoly the CBC held was the ability to form a network, the implication was clear: if not for the commercial stations – the collective "little guy" standing up to an imperious broadcasting bureaucracy – Canadian listeners would be scarcely better off than their counterparts in Goebbels' Germany. CAB president Glen Bannerman wondered if Canada would take the "road of community responsibility; of community strength and effort, or is it the road of state centralization with its bureaucracy and red tape?"[48] After the war, the CAB took on the "monopoly" even more aggressively, painting the CBC as an obstacle to "free and fair competition" and arguing that ratings proved the CBC's tendency to produce "unpopular" programming was herding more listeners towards American networks[49] – exactly the effect the CBC was supposed to halt.[50] In 1948, the association's public relations director came up with the idea of broadcasting a drama festival to put the CBC's efforts to shame. Yet, with no follow-up programming or suggestions that the event would be held annually,[51] it seemed the idea was announced chiefly to prove that private stations took an interest in "high" culture. Further statements followed, citing the CBC's "wide, stifling, and restrictive power" to ignore "the programme tastes of other segments of the community" and reflecting commercial stations' conviction[52] – a justified one – that they too were serving the public by airing well-produced entertainment.

Although the appeal of star-studded commercial programs remained undeniable – for instance, a struggling CRBC kept such programs prominent in its schedule, noting: "popular demand brings them back on the air this fall"[53] – public broadcasters and their allies mounted their own extended critique of commercial stations' aggressive populism. Even public broadcasting veterans like Donald Manson sometimes found themselves using the phrase "what the public wants" to denote the commercial programming they considered "very seldom compatible with the ideals of men interested in social and intellectual welfare."[54] While Manson and his colleagues at the CBC saw radio as a site of investment in listeners' cultural capital and civic habits, they were stuck contending against a familiar slogan and had to use their competitors' more simplistic definition of public preference, even to articulate their own. The widespread acceptance of lively musical programs or melodramatic plays did not concern them as much as did the tendency of such shows to crowd out other kinds of programming or commercial broadcasters' claims that "popular demand" should be the only factor dictating what aired. Indeed, the less credited idea that broadcasters themselves were the parties most responsible for shaping public tastes easily predated the CRBC and the CBC. During the Aird Commission hearings in 1929, Augustin Frigon, still an engineering professor seconded to the commission, noted: "If you keep on serving to the public a low grade of things, they will ask for it, but if you keep your level up, you will find that they like good things. In England, when they started these good programmes, there was criticism, but now the people are asking for more because they like it."[55] Frigon's assessment was based on little more than an anecdotal understanding of audience preferences, and his notion of what was "good" reflected his class and educational experience. However, the contrary position – that listener preferences were a pure and irresistible force that governed programming – was just as impressionistic, relying on ratings of only the shows broadcasters had chosen to air and discounting listeners who had turned their sets off because nothing had compelled them to listen. Public broadcasters like Ernest Bushnell, who asked "What is entertainment? Is it music? – Is it drama? – Is it comedy? Yes it is all of those and a lot more,"[56] maintained that it would be impossible to know what the public wanted at any moment and that claims to certainty should be treated with suspicion.

Suspicion was only a sideline. Creating programs took up much of the public broadcasters' time, and their supporters – members of the Canadian Radio League or crusaders for a "better" sort of schedule – chimed in only occasionally. One of the earliest was the manager at the CRBC-affiliated CKY Winnipeg, Darby Coats, whom Mary Vipond saw as inclined

> not merely to amuse and entertain the largest possible number of listeners, as the private stations bragged they did, but to try to change listeners' habits and expectations of radio, to teach them to be more accepting of others, and of more educational programs. By 1936 he had adopted an authoritative role for himself as a broadcaster. While he did indeed want to understand the

listeners' wishes and desires, he also accepted his responsibility to override them for what he believed to be the greater good.[57]

Historian and public intellectual Arthur Lower correctly observes that most of the time the CBC "cannot carry its own case to the public."[58] When CBC staff advanced their views on the supply of programming and public service, relatively few listeners got to hear the message. Still, their attempts to counter the dominant interpretation of "what the public wants" were vigorous, not blaming listeners but viewing them instead as the underserved clients of broadcasting's ruling impresarios. Lower echoed Robert Hutchins of the University of Chicago, who told British readers: "American radio is not made in the image of the American people; it is made in the image that advertising men would like to create." Hutchins sympathized, as Lower would later, with listeners lost in the shuffle of ratings and with listeners having access to only one or two kinds of programming, noting that "an audience cannot be expected to demand something it has never heard of."[59]

Sometimes it was difficult to separate nationalism from this sense that people might not be getting what they wanted. In 1931, radio columnist Arthur Wallace quoted a reader in North Bay, Ontario, who suggested: "people are getting more and more accustomed to the programmes from across the line and if a vote was taken on the programmes most desired everyone would demand to hear these programmes in preference to our Canadian talent simply because they have been accustomed to hear them and not because they are really any better than our people can put on."[60] More than a decade later, critic Frank Chamberlain concluded that homegrown programming suffered from another disadvantage in that "a lot of people listen to radio programs they don't like, some from a strange force of habit. They listen, perhaps hoping for unexpected pleasures."[61] Just after the war, CBC Dominion Network manager Bud Walker doubted many highly rated programs would do as well had they not been scheduled among other more durable habit-forming (usually American) favourites.[62] Mostly, however, public broadcasters and their allies avoided comparing programs in this way because the numbers would never be on their side. Instead, they expressed discomfort with the dominant system by challenging the myth of the sovereign audience. This part-time critique of "giving the public what it wants" rested on a couple of pillars. First, although some programs would draw more listeners than others, critics believed that factors like advertiser input, programming categories, or ratings for previous shows shaped those numbers. In their estimation, all programs were gestures towards pleasing an audience, but they were gestures frequently affected by things that had little to do with a program's aesthetic value. Second, they argued that, while commercial broadcasters paid close attention to ratings information, these same broadcasters avoided doing more to monitor public preferences, as though they did not want to discover that radio audiences could be fragmented and moody or that listeners might appreciate a wider range of programming.

While attention to the psychological aspects of broadcasting blossomed in the United States, most notably at the Office of Radio Research and via studies underwritten by the big networks from the mid-1930s through the early war years,[63] in Canada such curiosity about broadcasting was not so structured or well funded, at least until the late 1940s, when the Massey Commission had its mandate to ask. Nonetheless, interested parties offered their opinions regarding the formation of tastes by radio and had been doing so in more than one jurisdiction before any public broadcasting authority emerged.[64] At the Aird Commission hearings in 1929, commissioners' concern about the effects and extent of sponsorship led a commercial broadcaster in Windsor to admit that the programs offered "for free" to listeners were not free because advertising was a production cost: "the public pays for all advertising [in] the ultimate purchase; we get nothing for nothing."[65] In 1931, Graham Spry noted that applications for new licences were for small stations not reaching underserved areas or for city stations that would crowd airwaves and result in "a further sharing of wave-lengths, an increase in the cost to be borne by the advertisers and of the total overhead of broadcasting operations, and a division of the limited revenue obtained from advertising and available for programmes. These costs, needless to remark, would be paid ultimately by the consumer."[66] A Nova Scotian ally of Spry's Canadian Radio League complained about intrusive sponsors and the tendency of private broadcasting's advocates to dismiss public service broadcasting as bureaucratic, adding: "An advertiser's job is primarily to sell his wares, not to provide entertainment, and he is certainly no better qualified to gauge public taste than 'the bureaucracy' to which Mr. Maxwell refers."[67]

In 1936, as the new public broadcasting institution took up operation, CBC Board of Governors chair Leonard Brockington took pains to announce that the new network would operate under a different set of assumptions: "It is our desire to give the Canadian listeners what they want. Whatever they want[,] and tastes must differ, we believe that they desire the best in music, in dance, in drama, in speech, in announcement."[68] That pledge was barely a murmur in the long and clamorous international conversation about broadcasting's present and future. The BBC's former foreign director, C.F. Atkinson, assessed the North American broadcasting scene a year earlier, calling its programming

> what the listener appears to want, as affected by what the citizen appears to approve. And the listener and the citizen are the same person under different aspects. Further, there are millions of him, with every conceivable shade of difference in taste qua listener and in opinions qua citizen. The "average" listener and the "average" citizen alike are abstractions, myths, or at any rate mere assumed datum-points from which one may try to cope with human phenomena with the least possible mean error.[69]

Back in Canada, Brockington's belief that "tastes must differ" and that there was no reliable way to account for all of them found support among radio critics and found embodiment in the CBC's approach to what the public wants. This uncertainty about public desires contrasted sharply with commercial broadcasters' faith in listener surveys and ratings. An article in the *Canadian Author* cites Brockington's speech favourably, disparaging a radio scene in which: "Popularity survey is practically a substitute for judgment [and station owners'] quick willingness to throw out the program no matter how promising. The industry is prone to call this whole situation 'response to the known will of the public."[70] Conductor Sir Ernest MacMillan warned: "Giving people what they want sounds reasonable enough from certain points of view, but as generally interpreted, this practice turns this mighty force into a mere medium for ephemeral amusement with an occasional sop thrown to appease the 'highbrows.'" He feared putting too much emphasis on the "consumer side of the question" and thought programming that offered "stronger meat" would be best not only for fostering Canadian talent but also for better determining over time what it was that listeners genuinely liked.[71]

Throughout radio's heyday in Canada, those who considered broadcasters to be the leaders, not followers, of public taste also tended to view commercial broadcasting as a public trust betrayed by stations that only begrudgingly carried sustaining material or promoted local talent.[72] Worth quoting at length because he encapsulated almost the entire position in one go, R.B. Tolbridge – reliably pessimistic about the broadcasting game in Canada – wrote in 1942 that commercial broadcasting was

> not concerned in the least with raising popular taste or with giving people what is good for them, or even what people, when not habituated to the inferior, might themselves come to want. It is concerned solely with reaching the masses by appealing to the lowest common denominator of existing taste. The advertiser is seldom keen enough to see that the socially desirable can be invested with more interest for ordinary people than the meretricious, and hence might ultimately be the more profitable for him. Still, even if he were, he would hesitate to undertake the job, for it is an extremely difficult one. It is so much easier to "give the people what they want." And the pathetic, good-natured readiness of plain people to "make allowances" for their entertainers, their eagerness to persuade themselves that they are really "having a good time," make it possible for commercial interests to continue palming off the shoddiest kind of stuff without rousing the mass audience to revolt. The hungry sheep look up and are not fed – except with the husks they have been led to think are nourishing.[73]

Tolbridge exhibited minimal regard for those he called "plain people," leaving it to other disgruntled observers to hold listeners blameless for the state of broadcasting. This more circumspect lot emphasized that, while public broadcasters needed to be careful they did not broadcast only what they thought listeners ought to hear, the same principle should apply to the whole industry. J.S. Thomson, who succeeded Murray as CBC general manager, told Canada's commercial broadcasters that, having led "the horse to the water," they needed to let him "find what he wants to drink." While reminding private broadcasters of their privilege as broadcast licence holders, Thomson also questioned their commitment to the public by suggesting that "edging" listeners into civilized life via the occasional challenging program was a nobler calling than producing sponsor-friendly material practically all the time.[74]

Instead of writing off most listeners en masse, as Tolbridge was more likely to do, broadcasters, critics, and listeners wary of commercial broadcasting's dominance during the 1940s and early 1950s expressed disbelief that commercial broadcasters' self-cultivated image as diviners of the popular will had taken hold so firmly. When Tolbridge spoke up again in 1946 and 1947 to note private stations' frustration at the CBC's wartime growth, he lamented the "posturing of private radio as the injured and oppressed friend of the listener," "cribbed, cabined and confined by an autocratic and bureaucratic CBC," and ridiculed its insistence that it had always been "giving the people what they want."[75] In contrast, the CBC was an outlet – at least part of the time – for alternative programming, and even its more fervent supporters admitted that the network's impact on listening habits would be modest or incremental at best. A Manitoba listener suggested in 1945 that the CBC should "enclose a questionnaire when one buys a radio license, and get first-hand information of what the people want." "F.L.J." supposed that the result would probably be "less 'jive,' 'swing' and tin can music, also the soap and pill advertising with their same rigmarole every day," but concluded that "as long as big business owns the radio I guess we'll have to take the bitter with the bitter."[76]

Despite this type of support for the notion that commercial broadcasters had poisoned the industry by not taking all listeners into account, CBC staff members only occasionally risked denouncing the status quo in hopes of presenting their preferred mode of broadcasting as a more sensitive one. In 1948, CBC Board of Governors chair Davidson Dunton, echoing sentiments aired more than a decade earlier by Graham Spry, declared that "freedom of the air" had been harmed by some broadcasters controlling most of the precious few "air channels" available in Canada and that only national radio safeguarded listeners' "freedom to get different ideas and views and material for varying tastes if they choose."[77] Within about a year, Dunton addressed popular tastes and the commercial stations' favourite trump card more directly: "In planning its programs the CBC does not believe that there is any simple criterion of 'what people want.' In the field of program tastes there is not one 'public,' there are a number of 'publics.'"[78] This pronouncement reflected discomfort with commercial broadcasters' long-standing claims of majority pre-approval for their programming. For a 1953 CBC series, Len Peterson wrote a play in which Ed McIntyre, a producer at a thinly veiled CBC, cast around for new show ideas and had revelatory chats with his manager, his secretary, a radio critic, an actor, and a writer about what the public wanted and why radio needed to be done differently. The sort of shows he had worked on previously discouraged McIntyre, but the prospect of doing something new inspired him. Peterson had his fictional producer reject the idea of a unitary public and, with it, the well-worn appeal to a uniform set of tastes. At one point, the producer mocks established broadcasting wisdom, claiming: "I would willingly journey all the way to the oracle at Delphi, and pay my own expenses, if I thought it could tell me what the public wants."[79]

Amid such uncertainty, a predictable response emerged. The way forward for the conscientious broadcaster was to engage listeners' fears that they were not getting the range or quality of programming they deserved. Charles Siepmann, the British-born crusader for public service broadcasting in the United States, put the onus on listeners to demand more imaginative programming, warning: "we can get what we like, as Bernard Shaw puts it, or we shall grow to like what we get."[80] Staff members at the CBC, along with their allies, embraced Siepmann's call to listener action, arguing that the listening public had been conditioned to expect schedules dominated by familiar shows, as though broadcasting had found a kind of homeostasis. CBC farm broadcaster (and later director of television in Toronto) Fergus Mutrie expressed his frustration that some Canadian listeners were left wondering if there might ever be programming for them: "When a storm of protest arises the answer is 'That's what the public wants' and 'If they don't like it they can turn it off.' I don't agree with either answer. It might not be what the public wants if it had more opportunity to get acquainted with something better."[81] Mutrie's "something better" meant precisely what the CBC's adversaries assumed it did: shows that had little apparent appeal – except to what one of McIntyre's fictitious fellow producers called "queer minorities"[82] – shows that could be used to tie the corporation's programming choices to BBC-style high-handedness. Statements like prominent artist Lawren Harris's wartime declaration that "the best in art in any country never originates in terms of 'What the public wants'" did not serve the cause, either.[83] The idea that the "artist trains the public" seemed most obvious to those who doubted that mainstream commercial programming would produce the opposite result.[84] In other words, they believed that the public was not training artists because tastes formed around programming *as it emerged* – public taste was instead *reacting* to what artists or broadcasters were already providing, not inspiring it. As a listener from Lipton, Saskatchewan, wrote: "If I am exposed gradually to a variety of programs, I am developing my taste by way of comparison, and one fine day I find myself a more appreciative and discriminate listener ... The CBC must never proceed on the basis of giving people what they like. People must be conditioned to the best and they will develop a taste for it in the end."[85] However, commercial broadcasters had done a better job conditioning listeners – and even some other broadcasters – to accept the idea that "popular" programming was somehow found, not made.

MINORITIES AND VARIETY

We tend to take examples like the Lipton listener's tough-minded optimism – along with other declarations like Gladstone Murray's that the CBC needed to set high standards, and J.S. Thomson's that the duty of every broadcaster towards the public was to "leave them better than we found them"[86] – as evidence that public broadcasters and their supporters had only the "improvement" of listeners' tastes in mind. Although unlikely to convince many that what the public wanted was already plentiful enough on the radio, public broadcasters defended the right of "minority" audiences to hear programming that commercial stations were neither obligated nor inclined to provide. Sociologists have more recently attached the label "cultural omnivore" to those who sample and consume works from all along the spectrum of possibilities,[87] but around the mid-twentieth century, binary distinctions (or at least Russell Lynes's high-, middle-, and lowbrow) prevailed.[88] Murray found his CBC castigated for paternalism and found himself personally criticized for courting radio moguls who controlled shows the corporation wanted to carry so that it could appear less paternalist.[89] Early plans for a CBC print publication, to be a program guide and companion to careful listening, differentiated more starkly between the discriminating listener and the "casual knob-twiddler," implying that the latter group was larger and already catered to extensively.[90] As well, within North America, Canadians themselves were a minority, and any broadcaster attempting to present Canadian programming to Canadian listeners was already seeking a somewhat limited audience. Within Canada, in contrast to a more densely populated American listenership, rural listeners and those in "the lonely lanes of the little places" made up a still smaller minority, reliably invoked as a reason for maintaining and expanding the public broadcasting system.[91] The public could be sliced into almost any number of minorities, and serving these smaller audiences called for a greater variety of programs.

While they sometimes created specialized programs that failed to rate much advertiser attention, public broadcasters further acknowledged that members of taste minorities were not reflexively opposed to mainstream entertainment. Dunton's idea of multiple publics or a fragmented listenership invited broadcasters and listeners to think of listening as an activity mirroring the other parts of a person's life in that one might be a member of several discrete social groups that, in a democratic society, could each expect some consideration no matter how small they were. Public broadcasters extended such consideration to listening minorities, ensuring that programming had, at least part of the time, more range and depth than it otherwise would.[92] Expressions of support for serving listener minorities by presenting a broader range of programming took several forms.

For some in the broadcasting industry, one hoped-for side effect of producing programs for small and specialized audiences was the exposure of average listeners to programming they usually would not hear. Another was the encouragement of talent that might otherwise be overlooked.[93] Predictably, organizations dedicated to cultural development approved of a steady stream of fare that could supplement sponsored mainstream programming.[94] While plainly optimistic, the CBC Press and Information Department's assertion that "music of the masters has become music of the masses" exemplified the existing artificial distinctions between the types of programming available.[95] It became necessary for "worthy" stuff to be brought to the attention of listeners accustomed to getting something else, and this might result at least in larger minority audiences. In his report on the state of broadcasting in Canada, BBC chairman Lord Simon speculated that, if all the money spent on radio went to the CBC, "[it] would undoubtedly give a much better service both to the mass of listeners and to the significant minorities than is at present possible."[96] For others, like George Chandler of commercial station CJOR Vancouver, only "very small minority groups" listened to the CBC's own programs, but, as he said, "unfortunately" the tendency of these minority groups was to be vocal,[97] suggesting that they influenced programming more than he thought they should. This perspective on programming, that "the great rank and file of listeners consume their daily radio schedules gratefully and zestfully" and that it was only "our class minority"[98] that demanded alternatives, had been current in the mid-1930s. Davidson Dunton reprised his "multiple publics" idea in rejecting this long-standing division:

> Some sections of the public seem to like some types of programs and some another; but the sections are not clearly defined and their membership often overlaps. Actually it is doubtful if there are any single programs, or more than a few, to which a majority of the whole public want to listen. It seems to be more a question of relative size of minority groups. One fairly large group of the public may wish to listen to a certain type of comedy program, a smaller group may like a type of musical program, but may still be in itself a very sizeable section of the public.[99]

The CBC's identification of ill-served sections within "the public" signalled the public broadcaster's determination to promote greater diversity in programming. CBC programming managers like Charles Jennings further articulated their stance by noting: "a great many of the intelligent and serious-minded men and women, to whom we felt we had a definite responsibility, were more and more leaving their radios turned off."[100] Jennings suggested on another occasion that, among listeners who could be considered local opinion leaders, there had developed a "distressing tendency to dismiss radio as nothing but a tool for hucksters."[101] This pointed reference to Frederic Wakeman's 1946 novel *The Hucksters*, an indictment of the advertising industry that became a Book-of-the-Month Club selection, and before long a film starring Clark Gable, would not have been lost on Jennings' colleagues. Harry Boyle, for instance, declared broadcasting had all gone downhill once the "ad men stepped in."[102] In its public pronouncements, the CBC displayed its reluctance to treat listeners as part of a great herd sold to advertisers because that transaction seemed like a betrayal of the intimate link between broadcaster and listener and an affront to listeners' own potentially widely variable preferences. As Winnipeg-based CBC representative

J.R. Finlay told a group of local clergy concerned about program standards: "both religion and radio listening are very personal matters. There are almost as many opinions about radio programme[s] as there are people listening."[103]

Public broadcasters could *afford* to support this view, not in the financial sense, as they were able to spend only what licence fees and limited commercial traffic earned, but in the sense that their vision of broadcasting assumed that the various smaller taste factions would take it in turns to have their desires met. Ernest Bushnell established this position in defending "thriller" programs during the war, and in 1949 director of presentation John Kannawin reminded CBC *Times* readers that "to please all at varying times is our sincere aim," a sentiment quite distinct from R.W. Ashcroft's "most of the people most the time."[104] Leonard Brockington, more than a decade earlier, told listeners that morality also played a role: "We should all recognize, if we can, the other fellow's point of view in connection with radio programmes, as with all other things ... [t]here is scarcely one of our programmes which has been on the air for some considerable time which some people have not told me is at once the worst and the best entertainment offered in the Dominion."[105] Having heard similar praise and complaint over the years, CBC programming officials decided in 1943 to place greater emphasis on evaluating the sponsored programs they carried for talent and overall quality instead of on the basis of big audiences or prior occupation of a particular broadcast time.[106] To the BBC's representatives in Canada, the CBC appeared to be pulled in several directions: "[It seemed] obliged to ignore the predominance of some desire at a given moment, in order to protect the interests of a minority. CBC must also always bear in mind the interests of the scattered population living in country districts, whose tastes differ from those of the people in the big cities, but whose need of radio was even greater."[107] The CBC would, as Bushnell confessed to a group of radio students, air some programs with minority appeal during peak listening times, but it would not juggle its schedule to cater only to listeners whose preferences or desires it might revere most.[108]

Public broadcasters viewed such practices as not only ethically sound but also as the fulfilment of a *responsibility* to "meet the listening public on a variety of levels" and an affirmation that the available broadcast frequencies were a commons in which one could expect a variety of activities to take place.[109] It was Bushnell again who saw this responsibility as an inclusive one, noting: "Broadcasters today are more conscious of their responsibility to all listeners – to those who like cultural and education programmes as well as to those who enjoy jive and the so-called 'popular' music."[110] The idea of a public network responsible for public service was easy to sell during wartime, when allowing a national public radio network to coordinate the distribution of war bulletins and national directives was plainly desirable.[111] Andrew Cowan, who spent a good portion of his years at the CBC representing the corporation abroad, called on his colleagues to think of average listeners, not just the regular CBC audience, and to "go out of our way to inform them, just as we go out of our way to sell them soap and movies."[112] Taking responsibility for maintaining a postwar balance in programming proved more difficult. Once peace returned, broadcasters of all descriptions had more to say about how vigorously minority audiences could, or should, be accommodated. The CBC had, almost from its inception, been cautioning taste minorities that they would have to take some role in managing their own radio diets, especially since, in a nominally democratic system, shows with bigger audiences (however those listeners had been gathered) could justifiably claim a greater share of airtime.[113] A postwar listener who had written to the *Ottawa Citizen* to complain about Max Ferguson's *Rawhide* program as an unwelcome example of the "lower type of entertainment" later heard back from the CBC's Ron Fraser, who advised the usual patience, adding: "selective listening has always seemed to me to be essential where radio must do its best to meet all tastes."[114] Yet, early in peacetime, the CBC declared its reluctance to simply banish programming for minorities to odd hours, casting such shows as "an active and stimulating force in the mental and artistic mind of the nation."[115]

Linking programming choices and scheduling so overtly to national development implied that other broadcasters were doing little to stimulate listeners, and little to help Canadian culture come into its own, but this was not a connection public broadcasters made often. Public broadcasters' reputations preceded them, and listeners came to expect that CBC productions would frequently be contrary in tone to what aired elsewhere on the dial. Critic Graham McInnes wrote: "amid the avalanche of whipped cream and fudge which clogs the networks," "mature" listeners formed a distinct minority whose presence ensured that "someone like Andrew Allan or Norman Corwin or Bernard Braden or Lawrence Gilliam or Frank Willis refuse[d] to be bound by the silly convention of adolescence so carefully fostered by the agency boys, and insist[ed] that the Canadian audience be treated as adults."[116] Freelance script contributor Ted Allan (no relation to Andrew) wanted to do a series on the Knights of Malta in 1952, and the CBC's chief objection to the project was not that it might not draw a big audience but that: "since this is a story of a charitable institution, we will have to think of it as compared with the kinds of things we do for other organizations of this general type."[117] Allan did not even bother pitching the idea to commercial stations because taking risks by running programming with limited appeal suited neither the commercial stations' operational model nor the market ideology underpinning it. A highly distilled example of the pro-market view came from Bert Jacobs of London, Ontario, who wrote to Minister of Marine C.D. Howe in 1938, citing extensive broadcasting experience and contacts, calling CBC programming stodgy, and declaring that neither listeners in sparsely settled areas nor taste minorities deserved the attention they got from what appeared to him to be a failed experiment. If these minorities were meant to be served, Jacobs suggested, private stations would have done so already.[118] While Jacobs' confidence in commercial broadcasters dates from a particular moment before the CBC's wartime growth spurt, the Canadian Association of Broadcasters, its members, and their allies returned to the question of minority programming over several years, especially from the Second World War into the 1950s.

Like public broadcasters, commercial broadcasters had a *responsibility* to listeners but believed it could best be met by taking into account the tastes of most people, seeking variety where numbers warranted but acknowledging that some audiences might be simply too small to pursue. In Clause 1 of its 1943 Code of Ethics, the CAB made this plain: "as far as possible, all groups of listeners shall have some part of the programming devoted to their special likes and desires in proportion to the relation of the numbers of each group to all other groups." The association's code also alluded to the "present structure" of the broadcasting industry,[119] which prevented commercial stations from forming networks of their own and meant that these stations could only consider the potential local or regional audience for any programming they might run. If sponsorships or advertising spots could not be sold against low to negligible audience projections for "minority" programming, stations could claim they had accommodated minorities to the "utmost practical extent."[120]

Running a solvent broadcasting business demanded such hard choices, and not all these choices broke in the direction of profit. As David Goodman argues in the American context, critics of commercial broadcasting often ignored its "civic function."[121] When asked to produce evidence of their commitment to public service, Canadian commercial stations proudly reported examples of the unsponsored "sustaining" programs they broadcast in their communities and noted that much or all of this airtime could have been sold to sponsors. With its sustaining output of almost six hours of religious programming per week, a shade under thirty minutes every weekday for children's programming and forty-five minutes per week devoted to "child training," CJVI in Victoria was one of the association's stars.[122] In view of its status as an exemplar within the CAB, the station operated, presumably, closer than most to the point beyond which it became financially risky to produce more unsponsored programs. American critic Gilbert Seldes, visiting Toronto in 1952, noted how careful commercial outfits had become, quipping that "efforts to supply minority demands have been pretty good in radio, except for the minorities of less than 37 percent".[123]

Responsiveness to local conditions became a point of strength, at least rhetorically, for commercial broadcasters as they sought to differentiate what they did from the CBC's mode of operating. In programming for local audiences, CAB member stations offered "alternative" programming almost as a matter of course because it would be commercially foolish to do otherwise. As the association declared in its report to Parliament: "If one station or network in the area is aiming at the mass audience with Charlie McCarthy, a policy of sound logic dictates that the other station or stations must appeal to the minority audience to get listeners. The reverse is also true."[124] When the CAB referred to *the* minority audience, it was referring to non-McCarthy listeners as a lump, not necessarily to a fragmented listenership that might have wandered off to a variety of other programs or switched off its sets. The best commercial strategy when up against a lavishly produced show like McCarthy was to present a program that differed but still aimed to draw the bulk of those who were not already listening to the dummy and his sidekick. The CAB's corollary, "the reverse is also true," suggested that when the CBC – often commercial operators' main competition outside Canada's larger urban markets – was presenting a program of minority interest, commercial operators should take every opportunity to capture the largest possible audience by broadcasting something else.

The CBC's status as the only national network also provided an angle for commercial stations to claim that they, not the CBC, could best interpret local desires. During wartime, the association suggested that national network programming might be set aside "where special regional interests and tastes exist," but it did not specify what might emerge to satisfy these interests.[125] After the war, when the need to have a national network to pass along war news and wartime directives had vanished, the CAB could more openly portray the CBC as a niche broadcaster and insist that only private operators could be relied upon to cater to local or regional audiences. Otherwise, they would face the extinction that was supposed to follow failure to respond to local majority demand. For its part, the CBC recognized that, when it ran national programs instead of local ones, it was not serving listeners who wanted more local programming.[126]

Commercial stations claimed they carried more minority programming than they had twenty years earlier not because of "rules and regulations" but because they had made a "significant contribution to the development of expanding cultural horizons in their communities," a shift that, for the "sake of stability and permanence," should be slow. Predictably, the CAB also saw as scaremongering the suggestion that giving more power to private stations through deregulation would lead to the import of more cheap US block programming.[127] The BBC's Canadian representative in the late 1940s reported that, even under the supervision of the CBC, private stations' output was already "aimed at a low level audience and [they] make little or no attempt to cater for minorities. Use of live talent is rare and the mainstay of the programmes consists of American transcriptions and recorded music from the American transcription libraries."[128] Humorist Eric Nicol put it more colourfully when he called the private stations' output a "mixture of dishpan drama, give-away garbage and the recorded retchings of American crooners calculated to appeal to the mentality of a cretin and the instincts of the saffron-seated baboon."[129]

It's fairly plain that the task of catering to minorities fell largely to public broadcasters, and this task suited their vision of broadcasting. However, this vision did not rely solely on "mopping up" after commercial stations by catering to pockets of listeners who remained dissatisfied. There was also the question of variety, or diversity.[130] Gladstone Murray suggested late in his tenure as general manager that the CBC was serving the public even when it earned revenues by carrying sponsored programs. People were going to listen to those shows anyway, and money earned would be put back into the rest of the CBC's productions, providing listeners with a more varied schedule.[131] Also during the war, the Dominion Network's creation came as a result of a parliamentary recommendation in support of alternative listening. Private stations had expressed their support for alternatives to CBC's Trans-Canada service but wanted any new networks to be *their* new networks.[132] American shows with large followings, too, were part of the range of programming the CBC could provide to more remote or rural regions, so these programs had earned a place in the reckoning as vital to an overall variety in programming.[133] For Davidson Dunton, exposing Canadians to unfamiliar programming was the essence of democratic stewardship, and, as he noted just after television arrived on the scene, "trying to maintain a sensible, impartial balance between different kinds of ideas, different opinions, different kinds of tastes, different types of material" would be even more important as TV caught on.[134]

To commercial broadcasters, the CBC's mantra of variety was more than a competitive challenge: it was a perversion of the natural order. They deeply resented having broadcasting characterized as a special case apart from "newspapers, magazines, weeklies, billboards and other means of dissemination." They contended that treating broadcasting like those industries, which were governed only by the "law of the land" and not some caretaker/competitor like the CBC, would help program makers draw upon the "cumulative result of years, even centuries, of experience, whereas regulation [was] a matter of a few years experience at best, and frequently of hasty judgment."[135] The Dunton-era CBC responded to such provocations, arguing broadcasting was not a business, but "both an art and a science." and, unlike most businesses, needed to be more judiciously managed because it used "resources that belong to the State." The corporation greeted the private stations' declaration that they too aired some minority interest programming not with disbelief or congratulations but with "why not?"[136] The standard to which the CBC aspired was as much inclusionary as it was aesthetically ambitious.

Yet aesthetic standards must not be dismissed. Creating programming for minority tastes often meant producing material drawn from the literary, musical, and intellectual canons, and involved judgments of value. Most often, broadcasters assumed that minority programming would be "earnest" or esoteric, "better" than the bulk of what made it to air and more potentially taste-altering for those who might be tempted to venture beyond the mainstream. Broadcasters, critics, and listeners themselves paid attention to the class distinctions, educational gaps, and variations in daily rhythms that divided radio set owners, and they linked these social markers with expectations about what made worthwhile programming. The BBC's Gordon Winter cheerfully noted that BBC programming imported to Canada was making an impact among the "thinking minority,"[137] a group with influence presumably out of proportion to its numbers. This reading of audience preferences implied that programming aimed at such a group might exclude other listeners. However, by importing or producing programming not usually found in commercial schedules, the CBC gave taste minorities something to anticipate and hoped to demystify new material for listeners acclimatized to mainstream fare. An industrial designer in Montreal said of one ballet music broadcast: "I didn't like it, but programs like this are very necessary."[138] A listener in Kamloops sounded a familiar refrain, suggesting that neither local stations nor the national broadcaster should be "entirely governed by those who applaud the poorest of stuff because they have rarely been exposed to anything better."[139] When the public broadcaster embarked on its *Wednesday Night* slate of "high-tone" programming, academic and occasional broadcaster Arthur Phelps introduced the first evening of entertainment as a bold gamble, one that was meant to sweep away the assumption that the majority of listeners would not be interested in shows or features that broadcasters themselves had for so long associated with small and presumably self-important audiences. Phelps equated uncommon programming with common humanity:

I believe in *people*. The social and economic and educational stratifications dissolve as incidentals·when we talk discerningly of that human intelligence, human taste and human culture which, in its essence, exists everywhere among all of us. Good listeners, ready and eager for good listening, are everywhere, I believe, in all the so-called strata of our society.[140]

When it began operations in 1953, the CBC Audience Research Branch vowed to look out for minorities by accounting for qualitative as well as quantitative measures of who was listening and how.[141] Individual departments and producers at the CBC and commercial stations had been monitoring listener mail informally for a couple of decades, but the corporation's decision to approach more systematically the data from its favoured listener surveys represented a departure from its common practice, which made a point of defending minority programming.[142] Employing a more explicit system for gauging audience size did not, however, alter the conviction that what Davidson Dunton called "commercial arithmetic" rarely added up.[143] He resisted the temptation "to make surveys and determine what the largest number of people like the best – then run only that kind of program," telling what could best be described as a "free-enterprise" audience at the Canadian Club: "it isn't our democratic way in Canada to crush the legitimate desires of minorities with the mass of majorities."[144]

CULTURAL DEMOCRACY

In his study of the CBC's belated and relatively weak audience research efforts, Ross Eaman writes that the corporation had "seldom been *associated* with the idea of cultural democracy" because cultural democracy "is usually *identified* with serving the lowest common denominator, which is *thought* to be alien to the ideal of public service broadcasting."[145] As suppositions go, Eaman's seems a safe one, part of a pervasive story casting pioneer Canadian broadcasters as either mercenaries or hopeful utopians. Yet it is difficult to tell who was doing all this associating, identifying, and thinking in the past as broadcasters otherwise kept themselves quite busy. Spending too much time noticing that commercial broadcasters promoted their sponsored material and public broadcasters trumpeted their unconventional productions might keep historians from noticing how all of them viewed the public, or publics, they served. Eaman went on to define cultural democracy sharply, as a system that reserves for the public the right to "decide priorities in those areas of cultural creation where its resources provide economic means for production and distribution." This definition borrows from a common understanding of political democracy and suggests that boosting audience input or polling would make public broadcasting more democratic. While Eaman acknowledges that it has always been impractical for listeners to be directly and intimately involved with the selection of programming, he dismisses the defenders of minority tastes as "opponents of cultural democracy."[146] The historical record begs to differ.

In the various communications media that accompanied modernity, direct democracy – with all citizens voting on the output of
presses, broadcasting stations, or news operations – could not be
practical. John Keane saw this pattern already set by the eighteenth
century, noting: "in large-scale societies *representative* mechanisms in
the field of communications cannot be bypassed, so that some will
necessarily communicate on behalf of others, if only for a time." Such
arrangements tend to endure, however, and the danger of "irrespon-
sible or unaccountable communication" loomed larger.[147] As societies and their modes of communication became more complex, those
complexities needed to be acknowledged, and broadcasting looked
to be a "great democratizer." As communications historian Paddy
Scannell contends: "The fundamentally democratic thrust of broadcasting lay in the new kind of access to virtually the whole spectrum
of public life that radio first, and later television, made available to
all. By placing political, religious, civic, cultural events and entertainments in a common domain, public life was equalized in a way that
had never before been possible."[148] It followed that broadcasters of
all types would want to engage as many listeners as they could in
offering access to ceremonies, speeches, and concerts. However, pursuing big audiences was not the only way broadcasters could serve
listeners or satisfy their democratic impulses. In Canada, programs
like topical talks, for example, hardly likely to pull in the crowds,
allowed C B C producers "to embrace democratic principles at home,
with radio playing an important role. By presenting a diversity of
opinion through open discussion, the medium could serve as both an
instrument and example of democracy."[149] Even outside Canada,
and outside the realm of programs that were explicitly about citizens'
rights and obligations, the resonance between broadcasting and
democracy for listeners of all ages and backgrounds was plain.[150]

In 1949, W.M. Haugan, an official with the Canadian government's Citizenship Branch, offered his perspective on cultural democracy. His advice had mainly to do with embracing the diversity
represented in the postwar flood of immigrants, who would in time
recognize that they were no longer in their homelands. It would be
foolish to force new arrivals to conform to codes of behaviour established by the majority, Haugan writes, because that sort of coercion
was simply undemocratic and would abort the "unity of purpose
and mutual respect" so venerated during the postwar reconstruction
era.[151] In advocating a cautiously pluralist society, Haugan transmits

a powerful message: practising democracy is an imprecise activity, and newcomers/minorities would adjust to their new and evolving surroundings best if their traditions and preferences were respected. Likewise, in broadcasting, the CBC championed minority audiences because it could not pretend to be sure of the shifting tastes of the majority and because keeping listeners engaged could mean a stronger Canadian entertainment and artistic scene. In modelling the democratic society via talks and public affairs programming, and producing entertainment for minority audiences, Canadian public broadcasters and their allies straddled two worlds. They resembled transplanted American art educator Walter Abell, who was "simultaneously a cultural radical and a member of the cultural elite." Abell's complaints about the concentration of wealth and power might have marked him as a political democrat (if not a democratic socialist), but he also courted art patrons whose tastes ran to work that was neither populist nor budget-friendly.[152] Broadcasters, however they chose to ply their trade, were artists *and* patrons. At the CBC, producers, performers, and management took into account listeners who were accustomed – via commercial programming over the CBC and elsewhere – to being patronized more covertly. These public broadcasters practised cultural democracy but struggled to convince many that they were doing so.

While "giving the public what it wants" gained currency as an all-purpose creed for commercial broadcasters, public broadcasters had to challenge the default populist view of what was in the public interest. Again, talks were one area in which public broadcasters could defend their democratic credentials. Presenting current issues via expert lectures or panel programs constituted part of broadcasters' duty to listeners in a democratic society, and the CBC pushed in that direction immediately upon its incorporation, with some success. While she considered broadcasting to be a "rival of the pleasant evenings at home," Nellie McClung also declared that "'The Radio' belongs to us all, and [t]he great University of the Air is open for any one who will enroll."[153] Visiting some colleagues at NBC and CBS in 1938, the CBC's Roy Dunlop told his hosts: "while some of our talks did not appeal to the majority of listeners, we tried to build them and vary them in such a way that the majority of listeners could hear authoritative talks on topics of genuine interest to them."[154] Wartime's drumbeating for democracy limited the time available for the corporation's examinations of the topical and the timeless, but even during the war the CBC could report, based on listener response and expert opinion, that "the despised 'talk' ha[d] grown in importance and won greater appreciation among listeners."[155] The postwar period saw the CBC returning to earnest and sometimes bracingly frank discussions, and forum programs maintained the momentum they had acquired during the war, emphasizing civic responsibility and participation as core democratic values.[156] Certainly program producers still chose the show topics and prepared the programs, but the results were hardly anodyne or irrelevant to the lives of listeners. Putting these shows out carried considerable risk during a period when returning to normal patterns of life and leisure seemed the best antidote to stress. In support of a CBC series on psychological problems, a listener from Toronto wrote that such programming helped to "strengthen democracy by strengthening its basis, an alert and well informed, intelligent populace."[157] In contrast, playing "safe," as historian Arthur Lower said commercial stations had done to avoid revenue-jeopardizing controversy, seemed like a shackling of free thought.[158]

The extent to which any broadcast outlet could be seen to control its own programming (or the programming of others) also affected its credibility as democratic. Among broadcasters, one's relationship to the means of production (owner-operator or operator in the public trust) played a significant role in determining how these outlets approached the question of control over programming. Private broadcasters resented the regulations the CBC could use to trammel their plans, and the CBC defended its regulatory role as vital to listener "welfare." Commercial operators contended that the radio marketplace could and should be less restricted than it was. The CBC's decision makers were too wary of being labelled as eager monopolists to do much more than alter their own schedules to include minority programming. The question of control was a live one outside of broadcasting as well. Paul Litt's history of the Royal Commission on National Development in the Arts, Letters and Sciences during the late 1940s and early 1950s tells the story of a commission "unwilling to debase high culture in order to popularize it, but neither would they [the commissioners] force it down people's throats. In the end, their liberal democratic consciences ensured that their elitist dream of edifying the masses would never be realized."[159] This interpretation applies to broadcasting as readily as it does to ballet or sculpture. Litt points out a paradox that escaped critics of public broadcasting, who continued to behave as though elitism was the whole story and that any amount of minority programming would erode the "natural" or "popular" order. The CBC's efforts to produce unsponsored programming or regulate some aspects of commercial stations' activities were not directed at creating or consolidating a monopoly. The good ship monopoly had in fact sailed when Parliament declined to nationalize privately owned stations in 1932, and Gladstone Murray made it clear in his testimony to Parliament that the CBC could not impose its will on private stations.[160] Broadcasters of all stripes became adept, over time, at arguing that *control* was what their competitors sought or had already attained.

To label the CBC as a controlling force, the image of a horde of bureaucrats aiming to stifle a lively broadcasting business seemed to serve well. When the Canadian Radio League advocated a national system in 1931 "as a way of raising the level of public entertainment," it was careful to note: "this does not mean that the best foreign and American programmes would be excluded – Rather it would ensure that all listeners could hear them."[161] However, CPR publicity officer Murray Gibbon damned this vision of public broadcasting, declaring that any prospective public broadcasting authority had better not overstep the bounds the government's own appointees had set: "If the advocates of Government monopoly of radio broadcasting in Canada hope to monopolize the attention of Canadian radio listeners, they will have to secure a much larger subsidy for talent than is allowed for in the recommendations of the Aird Commission."[162] The implication here was that "subsidies" for talent were artificial – state meddling – and that more traditional commercial methods respected the spirit of competition. More than fifteen years later, when the CBC had been in operation for a decade, Gibbon's fears seemed to have been realized. Political pundit Austin Cross accused the CBC and its parliamentary overlords of having developed "Star Chamber methods" that distorted an otherwise promising broadcasting marketplace. The editorial cartoon accompanying Cross's magazine piece portrayed C.D. Howe, the minister responsible for broadcasting, as a trick rider unable to control his most dangerous mount, Canadian Radio, because, as Cross suggested, the animal had been fed for too long at the public trough.[163] Effectively in tandem with independent commentators like Cross, the CAB's long-developing strategy sought to equate regulation of the broadcasting business with denial of free speech, trading heavily on the idea that a station was notionally the same as a printing press. If that part of its case seemed too high-flown for listeners, the CAB more plainly identified its rival with the decline of Canada, judging "public control" to have failed in its effort to represent Canada internationally and at home: "the CBC monopoly of experts and elites stifles Canadian nationality, contributing to the very problem it was trying to eradicate."[164] With television already reaching many Canadian homes in the mid-1950s, commercial broadcasting interests were still arguing along freedom of speech lines as they sought a freer hand in creating networks. They continued to denounce minority programming as elitist and/or targeted at one segment of the audience, excluding others.[165] This sort of targeting, however, had always been the basis of effective advertising on radio. To make their investments in broadcasting pay, sponsors relied on suppositions about who was listening to which programs.

Public broadcasters and their allies fired back and accused sponsors of cultivating a "deceptive air of disinterestedness" and of exerting control over the industry by defining what the public wants through their selective patronage,[166] which tailored programming to serve their own interests. American broadcasting had shown that commercial firms and networks exerted at least as much power as cultural elites, resulting in some concern that a radio trust comprising sponsors and station owners could be as formidable an antidemocratic force as any potential state monopoly.[167] By the mid-1930s, Graham Spry could lament what he considered corporate control over the CRBC, and he cited the scarcity of frequencies available as the main difference between broadcasting and a free, democratic press. To Spry, William Aberhart, Alberta Social Credit's chief evangelist, had "practically turned the Province of Alberta inside out by using the radio, and he can keep anyone who doesn't agree with him off that radio station, of which he has a monopoly. I can start a newspaper opposing that man but I can't start a radio station to oppose him."[168] It took capital to acquire and run a broadcasting station, and early in its mandate, the CBC justified its policy against the formation of private networks on the basis that it prevented the wealthy, who already had friends (or employees) in the press, from getting even wider airings for their views.[169] In response to a postwar CAB campaign equating regulation with monopoly, Vancouver journalist Jack Scott did all but call private station owners a cartel and accused them of misleading listeners who "are understandably less concerned about competition than what comes out of our loud-speakers."[170] Like many of his contemporaries, Davidson Dunton cast the disinterested individual – citizen and listener – as the foundation of democracy, but he insisted that broadcasting authorities must be vigilant against concentration of ownership and conformity, "with no one taste or opinion having domination."[171] An otherwise free-enterprise-oriented reader later reminded the editors of *Saturday Night* magazine that commercial broadcasting was different from the magazine business because advertising and the desire to sell "every news spot, even the announcement of the time of day," had permeated radio in a way that print had resisted.[172]

Despite their interpretation of broadcasting as a close cousin to the print media, where ownership of a printing press likewise granted a "voice" in the community, commercial broadcasters claimed that their long-term programming strategies and daily program selections were eminently democratic. Locally operated, yet attuned to the nation's needs and "serving its only master, the listening public," the privately held station could be "a bulwark for freedom and democracy."[173] Selling the impression that commercial stations were fulfilling a kind of covenant with listeners and not simply serving those paying the bills was perhaps the most difficult advertising campaign they would undertake. J.R. Radford, who worked during his career in both public and private broadcasting, saw the private stations as a local trust and as plausibly democratic when they carried out these local responsibilities. However, he viewed commercial stations' quest to form networks and the practice of absentee licence-holding as a perversion of their appropriate role. Radford was particularly concerned, along with his CBC colleagues during the war, with the danger of some private broadcasters exploiting war-related events and programming for commercial gain.[174] The usual pressure to make broadcasting pay was one thing, but the potential for commercial broadcasters to aid demagogues was another. Just as Graham Spry worried about Aberhart, exiled Canadian author/critic Merrill Denison reasoned that the same people who "manufactured" soap operas could be persuaded or coerced into more sinister manipulations. "One cannot help wondering," he writes, "what would happen were the same technics used to serve political ends."[175] Denison likely overestimated the capacity of listeners to be brainwashed, but he was expressing a common belief that broadcasting needed to restrain itself and to be examined with a critical eye. For Gladstone

Murray, there was no danger in sticking to less controversial topics and putting on shows of varying gravity, tone, and ambition. As he told an American audience: "radio in the modern democratic state should assume the role of a Ministry of the Arts."[176]

Some listeners bridled at the suggestion that minority audiences needed to be served or that broadcasting should be overseen in the interest of assuring varied programming. A concerned correspondent from Fort Saskatchewan, Alberta, wrote to CBC host John Fisher denouncing a program Fisher had done on Canadian literature for children and claiming: "We would be far better off as Canadians if there were more like me, working to get the supply of goods and services caught up to the demand, and fewer like you, spending their time roaming the country on the taxpayer's money."[177] To this man, any efforts beyond hewing wood and drawing water were wasted, especially when he, the taxpayer/citizen, had not consented to making them. His role in democracy ended at the polling place, and the results he expected from his vote were to be tangible and immediate. Contributing to cultural democracy, however, meant more than satisfying listeners like that practical fellow. It meant understanding how programs like a broadcast about the Antigonish Turkey Pool would not only "brighten the life of the farmer's daughter" but bring an entirely new (though still mediated or curated) experience to listeners who were not expecting it.[178] Private broadcasters stuck to their guns, having the advantage of portraying the programming market as an organic force and the CBC as full of would-be social engineers who purported to care about listeners in remote regions and daytime listeners. Contrary to the widely held conception of the CBC as an institution concerned only about remaking listeners in the image of its middle- and upper-class staff, the corporation did more to cater to the programming needs of all Canadians than private stations could, or would.

Early in the 1930s, Graham Spry insisted that the way broadcasting worked on the North American continent could not be democratic as long as commercial interests who "cannot be chastened" were in control.[179] "Giving the public what it wants" was profitable from the beginning, and commercial broadcasters were wise to exploit that strategy. However, it was not as equitable or responsive as it sounded because it was based on broadcasters' self-interested suppositions about listeners and their inner lives. In the late 1940s, Davidson Dunton suggested that it would certainly be more convenient if people had predictable and uniform tastes, but he concluded that we don't live in that sort of world and that chasing high ratings would only confine the horizons of listeners to the spectacular and the sensational, at the expense of "other things."[180] Assuming that listeners share a median taste that can be identified and effectively satisfied seems plainly anti-democratic. Scannell writes that programming needs to be both for anyone (a general audience) and for someone (the individual listener or viewer) but, more importantly, he warns: "those whose beliefs, thoughts and feelings are publicly denied or suppressed or ignored are not persons: they are not allowed to be themselves."[181] If the broadcasting industry doesn't serve taste minorities some of the time, it is not a democratic space. Totalitarian states like North Korea run repressive broadcasting systems, and we readily and rightly see this as a denial of democracy. Yet we say nothing when content is chosen by a handful of program directors or when it converges on one type of sponsor-friendly fare, be this easy listening or "reality" programming. While it was not necessary or practical for listeners to construct their own broadcasting environment by running community stations,[182] listeners needed to be treated as more than "the public," more than a commodity. The CBC's programming policy was often blatantly nationalist and appeared disdainful of mass entertainments, but it also left listeners to recognize their own tastes by allowing them, as often as could be managed, to float free of a rigged market.

Conclusion

Broadcasting's past, like the past of any other human activity, was a series of moments in which people acted upon and reacted to their present circumstances, sometimes revealing their thoughts or interests. Looking back at what broadcasters and others did or said as they met radio's unfolding present with confidence, anxiety, and everything in between is to look back at people who had more than serving listeners in mind. Broadcasters and listeners alike may not have spent much time describing, as David Cleghorn Thomson did, how *Radio Is Changing Us*,[1] but they could see that broadcasting was not just a fad. Radio's path to a generation or so of dominance led through contested territory, and its history and legacy are still contested because the debate over broadcasting policy remains rooted in opposing, or at least discordant, worldviews. Broadcasting is a complicated and historically rooted activity, involving conflicting impulses and encompassing everything from wholesome family listening to corporate mergers to *War of the Worlds* panic. As I've tried to show in this study of programming and taste, radio changed us, but we changed radio.

When historians address what (or who) made a difference anywhere or anytime in the past, we often point to powerful or strong-willed individuals, governments, movements, or corporations as catalysts. Factors like class position, religious affiliation, or even the combined actions of the apparently weak also frequently play a role in our interpretations. Abstractions like taste or democracy need to take their rightful place, especially when we write the history of a medium like radio, with its unseen but readily acknowledged capacity to soothe, to stimulate, or to motivate people en masse. Programming often included vital information about local or world events, but what broadcasters did to keep listeners entertained was also revealing. In preparing their entertaining or informative programming, broadcasters anywhere could claim to have a decent grasp of what listeners wanted or needed, but broadcasters' sense of what to put on the air also depended on such variables as: their financial stake in the station, their location, the availability and cost of talent, the ease of getting recorded programs, advertisers' patience, regulators' judgments, the political climate, and past attempts at making shows that listeners might "invite" back into their homes. As we've seen in the previous chapters, there was a whole system operating behind the scenes as audiences large and small consumed programs, and until now we have paid scant attention to the linkages between this backstage action, what listeners got, and what it all meant.

During radio's "golden age," broadcasting in Canada was plainly entangled with historical realities like war, political divisions, and economic cycles. This really wasn't much of a surprise. Near the tail end of that period, economic historian Harold Innis reminded us that such entanglements had been the pattern for communications media long before electronic technologies of transmission emerged. The radio era, however, marked a decisive victory for what Innis called space-biased (widely and quickly available, but less permanent) media,[2] and this was a notable historical departure. Recurring programs drew listeners, becoming intangible – but eminently exploitable – venues for advertising, entertainment, information, and taste-making. In all its forms, radio served the public by delivering something, *anything*. Station owners took the programs they could get from a variety of sources and, when possible, produced their own. While broadcasters used existing taste categories to describe and plan their programming, it's important to note that broadcasts differed markedly from books, magazines, newspapers, and recorded music, which were consumed at a discrete and visible cost and had to be transported. Live performances and films required their audiences to go somewhere. Radio (the technology) enabled broadcasting (the activity) to transcend these constraints, and the "spell" some thought it cast on listeners sparked considerable debate about programming and the uses to which programs might be put by advertisers, demagogues, or any other busybodies with access to a transmitter. Broadcasting's emergence and growth occurred as the world recovered from one war fought to make the world safe for democracy and slid slowly towards another in which broadcasting would figure prominently. Peacetime and wartime concerns about freedom of choice, the role of the market, and protection for minorities echoed through the contest over programming and in whose interest it would be made.

As American networks cornered talent and promoted their shows vigorously beyond the US border, Canada's public broadcaster attempted to use its programming to represent Canada at home and abroad and to "round out" the broadcast schedule. Working out what made it to air in Canada may have seemed like a simple contest between competing aesthetic visions, but it was more. About fifty years ago, Austin Weir wrote of the "Struggle for National Broadcasting," telling a story of qualified triumph. The triumph, for Weir and his colleagues at the CBC, was establishing a public broadcasting institution on a continent where commercial broadcasters reigned. The CBC's struggle to take root and flourish also entailed compromise. Modern public institutions, especially those in the cultural field, must be seen to be "paying their way," and the CBC in its radio days had to supplement revenue from receiving licences with the proceeds from advertising. Having to schedule programs without knowing exactly what listeners will make of them is an uncertain proposition at best, but it is one that was well suited to an organization whose goals did not demand the kind of certainty wholly commercial enterprises prefer. The CBC's only ostensible job was to bring programs from Canada (and elsewhere) to Canadians, regardless of where they lived or how reliably they could be counted on to buy advertised products.

The corporation also fulfilled less obvious roles. Its staff grappled with the intimate power of broadcasting, maintained relationships with American and British broadcasters, regulated the airwaves, affected (and effected) musical tastes, and tried to bring the public a variety of shows. These activities reminded us, decades later, that programs are not heard and forgotten but resound across the aural landscape in our communities and nations. A culturally democratic view of broadcasting would prove incapable of treating programs as commodities without artistic, psychological, or even political weight. We expect, as Peter Dahlgren suggests, that "media culture generally, with its emphasis on consumption and entertainment, has undercut the kind of public culture needed for a healthy democracy."[3] Historically, broadcasters interested primarily in turning a profit have not prioritized the building of a robust public culture, nor do we expect them to fritter away their capital on such self-defeating behaviour. In contrast, public broadcasters and their supporters treated broadcasting policies and strategies as crucial to life away from the radio set. For them, embracing entertainment and exposing listeners to the unfamiliar were *complementary* actions. In looking at the same period from various angles, the foregoing discussion depicts this other struggle: the effort to anticipate and serve listeners' needs while still accounting for contemporary values and, above all, giving even tiny audiences what they might want, if only for a half hour every second Thursday.

At the outset, I supply a few "central questions" to help highlight some of the major themes that emerge as my research progresses. The aim is also to emphasize how quickly and deeply radio pervaded its historical environment. People shifted within the space of a few years from other leisure or work activities to spending part of the day, usually at home but not always, listening with varying levels of attention to programs. The boom in station building reflected this quick expansion. The early broadcast era represented a revolution in media, but we can also see how established media, social, business, and aesthetic patterns came in to play. Let's revisit those questions in the light of the evidence I've been presenting.

First, how did broadcasters allow for audience tastes as shows were planned, produced, and scheduled? As they gained experience making programs, broadcasters gained confidence in their ability to categorize and subdivide the listening public into discrete audiences. They could, in the case of music programming, point to interest in various types of music as reflecting Canadians' collective radio preferences. Dance music had "worked" to bring enough patrons to the dance halls, and broadcasters presumed it would work on the air, so it appeared in broadcast schedules, regardless of what else a station wanted to put out. Evenings were a time for family oriented radio fare, and broadcasters produced and scheduled their variety shows to suit that pattern. Female-oriented programming, to the extent that it could be said to dominate, dominated the daytime, when broadcasters assumed their audiences were largely composed of women. Much of the well known American programming made a splash because, even though Canadian broadcasters rarely had the resources to gather data about what listeners liked, the publicity attending the big network shows and stars guaranteed that at least one station in each main radio market would see the sense in relaying them. The people who planned and produced programs could not stray too far from older aesthetic categories because the question of who might listen always came up, and the novelty or appeal of a new program had to be expressed in terms of existing ones. The imprecision of gauging where the listener might want to go in the future meant that most broadcasters could not afford to make grand gestures or take bold steps into uncharted programming territory. In making their own deliberate gestures and taking their own tentative steps, CBC programming staff were an exception to this common practice, but they remained more cautious than we might suppose, and more cautious than we might expect of an out-of-touch "elitist" institution. The corporation's stations carried their share of mainstream programs as part of their commitment to serve listeners, but they also produced and scheduled riskier material as the *other* part of that commitment. Service could come with a smile – and a nudge.

Next, did influences from elsewhere make much difference? The examples of the more mature US and British broadcasting industries provided daily guidance and daily cautionary tales for Canadian broadcasters. Canadians became familiar with performers and show formats from these other places, but sustained or direct external control would not fly in an age of waxing nationalism and waning empire. To import programs wholesale from these places might have been technologically possible, but in practice commercial stations and the CRBC / CBC needed to produce their own material to serve local/regional/national listeners. The output of American networks and individual stations arrived unbidden, but Canadian listeners generally welcomed it as familiar enough to become part of their radio routine. This familiarity presented a problem for cultural "protectionists," but it was the foil they needed to argue that producing more Canadian programming to accompany the ubiquitous and undeniably entertaining American stuff was the best way forward. The CBC, for its part, had to nurture Canadian talent where it could while continuing to operate alongside, and stay on good trading terms with, the various programming sources in a formidable American broadcasting industry. The relentless showmanship and commercial opportunism that went along with the American style of broadcasting did not always play well in Canada, though these qualities effectively masked its cultural limitations. Shackled to advertising, the American model tended to discourage experimentation, favouring the types of entertainment that were already in production and generated enough interest to meet profit margins.

Public broadcasters in Canada envied the BBC's reach and generally welcomed its assistance in establishing programs that would set Canada apart from the dominant North American commercial pattern. Commercial broadcasters in Canada, unlike those in the United Kingdom that reached their audiences from the European continent, maintained a cordial relationship with the BBC because they occasionally bought its programs, but they did not benefit from its aid. Structurally, Canada's public broadcasting entities could not duplicate the BBC's control, and, in terms of producing programs, the costs of becoming North America's BBC were prohibitive. The most important influence the BBC exerted was in advising the CBC to become the sort of public broadcasting organization that its historical baggage and surroundings would allow. The burden of representing the main public service alternative to the prevailing North American way meant that the CBC faced a more difficult set of circumstances than did the BBC and that it had to develop its own manner of reconciling modest cultural ambitions with everyday entertainment and its role as a national broadcaster.

When I ask "Why were certain programs thought to be in 'good taste' or 'bad taste,' and how were these regulated?" I mean to show that taste entailed more than aesthetic preference. Programming and advertising represented the writers, firms, and performers who made it, and these people did not want to court controversy by offending listeners. Making radio programs took ingenuity and a flair for presenting compelling performances or scripts, but it also relied upon broadcasters' readings of existing domestic and social rhythms and norms. As we've seen in the discussion of regulation, broadcasters were generally eager to support free speech, and the timely and well known examples of fascist broadcasting only strengthened that commitment. Yet the problem of speakers or performers who might abuse the collective trust by misleading, disturbing, or even defrauding listeners raised genuine concern. While in theory they had considerable power over station licensing and could compel broadcasters to adhere to their rulings, regulators at the CBC did not fashion new codes of morality to accompany the radio age. What had been "in bad taste" before broadcasting came along remained so, though the reach and widespread acceptance of broadcasting pushed regulators to act quickly in defence of community standards. The intimacy of broadcasting came into play here as regulators and program makers applied the standards of personal conversation in "mixed company" to decide what sort of speech would be appropriate for thousands of people to hear at the same time. Commercial broadcasters were most attuned to what broadcasting controversial material would do to their bottom lines, and public broadcasters despaired of the good-will they might squander if they appeared to flout the sensibilities of licence-fee-paying citizens, many of whom had been conditioned to resent "government" broadcasting. Whenever vigilant listeners per-ceived a program to be offensive and wrote letters of protest (usually to the CBC), both the CBC and commercial stations had to weigh their options. In some cases, upcoming programs could be altered, in others, stricter enforcement or bans could be threatened or enforced. Because the Canadian broadcasting industry was not composed of wealthy individual stations or a national broadcaster flush with money, regulation brought warnings and awkward cooperation far more often that it brought definitive bans or legal action.

How did differing notions of "what the public wants" relate to programming strategies and choices? In the final chapter, I spend considerable time on this notion because it was so central to the identity of commercial broadcasters, whose interests ideally suited linking listeners and advertisers through "tried-and-true" forms of entertainment. Commercial broadcasters assumed that they some-how innately understood and continued to serve the popular will. In contrast, public broadcasters struggled to recognize that most listen-ers were not much like them, and they tended to provide radio pro-grams that were more challenging and more plainly didactic because that was the sort of thing they wanted to hear. Today, public broad-casters, in English Canada at least, continue to face a "legitimation crisis," perhaps because they have failed, just as Michael Bérubé says practitioners of cultural studies have failed, to ask themselves: "What ... actively makes sense to people whose beliefs you do not share?"[4] In the end, whose beliefs, tastes, and patterns of cultural consumption are going to converge so neatly as to enable any broad-caster to supply exactly what's needed? The listening public divided itself up daily, and not always along predictable lines. Davidson Dunton's idea of multiple publics acknowledges, and operates from, the idea that people are gloriously fickle. This was not at all the sort of admission that suited radio as a business, so commercial broad-casters and their allies accused the CBC of ignoring the common radio listener in favour of the highbrow, and it worked. This strategy echoed the sort of mid-twentieth-century populist shift Michael Kammen sees in the United States, a shift embodied in a contrast between the "taste levels people felt most comfortable being identified with (*not* high) and the cultural aspirations conveyed by critics for the society as a whole (upward)."[5] When examining a broadcasting environment that rewarded the cultivation of mass audiences, my assertion that public broadcasters' attempts to diversify programming were culturally democratic might initially seem misguided, looking at first like an *anti*-democratic defence of unconventional tastes against the "popular." However, please consider how much guesswork went into making programs in both the private and public broadcasting sectors. Broadcasters had to make shows in advance, and they had to make them based on their perceptions of listeners' desires. These advance perceptions were prone to be interpreted in terms of programming that broadcasters already knew how to make and knew how to categorize. The CBC's preservation of less "popular" fare and the introduction of new programming initiatives were in this way more culturally democratic than was selling pre-packaged audiences to advertisers.

Public broadcasters also followed a culturally democratic path in that they rejected the notion that radio operated like the efficient marketplace commercial broadcasters assured everyone it was, yet public broadcasters also attempted to serve the public *within* the existing industry, providing "the hits" as well as distinctive or aspirational programs for smaller audiences. Despite the existence of ratings, surveys, and letters of praise or condemnation, these reports from the past need to be regarded with caution. We can't *know* what listeners liked, at least not in the way that we can know what broadcasters said or wrote about their attempts to serve audiences. While many listeners responded warmly to commercial programming, historians should be careful of falling into the same trap the commercial broadcasters did – equating what scored well in ratings with "what the public wanted." Ratings served to rank what was broadcast in a given region – effective for selling ad spots – but ratings could never reveal who *wasn't* getting programming they appreciated. Ratings agencies never asked *what else* listeners might want. Put a burger up against quiche on a menu, then track diners' choices. You'll get measurable results, but you won't know if people chose quiche over burger because they found exactly what they wanted or because pan-fried pickerel or any number of other choices never appeared on the menu. Fewer choices make matters simpler, but they hardly reflect the range of tastes "out there." Listeners spent money on advertised products, and there can be little doubt that they appreciated what they got on the radio. The affirmation of even tiny purchases multiplied by thousands of listener-customers became cultural privilege that started to look genuine when broadcasters went back to the same wells of talent and genre to keep up their audiences. Broadcasting was, in Gladstone Murray's words, "fashioned as we go along," and what it was fashioned into was an industry in which commercial broadcasters could more easily (but no more justifiably) claim to know the public will.

The history of broadcast programming also reminds us how, even in the earliest stages of a medium's development, old habits and assumptions can limit the pace and direction of cultural change. Radio and radio programs were plainly new arrivals during the first half of the twentieth century, but they took up and adapted existing forms of entertainment, along with existing categories and codes of taste and conduct. Paradoxically, in the fast-moving radio field, programming had to be new, but it had to be familiar. Commercial stations in North America thrived on familiarity, leaving public broadcasters looking, in comparison, like insurgent prigs bent on ending the party. Public broadcasters advertised their intentions ineffectively, failing to show listeners that broadcasting could be eminently democratic when its priority was simply to represent a wider range of tastes and moods. The cost of maintaining a public broadcasting entity has always been a matter of public record, another strategic disadvantage for the CBC and organizations like it. Commercial broadcasters proved particularly adept at establishing their brand of "truth" by repeating the line that sponsored programming came to listeners at no financial cost. We can rest assured, however, that advertisers folded the cost of broadcast advertising into the price of each advertised product. Presumably, intrepid historians of business and fiscal policy could also tell us whether advertisers also claimed advertising costs against their reported revenues at tax time.

The broader history of broadcasting has shown that programs have power to influence everything from public policy to the pop charts. In societies subscribing to democratic principles, broadcasting stations, networks, and personalities do not stand for election or precipitate financial crises, so they appear to occupy less prominent and potent positions than do politicians or captains of industry. For most broadcasters, discussing the fact that they *control* what listeners or viewers get has always been unappealing. Better to play the messenger, the impresario, or the public servant bringing the world to everyone's radio or TV than to draw attention to the continuous and necessarily arbitrary curation that broadcasters, artists, and even advertisers perform. Broadcasters construct programs according to their own tastes, and they imagine what their target audiences or "the public" as a whole might appreciate. Since they cannot predict how gullibly or sceptically listeners will take up or use any program, broadcasters have to operate on the premise that their output stands on its own, to be used as the manufacturer intended. Radio listeners, television viewers, and consumers of cultural products in general are hardly a uniformly passive lot. Subversive readings happen, and cataloguing the ways in which listeners could and did use these things differently is valuable. However, this book draws its evidence from the production side, where it is plain that broadcasters could only imagine or plan for a limited range of listening outcomes, namely: continued interest in a program, tuning in something else, or switching off altogether. Listeners were not present in the studio giving their opinions, and this was both one of broadcasting's greatest strengths and one of its greatest weaknesses.

Radio's power to conquer time and space brings us back briefly to Innis, especially to the notion that time- and space-biased media are vastly different or mutually exclusive. Some programs are made to be transmitted and to fade in the moment, leaving satisfaction and the bankable likelihood that listeners will return. Other programs are made to endure, instilling an appetite (their creators fondly hope) to appreciate, evaluate, and choose one's entertainment as well as one's social and cultural surroundings. The way that broadcasters in Canada did their jobs and thought about the listening experience indicates that, in radio (and by extension in other media), these differences or apparent exclusions are not so hard and fast – a broadcaster need not dwell on one side or the other of Innis's time-space divide. Taken as a whole, Canadian broadcasting during radio's era of dominance had it both ways: churning out hours of "space-biased" variety shows, soap operas, and light music, and leavening those indispensible hours with likewise indispensible "time-biased" alternative programming. The result was an overall radio slate that gave listeners more leeway than they knew they had, and more leeway than we acknowledge when we moralize about which sorts of programming were good or bad or about which broadcasters were pandering and which were patronizing.

Because it took place during a period when various large- and small-scale modernist experiments were under way around the world, any history of broadcast programming should remind us of a couple of basic modern questions – questions that themselves have a great deal to do with who holds cultural power in "democratic" societies: Can we deliberately alter our living or working conditions, or our leisure experiences? Are we inclined to interpret "the way things are" as predestined or somehow natural and to see challenges to established norms as artificial or unwarranted? Our responses might well be primarily conditioned by how we view the legitimacy of any society's status quo. If we see the possession of political or cultural power as a sign that those with power must have justifiably won the approval of most people, we are likely to reject ambitious schemes to question the way things are, especially when such schemes appear to be imposed by unelected bodies like a public broadcasting organization pushing opera, or the staff of federal research institutes telling us the cod are all gone or the oilsands are more trouble than they're worth. If we see political or cultural power as held by people or organizations whose assets or influence have enabled them to consolidate and perpetuate their hold on power, we are likely to seek ways to dismantle or at least provide a counterpoint to the hegemony enjoyed by those at the controls. In essence, while we may think much depends on the choices we make, even more depends on knowing about the range of choices we have available to us. In the case we've followed through the foregoing chapters, control resided with broadcasters at the centre of the whole struggle over radio programming. Attempts to do something else with programming other than putting hotel orchestras behind a microphone prompted accusations of meddling with what the public wanted to hear, and those accusations have echoed loudly ever since.

From the interwar through the early postwar years, broadcasting found a place in most Canadians' daily lives. For broadcasters, there was much to be worked out, to be managed and balanced as broadcasting grew to become the frequent companion of individual listeners and the frequent focus of family time. Listeners also became familiar with the programs that filled their listening time and learned rather quickly to distinguish between what they liked immediately, what they could ignore, and what might rate some attention later. Commercial broadcasters worked feverishly to discern what they should do next for identifiable audiences, in effect unable to acknowledge that individual listeners were making these choices. Public broadcasters could afford to be somewhat more sensitive to diversity among listeners, but neither group could provide the sublime listening experience that marked a true communion between producer and consumer. Television arrived in the 1950s, and from the late 1970s onward, neoliberal thought and policies transformed the world – media included – so that now we slip rather easily into justifying programming in terms of its exchange value in multiple markets, in syndication, in translation. Most recently, the arrival of hundreds of channels and an expanding universe of online options for audio, video, and textual communication might lead us to infer that enough diversity exists, that public broadcasting is irrelevant or unnecessary, or to infer that standards have fallen badly and to dismiss commercial broadcasting as a cesspool. Neither conclusion seems warranted.

For about a decade, the elephant in my writing room has been the defunding of – and existential angst surrounding – the CBC. As its allocated budgets have been cut in the name of efficiency, the corporation's defenders and detractors regularly shout at each other in the comments sections of various newspapers and websites, and sometimes even on the air. Each group looks at broadcasting through lenses ground over nearly a century and tempered by diverging ideologies. Such debates are part of life in a liberal democracy. While we may now have an embarrassment of riches when it comes to the number of media sources to which we have access, the stakes remain as high as they were in the early 1930s. The decisions taken and habits developed in Canadian broadcasting's early days continue to be relevant wherever commercial and public systems co-exist, and they remind us of broadcasting's fundamental promise: entertainment and information for all. Consolidating control over broadcasting by acquiring or sidelining one's rivals, expecting broadcasting to reflect generic or carefully focus-grouped tastes and interests, invoking the sainted taxpayer as the sovereign authority, or pretending that what's "popular" somehow organically emerged from "the people" have always been activities that diminish our hopes for cultural democracy. The struggle continues.

Notes

INTRODUCTION

1 "Popular" is a particularly loaded term. It implies that the material broadcast somehow emerged spontaneously from listeners themselves as an expression of what they would like to hear. I use the term sparingly here, most often to mean material that drew large audiences, and most often between double quotation marks to remind readers to examine the idea critically. What became "popular" frequently became so because of excellent distribution. For an unorthodox take on popularity and triviality, see Dahlhaus, "Trivialmusik," 335–6.

2 Nineteenth-century English school inspector, poet, and literary critic Matthew Arnold (1822–88) is often identified with "high culture" and an uncompromising attitude towards selecting works for one's own consumption. His *Essays in Criticism* (two parts, various editions starting about 1865) offers an introduction to his thought. Raymond Williams (1921–88) was one of the pioneers in the field of cultural studies and found culture worthy of attention in all contexts, especially in the working-class lives Arnold considered all but devoid of cultural hope. Williams's short essay, "Culture Is Ordinary," is a window on his approach and has been reprinted in various anthologies.

3 While politically wedded to the Rest of Canada and possessing both public and private components, Quebec radio and the francophone broadcasting industry developed along a separate path from the anglophone system discussed in this book. Within the public broadcasting sector, the early trend, in which each linguistic branch of the national network "operated under entirely distinct programme supervision and policy," changed little over time. Quotation from: House of Commons Special Committee on Radio Broadcasting, "Third and Final Report," n.d. [1942], 8, Library

and Archives Canada, Records of the Canadian Broadcasting Corporation, Ottawa (hereafter CBC), vol. 342, file 15-3, pt. 3. See also Raboy, *Missed Opportunities*, 62. On francophone broadcasting, see Luneau, "Radio-Canada et la promotion de la culture francophone (1936–1997)," 112–23; Michel Filion, "Broadcasting and Cultural Identity: The Canadian Experience," 447–67; and Michel Filion, *Radiodiffusion et société distincte*. In comparison to the sort of forced unity that the BBC in Northern Ireland had to maintain, the linguistic division in Canada seems tame. See chapter 3 of McIntosh, *The Force of Culture*. On Newfoundland broadcasting outlets, some of which were absorbed in 1949 by the CBC, see Webb, *The Voice of Newfoundland*.

4 "Re-orientation of Programming in Radio," n.d. [1953], CBC, vol. 161, file 11-1, pt. 1.

5 Skinner, "Divided Loyalties: The Early Development of Canada's 'Single' Broadcasting System," 136–55; Godfrey and Spencer, "Canadian Marconi: CFCF Television From Signal Hill to the Canadian Television Network," 437–55; Vipond, "'Please Stand By for That Report': The Historiography of Early Canadian Radio," 13–32; Nolan, "An Infant Industry: Canadian Private Radio, 1919–36," 496–518; Butsch, "Canada's Broadcasting Pioneers: 1918–1932," 1–26; Godfrey, "Canadian Marconi: CFCF, the Forgotten Case," 56–71.

6 Martyn Estall, "The War Has Changed Things," 1945, 4, Archives of Ontario, CAAE Papers, series B-I, box 3.

7 Eichner, *Agency and Media Reception*, 68.

8 Scannell, *Radio, Television and Modern Life*, 5.

9 G.A., Newton Robinson, Ontario, to "In Reply," 9 May 1956, CBC, vol. 161, file 11-1, pt. 2.

10 W.E. Gladstone Murray, "Broadcasting – Everybody's Business," address to the Canadian Club, Ottawa, 14 January 1942, 3, Library and Archives Canada (hereafter LAC), Neil M. Morrison Papers, vol. 6.

11 Taylor, "Other People's Poison," 269–70.

12 E.P.H. James to J.E. Mason, 28 January 1929, National Broadcasting Company Records, Wisconsin Historical Society Archives, Madison (hereafter NBC), box 4, fol. 33.

13 Napoli, "Revisiting 'Mass Communication' and the 'Work' of the Audience in the New Media Environment," 505–16; Scannell, "Public Service Broadcasting and Modern Public Life," 135–66.

14 McFadden, "'America's Boy Friend Who Can't Get a Date': Gender, Race, and the Cultural Work of the Jack Benny Program, 1932–1946," 114.

15 Scannell, "Public Service Broadcasting: The History of a Concept," 11–29.

16 Klancher, *The Making of English Reading Audiences, 1790–1832*, 8.

17 Waldfogel, *The Tyranny of the Market*, 3.

18 Slotten, *Radio's Hidden Voice*; Steemers, "In Search of a Third Way: Balancing Public Purpose and Commerce in German and British Public Service Broadcasting," 69–87; McChesney, "Graham Spry and the Future of Public Broadcasting: The 1997 Spry Memorial Lecture," 25–47.

19 Briggs, *Serious Pursuits*, 2; McKay, "The Liberal Order Framework: A Prospectus for a Reconnaissance of Canadian History," 621.

20 Lewis, "Referable Words in Radio Drama," 26.

21 Joseph Schull, "What Is Radio Headed For?" *CBC Times*, 11–17 March 1952, 2.

22 Michele Hilmes, "Rethinking Radio," 2.

23 Lears, *Fables of Abundance*, 19.

24 Cardiff, "Time, Money and Culture: BBC Programme Finances, 1927–1939," 374.

25 Peers, *The Politics of Canadian Broadcasting, 1920–1951*; Peers, "The Nationalist Dilemma in Canadian Broadcasting," 252–67; Weir, *The Struggle for National Broadcasting in Canada*; Prang, "The Origins of Public Broadcasting in Canada," 1–31.

26 Jamieson, *The Troubled Air*; Allard, *Straight Up*.

27 Stursberg, *Mister Broadcasting*; Rickwood, "Canadian Broadcasting Policy and the Private Broadcasters: 1936–1968"; Hudson, "The Role of Radio in the Canadian North," 130–9; Godfrey, "Canadian Marconi: CFCF, The Forgotten Case," 56–71; Nolan, "Canadian Election Broadcasting: Political Practices and Radio Regulation, 1919–1939," 175–88; Nolan, "An Infant Industry: Canadian Private Radio, 1919–36," 496–518; Spencer and Bolan, "Election Broadcasting in Canada: A Brief History," 3–38; Babaian, *Radio Communication in Canada: A Historical and Technological Survey*; Parnis, "'Tuning in': The Political Economy of Commercial Radio Broadcasting in Canada."

28 Wilson, *Citizens' Forum*; Bruce, "Women in CBC Radio Talks and Public Affairs," 7–18; Berland, "Cultural Re/percussions: The Social Production of Music Broadcasting in Canada"; Baillargeon, "The CBC and the Cold War Mentality, 1946–1952"; Spencer, "The Social Origins of Broadcasting: Canada, 1919–1945," 96–110; Rothwell, "Andrew Allan, Nathan Cohen, and Mavor Moore: Cultural Nationalism and the Growth of English-Canadian Drama, 1945 to 1960"; Johnston, "The Early Trials of Protestant Radio, 1922–38," 376–402; Klee, "'Hands-Off Labour Forum': The Making and Unmaking of National Working-Class Radio Broadcasting in Canada, 1935–1944," 107–32; Vipond, "Please Stand

By"; Russell Johnston, "The Emergence of Broadcast Advertising in Canada, 1919–1932," 29–47; Webb, "Constructing Community and Consumers: Joseph R. Smallwood's Barrelman Radio Programme," 166–86; Parnis, "Representation, Regulation and Commercial Radio Broadcasting in Canada," 177–91; Vipond, "Desperately Seeking the Audience for Early Canadian Radio," 86–96; Cupido, "The Medium, the Message and the Modern: The Jubilee Broadcast of 1927," 101–23; Vipond, "British or American? Canada's 'Mixed' Broadcasting System in the 1930s," 89–100; Webb, "Who Speaks for the Public? The Debate over Government or Private Broadcasting in Newfoundland, 1939–1949," 74–93; Graham, "Radio Revolution, Classic Concerns: The Development of Canadian Broadcasting, 1927–1936"; Vipond, "The Royal Tour of 1939 as a Media Event," 149–72.

29   Vipond, *Listening In*; Raboy, *Missed Opportunities*. Special mention is due here for Litt's *The Muses, the Masses, and the Massey Commission*, which recognized the importance of broadcasting in determining cultural policy in the early interwar period.

30   Friesen, *Citizens and Nation*, 219.

31   Vipond, "Royal Tour of 1939"; Mary Vipond, "'A Living, Moving Pageant': The CBC's Coverage of the Royal Tour of 1939," 335–50; Potter, "The BBC, the CBC, and the 1939 Royal Tour of Canada," 424–44.

32   Raboy, "Making Media: Creating Conditions for Communication in the Public Good – The 1997 Spry Memorial Lecture," 289–306.

33   Raboy, *Missed Opportunities*, 335.

34   "The Voice of Canada on the Air," *Ottawa Journal*, 6 April 1937; Merrill Denison to Weir, 18 March 1931, LAC, Weir Papers, vol. 2, file 8; Vipond, "Cultural Authority and Canadian Public Broadcasting in the 1930s: Hector Charlesworth and the CRBC," 59–82.

35   Tallents, *The Projection of England*, n.p.; Neulander, *Programming National Identity*.

36   Poulot, "The Changing Roles of Art Museums," 89–118.

37   Smith, "Canadian Culture, the Canadian State, and the New Continentalism," 9; Charles Jennings, "The National System – Programmes," 24 February 1948, CBC, vol. 161, file 11-1, pt. 1.

38   "Some Aspects of Commercial and Public Service Broadcasting," 20 August 1948, British Broadcasting Corporation Written Archives Centre, Caversham, Berkshire (hereafter BBC), E1/489.

39   Spry, "The Origins of Public Broadcasting in Canada: A Comment," 134–41; Gilbert, "'On the Road to New York': The Protective Impulse and the English-Canadian Cultural Identity, 1896–1914," 405–17. On a similar

theme elsewhere, see Mahony, "Memory and Belonging: Irish Writers, Radio, and the Nation," 10–24.

40 Adria, *Technology and Nationalism*.

41 See, for example: Butsch, "Introduction: How Are Media Public Spheres?" 1–14; Glynn, *Tabloid Culture*; Scannell, "For-Anyone-as-Someone Structures," 5–24; Shaw, *Deciding What We Watch*; Monroe Shrum, Jr., *Fringe and Fortune*; Riccio, "Popular Culture and High Culture: Dwight Macdonald, His Critics and the Ideal of Cultural Hierarchy in Modern America," 7–18; Alasuutari, "'I'm Ashamed to Admit It, But I Have Watched Dallas': The Moral Hierarchy of Television Programmes," 561–82.

42 Hilmes, *Network Nations*.

43 McChesney, "The Personal Is Political: The Political Economy of Noncommercial Radio Broadcasting in the United States," 379–87; McChesney, *Rich Media, Poor Democracy*; McChesney, *Telecommunications, Mass Media, and Democracy*; Raboy, *Missed Opportunities*; Lacey, *Listening Publics*, 92–103; Razlogova, *The Listener's Voice*.

44 MacLennan, "Women, Radio Broadcasting and the Depression: A 'Captive' Audience from Household Hints to Story Time and Serials," 616–33; Hendy, *Life on Air*; Craig, "'The More They Listen, the More They Buy': Radio and the Modernizing of Rural America," 1–16; Loviglio, *Radio's Intimate Public*; Doerksen, *American Babel*; Hangen, *Redeeming the Dial Radio, Religion, and Popular Culture in America*; Vipond, "The Beginnings of Public Broadcasting in Canada: The CRBC, 1932–1936," 151–71; Johnson, *The Unseen Voice*.

45 Gurstein, "Taste and 'the Conversible World' in the Eighteenth Century," 203–21; Heesen, *The World in a Box*.

46 Hahn, "Consumer Culture and Advertising," 392–404; Cross and Proctor, *Packaged Pleasures*; Epp, "'Good Bad Stuff': Editing, Advertising, and the Transformation of Genteel Literary Production in the 1890s," 186–205; Gendron, *Between Montmartre and the Mudd Club*.

47 "A Culture for Canada," *Royal Bank of Canada Monthly Letter*, September 1954, 2.

48 Gronow, *The Sociology of Taste*; Gronow, *Caviar with Champagne*.

49 Mennell, "Indigestion in the Long Nineteenth Century: Aspects of English Taste and Anxiety, 1800–1950," 135–58; Potolsky, *The Decadent Republic of Letters*; Castronovo, *Beautiful Democracy*; Ewen and Ewen, *Typecasting*; Swirski, *From Lowbrow to Nobrow*; Kammen, *American Culture, American Tastes*; Bayley, *Taste*; Schwartz, *Vertical Classifications*;

Ohmann, "The Shaping of a Canon: US Fiction, 1960–1975," 202; Gans, *Popular Culture and High Culture*.

50 "What about the CBC?" *Citizenship Items* 8, 5 (1955): 3.

51 G. Hodges to Programme Correspondence, 8 March 1934, BBC, R34/281.

52 Bourdieu, *Distinction*; Prieur and Savage, "On 'Knowingness,' Cosmopolitanism and Busyness as Emerging Forms of Cultural Capital," 307–17; Chan and Goldthorpe, "Social Stratification and Cultural Consumption: Music in England," 1–19.

53 Godfried, "Identity, Power, and Local Television: African Americans, Organized Labor and UHF-TV in Chicago, 1962–1968," 121.

54 Smulyan, "Live from Waikiki: Colonialism, Race, and Radio in Hawaii, 1934–1963," 63–75; Vaillant, "Sounds of Whiteness: Local Radio, Racial Formation, and Public Culture in Chicago, 1921–1935," 25–66; Savage, *Broadcasting Freedom*); Pickering, "The BBC's Kentucky Minstrels: Blackface Entertainment on British Radio," 161–95; Hilmes, "Invisible Men: *Amos 'n' Andy* and the Roots of Broadcast Discourse," 301–21.

55 Pauline Boutal, "National Art Exchange," in the series "Speaking as a Canadian," 13 July 1945; Elizabeth D. Long, Women's Interests, Programme Division, CBC, to W.B. Herbert, 2 March 1946, LAC, Canada Foundation, vol. 25, file 4b.

56 Kuffert, "'Needful Supervision': Talks and Taste on Canadian Radio," 1–15.

CHAPTER ONE

1 *From Sea to Sea/A Mari Usque ad Mare: Canada's Jubilee Radio Broadcast* (Ottawa: National Committee for the Celebration of the Diamond Jubilee of Confederation, 1927), 3, Library and Archives Canada, Records of the Canadian Broadcasting Corporation, Ottawa (hereafter CBC), vol. 249, file 11-38, pt. 1, Programming – Documentary and Commemorative Broadcasts – General.

2 *From Sea to Sea/A Mari Usque ad Mare*, 34–5.

3 Vipond, *Listening In*, 14.

4 Curran and Seaton, *Power without Responsibility*, 103.

5 The origins of radio broadcasting in Canada are fascinating and complex, linking technology, culture, politics, social change, business, and a variety of colourful characters. Recounting this history is not the purpose of this book. The best single source remains Vipond's *Listening In*, especially

pp. 13–53. For a more technical account, see Babaian, *Radio Communication in Canada*.

6   See, especially, chapter 3 of Johnson, *Unseen Voice*; Johnson, "Intimate Voice of Australian Radio," 44–5; Johnson, "Radio and Everyday Life," 167–78. In the United Kingdom, David Hendy sees radio as closely linked to evolving standards in film, stage, and television in "Bad Language and BBC Radio Four." Jacobs's *Intimate Screen*, while arguing that television exceeded radio and film in intimacy, stresses the centrality of a personal connection to the audience. See, especially, pp. 28–31. "In the beginning," there was Cardiff's "Serious and the Popular."

7   Lenthall, *Radio's America*; Craig, " More They Listen"; Vaillant, "Your Voice Came in Last Night"; Craig, "Farmer's Friend"; Lum, "Intimate Voice"; Douglas, *Listening In*; Hilmes, *Radio Voices*.

8   Patnode, "What These People Need."

9   Sconce, *Haunted Media*, 64–6.

10   Taylor, "Music and the Rise of Radio"; McCracken, "God's Gift to Us Girls"; McCusker, "Dear Radio Friend."

11   Bailey, "Angel in the Ether"; Lloyd, "Intimate Empire"; Moores, "Box on the Dresser.".

12   Loviglio, *Radio's Intimate Public*.

13   Shapiro, "Places and Spaces." On this blurring of boundaries in public affairs broadcasting, see Loviglio, "Eleanor Roosevelt and Radio's Intimate Public."

14   Parliament of the Commonwealth of Australia, *Report of the Joint Committee on Wireless Broadcasting*, 53.

15   Ward, "Early Use of Radio"; Webb, "Constructing Community and Consumers."

16   McLuhan, *Understanding Media*.

17   Sconce, *Haunted Media*, see esp. chap. 2; Powell, "You Are What You Hear"; Covert, "We May Hear Too Much"; Moss and Higgins, "Radio Voices."

18   Gitelman, "Unexpected Pleasures," 335–6.

19   The narrative of mind control through electronic means was frighteningly expressed during the early 1930s in a translation of a 1919 article by Victor Tausk. See Tausk, "Origin of the Influencing Machine."

20   Vipond, *Listening In*, 37.

21   M.J. Caveney, "New Voices in the Wilderness," cited in Peter Edidin, "Confounding Machines: How the Future Looked," *New York Times*, 28 August 2005.

22   Peters, *Speaking into the Air*.

23 "What about the Hit Parade?" CBC *Times*, 23–29 November 1952, 3. See also McCusker, "Dear Radio Friend," 179.

24 Graham McInnes, "Speaking as a Listener," broadcast 13 August 1948, CBC Trans-Canada Network, CBC, vol. 193, file 11-18-11-6, pt. 1, PG8.

25 John Fisher, "Helping Sew the Fabric of Unity," CBC *Times*, 18–24 December 1949, 2.

26 "Policy of the Corporation," n.d. [1939], 6, CBC, vol. 287, file 14-1-5, pt. 1.

27 "Special Events," 2.

28 McKenzie, "Radio as Instrument of Democracy"; McKenzie, "Radio, Instrument of Democracy."

29 Canadian Broadcasting Corporation, "Notes on CBC Regulations for Broadcasting Stations," 1950, CBC, vol. 304, file 14-2-2, pt. 7, Massey Commission.

30 Graham McInnes, "Speaking as a Listener," broadcast 30 July 1948, CBC Trans-Canada Network, 1, CBC, vol. 193, file 11-18-11-6, pt. 1, PG8.

31 Landry, *This Fascinating Radio Business*, 87.

32 Scannell and Cardiff, *Social History of British Broadcasting*, vol. 1.

33 "Policy of the Corporation," n.d. [1939], 6, CBC, vol. 287, file 14-1-5, pt. 1, Reports and Memoranda for Parliamentary Committee 1939.

34 Denison, "Romance of Canada."

35 Scott, *Seeing Like a State*, 346.

36 "Statement from Dr. Lee DeForest sent to the Canadian Radio League and submitted to the Special Parliamentary Committee on Radio Broadcasting," 1932, Library and Archives Canada (hereafter LAC), Graham Spry Papers, vol. 158, file 158-2.

37 McClung, "Radio," 5; Kirstein, "Radio and Social Welfare," 129.

38 W.D. Robb, "Radio," broadcast 25 July 1924, CFCA Toronto, LAC, Weir Papers, vol. 5, file 12.

39 W.H. Swift, Jr., "Radio Activities of the Canadian National Railways," March 1925, LAC, Weir Papers, vol. 19, file 1. According to an untitled source collected for a later parliamentary committee, the CNR did not establish a network worthy of the name until near the end of 1928. "Untitled", n.d., 1, CBC, vol. 289, file 14-1-12, pt. 6.

40 "Radio Travels Rapidly But Plodding Sun Wins," n.d. [1928], LAC, Weir Papers, vol. 19, file 3.

41 Thomas Archer, "Speaking as a Listener," broadcast 9 July 1948, CBC Trans-Canada Network, 1, CBC, vol. 193, file 11-18-11-6, pt. 1, PG8.

42 Gladstone Murray to Phillip N. Morris, 2 December 1937, CBC, vol. 32A, file 1-18, pt. 2.

43 "Music," 1; David Adams, "Radio Brings Music Home," *Canadian Broadcaster*, 12 January 1946, 14.

44 Gordon Murchison, "CBC Broadcast – Metropolitan Opera Intermission," 27 January 1945, CBC, vol. 213, file 11-21-11, pt. 3.

45 Wayne and Shuster Show, broadcast 17 April 1952, LAC, Frank Shuster Papers, vol. 6.

46 CNR Press Release, 27 September 1930, 4, LAC, Weir Papers, vol. 19, file 1. See also Bathrick, "Making a National Family."

47 L.W. Brockington, "Chatting with the Listener," broadcast 3 February 1938, Rare Books and Special Collections, University of British Columbia (hereafter UBC Special Collections), Alan B. Plaunt Papers, box 17, file 5.

48 Charlotte Whitton to Murray, 12 March 1941, CBC, vol. 144, file 9-8, pt. 1, Station Relations, Radio Regulations – Matters of Public Health. On the idea of the electronic hearth as later developed by Marshall McLuhan, see Tichi, *Electronic Hearth*, esp. 42–61.

49 J.S. Thomson to J.R. Radford, 4 December 1942, CBC, vol. 142, file 9-5-1, pt. 1.

50 A.D. Dunton, "Radio 1946," broadcast 2 October 1946, British Broadcasting Corporation Written Archives Centre, Caversham, Berkshire (hereafter BBC), E1/500/2, countries: Canada, CBC Programmes, file 2, M-Z, 1939–49.

51 B.K. Sandwell, "Freedom of Speech by Radio," *Saturday Night*, 17 November 1951, 4–5.

52 Graham McInnes, "Speaking as a Listener," broadcast 16 July 1948, CBC Trans-Canada Network, 1, CBC, vol. 193, file 11-18-11-6, pt. 1, PG8.

53 Dr James R. Angell, "Programming in the Public Interest," address to the National Association of Broadcasters Convention, Chicago, 28 April 1943, LAC, Weir Papers, vol. 16, file 6; Morgan, "Question Time"; Rubin, "Information Please!"

54 Press kit for "Find Your Fortune," 1948, CBC, acc. 86-87/031, box 153.

55 Albert E.S. Whittaker to Chairman of CBC Board of Governors, 10 November 1951, CBC, acc. 86-87/031, box 198, file 18-16R-10 to W-9. Jason Loviglio addresses the idea of personification in his discussion of Roosevelt's addresses. See Loviglio, *Radio's Intimate Public*, 2–5.

56 Raymond Cardinal Rouleau to Aird, 1 February 1929, translation, LAC, Records of the Royal Commission on Radio Broadcasting, vol. 1, file 227-10-3.

57 "Real People" n.d. [1947], CBC, vol. 177, file 11-18. pt. 1.

58 Elizabeth Long to Margaret Cuthbert, 23 April 1940, National Broadcasting Company Records, Wisconsin Historical Society Archives, Madison (hereafter NBC), box 75, fol. 33.

59 Graham McInnes, "Speaking as a Listener," broadcast 4 June 1948, CBC Trans-Canada Network, 3, CBC, vol. 193, file 11-18-11-6, pt. 1, PG8;

Elizabeth Long, "A Welcome Guest in Every Home," CBC *Times*, 18–24 June 1950, 2. For a more pessimistic view of invaded privacy, see Gruenberg, "Radio and the Child," 123.

60 Ted Allan to Robert Weaver, 13 June 1949, LAC, Ted Allan Papers, vol. 20, file 2; Wendell J. Munn to Ted Allan, 22 July 1949, LAC, Ted Allan Papers, vol. 20, file 1.

61 Clara Virginia Barton, "The Romance of Radio," *Canadian National Railways Magazine*, October 1925, 31, LAC, Weir Papers, vol. 18, file 7.

62 J.R. Mutchmor, memo regarding the half-hour broadcasts of the National Religious Advisory Council, n.d. [1938], University of British Columbia Archives, N.A.M. MacKenzie Papers, box 103, fol. 48.

63 Frank Chamberlain, "I Love Radio, Even If ..." *Saturday Night*, 22 March 1941, 24.

64 Gladstone Murray, "Broadcasting the Royal Tour" (synopsis of the remarks of the general manager), Meeting of Commentators, CBC Headquarters, Ottawa, 11 May 1939, UBC Special Collections, Alan B. Plaunt Papers, box 17, file 4.

65 *Sweet Hour of Prayer* letterhead, LAC, Winston Curry Papers, vol. 1, file 1.

66 Canadian Catholic Conference, "Brief submitted to the Royal Commission on National Development in the Arts, Letters and Sciences," March 1950, 9, CBC, vol. 306, file 14-2-2, pt. 23.

67 Scannell and Cardiff, *Social History of British Broadcasting*, 1:14–15.

68 Gladstone Murray, "National Radio in Canada," 25 July 1933, LAC, Gladstone Murray Papers, vol. 1.

69 Gladstone Murray, "Chatting with the Listener," broadcast 22 December 1936, CBC Trans-Canada Network, LAC, Graham Spry Papers, vol. 108, file 24.

70 Barnouw, *Golden Web*, 288.

71 Spot announcement for broadcast over station CKCK Regina, approved by Station Relations Division, 29 January 1944, CBC, vol. 144, file 9-8. pt. 2.

72 Gladstone Murray to Felix J. Lafferty, 9 November 1937, CBC, vol. 144, file 9-8, pt. 1.

73 Minutes, CBC Board of Governors, 8 September 1937, CBC, vol. 615, microfilm reel T-3041 (emphasis mine).

74 See Loviglio, *Radio's Intimate Public*, for a more complete and nuanced discussion of this idea.

75 Gladstone Murray to Alan Plaunt, 30 March 1936, LAC, Weir Papers, vol. 4, file 7.

76 "CBC General Manager Sets New Standard for Radio Advertising" n.d. [November 1942], CBC, vol. 142, file 9-5-1, pt. 1.

77 J.R. Radford to Manson, teletype, 12 December 1940, CBC, vol. 144, file 9-8, pt. 1.

78 Butsch, "Crystal Sets and Scarf-Pin Radios."

79 "Programs for Women," CBC Times, 31 October–6 November 1948, 4; James Scott, "Women versus Men," CBC Times, 30 October–5 November 1949, 11; James Scott, "Soapsud Music Must Be Sweet," CBC Times, 20–6 February 1949, 8.

80 "Price Mention Regulation," 1939, 1, CBC, vol. 32A, file 1-18, pt. 2.

81 "Points of View on Price Mention," broadcast 7 December 1948, CBC Trans-Canada Network, CBC, vol. 155, file 9-35, pt. 5. A strong showing from consumer groups in the late wartime and early postwar period probably aided these changes. On the movement, see Fahrni, "Counting the Costs of Living."

82 "Policy of the Corporation," n.d. [1939], CBC, vol. 287, file 14-1-5, pt. 1; Merrill Denison, "Soap Opera," Harper's, April 1940. 498–505. On the genesis of the gendered approach in radio advertising, see Smulyan, "Radio Advertising to Women"; Smethers and Jolliffe, "Homemaking Programs"; Hill, Advertising to the American Woman.

83 Columbia Broadcasting System, Radio's Daytime Serial, 21.

84 George Taggart to Ira Dilworth, 2 October 1939, CBC, vol. 237, file 11-29; Elizabeth Long to Assistant Supervisor of Programmes, "Agreed Policies and Procedure – Talks Dept. Department of Women's Interests," 5 September 1945, CBC, vol. 164, file 11-2, pt. 1.

85 Canadian Broadcasting Corporation, "Radio Talks For Women," 1945, LAC, Robert Alexander Sim Papers, vol. 3, file 24.

86 Giles, "Help for Housewives."

87 H.G. Walker to Weir, 14 December 1945, CBC, vol. 290, file 14-1-12, pt. 9.

88 A.D. Dunton, address to the Canadian Club, Toronto, 18 March 1946, LAC, Ernest Bushnell Papers, vol. 4.

89 "Commercial Division" n.d. [1944], 1, CBC, vol. 49, file 2-3-5, pt. 2.

90 CBC Programme Division, "[Report on] Sound Broadcasting," March-April 1952, 3, CBC, vol. 46, file 2-3-2-2, pt. 3.

91 W.H. Brodie to Regional Representatives, 14 January 1941, CBC, vol. 174, file 11-17-4-1.

92 Stursberg, Mister Broadcasting, 109.

93 Balzer, "In Case the Raid Is Unsuccessful."

94 C.E. Silcox, "Is the Power of the Press Waxing or Waning?" MS for Saturday Night, 1949, 4, United Church of Canada Archives, Claris Edwin Silcox Papers, box 9, file 60.

95   Earle Kelly, "National Canadian News Broadcast," 1937, LAC, Graham Spry Papers, vol. 108, file 24.

96   Gladstone Murray, "About the CBC Overseas, News, and Plays," broadcast on CBC Trans-Canada Network, 1 January 1941, 4, CBC, vol. 466, file 31-1.

97   Christopher V. Salmon, "Talks Presentation," 1938, CBC, vol. 177, file 11-18, pt. 1. On BBC talks culture and the audience of one, see Scannell, "For-Anyone-as-Someone Structures," 10.

98   "So You're Going on the Air – Tips to Talkers," 1942, 1, LAC, Marjorie McEnaney Papers, vol. 1, scripts for Talks Department.

99   CBC Talks Department, "Hints for *Canadian Roundup* Reporters," December 1943, CBC, vol. 177, file 11-18 pt. 1.

100   Broadcast Talks: Hints to CBC microphone Speakers," n.d. [1944], CBC, vol. 177, file 11-18, pt. 1.

101   Coulter and Lewis, *Radio Drama Is Not Theatre*, v. Lewis was perhaps best known for his statues of Timothy Eaton in the company's Toronto and Winnipeg stores.

102   W.H. Brodie, "Notes on Continuity," 16 May 1944, CBC, acc. 86-87/031, box 24.

103   Ernest Bushnell, "CBC Programme Standards," address at Queen's University, Kingston, 9 July 1945, 3, LAC, Ernest Bushnell Papers, vol. 4.

104   Lamont Tilden, "Getting Across to You," *CBC Times*, 25–31 March 1951, 5.

105   John Herries McCulloch, "Giving Canadian History the Air," *Toronto Star Weekly*, 7 March 1931, 5.

106   Edgar Stone, "Suggestions for the Development of Actors, Producers and Writers for Broadcasting," 29 July 1938, 2–3, CBC, vol. 851, file PG1-15, pt. 1.

107   E.L. Bushnell, "Horror Programmes," 6 January 1945, 1, CBC, vol. 861, file 4-2-1, pt. 1.

108   Constance McKay, "Speaking as a Listener," broadcast 30 October 1948, CBC Trans-Canada Network, CBC, vol. 193, file 11-18-11-6 (pt. 1), PG8.

109   Paul Standard to D.R. Buckham, 17 October 1940, NBC, box 75, fol. 36.

110   Dorothy Brister Stafford, "Educating the Children by Radio," *Canadian National Railways Magazine*, October 1925, 31.

111   CBC Press Release re: "thrillers," CBC, vol. 276, file 11-42-9, pt. 3.

112   G.P. "Regarding a Loan," n.d. [1932], LAC, Weir Papers, vol. 4, file 6.

113   "Report of the General Supervisor of Programmes on the Proceedings of the Programme Conference, Held, Toronto, August 8th and 9th, 1938," CBC, vol. 850, file PG1-13, pt. 1.

114 "Children's and Thriller Programmes," 10 June 1946, CBC, vol. 276, file 11-42-9, pt. 3.

115 W.H. Brodie, "Bulletin #1: Royal Tour Broadcasts," 31 August 1951, 2, CBC, acc. 86-87/031, box 198, file 18-16R-10 to W-9.

116 W.H. Brodie, "Bulletin #6: Royal Tour Broadcasts," 21 September 1951, CBC, acc. 86-87/031, box 198, file 18-16R-10 to W-9.

117 "Around the Studios," CBC Times, 14–20 December 1952, n.p., CBC, acc. 86-87/031, box 150.

118 Jean Pratt, "The Intimate Quality in Radio," CBC Times, 10–16 September 1950, 2.

119 "Real People" n.d. [1947], CBC, vol. 177, file 11-18, pt. 1.

120 Jennings and Gill, Broadcasting in Everyday Life; Pegg, Broadcasting and Society.

121 Craig, Fireside Politics, 259.

CHAPTER TWO

1 In the 3 June 2011 Speech from the Throne, Prime Minister Harper's government kept up a long tradition, calling the United States "our most important trading partner, ally and friend." One recent study of cross-border opinion sees the overall similarity between the two nations as a useful basis for comparing American and Canadian responses to the same questions. See Anderson and Stephenson, "Moving Closer or Drifting Apart," 3.

2 MacLean, "Canadian Studies and American Studies"; Thompson and Randall, Canada and the United States; Adams, Fire and Ice; Lipset, Continental Divide; Martin, Presidents and the Prime Ministers.

3 Two Royal Commissions on Broadcasting, begun in 1929 and 1955, respectively – the Royal Commission on National Development in the Arts, Letters and Sciences (1949) and the 1960 Royal Commission on Publications – were the most formal markers of concern with the communications media. On the penetration of American influence/philanthropy and the paradox of its enabling of Canadians to declare their distinctness, see Brison, Rockefeller. For a number of essays on cultural friction, see Flaherty and Manning, Beaver Bites Back, 260–80. Smythe, Dependency Road; and Grant, Lament for a Nation, approach a similar problem from divergent political perspectives.

4 The Princeton University team led by sociologist Paul Lazarsfeld began studying radio's interaction with its audiences in the later 1930s. This team included Theodor Adorno, who would write a good deal more about

radio and media. Barnouw's three-volume *History of Broadcasting in the United States* chronicles not only the rise of a business but also radio's "ability to move and persuade" (Barnouw, *Golden Web*, 2–3.); Douglas, *Listening In*, esp. chap. 6.

5 Douglas, *Inventing American Broadcasting*; McChesney, *Telecommunications*; Douglas, *Listening In* ; Hilmes, *Radio Voices*. A short sampling of more recent books and edited collections includes: Goodman, *Radio's Civic Ambition*; Slotten, *Radio's Hidden Voice*; Hilmes, *NBC*; Doerksen, *American Babel*; Fortner, *Radio, Morality, and Culture*; Loviglio, *Radio's Intimate Public*; Newman, *Radio Active*; Hangen, *Redeeming the Dial*; Hilmes and Loviglio, *Radio Reader*; Savage, *Broadcasting Freedom*.

6 Griffen-Foley, "Australian Commercial Radio"; Romanow, "Picture of Democracy"; Filion, "Broadcasting and Cultural Identity"; Pickering, "BBC's Kentucky Minstrels"; Day, "American Popular Culture"; Rutherford, "Made in America"; Litt, *Muses*; Smith, "Canadian Culture"; Frick, *Image in the Mind*.

7 "Pro Radio Publico," quoted in Arthur Wallace, "On the Air," *Saturday Night*, 7 February 1931, sec. 2, 12.

8 Hugh Garner, "Remember When We Raved about Radio?" *Maclean's*, 1 September 1956, 18.

9 Jewell, "Hollywood and Radio."

10 Beaty, "High Treason," 87.

11 Spry, "Radio Broadcasting," 106.

12 Arthur L. Phelps, "This Canada: No. 11 Canada Looks South," broadcast 19 February 1940, 2, National Broadcasting Company Records, Wisconsin Historical Society Archives, Madison (hereafter NBC), box 79, fol. 53, Phelps, Arthur L., 1940.

13 James Buckley to Donald Manson, 7 January 1929, Library and Archives Canada (hereafter LAC), Records of the Royal Commission on Radio Broadcasting, vol. 1, file 227-10-3.

14 Adria, *Technology and Nationalism*; Neulander, *Programming National Identity*; Edwardson, *Canadian Content*; Igartua, *Other Quiet Revolution*; Smith and Phillips, "Collective Belonging"; Haussen, "Radio and Populism"; Romanow, "Picture of Democracy"; Hayes, *Radio Nation*; Bathrick, "Making a National Family"; Scullion, "BBC Radio in Scotland"; Berland, "Marginal Notes"; Collins, *Culture, Communication, and National Identity*; Raboy, *Missed Opportunities*.

15 Glancy, "Temporary American Citizens"; Jewell, "Hollywood and Radio."

16 Gladstone Murray, "National Radio in Canada," 25 July 1933, LAC, Murray Papers, vol. 1.

17 Doris Hedges, "Report", 10 April 1943, LAC, Canadian Authors Association Papers, vol. 1.

18 "The Future of Radio," Montreal *Daily Herald*, 21 September 1933; "U . Broadcasts in Canada Stir Ire of Commons," *Advertising Age*, 4 March 1933.

19 Vipond, "Continental Marketplace."

20 "Notes on Programme Meeting – A.M. Wednesday 12 March 1947," 1947, 2, Library and Archives Canada, Records of the Canadian Broadcast Corporation, Ottawa (hereafter CBC), vol. 166, file 11-5-1.

21 Lower, "Question of National Television," 275. Lower expressed similar alarm to a future prime minister a few years earlier: Arthur Lower to John Diefenbaker, 16 December 1952, Queen's University Archives, Lower Papers, box 7, A 119.

22 "CBC 1946: A Digest of Statements and Policies, Administration and Programs of the Canadian Broadcasting Corporation," 1946, 11, LAC, Bushnell Papers, vol. 2.

23 MacLennan, "American Network Broadcasting."

24 Goodman, *Radio's Civic Ambition*, esp. pt. 1.

25 Few historians dispute the march of commercialism through American broadcasting, but David Berkman argues that the public service lobby was stronger than many suspected before about 1924. See Berkman, "Not *Quite* So Inevitable Origins."

26 Foust, "Technology versus Monopoly"; Pickard, "Battle over the FCC Blue Book"; Socolow, "Questioning Advertising's Influence"; Slotten, *Radio and Television Regulation*.

27 Meyers, "Problems with Sponsorship"; Fones-Wolf, "Creating a Favorable Business Climate."

28 R.C. Witmer to Edgar Kobak, 5 February 1935, NBC, box 35, fol. 10; George F. McClelland to H.L. Sheen, telegram, 31 March 1928, NBC, box 2, fol. 86.

29 E.A. Weir, "Network Broadcasting Rates in Canada – Some Reasons Why They Should Be Reduced," 14 August 1931, LAC, E.A. Weir Papers, vol. 19, file 2.

30 Vipond, *Listening In*, xiv-xv; Weir, *Struggle for National Broadcasting*, 128.

31 House of Commons Special Committee on Radio Broadcasting, "Minutes of Proceedings and Evidence, No. 4," 19 April 1944, witness: Augustin Frigon (Ottawa, King's Printer, 1944).

32 "'Thar's Gold ... in Them Thar Hillbillies,'" *Canadian Broadcaster* 1, 3 (1942): n.p.; "Some Aspects of Commercial and Public Service

Broadcasting," 20 August 1948, British Broadcasting Corporation Written Archives Centre, Caversham, Berkshire (hereafter BBC), E1/489.

33 American broadcasters produced unsponsored programs, but these were most often made to attract a sponsor eventually. Roy Dunlop, "Report from Hollywood," September 1938, 19, LAC, Roy Dunlop Papers, vol. 1; Hutchins, "State of American Radio"; Advisory Council of the National Broadcasting Company, the President's Report and Resume of Programs, committee reports, fifth meeting, 1931, NBC, box 107, fol. 5; Sangster, "On the Air."

34 Blackburn, "Radio in Canada."

35 A.B. Oldfield-Davies, "A Report on C.W.'s visit to USA and Canada, April–May 1949," BBC, E1/584/2. Former Yale University president and NBC public service counsellor James Angell's vision for American radio was to have top writers producing minority taste programs instead of "the apprentices and the culls that now too often, in the sustaining field at least, get these unwelcome public service jobs." See Dr James R. Angell, "Programming in the Public Interest," address before the National Association of Broadcasters Convention, Chicago, 28 April 1943, LAC, Weir Papers, vol. 16, file 6.

36 MacLennan, "Resistance to Regulation," 44; Fowler and Crawford, *Border Radio.*

37 Spry, "Radio Broadcasting," 126.

38 On *Town Meeting*, see Goodman, "Programming in the Public Interest."

39 Phillips Carlin to Keith Higgins, 28 April 1939, NBC, box 67, fol. 3.

40 Arthur Wallace, "On the Air," *Saturday Night*, 7 March 1931, 20; Thomas Maher to M. Aylesworth, 4 January 1934. NBC, box 24, fol. 47.

41 (Miss) Frederica Von Charles to Rupert Caplan [24 January 1934], CBC, vol. 41, file 2-2-8-3, pt. 1.

42 Stallsworthy, "What Price Radio?," 18.

43 [Orville Shugg], "Rural Canada and National Radio" [1936], LAC, O.J.W. Shugg Papers, vol. 1. Vancouver's *Western Canada Radio News* also prominently featured American acts, with some coverage of the Canadian scene and BBC output. Its extensive schedules reflected what was available to listeners, but most featured stories in the paper were about American shows. See *Western Canada Radio News*, 20 September 1936.

44 *Western Canada Radio News*, 20 September 1936.

45 Bushnell to Frigon, 12 March 1946, CBC, vol. 161, file 11-1, pt. 1.

46 "Special Parliamentary Committee on Radio Broadcasting – 1946, Statement by E.L. Bushnell, Director General of Programs, Canadian Broadcasting Corporation," CBC, vol. 288, file 14-1-12, pt. 2.

47 Bandleader Mart Kenney, quoted in Mavor Moore, "What We'll Do with TV," *Saturday Night*, 24 May 1952, 20.

48 Royal Commission on Radio Broadcasting, "Summary of Public Hearings held at Windsor, 13 May 1929," 10–15, and "Summary of Public Hearings held at Hamilton, 15 May 1929," 11–13, LAC, Records of the Royal Commission on Radio Broadcasting, vol. 1, file 227-9-6.

49 M.A. Frost to D.B.R.-D.E.F.S., n.d. [February 1934]. BBC, E4/48, Empire Service, M.A. Frost's Tour: V, 1933–1934. Quotation from: "Summary of Correspondence relating to programmes," February 1933, BBC, E4/37; Michael Barkway to MacAlpine, 21 May 1946, BBC, E1/509/3.

50 "Meeting with Basic and Affiliated Stations held in Hall "C," Royal York Hotel, 10.00 AM, February 18, 1943," CBC, vol. 342, file 15-3, pt. 3.

51 [Decisions of Sub-Committee on News Commentaries], 15 March 1944, 8, LAC, Bushnell Papers, vol. 2.

52 Hill, "Broadcasting in Canada."

53 William S. Hedges to Witmer and Edgar Kobak, "Canadian Broadcasting Corp. – Alternative Network," 6 January 1942, NBC, box 87, fol. 32.

54 Augustin Frigon, address to the Royal Canadian Institute, 11 December 1943, CBC, vol. 472, file 31-9, pt. 5.

55 Weir, *Struggle for National Broadcasting*, 278.

56 L.W. Brockington, "Chatting with the Listener," broadcast 3 February 1938, Rare Books and Special Collections, University of British Columbia, Alan B. Plaunt Papers, box 17, file 5 (emphasis in original).

57 "Up Goes the Price of Radio Licences," *Kelowna Courier*, 27 January 1938; Mrs H.A. [McKerrall] to CBC, 14 February 1938, CBC, vol. 394, file 21-17, pt. 1.

58 CBC brief submitted to the Royal Commission on National Development in the Arts, Letters and Sciences, 1949, LAC, Bushnell Papers, vol. 2.

59 *This Is the CBC* (1946), 6, CBC, acc. 86-87/031, box 43.

60 Drew Crossan, "Juke Box Jury" (1950), CBC, acc. 86-87/031, box 153.

61 H.G. Walker, "Promotion," memo to general supervisor of programmes, 10 December 1945, CBC, bol. 164, file 11-2, pt. 1.

62 Royal Commission on Radio Broadcasting, "Summary of Public Hearings held at Hamilton, 15 May 1929," LAC, Records of the Royal Commission on Radio Broadcasting, vol. 1, file 227-9-6.

63 Lawren Harris, "Commercialism and Art," n.d., 4, LAC, Lawren Stewart Harris Papers, 5-7.

64 D.G. Bridson, "A Consideration of Short-Wave Broadcasting to America," 10 April 1942, BBC, E1/128; Atkinson, "European View."

65 Ted Allan to Lovell Mickles, Jr, 16 June 1951, LAC, Ted Allan Papers, vol. 20, file 13 (emphasis in original).

66 "High Ratings for CBC Network Shows at the Annual 'Exhibition' in Ohio," *CBC Times*, 26 April – 5 May 1953, 5; William A. Taylor, "Music on the Air in Canada Includes Non-Commercial CBC 'Wednesday Nights,'" *Musical Courier*, 1 March 1948; "List of Awards and Judges Report for the Ninth American Exhibition of Educational Radio Programs," May 1945, CBC, vol. 264, file 11-42, pt. 1; Jack Gould, "Canada Shows Us How," *New York Times*, 19 November 1944, X7; "Words in Behalf of Canadian Drama – Miss Francis Says It All," *New York Times*, 1 September 1946.

67 George Rosen, "Showmen Hit Radio Drabness," *Variety*, 26 December 1945; Jennings to Bushnell, 5 February 1946, CBC, vol. 288, file 14-1-12, pt. 1.

68 Royal Commission on Radio Broadcasting, "Summary of Public Hearings held at Fredericton, 13 June 1929," 12, LAC, Records of the Royal Commission on Radio Broadcasting, box. 1, file 227-11-5.

69 "2nd Meeting," minutes of a meeting of the Committee Studying Commercial Continuity (1944), CBC, vol. 342, file 15-3, pt. 4; E.A. Weir to Ernest Bushnell, 15 February 1947, CBC, vol. 161, file 11-1, pt. 1; "Supplementary Joint Report from Programme and Commercial Divisions for Board of Governors re Recommendation (h) of the Massey Report," September 1951, CBC, vol. 46, file 2-3-2-2, pt. 3.

70 Roy Dunlop, "Report from Hollywood," September 1938, LAC, Roy Dunlop Papers, vol. 1.

71 "Destructive Radio Policy," *Montreal Gazette*, 19 January 1938.

72 J.E. Mason to E.P.H. James, 28 January 1929, NBC, box 4, fol. 33, A. McKim Advertising Agency; Johnston, "Emergence of Broadcast Advertising."

73 Gibbon, "Radio as a Fine Art," 213.

74 J.M. Beaudet to David M. Adams, 14 December 1945, CBC, vol. 212, file 11-21, pt. 1.

75 H.H. Murphy M.D. to Department of Transport, 14 February 1938, CBC, vol. 394, file 21-17, pt. 1.

76 Marjorie McEnaney, "E.A. Corbett – views on radio," 1951, LAC, Marjorie McEnaney Papers, vol. 1.

77 Brockington, "Chatting with the Listener," 8.

78 Yorke, "Radio Octopus"; Hutchinson, "Freedom of the Air."

79 Columbus was the site of a prestigious conference/award ceremony for broadcasting, especially in the educational field. See Spry, "Canadian Radio Situation."

80 Frigon to Bushnell, 12 March 1946, CBC, vol. 161, file 11-1, pt. 1.

81 V. van der Linde to R.C. Witmer, 3 February 1933, NBC, box 16, fol. 41.

82 Bowman to Macgregor, 22 April 1938, BBC, E1/522/4.

83 David Sarnoff was a leading executive at the Radio Corporation of America (RCA), which created the National Broadcasting Company (NBC) network. Radio City was/is the network's New York City headquarters. See Murray to Graves, 16 April 1937, BBC, E1/585/2.

84 W.A. Steel to [Donald] Withycomb, 18 May 1934, and J.A. Dupont to Donald Withycomb, 26 September 1934, NBC, box 24, fol. 47.

85 Donald Withycomb to R.C. Patterson, 21 February 1934, NBC, box 24, fol. 47; A.L. Ashby to Edgar Kobak, 29 March 1935, and Reginald Brophy to R.C. Witmer, 10 April 1935, NBC, box 35, fol. 10.

86 Denison, "Radio in Canada," 49.

87 R.W. Ashcroft, "Government vs. Private Ownership of Canadian Radio" [1931], LAC, Graham Spry Papers, vol. 97, file 10; Frank Chamberlain, "Canadian Stars Return to Canada," Saturday Night, 24 October 1942, 29; "Script Writer Thinks Canadian Scripts Better Than American," Saturday Night, 16 December 1944, 22; Robert Dunbar, "Ace Radio Impresarios Are Statisticians," Saturday Night, 30 November 1946, 22-3; Ron Fraser to A.D. Dunton, 30 December 1949, CBC, vol. 851, file PG 1-15, pt. 1.

88 Weir to Dunton, "Give-Away Programs," 12 March 1947, CBC, vol. 161, file 11-1, pt. 1.

89 Gladstone Murray to J.J. Heagarty, 27 October 1942, CBC, vol. 142, file 9-5-1, pt. 1; Weir to Bushnell, 15 February 1947, and Weir to Dunton, "Give-Away Programs," 12 March 1947, CBC, vol. 161, file 11-1, pt. 1.

90 Quotation from "Decisions of Sub-Committee on News Commentaries," 15 March 1944, LAC, Bushnell Papers, vol. 2, CBC Correspondence and memoranda relating to programming, 1944; Minutes of the 1st General Administrative Conference, Ottawa, 2–3 November 1943, app. C, CBC, vol. 466, file 30-16, pt. 1.

91 Ira Dilworth, "Statement re Programme Policy," 14 March 1952, 2–3, CBC, vol. 164, file 11-2, pt. 2.

92 Landry, "Wanted," 626.

93 "Some Aspects of Commercial and Public Service Broadcasting," 20 August 1948, BBC, E1/489. The "trend" never really took hold, and an FCC regulation governing giveaway shows was easily circumvented. See Waller, Radio, 40–2.

94 J.R. Finlay to Bushnell, 13 February 1947, and Charles Jennings to Bushnell, 18 February 1947, CBC, vol. 161, file 11-1, pt. 1.

95 Roy Dunlop, "New Vistas in Radio," address to the Vancouver Rotary Club, March 1946, LAC, Roy Dunlop Papers, vol. 1. Dunlop was

probably referring to the buzz surrounding: Wakeman's *Hucksters* or Siepmann's *Radio's Second Chance*, but calls for reform were not strictly a postwar phenomenon. See Brindze, *Not to Be Broadcast*.

96 Kathleen Pratley to Graham Spry, 26 March 1931, LAC, Graham Spry Papers, vol. 94, file 11.

97 Landry, *This Fascinating Radio Business*, 193.

98 Thomas Archer, "Speaking as a Listener," broadcast 20 August 1948, CBC Trans-Canada Network, CBC, vol. 193, file 11-18-11-6, pt. 1, PG8.

99 Edgar Stone, "Suggestions for the Development of Actors, Producers and Writers for Broadcasting," 29 July 1938, 1, CBC, vol. 851, file PG 1-15. pt. 1.

100 The CBC and Canadian Broadcasting: Statements by Dr James S. Thomson, General Manager, and Dr Augustin Frigon, Assistant General Manager, Canadian Broadcasting Corporation, before the House of Commons Special Committee on Radio Broadcasting, June – July 1943, CBC, vol. 472, file 31-9, pt. 5.

101 Overseas Intelligence Department, "Empire Correspondence, Summary of Analysis – October 1938 – March 1939," n.d. [April 1939], BBC, E4/38.

102 Max Ferguson to BBC Bursary Committee, CBC, 9 March 1951, 3, CBC, vol. 238, file 11-36, pt. 1.

103 Canadian Association of Broadcasters, Statement to the Royal Commission on National Development in the Arts, Letters and Sciences, 1950, LAC, Allard Papers, vol. 5, file 10.

104 Cecil Lamont to Graham Spry, 8 January 1931, LAC, Graham Spry Papers, vol. 94, file 4.

105 Although Raymond Williams discourages the application of Gresham's idea about currency to culture, it remains a useful notion when discussing cultural situations in which one strain of culture was thought to "displace" another. See Williams, "Gresham's Law."

106 Gordon Shrum to Gladstone Murray, 20 January 1938, BBC, E1/522/4; Robert Dunbar, "Ace Radio Impresarios Are Statisticians," *Saturday Night*, 30 November 1946, 22-3.

107 Weir to Frank Starr, 27 December 1945, CBC, vol. 290, file 14-1-12, pt. 9.

108 Edgar Stone to Weir, 14 December 1945, CBC, vol. 290, file 14-1-12, pt. 9.

109 "CBC Drives Listeners to U.S. Stations," *Canadian Broadcaster*, 26 January 1946, 1.

110 Gladstone Murray, "About the CBC Overseas, News, and Plays," broadcast on CBC Trans-Canada Network, 1 January 1941, CBC, vol. 466, file 31-1.

111 Perry, "Weak Spots."

112 H.W. Morrison, "Response to John Collingwood Reade," n.d. [December 1938], CBC, vol. 287, file 14-1-5, pt. 1.

113 William Burke Miller to Marley Sherris, 8 February 1934, and J.A. Dupont to Marley Sherris, 8 February 1934, NBC, box 24, fol. 47.

114 James Law to the Manager, Station CRCT, 20 September 1936, NBC, box 44, fol. 65.

115 J. Barclay to Canadian Radio Commission [*sic*], 9 January 1939, CBC, vol. 153, file 9-31, pt 1.

116 Maurice Goudrault to J.R. Radford, telegram, 16 December 1943, CBC, vol. 151, file 9-19, pt. 3; Goudrault to A.D. Dunton, 22 November 1951, CBC, vol. 147, file 9-11-1, pt. 3.

117 Greene to Graves, 16 January 1936 (completed 22 January 1936), BBC, E1/113/2.

118 E.A. Weir to J.H. McCulloch, 3 May 1940, LAC, Weir Papers, vol. 4, file 4.

119 John Fisher, "Leonard Was Right," *CBC Times*, 13–19 February 1949, 2.

120 Allen, *Chartered Libertine*, 62.

121 J. Strathallan D. Nation to General Manager, CBC, 3 October 1937, CBC, vol. 255, file 11-40-1, pt. 2.

122 Royal Commission on Radio Broadcasting, "Summary of Public Hearings held at Fredericton, 13 June 1929," 12, LAC, Records of the Royal Commission on Radio Broadcasting, vol. 1, file 227-11-5.

123 Theo and [La?] Wallgate to L.W. Brockington, 14 March 1939, CBC, vol. 540, file 13-7-1, pt. 2 (emphasis in original).

124 Murray to F.W. Ogilvie, 22 November 1939, BBC, E1/561/1.

125 James S. Thomson to Murray, 4 January 1941, CBC, vol. 171, file 11-17, pt. 1.

126 "Radio's Responsibility in Juvenile Delinquency," 9 April 1946, LAC, Bushnell Papers, vol. 2.

127 Spencer, "We Went to the People."

128 Ira Dilworth, "Statement re Programme Policy," 14 March 1952, CBC, vol. 164, file 11-2, pt. 2.

129 "CBC in Montreal Calls Hollywood," *CBC Times*, 16–22 January 1949, 12.

130 W. George to Frances Rockefeller King, 7 September 1932, NBC, box 7, fol. 41; George Engles to W. George, 14 October 1932, NBC, box 7, fol. 41; R.A. Rendall to S.J. de Lotbinière, 12 December 1943, BBC, E1/509/1, file 1; Horace Stovin to Stephen Fry, 11 March 1943, BBC, E1/488.

131 "CBC Programming," n.d. [1949], LAC, Bushnell Papers, vol. 14.

132 Gruneau Research Ltd., *A Survey of Canadian Public Opinion towards Radio and the Canadian Broadcasting Corporation*, Toronto, March 1952, LAC, Weir Papers, vol. 16, file 2.

133 Hendy, *Life on Air*, 1-2.

134 Irvin Cooper, "Address to the Royal Commission on Radio Broadcasting," 29 May 1929, LAC, Records of the Royal Commission on Radio Broadcasting, vol. 1, file 227-10-6.

135 Rev. George N. Luxton, "Radio Vesper Hour Enjoyed by Thousands," *Calgary Herald*, May 1931.

136 Extracts from Correspondence to Gladstone Murray, November 1938, CBC, vol. 466, file 31-1.

137 "Report: Empire Broadcasting in Canada," n.d. [1936], BBC, E1/492.

138 "(for example, Schools Broadcasts, full attention to serious music, balanced but comprehensive political broadcasting, the full conception of Radio Drama)," "Some Aspects of Commercial and Public Service Broadcasting," 20 August 1948, BBC, E1/489.

139 Arthur L. Phelps, "Good Listening," broadcast 3 December 1947, BBC, E1/586/1.

CHAPTER THREE

1 Bridget Griffen-Foley makes a similar distinction between attention and influence. See Griffen-Foley, "Australian Commercial Radio."

2 C.E. Silcox, "The Future of Patriotism," *Saturday Night*, 15 September 1949, United Church of Canada Archives, Claris Edwin Silcox Papers, box 9, file 58.

3 Champion, "Mike Pearson at Oxford"; Mathews, *Canadian Identity*; Allen, *Ordeal by Fire*, 473-6.

4 *This Is the CBC* (1946), 6, CBC, acc. 86-87/031, box 43.

5 Nicholas, "Brushing Up Your Empire."

6 Gilbert Harding to Laurence Gilliam, 25 January 1946, BBC, E1/510.

7 Michael Barkway to J.B. Clark, 21 May 1946, BBC, E1/488, files 1-2, 1941-53.

8 Hilmes, *Network Nations*; Potter, *Broadcasting Empire*. My profound gratitude to Simon for access to the book in manuscript.

9 Works approaching the broadcasting culture of a nation or nations in a similarly sensitive way include: Goodman, *Radio's Civic Ambition*; Lenthall, *Radio's America*; Loviglio, *Radio's Intimate Public*; Lacey, *Feminine Frequencies*; Vipond, *Listening In*; LeMahieu, *Culture for Democracy*.

10 Hilmes, *Network Nations*, 85.

11 Potter, *Broadcasting Empire*, intro.

12 Given, "Another Kind of Empire," 41.

13 Briggs, *History of Broadcasting*, 1:53.

14 Lemahieu, "John Reith," 193–4; Cardiff, "Time, Money and Culture."

15 Hilmes, *Network Nations*, 39–50. The BBC charter came into effect on 1 January 1927, but the relevant discussions happened during the previous year.

16 Curran and Seaton, *Power without Responsibility*, 104. The most detailed and comprehensive work on the formation and career of the BBC remains Asa Briggs's five-volume series *History of Broadcasting in the United Kingdom*, but other works also treat the pre-television era. See, for example, Hajkowski, *BBC and National Identity*; Street, *Crossing the Ether*; Scannell and Cardiff, *Social History of British Broadcasting*, vol. 1; Pegg, *Broadcasting and Society*.

17 Potter, "Who Listened."

18 Robertson, "I Get a Real Kick."

19 Weir, *Struggle for National Broadcasting*, 55, 76–7, 124, 132; Vipond, *Listening In*, 261, 283. The most notable exception is Raboy's *Missed Opportunities*, in which BBC director general John Reith's cultural style is eventually aped by the CBC (see pp. 23 and 60), but little contact was otherwise reported.

20 Potter, "Britishness," 81; Vipond, "Canadian Radio Broadcasting Commission."

21 On the various institutional connections, see Potter, *Broadcasting Empire*, chap. 3; Vipond, "Mass Media in Canadian History."

22 Vipond, "Royal Tour of 1939"; Vipond, "Living"; Potter, "BBC."

23 Briggs, *History of Broadcasting*, 2:8; Briggs, *History of Broadcasting*, vol. 3; Hajkowski, "BBC."

24 Potter, *Broadcasting Empire*, chap. 4.

25 Raboy, *Missed Opportunities*, 83.

26 Potter, *Broadcasting Empire*, chap. 5.

27 Vipond, "Cultural Authority," 62.

28 Vipond, "British or American."

29 Vipond, "Going Their Own Way." On inspiration, see Potter, "Webs, Networks, and Systems," 639.

30 Address by Mr W.D. Robb, vice-president, Canadian National Railways, from CNRA, Moncton, broadcast 6 November 1925, Library and Archives Canada (hereafter LAC), Weir Papers, vol. 19, file 1.

31 Val Gielgud to Director of Programmes, 16 October 1930, BBC, E1/506.

32 Press Release on CNR radio, n.d. [1929], LAC, Weir Papers, MG 30 D 67, vol. 19, file 1.

33 Weir to Hector Charlesworth, 12 November 1932, LAC, Weir Papers, vol. 17, file 4.

34 Royal Commission on Radio Broadcasting, "Views of the Canadian Legion of the B.E.S.L. on Radio Broadcasting in Canada," submitted 3 July 1929, 4, LAC, Records of the Royal Commission on Radio Broadcasting, vol. 1, file 227-9-10.

35 Canadian Manufacturing Association, "Brief Respecting Radio Broadcasting submitted to the Royal Commission on Radio Broadcasting," Toronto, 17 May 1929, 2, LAC, Allard Papers, vol. 5, file 9.

36 Dozens of factors figured into the commission's recommendations, and the process is best outlined in Part 3 of Vipond's *Listening In*.

37 Weir to Howgill, 12 February 1931, BBC, E1/506; Press Release on CNR radio, n.d. [1929], LAC, Weir Papers, vol. 19, file 1.

38 Arthur Wallace, "On the Air: Helpless Canadians," *Saturday Night*, 7 March 1931, 20; Yorke, "Radio Octopus"; Hutchinson, "Air Already Monopolized"; Hutchinson, "Freedom of the Air"; James Montagnes, "Canada Plans to Rule Her Ether Waves," *Baltimore Sun*, 16 February 1930.

39 The most prominent exceptions were stations owned by newspapers, who saw a public system as less of a threat to their stake in advertising. Canadian Association of Broadcasters, "Radio Broadcasting under Private Ownership," 1929, CBC, vol. 342, file 15-3, pt. 8.; Canadian Manufacturing Association, "Brief Respecting Radio Broadcasting submitted to the Royal Commission on Radio Broadcasting," Toronto, 17 May 1929, LAC, Allard Papers, vol. 5, file 9; Canadian Radio League, "The Canadian Radio League: Objects, Information, National Support," 1931, LAC, Spry Papers, vol. 158, file 158-1; Canadian Radio League, statement of objectives, "Radio Broadcasting" [1930], LAC, Spry Papers, vol. 97, file 8; Spry, "Canadian Radio Situation"; F.R. McKelcan to Graham Spry, 2 January 1931, LAC, Spry Papers, vol. 94, file 4; Ernest Thomas to Editor, "National Control of Broadcasting," *Ottawa Citizen*, 7 February 1931. Thomas was field secretary, Board of Evangelism and Social Service, United Church of Canada. See Duncan Johnson, Ottawa, to Editor, "For National Broadcasting," *Ottawa Citizen*, 8 March 1930.

40 R.W. Ashcroft, "Government vs. Private Ownership of Canadian Radio," [1931], LAC, Spry Papers, vol. 97, file 10. In the same vein: Arthur Wallace, "On the Air," *Saturday Night*, 7 February 1931, sec. 2, 12.

41 Gibbon, "Radio as a Fine Art." Canada had a monopoly broadcaster, but it was not a national network. See Vipond, "CKY Winnipeg." NBC also

used this characterization of public broadcasting to celebrate the commer-
cial model. See Advisory Council of the National Broadcasting Company,
*The President's Report and Resume of Programs, Committee Reports,
Seventh Meeting, 1933*, National Broadcasting Company Records,
Wisconsin Historical Society Archives, Madison (hereafter NBC), box 107,
fol. 7.

42 Spry, "Canadian Broadcasting Issue."

43 W.T. Maxwell, "Broadcast Problems in England," *Saturday Night*,
28 February 1931, 3.

44 Evershed Heron to Graham Spry, 15 March 1931, LAC, Spry Papers,
vol. 95, file 1.

45 Chapter 2 of Potter's *Broadcasting Empire* deals with the BBC-Canada
relationship, and compares it with the development of broadcast control
in other dominions. On the CRBC as a creature of "red Toryism," see
Spencer, "Social Origins of Broadcasting"; Vipond, *Listening In*, 225–54;
Raboy, *Missed Opportunities*, 29–47; Nolan, *Foundations*, 83–93; Peers,
Politics of Canadian Broadcasting, 63–107; Weir, *Struggle for National
Broadcasting*. For an alternative view of this process, see Allard, *Straight
Up*, 59–90.

46 Raboy, *Missed Opportunities*, 8–9.

47 "Summary of Correspondence relating to programmes," February 1933,
BBC, E4/37.

48 M.A. Frost to D.B.R. – D.E.F.S., n.d. [February 1934], BBC, E4/48.

49 Col. W.A. Steel to C.G. Graves, 24 August 1935, BBC, E1/522/2, file 1B;
Murray to Reith, 12 March 1934, BBC, E1/522/1, file 1A.

50 "The Future of Radio," *Montreal Daily Herald*, 21 September 1933.

51 Murray to Reith, 12 March 1934, BBC, E1/522/1, file 1A.

52 Col. W.A. Steel to C.G. Graves, 24 August 1935, BBC, E1/522/2, file 1B,
1935.

53 J.B. Clark to Col. W.A. Steel, 16 October 1935, BBC, E1/113/1, file 1.

54 G. Fred McNally to Alan Plaunt, 27 May 1931, Rare Books and Special
Collections, University of British Columbia (hereafter UBC Special
Collections), Alan B. Plaunt Papers, box 1, file 1.

55 Major Frederick Ney to Gladstone Murray, 4 June 1935, BBC, E1/552.
Lambert was a subordinate of Murray's who came to Canada just before
the Second World War and ended up running the CBC's School Broadcasts.

56 Orrin E. Dunlap, Jr., "Where the Listeners Pay," *New York Times*, 2 April
1933.

57 MacMillan, "Problems of Music," 194.

58 Frost to Graves, 11 January 1934, BBC, E4/50.

59 Vipond, "Going Their Own Way," 71–7.

60 "British Programs Soon to Be Coming Direct to Canada," *Telegraph-Journal* (St John), 5 December 1934. On the difficulties behind arranging such broadcasts, see Potter, *Broadcasting Empire*, chap. 2.

61 Potter, *Broadcasting Empire*, intro.

62 John Craig to Val Gielgud, 20 June 1936, BBC, E1/523; Gielgud to Craig, 3 July 1936, BBC, E1/523.

63 Potter, *Broadcasting Empire*, chap. 2.

64 Gladstone Murray to M.H. Aylesworth, 10 May 1933, NBC, box 19, fol. 56.

65 Gladstone Murray, "National Radio in Canada," 25 July 1933, 25, LAC, Gladstone Murray Papers, vol. 1; Gladstone Murray to M.H. Aylesworth, 10 May 1933, NBC, box 19, fol. 56.

66 Murray, "National Radio in Canada," 24.

67 Ibid., 15.

68 C.G. Graves to M.A. Frost, 4 July 1933, BBC, E4/47.

69 "Summary of correspondence relating to programmes," February 1933, BBC, E4/37.

70 Cull, "Radio Propaganda," 403–4.

71 Frost to Graves, 20 January 1934, BBC, E4/50.

72 Graves to Controller (P), 29 January 1934, BBC, E4/50; Reith to Charlesworth, 8 February 1934 (C.G. Graves wrote Reith's letter to Charlesworth) and Graves to Reith, 8 February 1934, BBC, E4/50, Empire Service.

73 C.G. Graves to Sir Charles Carpendale, 1 August 1934, BBC, E2/1139.

74 "Report: Empire Broadcasting in Canada," n.d. [1936], BBC, E1/492.

75 John Royal to R.C. Patterson, 6 November 1935, NBC, box 35, fol. 10.

76 Murray to Plaunt, 26 June 1935, UBC Special Collections, Alan B. Plaunt Papers, box 3, file 14.

77 Murray to Plaunt, 5 November 1935, UBC Special Collections, Alan B. Plaunt Papers, box 3, file 15.

78 Felix Greene to C(P), 27 December 1935, BBC, E1/486.

79 Felix Greene to C.D. Howe, 4 January 1936 and Felix Greene to C.G. Graves, 1 March 1936, BBC, E1/528.

80 Felix Greene to John Reith, 23 February 1936, BBC, E1/528.

81 Felix Greene to BBC, n.d. [January 1936], telegram, BBC, E1/528; Felix Greene to C.G. Graves, 10 January 1936, BBC, E1/528.

82 "A Brief Presented by the Association of Canadian Advertisers and the Canadian Association of Broadcasters to the Parliamentary Committee on Radio – 1936," (1936), 6, CBC, vol. 46, file 2-3, pt. 4.

83 John Royal to Fred B. Bate, 3 March 1936, NBC, box 44, fol. 65.

84 Nolan, *Foundations*, 130–4; Vipond, "Going Their Own Way," 80–1.

85 Gladstone Murray, "Chatting with the Listener," broadcast 22 December 1936, CBC Trans-Canada Network, LAC, Graham Spry Papers, vol. 108, file 24.

86 CBC Programme Schedule, week of 1–7 August 1937, BBC, E1/522/3, file 1C; Ernest Bushnell to Felix Greene, 9 March 1937, BBC, E1/522/3, file 1C.

87 Bowman to Macgregor, 22 April 1938, BBC, E1/522/4, file 2A.

88 William C. Gibson to Graham Spry, 10 February 1939, LAC, Spry Papers, vol. 65, file 31; "Report by H.N.A.S. on Duty Visits to Canada and U.S.A." [1949], BBC, E15/133.

89 "Minutes of the twenty-fifth meeting of members of the National Programme Office," 22 May 1940, LAC, Bushnell Papers, vol. 1, file 12.

90 Gilbert Harding, "The Canadian Personality," broadcast 15 September 1948, CBC Trans-Canada Network, CBC, vol. 193, file 11-18-11-6, pt. 1, PG8.

91 Hilmes, "British Quality."

92 Harold Clark to Gladstone Murray, 15 November 1937, LAC, CBC, vol. 40, file 2-2-8-2, pt. 4.

93 Egerton Lovering to C.D. Howe, 23 December 1937, and Lewis to Murray, 27 November 1937, CBC, vol. 151, file 9-19, pt. 1; Minutes of Proceedings, Special Committee on Radio Broadcasting, 7 July 1942, RG 14, reel M-467, 888-902.

94 D.R.P. Coats to Donald Buchanan, 12 March 1937 and Buchanan to Coats, 15 March 1937, telegram, CBC, vol. 240, file 11-37-2, pt. 1. On Coats and his listener surveys during this period, see Vipond, "Public Service Broadcasting."

95 William C. Gibson to Graham Spry, 10 February 1939, LAC, Spry Papers, vol. 65, file 31.

96 Mrs. R.L. Elliott to CBC, 14 February 1938, CBC, vol. 394, file 21-17, pt. 1; Ira Dilworth, "Report from BC Region," 1945, CBC, vol. 166, file 11-5-1.

97 "The Way of the Spirit," 1948, CBC, vol. 292, file 14-1-21, pt. 6.

98 John Polwarth to A.E. McDonald, 2 December 1948, BBC, E17/29/6, file 3C.

99 Ferguson to BBC Bursary Committee, 9 March 1951, CBC, vol. 238, file 11-36, pt. 1.

100 Greene to Graves, telegram, 18 November 1936 and Greene to Graves, 24 November 1936, BBC, E1/113/2, file 2; Greene to Graves, 24 September 1937 and Greene to Graves, 4 January 1937, BBC, E1/113/3, file 3.

101 Stephen Fry, "Canadian Survey," 23 March 1943, and Lindsay Wellington to R.W. Foot, 12 April 1943, BBC, E1/584/1, file 1. See especially Potter, *Broadcasting Empire*, chap. 4.

102 Michael Barkway to J.B. Clark, 28 November 1945, BBC, E1/509/2, file 2A.

103 Cardiff, "Mass Middlebrow Laughter."

104 Thelma Craig, "Central Authoritative Body on Proper Use of English Proposed," *Globe and Mail*, 17 May 1938.

105 CBC, CBC *Handbook for Announcers*, 1938, CBC, acc. 86-87/031, box 152; British Broadcasting Corporation, *Broadcast English*.

106 Gilbert Harding to H.C. Fenton, 29 January 1946, BBC, E12/97/1, file 1.

107 Program listings existed before 1948, but the CBC *Times* finally included *Listener*-like longer articles on broadcasting operations, performers, and upcoming programs. See R.S. Lambert, "Scheme for a Canadian National Weekly Linked with Radio and Other Cultural Interests," 1940, LAC, Weir Papers, vol. 13, file 5; R.S. Lambert to Plaunt, 5 April 1940, UBC Special Collections, Alan B. Plaunt Papers, box 2, file 18; Report on CBC National Programme Publication, 1943, LAC, Weir Papers, vol. 13, file 5; Weir, *Struggle for National Broadcasting*, 283–5.

108 Street, "BBC Sunday Policy."

109 Paper 13 – "Sunday Policy," 12 February 1945, BBC, R34/518.

110 Minutes of the 1st General Administrative Conference, Ottawa, 2–3 November 1943, app. C, CBC, vol. 466, file 30-16, pt. 1.

111 "Record of Proceedings," National Programme Conference, Toronto, 15–16 January 1945, LAC, Bushnell Papers, vol. 4, National Programme Conferences, n.d., and 1942–47, minutes; General Supervisor of programmes to Regional Representatives and Station Managers, 30 November 1949, CBC, vol. 164, file 11-2, pt. 2.

112 Badenoch, "Making Sunday," 578–9.

113 Tom Sloan to Overseas Liaison Officer, 16 April 1952, BBC, E1/500/1, file 1.

114 Ira Dilworth to Harry Boyle and others, 5 March 1952, CBC, vol. 166, file 11-5-1.

115 C.G. Graves to Hector Charlesworth, 23 November 1932, BBC, E4/44.

116 Murray to John Royal, 13 March 1937, NBC, box 52, fol. 42.

117 Murray to Graves, 27 June 1937, BBC, E1/555/1, Countries: Canada. Murray, W.E.G., 1937–1956, Lindsay Wellington, "Record of Interview at Broadcasting House," 22 September 1937, BBC, E1/522/4, file 2A.

118 Murray to T. Lochhead, 22 September 1939 and Murray to Lochhead, 6 October 1939, BBC, E1/502, Countries: Canada, CBC Staff, A-Z,

1939–47. Quotation from "Notes on Canadian Broadcasting Corporation," 22 August 1946, BBC, E1/493/2, file 1B; Report of the CBC for the fiscal year April 1st, 1938 – March 1st, 1939, n.d. [1939], CBC, vol. 287, file 14-1-5, pt. 1, Reports and Memoranda for Parliamentary Committee 1939. On these Commonwealth exchanges, see Potter, *Broadcasting Empire*, chap. 3.

119   R.A. Rendall to R.H. Eckersley, 19 April 1940, BBC, E1/522/5, file 2B.

120   R.A. Rendall, "Visit to Canada and the United States of America, October – November 1940," BBC, E15/180; R.A. Rendall to J.B. Clark, 17 September 1942, 3, BBC, E1/503; Potter, "Strengthening the Bonds," 195.

121   Howard B. Chase, "Talk by Howard B. Chase," broadcast 25 March 1945, CBC Trans-Canada Network, 4-5, LAC, CBC, vol. 33, file 2-2-4-1; "Canada – July 28 to August 3," n.d. [wartime], BBC, E1/490. On the origins and legacy of *Front Line Family*, see also Hilmes, *Network Nations*, 148.

122   "Drama and Features," 5, 8.

123   See Potter, "Strengthening the Bonds," 193–205.

124   Ivor Thomas to Harding, 18 April 1947, BBC, E1/585/2, file 2.

125   A.D. Dunton to George Barnes, 25 May 1949, BBC, E1/511.

126   Andrew Allan, "Report on Broadcast and Theatre Writing," 1950, 1, LAC, Andrew Allan Papers, CBC correspondence and memos, n.d.

127   "Public Announcement No. 15, Statement on Television by the Board of Governors," Canadian Broadcasting Corporation, Montreal, 17 May 1948, and "Public Announcement No. 22, Statement on Television by the Board of Governors," Canadian Broadcasting Corporation, Ottawa, 3 November 1948, BBC, E1/580.

128   Tom Sloan to MacAlpine, 29 August 1952, BBC, E1/580.

129   The CBC set up a listener research department in 1954, almost two decades later than had the BBC, and neither gave the data much weight in program policy. See Eaman, *Channels of Influence*; Silvey, *Methods of Listener Research*; Street, "BBC Sunday Policy"; Donald Manson to Sir William Haley, 23 January 1952, BBC, E1/511.

130   J.B. Clark to Overseas Programme Director, 26 March 1940, BBC, E1/500/2, file 2.

131   Gladstone Murray to Alan Plaunt, 2 November 1935, UBC Special Collections, Alan B. Plaunt Papers, box 3, file 15. On features, see Whitehead, *Third Programme*, chap. 6.

132   "Interchange of Programmes between CBC and BBC," 25 July 1939, BBC, E1/522/5, file 2B; Baillargeon, "CBC and the Cold War Mentality," 19.

133   Plaunt to G.M. Groves, 24 March 1938, BBC, E1/499/2, file 2.

134 C.A.L. Cliffe to J.B. Clark, 18 February 1938, BBC, E1/522/4, file 2A. Quotation is from Clarke's reply of 22 February on this same circulating memo.

135 The rate varied, but twenty pounds per hour was what CBC paid for recorded programming later in wartime. See C. Conner to C(OS), 28 September 1943, BBC, E17/29/1, file 1A; S.J. de Lotbiniere, "Note on the Marketing of L.T.S. Recordings in Canada," 30 March 1944. BBC, E17/31/1, file 1A. Michael Barkway reported sending half hours to CJOR in Vancouver for nine dollars in 1948. See Barkway to Gale, 30 June 1948 and Polwarth to R.L. Eastwood, 30 July 1948, BBC, E17/29/4, file 3A.

136 Mary Grannan to BBC, 1 August 1939 and Director of Overseas Service to Grannan, 7 September 1939, BBC, E12/97/1, file 1.

137 John S. Peach, "A Two-Way Street," CBC Times, 19–25 June 1949, 4; John Polwarth, "A Two-way Proposition," CBC Times, 5–11 March 1950, 2.

138 "Extracts from the Evidence of Mr. L.W. Brockington, Chairman of the Board of Governors of the Canadian Broadcasting Corporation," Standing Committee on Radio Broadcasting, 1938, CBC, vol. 288, file 14-1-12, pt. 1.

139 Gladstone Murray to Eric Maschwitz, 12 December 1936, BBC, E1/561/1.

140 "Memorandum on Overseas Programme Services," 20 March 1940, BBC, E2/1461/1, file 7A.

141 D.G. Bridson, "A Consideration of Short-Wave Broadcasting to America," 10 April 1942, BBC, E1/128.

142 "Extract from a Report by Laurence Gilliam on His Visit to the United States and Canada, 5th April 1943," BBC, E15/76.

143 Talks on or originating in Britain, CBC, vol. 893, file PG 8-1-1, pt. 1, 1939–61.

144 R.T. Bowman to Director, Empire Service, 18 January 1941, BBC, E1/500/2, file 2; R.A. Rendall to Overseas Programme Assistant, 19 April 1940, BBC, E1/522/5, file 2B.

145 C. Conner to C(OS), 28 September 1943 and C. Conner to C(OS), 18 October 1943, BBC, E17/29/1, file 1A; "Semi-Annual Canadian Report," January to June 1948, BBC, E1/509/4, file 3.

146 "Minute No. 2 of N.A.D. Meeting, 12th October 1943," BBC, E17/31/1, file 1A.

147 S.J. de Lotbiniere to Conner, 8 February 1945, Gilbert Harding to Conner, 22 March 1946, and Conner to Barkway, 5 December 1946, BBC, E17/31/2, file 1B; Barkway to Conner, 8 January 1947 and Robert McCall to DTS, 8 January 1947, BBC, E17/31/3, file 2A; "An Agreement," n.d. [1953], BBC, E17/31/5, file 2C.

148 Quotations from "Report on BBC's Canadian Office: January to June, 1947," BBC, E1/509/4, file 3; John Polwarth to R.L. Eastwood, 30 July 1948, BBC, E17/29/4, file 3A.

149 Thomas Archer, "Speaking as a Listener," broadcast 3 September 1948, CBC Trans-Canada Network, CBC, vol. 193, file 11-18-11-6, pt. 1, PG8.

150 Quotation from Canadian Representative to Chairman of BBC, n.d. [December 1948], BBC, E17/29/6, file 3C. Barkway was around the same time concerned with the CBC's "sponging" too much from the BBC. See Barkway to J.B. Clark, 3 August 1948, BBC, E17/29/5, file 3B.

151 "Home News from Britain," CBC Times, 4–10 March 1952, 2.

152 Pelletier to Barkway, 12 November 1947, correspondence between Barkway and Peggie Broadhead, 23–25 March 1948, Barkway to MacAlpine, 28 October 1948, Polwarth to Broadhead, 23 November 1948, BBC, E1/586/2, File 1B; Polwarth to Pelletier, 22 February 1950, BBC, E17/29/11, File 6A.

153 Polwarth to MacAlpine, 16 August 1948 and Barkway to J.B. Clark, 3 August 1948, BBC, E17/29/5, file 3B.

154 Polwarth to J.B. Clark, 27 September 1949, BBC, E12/100/3, file 3.

155 "CBC Presents the Light Operas of Gilbert and Sullivan," 1948, CBC, vol. 292, file 14-1-21, pt. 6, reports and Memoranda for parliamentary committee 1950; H.G. Walker, "Report by Manager of Dominion Network," 6 October 1948, CBC, vol. 166, file 11-5-1.

156 E.A Weir to Dawson Richardson, 13 March 1937, CBC, vol. 240, file 11-37-2, pt. 4; C.A.L. Cliffe to Murray, 6 July 1937, CBC, vol. 240, file 11-37-2, pt. 3.

157 Gladstone Murray, "Broadcasting the Royal Tour," synopsis of the remarks of the general manager, Meeting of Commentators, CBC headquarters, Ottawa, 11 May 1939, UBC Special Collections, Alan B. Plaunt Papers, box 17, file 4; "Special Events," 8; "Royal Visit Broadcasting Policies," 10 March 1939, CBC, vol. 242, file 11-37-14-2, pt. 1; Weir to Bushnell, "Commercial Sponsors and the Royal Visit," 7 March 1939, CBC, vol. 242, file 11-37-14-2, pt. 1; W.H. Brodie, "Bulletins #1-8: Royal Tour Broadcasts," 31 August – 1 October 1951, CBC, acc. 86-87/031, box 198, file 18-16R-10 to W-9.

158 Frigon to Bushnell, 27 March 1939, CBC, vol. 242, file 11-37-14-2, pt. 1.

159 Charles Jennings to Bushnell, 27 July 1951 and Jennings to Regional Representatives, "Demise of the Crown," 25 September 1951, CBC, vol. 241, file 11-37-9; F.R. Shaw to George Young, 23 February 1952, Ian Ritchie, "Network Arrangements on the Death of His Majesty King George Sixth," 18 February 1952, T.J. Allard to CAB member stations,

"Re: Broadcasting Procedure Day of Royal Funeral," 8 February 1952, and George Young to all broadcasting stations, 8 February 1952, CBC, vol. 242, file 11-37-10, pt. 2; Charles Jennings, "Outline of Procedure to be followed in Announcing the Deaths of Certain Persons," 20 March 1953, CBC, vol. 50, file 2-3-6-6, pt. 2.

160 "Report on Visit to United States," 1943, BBC, E15/76.

161 Seymour de Lotbiniere, "Report on Transcontinental Trip," 31 December 1943, BBC, E1/509/1, file 1.

162 Harding to MacAlpine, 23 March 1945, BBC, E1/509/2, file 2A; Michael Barkway to J.B. Clark, 12 October 1945, BBC, E1/509/1, file 1; J.B. Clark to AC(OS), 30 August 1946, BBC, E1/503.

163 Felix Greene to Gladstone Murray, 2 June 1938, CBC, vol. 378, file 20-3-5, pt. 2.

164 Val Gielgud to Archie MacCorkindale, 9 December 1944, BBC, E1/500/1, file 1; Patric Dickinson to George Barnes, 29 August 1946 and George Barnes to Gilbert Harding, 10 February 1947, BBC, E1/555/1, file 1. Quotation from Norman Luker to G.R. Barnes, 7 August 1941, BBC, E1/555/1, file 2.

165 George Barnes to Gilbert Harding, 15 June 1946, BBC, E1/509/3, file 2B.

166 George Barnes to Ira Dilworth, 12 September 1947, BBC, E1/520; Ivor Thomas, "Canada to Britain," 5 December 1947, BBC, E1/500/1, file 1; Robert Moyse, "Critically Speaking," broadcast 4 October 1953, BBC, E1/509/6, file 5.

167 Barkway to Listener Research Director, 15 November 1946, BBC, E12/97/2, file 2.

168 Stallsworthy, "What Price Radio?"; "CBC Freedom," *Saturday Night*, 27 November 1943, 1, 3; "CBC Drives Listeners to US Stations," *Canadian Broadcaster*, 26 January 1946, 1; John Chabot Smith, "Britain's Bid to Rule the Air Waves," *Saturday Evening Post*, 16 November 1946, 32–3, 58, 61–2; Chandler, "Case for Private Broadcasting."

169 Barkway to Cyril Conner, 15 November 1946, BBC, E12/97/2, file 2.

170 "Some Aspects of Commercial and Public Service Broadcasting," 20 August 1948, BBC, E1/489 (emphasis in original).

171 J.B. Clark to Canadian Representative, 29 November 1946, BBC, E1/479, files 1–2; Michael Barkway, "'What's the CBC Worth?'" CBC *Times*, 13–19 November 1949, 3, 10–11. (Orig. pub. in *Saturday Night*, 25 October 1949.)

172 Dunton, "T.S. Eliot on the Prairie."

173 "Canadian Representative's Report," 1 May 1952, BBC, E1/509/4, file 4.

174 Cyril Conner to AHF, 22 December 1953, BBC, E17/29/19, file 9B; Gordon Winter, "BBC in Canada," 4 October 1953, BBC, E1/509/6,

file 5; "It Has Old-Countrymen Rolling in the Aisles," CBC *Times*, 25 September – 1 October 1955, 3.

175 Cyril Conner to Gordon Winter, 20 January 1956, BBC, E1/479, files 1–2.

176 Gladstone Murray, "Some Thoughts on Broadcasting," typescript, June 1936, papers of R.S. Lambert, in the possession of Jessica Lambert Riddell, Ottawa.

177 Gladstone Murray, "Broadcasting in Canada," n.d. [1939], CBC, vol. 466, file 31-1.

178 Vipond, "Royal Tour of 1939," 150–1.

179 Felix Greene to J.B. Clark, 4 January 1937, BBC, E1/561/1, file 1.

180 Vipond, "Going Their Own Way", 76–7.

181 S.W. Fisher to Canadian Broadcasting Corporation, 8 May 1939, S. Bonneville to Canadian Broadcasting Corporation, 11 May 1939, CBC, vol. 393, file 21-8; Hill, "Broadcasting in Canada."

182 This was probably a joke about giving an arm for a drink. See Murray to J.B. Clark, 9 December 1937 and J.B. Clark to Murray, 24 December 1937, BBC, E1/522/4, file 2A.

183 Murray to Reith, 29 January 1938, BBC, E1/522/4, file 2A.

184 Gordon Shrum to Murray, 20 January 1938, Graves to Shrum, 14 February 1938, Graves to Murray, 14 February 1938, C.A.L. Cliffe to J.B. Clark, 18 February 1938, Bowman to Cliffe, 24 February 1938, Felix Greene to Clark, 22 March 1938 (source of quotation), BBC, E1/522/4, file 2A.

185 Bowman to Macgregor, 22 April 1938, BBC, E1/522/4, file 2A; Murray to Macgregor, 17 May 1938. BBC, E1/522/5, file 2B.

186 CRBC press release, "Distinct Canadian Flavor Permeates Fall Schedule," 16 September 1936, CBC, vol. 161, file 11-1, pt. 1, Programming – General; R.T. Bowman to J.C.S. Macgregor, 30 July 1937, BBC, E1/522/3, file 1C.

187 Frank Armstrong, "Let's Go to the Music Hall," *Radio Guide*, 3 May 1936, n.p., CBC, vol. 49, file 2-3-5, pt. 2.

188 Frank Chamberlain, "I Love Radio, Even If ..." *Saturday Night*, 22 March 1941, 24. "A Tour de Force of Simulation," CBC *Times*, 7–13 September 1952, 2.

189 Gladstone Murray to Stephen Fry, n.d. [March 1943], and Horace Stovin to Fry, 11 March 1943, BBC, E1/488, Canadian Association of Broadcasters, files 1–2, 1941–53; "Reading and Listening," *Canadian Forum* 20, 234 (1940): 101.

190 Felix Greene to ADES, 20 September 1937, BBC, E1/522/4, file 2A; Murray to Macgregor, 17 May 1938, BBC, E1/522/5, file 2B.

191 Charles Jennings to Macgregor, 25 November 1938, and R.A. Rendall to Overseas Programme Assistant, 19 April 1940, BBC, E1/522/5, file 2B.

192 Seymour de Lotbinière, "Fourth Report on the Working of the BBC's Canadian Office, 1 January to 21 May 1945," 21 May 1945, Barkway to A/NASD et al., 14 June 1945, and Barkway to MacAlpine, 8 September 1945, BBC, E1/509/2, file 2A.

193 Potter, *Broadcasting Empire*, chaps. 5 and 6.

194 MacAlpine to C(OS), 7 February 1946, BBC, E1/509/3, file 2B; "Report on BBC's Canadian Office: January to June, 1947," 1947, BBC, E1/509/4, file 3.

195 Barkway to MacAlpine, 21 May 1946, BBC, E1/509/3, File 2B and Barkway to T.P. Gale, 27 September 1946, BBC, E17/29/2, File 1B; Polwarth to MacAlpine, 30 October 1948 and "Semi-Annual Canadian Report," January to June 1948, BBC, E1/509/4, file 3. Quotation from "Semi-Annual Canadian Report," 8 January 1947, BBC, E1/509/4, file 3.

196 Harding to MacAlpine, 12 June 1947, BBC, E1/503; "Behind the Microphone," *CBC Times*, 9-15 March 1952, 15.

197 R.A. Rendall, "Report on a Visit to the United States, Canada, Mexico and Jamaica," BBC, E15/180; Polwarth to MacAlpine, 20 May 1949, BBC, E17/29/8, file 4B.

198 House of Commons Special Committee on Radio Broadcasting, *Minutes of Proceedings and Evidence, No. 5, 28–29 May 1942, Witness: Gladstone Murray*, 219–20 (Ottawa: King's Printer, 1942); Barkway to Controller (Overseas Service), BBC, 21 August 1946 and 15 November 1946, BBC, E1/493/2, file 1B; Lambert to Polwarth, 3 May 1949, BBC, E17/29/8, file 4B; MacAlpine to Polwarth, 6 May 1949. BBC, E1/509/4.

199 Simon of Wythenshawe, "Broadcasting in Canada," 3 January 1949, CBC, vol. 988, file 2.

200 James Buckley to Donald Manson, 7 January 1929, LAC, Records of the Royal Commission on Radio Broadcasting, vol. 1, file 227-10-3.

201 Scullion, "BBC Radio in Scotland," 64.

CHAPTER FOUR

1 MacLennan, "Resistance to Regulation"; Lipschultz, *Broadcast and Internet Indecency*; Hendy, "Bad Language"; Newman, *Radio Active*; Slotten, *Radio and Television Regulation*; Garay, "Guarding the Airwaves"; Benjamin, "Defining the Public Interest"; Brown, "Selling Airtime for Controversy."

2   "Procedure," n.d. [1947], 7, Library and Archives Canada, Records of the Canadian Broadcasting Corporation, Ottawa (hereafter CBC), vol. 32A, file 1-18, pt. 2.

3   Brewer, "What's Wrong with Commercial Radio?," 31.

4   Vipond, "Censorship in a Liberal State." On the idea of the liberal order, see McKay, "Liberal Order Framework."

5   Vipond, "Censorship in a Liberal State," 75–83.

6   Ibid., 87.

7   "Procedure," n.d. [1947], 5. CBC, vol. 32A, file 1-18, pt. 2.

8   "Radio's Role in the Election Campaign," CBC Times, 26 June–4 July 1953, 4; Spencer and Bolan, "Election Broadcasting in Canada," 3–5.

9   "A statement on good taste as prepared by Mr. L.A. [sic] Teevens, Chief of the Proprietary or Patent Medicine Division," cited in W. John Dunlop to J.S. Thomson, 14 November 1942, CBC, vol. 142, file 9-5-1, pt. 1.

10 On ratings and audience research during the early radio era, see Eaman, *Channels of Influence*, 49–83.

11 Kinahan, "Cultivating the Taste of the Nation"; Turvey, "Another of Those Sex Films"; Bingham, "Stream of Pollution"; Butsch, "Class and Audience Effects"; Gerson, *Purer Taste*, 28–32; Richards, "British Board of Film Censors." Moral panics involving smaller-circulation "newspapers" and books go back much further. See Lemmings and Walker, *Moral Panics*.

12 P.P. Eckersley to R.H. Eckersley, 6 March 1928, British Broadcasting Corporation Written Archives Centre, Caversham, Berkshire (hereafter BBC), R34/317/1, file 1A.

13 Vipond, *Listening In*, 134–49, esp. 145ff.

14 H.W. Thornton, "Agate Lines and Railway Lines," an address delivered to the Associated Advertising Clubs of the World, Philadelphia, PA, 21 June 1926, 5, Library and Archives Canada (hereafter LAC), Weir Papers, vol. 18, file 7.

15 Johnston, "Early Trials of Protestant Radio."

16 Raymond Cardinal Rouleau to Aird, 1 February 1929, translation, LAC, Records of the Royal Commission on Radio Broadcasting, vol. 1, file 227-10-3.

17 Krattenmaker and Powe, Jr., *Regulating Broadcast Programming*, 20–5.

18 James Montagnes, "Canada Plans to Rule Her Ether Waves," *Baltimore Sun*, 16 February 1930.

19 Raboy, *Missed Opportunities*, 11. The BBG existed for about ten years until it was replaced by the Canadian Radio-Television Commission

(CRTC), now the Canadian Radio-Television and Telecommunications Commission.

20   Vipond, "Censorship in a Liberal State," 89.

21   Gladstone Murray, "National Radio in Canada," 25 July 1933, 21-2, LAC, Murray Papers, vol. 1.

22   Vipond, "Beginnings of Public Broadcasting."

23   Ward, "Early Use of Radio"; Nolan, "Canadian Election Broadcasting," 181–2.

24   James Law to the Manager, Station CRCT, 20 September 1936. CRBC's regional director of programmes for Ontario, Stanley Maxted, noted that the commission had received numerous disapproving letters and telephone calls. See Maxted to Reg Brophy, 29 September 1936, National Broadcasting Company Records, Wisconsin Historical Society Archives, Madison (hereafter NBC), box 44, fol. 65. The show in question featured Eddie Cantor, who also tried the patience of American regulators. See Craig, "Out of Eden."

25   Spry, "Radio Broadcasting," 115, Claxton material at 125–6; Raboy, *Missed Opportunities*, 55.

26   "Report of the General Supervisor of Programmes of the Proceedings of the Second Semi-annual Programme Conference, Held in the National Research Building, Ottawa, June 7th to 11th, inclusive," [1937], app. A, 5, CBC, vol. 850, file PG1-13, pt. 1.

27   Kuffert, "Tempest in the Tea Leaves," 6.

28   Gladstone Murray to Phillip N. Morris, 2 December 1937, CBC, vol. 32A, file 1-18, pt. 2.

29   James S. Thomson, "A New Policy for Radio," n.d. [1942], 3-4, LAC, Weir Papers, vol. 6, file 10.

30   Minutes of Board of Governors meeting, 17 April 1942, CBC, vol. 616, ser. A.IV.2.a.ii.

31   Tolbridge, "Sabotaging the CBC," 175 (emphasis in original); Tolbridge, "Private Radio Gangs Up."

32   "Memorandum on Policy", 7 April 1942, CBC, vol. 33, file 2-2-3.

33   Minutes of the 1st General Administrative Conference, Ottawa, 2–3 November 1943, appendix C, 34, CBC, vol. 466, file 30-16, pt. 1.

34   Decisions of Sub-Committee on News Commentaries, 15 March 1944, LAC, Bushnell Papers, vol. 2; "Record of Proceedings," National Programme Conference, Toronto, 15–16 January 1945, LAC, Bushnell Papers, vol. 4.

35   Barkway to Controller (Overseas Service), BBC, 21 August 1946, BBC, E1/493/2, file 1B; "Note on the Canadian Broadcasting Corporation," November 1948, BBC, E1/489.

36 Gerald Pratley, "This Week at the Movies," broadcast 19 December 1948, LAC, Pratley Papers, vol. 1.

37 W.K. Moyer to Charles Jennings, 19 July 1949, CBC, fol. 237, file 11-29.

38 Neil M. Morrison, "The Social Sciences and Mass Communication: A Case History in Social Pressures," address to the Ontario Psychological Association, Toronto, 1 February 1952, LAC, Neil M. Morrison Papers, vol. 26.

39 A.L. Ashby to R.C. Patterson, 23 May 1933, NBC, box 16, fol. 42; Benjamin, "Defining the Public Interest," 90–7. Quotation from: "Statement from Dr. Lee DeForest sent to the Canadian Radio League and submitted to the Special Parliamentary Committee on Radio Broadcasting," 1932, LAC, Spry Papers, vol. 158, file 158-2.

40 On this reform movement, see McChesney, *Telecommunications, Mass Media, and Democracy*. On early American concern over the obtrusiveness of direct advertising, see Meyers, "Problems with Sponsorship," 356–8; Garay, "Guarding the Airwaves"; John Dunlop, "A Comparative Survey of the Clearance Methods for Copy Broadcast on the American Networks," 14 March 1942, CBC, vol. 142, file 9-5-1, pt. 1.

41 In a special issue of the *Annals of the American Academy of Political and Social Science* 177 (January 1935), see Perry, "Weak Spots"; Davis, "Regulation of Radio Advertising."

42 "Functions of the Continuity Acceptance Department, National Broadcasting Company," 1937, NBC, box 92, fol. 42. Consumer affairs journalist Ruth Brindze contested such claims the same year in Brindze, *Not to Be Broadcast*.

43 "Products Not Acceptable for Advertising over NBC Facilities," n.d. [1937], NBC, box 92, fol. 42; "CBC Commercial Policy re Unacceptable Accounts," n.d. [1951], CBC, vol. 46, file 2-3-2-2, pt. 3.

44 "Full Text of Final Code Adopted by NAB Convention" (as published in "Broadcasting," 15 July 1939), Rare Books and Special Collections, University of British Columbia (hereafter UBC Special Collections), Alan B. Plaunt Papers, box 17, file 4; "Practices and Principles," n.d. [1940], NBC, box 112, fol. 22; "2nd Meeting," minutes of a meeting of the Committee Studying Commercial Continuity, 1944, CBC, vol. 342, file 15-3, pt. 4; "NBC Program Policies and Working Manual," 1945, CBC, vol. 389, file 20-8-1; Mutual Broadcasting System Inc., "Program Standards," 1945, CBC, vol. 389, file 20-8-2; National Association of Broadcasters, "Standards of Practice," n.d. [1946], CBC, vol. 343, file 15-4, pt. 1.

45 Pickard, "Battle over the FCC Blue Book"; Socolow, "Questioning Advertising's Influence."

46 Felix Greene to C.G. Graves, 10 January 1936, BBC, E1/528.

47 Graves to DFD, DV, DOB and Regional Directors, 3 February 1937, BBC, R34/292/2, file 2A; J.B. Clark to C.G. Graves, 12 August 1942, BBC, R34/292/3, file 3; Director of Empire Programmes to Mr. Madden, 15 October 1942, BBC, R34/292/3, file 3; S.J. de Lotbiniere to Mr Madden, 27 November 1942, BBC, R34/292/3, file 3; Polwarth to T.P. Gale, 21 September 1948, BBC, E17/29/5, File 3B; "BBC Variety Programmes Policy Guide for Writers & Producers," 1948, BBC, R34/259.

48 Allard, *Straight Up*, 13, 99.

49 Canadian Association of Broadcasters, "Radio Broadcasting under Private Ownership," (1929), 9, CBC, vol. 342, file 15-3, pt. 8.

50 Memorandum of interview with Major Borrett (CHNS), 10 December 1936, CBC, vol. 146, file 9-11, pt. 1.

51 Canadian Association of Broadcasters, "Code of Ethics," 17 February 1943, LAC, Allard Papers, vol. 25, file 13.

52 Glen Bannerman, "Broadcasting in Canada (a Critique of the System)," 1944, CBC, vol. 342, file 15-3, pt. 5.

53 "CBC Cans Cantor," *Canadian Broadcaster*, 12 January 1946, 5.

54 "Canada's Radio Laws Spell Monopoly," print ad (1947), CBC, vol. 342, file 15-3, pt. 5; "Are 'Crystal Set' Radio Laws Good Enough for Canadians?," print ad (1947), CBC, vol. 342, file 15-3, pt. 5.

55 Quotation from: Canadian Association of Broadcasters, "Suggested Material for Massey Commission Questions," [1950], LAC, Allard Papers, vol. 5, file 9; George C. Chandler, "The Case for Private Broadcasting," *Public Affairs* (Spring 1952): 6-16. Chandler was manager of CJOR Vancouver.

56 "CBC General Manager Sets New Standard for Radio Advertising" n.d. [November 1942], CBC, vol. 142, file 9-5-1, pt. 1.

57 Fainmel and Eveleigh, "Proper Function of Advertising," 157.

58 Gladstone Murray to Felix J. Lafferty, 9 November 1937, CBC, vol. 144, file 9-8, pt. 1.

59 J.J. Heagarty to Horace Stovin, 28 January 1939, CBC, vol. 144, file 9-8, pt. 1; Heagarty to Stovin, 14 May 1940, CBC, vol. 144, file 9-8, pt. 1; Stovin to Effie V. Burnham, 15 May 1940, CBC, vol. 144, file 9-8, pt. 1.

60 Janet McRorie to Frank E. Mullen, 27 September 1940, NBC, box 95, fol. 14.

61 Notes on CBC relationship with the Department of Pensions and National Health, n.d. [1942], CBC, vol. 288, file 14-1-6, pt. 1.

62 J.S. Thomson to J.R. Radford, 23 March 1943, CBC, vol. 142, file 9-5-1, pt. 1.

63 J.R. Radford, "Station Relations Division," 10 July 1943, *Annual Report of the Canadian Broadcasting Corporation for the Fiscal Year ended*

March 31, 1943 (Ottawa: King's Printer, 1944), CBC, vol. 49, file 2-3-5, pt. 2.

64 Edgar Stone, memo to advertising agencies, 27 December 1943, CBC, vol. 210, file 11-19, pt. 1.

65 F.L.J., Ninga, Manitoba, to CBC, *CBC Program Schedule*, week of 15 April 1945, Prairie Region, 5.

66 "Procedure," n.d. [1947], 7, CBC, vol. 32A, file 1-18, pt. 2.

67 R.D. Whitmore to J.R. Radford, 1 February 1947, CBC, vol. 144, file 9-8, pt. 3.

68 Lister Sinclair, "What's on Your Mind? Chapter 1: The Crying Wren," 4 March 1946, LAC, Lister Sinclair Papers, vol. 2, radio scripts; Lister Sinclair, "What's On Your Mind? Chapter 2: The Exasperating Electrician," 11 March 1946, LAC, Lister Sinclair Papers, vol. 2, radio scripts; Chisholm et al., *Man's Last Enemy*; "Chasing Out the Ghosts That Haunt Our Lives," *CBC Times*, 20–26 September 1953, 2.

69 On an earlier struggle over patent medicine and alternative cures advertised in the United States, see Smith, "Quelling Radio's Quacks."

70 Charlesworth, "Broadcasting in Canada," 46.

71 Memorandum of interview with Major Borrett, 10 December 1936, CBC, vol. 146, file 9-11, pt. 1; R.E. Messer to Weir, 22 July 1937, CBC, vol. 167, file 7-1-1, pt. 1; Weir to Messer, 27 July 1937, CBC, vol. 167, file 7-1-1, pt. 1; J. Barclay to Canadian Radio Commission [*sic*], 9 January 1939, CBC, vol. 153, file 9-31, pt. 1; George Hebden Corsan, "Claims Millions Wasted on Nostrums Sold on Air," *Globe and Mail*, 3 May 1939; Harry Sedgewick, "Broadcasters Resent Attack on Advertising," *Globe and Mail*, 8 May 1939.

72 Weir to Frigon, 22 December 1941, CBC, vol. 142, file 9-5-1, pt. 1.

73 J.R. Radford to J.S. Thomson, 10 November 1942, CBC, vol. 142, file 9-5-1, pt. 1.

74 R.E. Wodehouse to Gladstone Murray, 8 January 1942, CBC, vol. 142, file 9-5-1, pt. 1.

75 J.S. Thomson to J.R. Radford, 4 December 1942, CBC, vol. 142, file 9-5-1, pt. 1.

76 Gladstone Murray to J.J. Heagarty, 27 October 1942, CBC, vol. 142, file 9-5-1, pt. 1.

77 J.R. Radford to J.S. Thomson, 10 November 1942, CBC, vol. 142, file 9-5-1, pt. 1.

78 Radford to G.M. Geldert, 19 August 1944, CBC, vol. 142, file 9-5-1, pt. 1.

79 J.S. Thomson to J.R. Radford, 23 March 1943, CBC, vol. 142, file 9-5-1, pt. 1.

80 J.R. Radford to J.S. Thomson, 10 December 1942, CBC, vol. 142, file 9-5-1, pt. 1.

81 Teevens report to Dunlop, cited in W. John Dunlop to J.S. Thomson, 14 November 1942, CBC, vol. 142, file 9-5-1, pt. 1.

82 W. John Dunlop to J.R. Radford, 15 October 1942, CBC, vol. 142, file 9-5-1, pt. 1.

83 W. John Dunlop, "A Comparative Survey of the Clearance Methods for Copy Broadcast on the American Networks," 14 March 1942, 9–11, CBC, vol. 142, file 9-5-1, pt. 1.

84 Dunlop, "Comparative Survey," 11.

85 C.R. Tetley to Neil Morrison, 9 May 1944, CBC, vol. 142, file 9-5-1, pt. 1.

86 Neil Morrison to C.R. Tetley, 22 May 1944, CBC, vol. 142, file 9-5-1, pt. 1.

87 C.R. Tetley to Neil Morrison, 9 May 1944, CBC vol. 142, file 9-5-1, pt. 1.

88 Frigon to S.B. Smith, 3 October 1944, CBC, vol. 142, file 9-5-1, pt. 1.

89 E.A. Weir to Frigon, 21 September 1944, CBC, vol. 142, file 9-5-1, pt. 1.

90 Frigon to Weir, 22 September 1944, CBC, vol. 142, file 9-5-1, pt. 1.

91 Weir to Frigon, 21 September 1944, 2, CBC, vol. 142, file 9-5-1, pt. 1.

92 Frigon to Bushnell, Weir, Radford, 3 October 1944, CBC, vol. 142, file 9-5-1, pt. 2.

93 Bushnell to Frigon, 9 November 1944, CBC, vol. 142, file 9-5-1, pt. 2. In the United States, the whole patent medicine connection with radio had just been vilified in a *New Republic* article calling for sweeping reform. See Cunningham Jr., "Medicine Men of the Air." See also Porter, "Radio Must Grow Up."

94 Ernest Bushnell, "What's In the Air?," address to the Canadian Club, Vancouver, 22 November 1944, LAC, Bushnell Papers, vol. 4.

95 Frigon to Bushnell, 13 November 1944, CBC, vol. 142, file 9-5-1, pt. 2.

96 Frigon to J.W. McKee, telegram, 30 November 1944, CBC, vol. 142, file 9-5-1, pt. 2; Frigon to Jennings, 30 November 1944, CBC, vol. 142, file 9-5-1, pt. 2.

97 Jennings to Bushnell, 1 December 1944, CBC, vol. 142, file 9-5-1, pt. 2.

98 H.G. Walker to Jennings, 9 December 1944, CBC, vol. 142, file 9-5-1, pt. 2.

99 Frigon to Walker, 11 December 1944, CBC, vol. 142, file 9-5-1, pt. 2.

100 Minutes of a meeting held at the National Office, Toronto, 22 December 1944, CBC, vol. 142, file 9-5-1, pt. 2; "CBC Commercial Policy re Unacceptable Accounts," n.d. [1951], CBC, vol. 46, file 2-3-2-2, pt. 3.

101 George F. French to CBC, 13 November 1939, CBC, vol. 238, file 11-34-2.

102 Gruenberg, "Radio and the Child"; Dennis, "Chills and Thrills"; Oswell, "Early Children's Broadcasting"; Dolan, "Aunties and Uncles"; Starker, *Evil Influences*, 114–19; Davies et al., "In the Worst Possible Taste."

103 Adams, "Youth."

104 Kuhn, "Children."

105 Preston, "Children's Reactions"; Razlogova, "True Crime Radio."

106 "Elliott Addresses US Association on Canadian Radio," *Canadian Broadcaster*, September 1942, 8; "They Like to Wake Up Screaming," *Canadian Broadcaster*, February 1942, 3.

107 "Drama and Features," 3.

108 Ibid., 1.

109 "Daytime Serials Report Finds Good Points Outweigh Bad," *Radio Daily*, 5 February 1943, 1, 3.

110 Ernest Bushnell, Commentary on thriller programmes, n.d. [1944], CBC, vol. 861, file 4-2-1, pt. 1; J.R. Radford, "Children's Thriller Programmes," 24 October 1944, CBC, vol. 861, file 4-2-1, pt. 1.

111 Radford, "Children's Thriller Programmes." On such concerns for the mental health of children in film, see Low, "New Generation."

112 Augustin Frigon, "Thriller and Horror Programmes: Memorandum by the General Manager," n.d. [1944], LAC, Bushnell Papers, vol. 14.

113 Val Gielgud to Archie MacCorkindale, 9 December 1944, BBC, E1/500/1, file 1.

114 Weir to Frigon, 5 January 1945, CBC, vol. 861, file 4-2-1, pt. 1.

115 E.L. Bushnell, "Horror Programmes," 6 January 1945, CBC, vol. 861, file 4-2-1, pt. 1.

116 Bushnell, commentary on thriller programmes.

117 Minutes of a meeting of the Policy Committee of the Canadian Association of Broadcasters, 15 January 1945, LAC, Allard Papers, vol. 5, file 10.

118 "Radio's Responsibility in Juvenile Delinquency," 9 April 1946, LAC, Bushnell Papers, vol. 2.

119 "Record of Proceedings," National Programme Conference, Toronto, 15–16 January 1945, LAC, Bushnell Papers, vol. 4; Minutes of the General Administrative Conference, Ottawa, 17–19 January 1945, LAC, Bushnell Papers, vol. 2.

120 Howard B. Chase, "Report to CBC Shareholders: A CBC Editorial," n.d. [1945], CBC, vol. 472, file 31-9, pt. 3.

121 Los Angeles Tenth District, California Congress of Parents and Teachers to Radio Stations, Radio Advertising Agencies and Sponsors of Radio Programs, 11 January 1946, CBC, vol. 288, file 14-1-12, pt. 1; Grace Johnsen to Mrs. Z.W. Logan, 25 February 1946, CBC, vol. 288, file 14-1-12, pt. 1; Rodney L. Brink, "Murder Plots on Radio Arouse Los Angeles," 23 March 1946, CBC, vol. 276, file 11-42-9, pt. 3. On the "Blue Book"

moment, see Pickard, "Battle over the FCC Blue Book"; and Socolow, "Questioning Advertising's Influence."

122 Meeting with Representatives of National Committee for Mental Hygiene, 3 May 1946, LAC, Bushnell Papers, vol. 2; Jennings to S.R. Laycock, 11 June 1946, CBC, vol. 276, file 11-42-9, pt. 3.

123 A.D. Dunton, "Parliamentary Committee," n.d. [1946], CBC, vol. 289, file 14-1-12, pt. 7.

124 "Children's and Thriller Programmes," 10 June 1946, CBC, vol. 276, file 11-42-9, pt. 3.

125 CBC Press Release re: "thrillers," n.d. [1946], 1-2, CBC, vol. 276, file 11-42-9, pt. 3; "Memorandum II Regarding Research Project on the Psychological Effect of Certain Types of Radio Programmes on the Behaviour of Children," 20 August 1946, CBC, vol. 276, file 11-42-9, pt. 3.

126 Louise Stone, "Society Feeds Its Children the Erotic Fare of Delinquency," *Saturday Night*, 12 October 1946, 38–9; Eda [Saile] to Ted Allan, n.d. 1949, LAC, Ted Allan Papers, vol. 20, file 1; Rev. Owen G. Barrow, Marathon, ON, letter to editor, "CBC's 'Horror' Newscasts," *Ottawa Citizen*, 12 March 1952, n.p.; "The War against Our Children's Minds," *New Frontiers* 3, 3 (1954): 1-3.

127 Ken R. Dyke, "Crime and Mystery Programs," 13 September 1947, NBC, box 115, fol. 15; Nick Kenny, "Day unto Day," *Daily Mirror* (New York), 19 September 1947.

128 Charles Jennings, "The National System – Programmes," 24 February 1948, CBC, vol. 161, file 11-1, pt. 1; "Books for Children Come Alive through Radio," *CBC Times*, 13–19 August 1950, 5.

129 Ira Dilworth, Statement re Programme Policy, 14 March 1952, CBC, vol. 164, file 11-2, pt. 2.

130 Kuffert, "Tempest in the Tea Leaves."

131 The regulation read: "No one shall broadcast (j)(i) programs presenting a person who claims supernatural or psychic powers, or a fortune teller, character analyst, crystal-gazer or the like, or programs which lead or may lead the listening public to believe that the person presented claims to possess or possesses supernatural or psychic powers or is or claims to be a fortune-teller, character analyst, crystal-gazer or the like; (ii) programs in which a person answers or solves or purports to answer or solve questions or problems submitted by listeners or members of the public unless such programs prior to being broadcast shall have been approved by a representative of the Corporation." See Parliament of Canada, *Regulations for Broadcasting Stations*.

132 Evans, "Divining the Social Order."

133 CBC, "Notes on CBC Regulations for Broadcasting Stations," (1950), 10, CBC, vol. 304, file 14-2-2, pt. 7.

134 Ibid.

135 Cited in letter from Gladstone Murray to Egerton Lovering, 14 January 1938, CBC, vol. 151, file 9-19, pt. 1.

136 Weir to Murray, 30 June 1937, CBC, vol. 146, file 9-11, pt. 2.

137 CBC Broadcast Regulations Division, "CBC Regulations," (1949), 9, file 14-2-2, pt. 8.

138 F.W. Savignac to Murray, 10 January 1938, CBC, vol. 151, file 9-19, pt. 1; F.P. Varcoe to Murray, 5 May 1942, CBC, vol. 151, file 9-19, pt. 3.

139 Gladstone Murray to C.D. Howe, 10 January 1938, CBC, vol. 151, file 9-19, pt. 1.

140 "Since this is a definite prohibition the enforcement rests with the individual station managers." See CBC Broadcast Regulations Division, "CBC Regulations," (1949), 9, CBC, vol. 304, file 14-2-2, pt. 8, Massey Commission.

141 *Astrolite* script, 27 October 1938, CFCF Montreal, CBC, vol. 151, file 9-19, pt. 2.

142 Exchange of telegrams re: *Astrolite*, December 1938, CBC, vol. 151, file 9-19, pt. 2.

143 D.W. Buchanan, "National Network," 19 June 1939, CBC, vol. 165, file 11-2-3. pt. 1.

144 Koram to Murray, 14 December 1937, CBC, vol. 151, file 9-19, pt. 1.

145 Stovin to Andrew M. Bell, telegram, 26 September 1939, vol. 151, file 9-19, pt. 2. "ASTROLITE SPEAKS," leaflet, September 1939; Stovin to Lewis, 15 September 1939, CBC, vol. 151, file 9-19, pt. 2 ; Stovin to Manson, 23 September 1939, CBC, vol. 151, file 9-19, pt. 2.

146 Koram to Murray, 5 February 1939, CBC, vol. 151, file 9-19, pt. 2.

147 Koram to Stovin, 9 March 1939, CBC, vol. 151, file 9-19, pt. 2.

148 Jane Gray to C. Arnold, 28 November 1938, CBC vol. 153, file 9-31, pt. 1, Station Relations – Radio Regulations, Advice to Listeners Re Personal Problems; Horace Stovin, "Circular Letter No. 83," 3 February 1939, CBC vol. 153, file 9-31, pt. 1, Station Relations – Radio Regulations, Advice to Listeners Re Personal Problems; Lucy Koserski, "Jane Gray's Own Life: A Real Crackerjack Plot," *Spectator* (Hamilton), n.d. [1967], printed material, file 1, Archives of Ontario, Jane Gray Papers, MU 7096.

149 Sangster, "On the Air."

150 Canadian Association of Broadcasters, "Comments on the Regulations of the CBC, part of CAB submission to the Royal Commission on National

Development in the Arts, Letters and Sciences, April 1950, CBC, vol. 306, file 14-2-2, pt. 24.

151 "Questions, Please, for the Answer Man," CBC Times, 11–17 December 1949, 3; CBC, "Notes on CBC Regulations for Broadcasting Stations," (1950), 10, CBC, acc. 86-87/031, box 165; S.W. Griffiths to Fergus Mutrie, 9 December 1952, CBC, acc. 86-87/031, box 165; "A New Challenge to Evening Radio?" CBC Times, 6–12 September 1953, 2.

152 Cited in Canadian Association of Broadcasters, "The Case for Freedom of Information," [1953], CBC, vol. 303, file 14-2-2, pt. 15.

153 Canadian Association of Broadcasters, "The Case for Freedom of Information,"[1953, 7, CBC, vol. 303, file 14-2-2, pt. 15; CBC Board of Governors, "Official Report of Proceedings to Consider Broadcast Applications and Proposed New Regulations," internal report, 22–23 January 1953, 158–9.

154 "Radio Discussion," Saturday Night, 14 February 1953, 6. New regulations as of 1 July 1953 did not mention programs of this sort and, therefore, did not prohibit them. See Dunton to Young, memo, n.d. [January 1954], CBC, vol. 151, file 9-19, pt. 4; George Young, Manager, Broadcast Regulations, to R.D. Alexander, CKSO Sudbury, 23 December 1955, CBC, vol. 151, file 9-19, pt. 4.

155 Canada, Royal Commission on Broadcasting, Report (Ottawa: Queen's Printer, 1957), 114.

156 Astrolite script, 22 October 1938, CFCF Montreal, CBC, vol. 151, file 9-19, pt. 2.

157 A.R.M. Lower, "Brief on the Question of Radio and Television Broadcasting for Submission to the Royal Commission of Inquiry on these Subjects," 1956, LAC, Royal Commission on Broadcasting, vol. 34, reel C-7020.

CHAPTER FIVE

1 Walden, "Toronto Society's Response." On the impact of the piano, see chapter 5, "The Musicking Machine," in Berland, North of Empire; O'Neill, "Impact of Copyright Legislation," 105.

2 "Music," 1. On the role of transient orchestras, see Warfield, "Amateur and Professional." On the rise of the commercial music industry, see Suisman, Selling Sounds.

3 Vipond, "London Listens." On the uneven early development of radio ratings and audience measurement, see Eaman, Channels of Influence, chap. 4.

4 Savran, Highbrow/Lowdown.

5 Gitelman, "Unexpected Pleasures, 331–2; Berland, "Radio Space and Industrial Time"; Owen, "Regulating Diversity."

6 Ray de Boer, "Report on CJBC," 15 August 1957, Library and Archives Canada, Records of the Canadian Broadcasting Corporation, Ottawa (hereafter CBC), vol. 164, file 11-2, pt. 2.

7 Levine, *Highbrow/Lowbrow*; Locke, "Music Lovers."

8 Vipond, *Listening In*, 86–9.

9 Gladstone Murray, "National Radio in Canada," 25 July 1933, Library and Archives Canada (hereafter LAC), Murray Papers, vol. 1; Ernest Bushnell, "Trends in Broadcast Programming 1935–1946 and Possible Trends for the Future", 23 June 1947, 1, LAC, Bushnell Papers, vol. 14.

10 Irvin Cooper, "Address to the Royal Commission on Radio Broadcasting," 29 May 1929, LAC, Records of the Royal Commission on Radio Broadcasting, vol. 1, file 227-10-6.

11 Charles Jennings to W.H. Brodie, 19 July 1951, CBC, vol. 237, file 11-29; Brodie to Jennings, 26 July 1951, CBC, vol. 237, file 11-29.

12 Douglas, *Listening In*, 149.

13 CBC Programme Division, "[Report on] Sound Broadcasting," March–April 1952, CBC, vol. 46, file 2-3-2-2, pt. 3; Herbert Murrill, "Broadcast Music and the Listener," *CBC Times*, 25 February – 3 March 1951, 4, 9; "A Listener" in North Kildonan, Manitoba, to Editor, *CBC Times*, 25–31 March 1951, 12. H.M., Lipton, Saskatchewan, to Editor, *CBC Times*, 8–14 April 1951, 9, 12.

14 W.G.S., London, Ontario, to CBC, "Letters," *CBC Times*, 10–16 July 1949, 5.

15 Douglas, *Inventing American Broadcasting*, esp. chap. 9.

16 Berland, "Cultural Re/percussions," iii.

17 Baade, *Victory through Harmony*; Mackay, "Being Beastly."

18 VanCour, "Popularizing the Classics"; Han, "Unraveling the Brow"; Taylor, "Music and the Rise of Radio," 425–9; van Eijck, "Social Differentiation"; Weber, "Mass Culture"; Biocca, "Media and Perceptual Shifts."

19 Ahlkvist, "Programming Philosophies"; Rothenbuhler, "Programming Decision Making"; Russo, "Defensive Transcriptions."

20 Frith, "Music and Everyday Life"; Bathrick, "Making a National Family"; Scannell, "Music for the Multitude"; Katz, "Public Patronage."

21 Huber, "Interstate Old Fiddlers Contest"; Patnode, "What These People Need"; McCusker, "Dear Radio Friend"; Grundy, "We Always Tried."

22 Chan and Goldthorpe, "Social Stratification"; Stamm, "Questions of Taste"; Bryson, "Anything But Heavy Metal"; Webb, "Cultural Intervention"; Francesconi, "Art vs. the Audience"; Geiger, "Radio Test of Musical Taste."

23 Vipond, *Listening In*, 55, 86, 137–8.

24 Barlow, "Black Music," 325.

25 A. Leger to Aird, 20 February 1929, translation, LAC, Records of the Royal Commission on Radio Broadcasting, vol. 1, file 227-10-3.

26 Extracts from Correspondence to Gladstone Murray, November 1938, CBC, vol. 466, file 31-1.

27 E.A. Weir, "Radio on the Run", n.d. [1930], 3, LAC, Weir Papers, vol. 19, file 1; Address by W.D. Robb, Second Anniversary CNRT, Toronto, broadcast 14 May 1926, LAC, Weir Papers, vol. 19, file 1.

28 Cooper, "Address to the Royal Commission," 29 May 1929, 2, LAC, Records of the Royal Commission on Radio Broadcasting, vol. 1, file 227-10-3; Jean Riddez to F. Rinfret, 24 April 1929, translation, 2-3, LAC, Records of the Royal Commission on Radio Broadcasting, vol. 1, file 227-10-3.

29 Royal Commission on Radio Broadcasting, "Summary of Public Hearings held at Hamilton, 15 May 1929," LAC, Records of the Royal Commission on Radio Broadcasting, vol. 1, file 227-9-6.

30 Press Release on CNR radio, n.d. [1929], LAC, Weir Papers, vol. 19, file 1.

31 Canadian Pacific Railway, "The Musical Crusaders, Programme No. 5," [1930], LAC, Jane Mallett Papers, vol. 1, file 1.

32 CNR Press Release, 27 September 1930, LAC, Weir Papers, vol. 19, file 1.

33 F.R. McKelcan to Graham Spry, 2 January 1931, LAC, Spry Papers, vol. 94, file 4.

34 Quotation from Gibbon, "Radio as a Fine Art," 213; Spry, "Canadian Broadcasting Issue."

35 Gladstone Murray, "National Radio in Canada," 25 July 1933, 15–16, LAC, Murray Papers, vol. 1.

36 Weir to Charlesworth, 23 June 1933, LAC, Weir Papers, vol. 17, file 4; G.F. Chipman to Weir, 1 May 1933, LAC, Weir Papers, vol. 17, file 8. The band remained popular through the CRBC era. Gladstone Murray to Alan Plaunt, 2 November 1935, Rare Books and Special Collections, University of British Columbia (hereafter UBC Special Collections), Alan B. Plaunt Papers, box 3, file 15.

37 Weir, "Prime Purpose of Radio," 255.

38 Ibid., 258.

39 "Summary of Correspondence Relating to the Empire Programme Service," April 1933; "Fourth Summary of Correspondence Relating to the Empire Programme Service," June 1933; "Eighth Summary of Correspondence Relating to the Empire Programme Service," n.d. [December 1933], British

Broadcasting Corporation Written Archives Centre, Caversham, Berkshire (hereafter BBC), E4/37.

40 "Sampling of Some of the Programs," week of 4 March 1933, LAC, Allard Papers, vol. 13, file 29.

41 Murray to Reith, 12 March 1934, BBC, E1/522/1, file 1A.

42 Thomas Maher to M. Aylesworth, 4 January 1934, National Broadcasting Company Records, Wisconsin Historical Society Archives, Madison (hereafter NBC) box 24, fol. 47; Thomas Belviso to John Royal, 28 August 1934, NBC, box 24, fol. 47; Merrill Denison, "The Educational Program and What to Do about It: An Article Prepared for the Radio Institute of Audible Arts," 13 February 1935, NBC, box 36, fol. 7. In 1935, NBC's load of musical programming was over half. See Advisory Council of the National Broadcasting Company, "The President's Report and Resume of Programs, Committee Reports, Ninth Meeting, 1935," NBC, box 107, fol. 9.

43 Quotation from CRBC press release, "Distinct Canadian Flavor Permeates Fall Schedule," 16 September 1936, CBC, vol. 161, file 11-1, pt. 1. See the 1935 run of CRBC Radio News Service held at CBC, vol. 41, file 2-2-9, pt. 1.

44 Quotation from E.A. Corbett to Weir, 11 February 1934, LAC, Weir Papers, vol. 2, file 4; J.E. McMurtrie to Weir, 24 June 1936, LAC, Weir Papers, vol. 4, file 5. These aspersions were cast about Horace Stovin, who joined the CBC for a time and then went back to commercial radio.

45 J.E. McMurtrie to E.A. Weir, 24 June 1936, LAC, Weir Papers, vol. 4, file 5.

46 MacMillan, "Problems of Music in Canada," 193.

47 "Report of the General Supervisor of Programmes of the Proceedings of the Second Semi-annual Programme Conference, Held in the National Research Building, Ottawa, June 7th to 11th, inclusive," 1937, app. B, 1, 4, CBC, vol. 850, file PG1-13, pt. 1.

48 Gladstone Murray, "Radio's Responsibility for National Culture," address given at Columbus, Ohio, 3 May 1937, BBC, E1/555/1.

49 Gladstone Murray, "Chatting with Listeners," broadcast 21 June 1937, CBC Trans-Canada Network, 4, CBC, vol. 472, file 31-9, pt. 1.

50 "Report of the General Supervisor of Programmes on the Proceedings of the Programme Conference, Held, Toronto, August 8th and 9th, 1938," CBC, vol. 850, file PG1-13, pt. 1; R.S. Lambert to Gladstone Murray, 18 November 1939, CBC, vol. 186, file 11-18-4, pt. 5.

51 Canadian Association of Broadcasters, "Suggested Material for Massey Commission Questions," 1950, LAC, Allard Papers, vol. 5, file 9.

52 D.R.P. Coats to Donald Buchanan, 12 March 1937, CBC, vol. 240, file 11-37-2, pt. 1.

53 O. Reidell to Chairman, CBC, 18 December 1939, CBC, vol. 238, file 11-34-2.

54 "Up Goes the Price of Radio Licences," *Kelowna Courier*, 27 January 1938.

55 "Broadcasters Seek News Freedom," *Canadian Broadcaster*, 10 March 1945, 12.

56 "Music," 2.

57 Station Relations Division, "Nature of Programmes," 12 December 1944, CBC, vol. 288, file 14-1-10, pt. 2; "Special Parliamentary Committee on Radio Broadcasting – 1946, Statement by A. Davidson Dunton, Chairman, Board of Governors, Canadian Broadcasting Corporation," 16, CBC, vol. 288, file 14-1-12, pt. 2.

58 H.W. Morrison, "Response to John Collingwood Reade," n.d. [December 1938], CBC, vol. 287, file 14-1-5, pt. 1.

59 "Nature of Sustaining and Commercial Programs, Year Ending March 31st 1945", CBC, vol. 288, file 14-1-12, pt. 1.

60 "Music," 2.

61 Gladstone Murray, "Programme Building, Season 1937–1938," 3 September 1937, LAC, Bushnell Papers, vol. 1.

62 Press Notes, "Evening – Ontario," 3 July 1942, LAC, Records of the Special Committee on Radio Broadcasting, ser. D4, acc. 87-88, box 27.

63 Keightley, "You Keep Coming Back."

64 R. Jamieson, Graham McInnes, and Percy Faith, "National Forum: Debate on Swing," 1 January 1939, CBC, vol. 185, file 11-18-4, pt. 2.

65 Minutes of the eighteenth meeting of members of the National Programme Office, 1 December 1939, 4, LAC, Bushnell Papers, vol. 1, file 10.

66 Canadian Association of Broadcasters, *Facts Respecting Radio Broadcasting under Private Ownership* (1929), pamphlet produced by CAB, CBC, vol. 342, file 15-3, pt. 8; John Collingwood Reade, "The Canadian Public Broadcasts," *Radio Mirror*, December 1938, n.p., CBC, vol. 287, file 14-1-5, pt. 1; "'Thar's Gold … in Them Thar Hillbillies,'" *Canadian Broadcaster*, March 1942, n.p.; "CBC Drives Listeners to US Stations," *Canadian Broadcaster*, 26 January 1946, 1; Canadian Association of Broadcasters, "Suggested Material for Massey Commission Questions," 1950, 15, LAC, Allard Papers, vol. 5, file 9.

67 H.B. Williams to Gladstone Murray, 29 March 1939, CBC, vol. 540, file 13-7-1, pt. 1.

68 "Extracts from Criticisms by Mrs. Elizabeth Morrison," n.d. [1942], LAC, Bushnell Papers, vol. 1, file 17.

69 "Audience Mail Analysis," n.d. [1945], CBC, vol. 345, file 16-11-1, pt. 1.

70 Graham McInnes, "Speaking as a Listener", broadcast 4 June 1948, CBC
Trans-Canada Network, CBC, vol. 193, file 11-18-11-6, pt. 1; Drew
Crossan, "Juke Box Jury," 1950, CBC, acc. 86-87/031, box 153.

71 Lister Sinclair, "Popular Morality and Good Taste," *Saturday Night*, 28
November 1953, 11; Hugh Garner, "The Boom in Bush League Be-Bop,"
Saturday Night, 13 June 1953, 9–10.

72 *CBC Program Schedule*, week of 1 April 1945, Prairie Region, 4.

73 "The Battle of Music," *CBC Times*, 6–12 August 1950, 4.

74 Robert McCall to DTS, 8 January 1947, BBC, E17/31/3, file 2A, 1947–
48; "Report on BBC's Canadian Office, January to June, 1947," BBC,
E1/509/4.

75 Minutes of the eighteenth meeting of members of the National Programme
Office, 1 December 1939, 2, LAC, Bushnell Papers, vol. 1, file 10 (emphasis in original).

76 "Our Singing Citizens," *CBC Times*, 20–26 December 1953, 15–16.

77 "Canadian Association of Broadcasters Statement to Parliamentary
Committee of Enquiry into Radio Broadcasting 1946," CBC, vol. 289,
file 14-1-12, pt. 5.

78 "Opportunity Knocks," *CBC Times*, 25–31 July 1948, 4; "'Opportunity
Knocks' with John Adaskin - Report for 12 months March 31st 1948 to
March 30th 1949," 1949, CBC, acc. 86-87/031, box 8; Charles Jennings
to Donald Manson, 13 November 1951, CBC, vol. 46, file 2-3-2-2, pt. 3.
The CBC also broadcast *Singing Stars of Tomorrow* on the Trans-Canada
Network and *Nos Futures Etoiles* on Radio-Canada. *Startime* was a simi-
lar program added in 1951. "The Spring Crop of Gifted Singers," *CBC
Times*, 21–27 March 1950, 2, 10; "Comment," *CBC Times*, 11–17 March
1951, 10.

79 There are dozens of examples of this. Here are three: "With McCarthy,"
CBC Program Schedule, week of 18 February 1945, 2; "Boston 'Pops'
Joins RCA Shows," *CBC Times*, 12–18 December 1948, 2; "London
Group Getting Around," *CBC Times*, 2–8 January 1949, 4.

80 Frank Chamberlain, "The School of the Air," *Saturday Night*, 20 September 1941, 16.

81 Weir to Messer, 2 July 1940, CBC, vol. 167, file 11-11, pt. 2.

82 Robert Anderson to T.O. Wicklund, 11 April 1940, CBC, vol. 251,
file 11-39-1.

83 Charles Jennings to W.H. Brodie, 11 October 1950, CBC, vol. 164,
file 11-2, pt. 2.

84 "Records Plus Personalities," *CBC Times*, 19–25 September 1948, 2; Ross
McLean, "Nine Neophyte Disk Jockeys," *CBC Times*, 2–8 July 1950, 2.

85 "CBC Programming", n.d. [1949], LAC, Bushnell Papers, vol. 14.

86 "Soapsud Music Must Be Sweet," CBC Times, 20–26 February 1949, 8.

87 Extracts from Correspondence to Gladstone Murray, November 1938, CBC, vol. 466, file 31-1; "Audience Mail Analysis", n.d. [1945], CBC, vol. 345, file 16-11-1, pt. 1; Boyle to Dunton, 21 October 1948, CBC, vol. 855, file PG1.

88 "What Is Your Musical Mood?" CBC Times, 4–10 February 1951, 4, 8. "What about the Hit Parade?" CBC Times, 23–29 November 1952, 3.

89 Andre Forget to Dunton, 19 January 1948, CBC, vol. 855, file PG1.

90 "CBC Programming," n.d. [1949], LAC, Bushnell Papers, vol. 14.

91 R.W. Ashcroft, "Government vs. Private Ownership of Canadian Radio," 1931, LAC, Spry Papers, vol. 97, file 10; Canadian Association of Broadcasters, "Answering You", n.d. [1943], CBC, vol. 342, file 15-3, pt. 4; Canadian Association of Broadcasters, "Report of the Public Relations Committee," n.d. [1943], CBC, vol. 342, file 15-3, pt. 4; Canadian Association of Broadcasters, Statement to the Royal Commission on National Development in the Arts, Letters and Sciences, 1950, LAC, Allard Papers, vol. 5, file 10; Minutes of the Programme Advisory Committee, 1945, sec. A, LAC, Weir Papers, vol. 13, file 7; T.J. Allard, "Memorandum to Directors No. 223, Re: CBC Propaganda Activities," 27 May 1952, LAC, Allard Papers, vol. 22, file 14. A strident contrary view may be found in Tolbridge, "Does Radio Need a Royal Commission?"

92 Arthur L. Phelps, "Good Listening", broadcast 3 December 1947, CBC Trans-Canada Network, 6, BBC, E1/586/1.

93 Ernest Bushnell to Dean W.E. Fuller, 1 October 1943, LAC, Bushnell Papers, vol. 1, file 19; J.M. Beaudet to David M. Adams, 14 December 1945, CBC, vol. 212, file 11-21, pt. 1; "Does Radio Cramp Their Style?" CBC Times, 22–28 March 1953, 4.

94 Roy Dunlop, "Radio Talk for Vancouver Symphony Society," broadcast 16 January 1940, LAC, Dunlop Papers, vol. 1.

95 Eveline A. Walker to CJCA Edmonton, 21 January 1940, CBC, vol. 212, file 11-21-2, pt. 1.

96 Extracts from D.F. Dorricott to BBC, n.d. [1948], BBC, E17/29/5.

97 Leonard Brockington, "Stenographic Report of Mr. Brockington's Speech Given during the Intermission of the Philharmonic Orchestra Broadcast, January 22nd 1939," CBC, vol. 212, file 11-21-2, pt. 1.

98 Byrne Sanders, "CBC Broadcast – Metropolitan Opera Intermission," 10 February 1945, CBC, vol. 213, file 11-21-11, pt. 3.

99 "Report of Sub-committee on Programme Content," app. B of minutes of the National Programme Conference, Toronto, 5-8 April 1943, LAC, Bushnell Papers, vol. 4.

100 F.S., Musgrave, BC, to Editor, *CBC Times*, 27 March–2 April 1949, 4.

101 W.H. Brodie, "Announcers' Continuity," 30 June 1937, CBC, vol. 53, file 2-3-8-3, pt. 1.

102 Ernest Bushnell, "CBC Programme Standards," Address at Queen's University, Kingston, 9 July 1945, 2, LAC, Bushnell Papers, vol. 4.

103 Roy Dunlop, "Savoy Opera Cavalcade," broadcast 15 February 1943, LAC, Dunlop Papers, vol. 1.

104 F. Renwick Brown, "A Mind to Be Musical?" *CBC Times*, 27 August–2 September 1950, 2. Quotation from: "Toward Greater Enjoyment – Some Simple Steps," *CBC Times*, 3–9 September 1950, 2.

105 "Whatever It Takes, Beethoven Has It!" *CBC Times*, 8–14 April 1951, 2–3.

106 "Canadian Composers," broadcast 1 January 1941, 1, CBC, acc. 86-87/031, box 7.

107 Harding to MacAlpine, 23 March 1945, BBC, E1/509/2.

108 "Assorted Opinions about Music," *CBC Times*, 16–22 December 1951, 4–5.

109 Robertson Davies, "For the Musical Amateur," *Saturday Night*, 2 April 1955, 13.

110 R.M.C., Almonte, Ontario, to CBC, "Comments on Last Year's Passion," *CBC Times*, 10–16 April 1949, 2.

111 Quotation from Damrosch, "Music and the Radio," 91; Howe, "NBC Music Appreciation Hour."

112 Adorno, "Social Critique of Radio Music," 212.

113 Taylor, "Share of the Air"; Thomas Archer, "Speaking as a Listener," broadcast 30 April 1948, CBC Dominion Network, CBC, vol. 193, file 11-18-11-6, pt. 2.

114 "CBC Music: Outstanding Programs to be Broadcast on CBC Wednesday Nights during the Fall and Winter Season 1948–1949," 1948, CBC, BBC, E1/586/2, file 1B; George Marek, "The Stuffed-Shirt Presentation of Music," *Good Housekeeping* (May 1948), 4, 171–2; Mr. W.H. Brodie's comments on "The Stuffed-Shirt Presentation of Music," 1948, CBC, vol. 161, file 11-1, pt. 1.

115 "A Layman's History of Music," *CBC Times*, 3–9 October 1948, 2–3; "Wednesday Night Brings Second Program of 'A Layman's History of Music,'" *CBC Times*, 18–24 October 1948, 3; Graham McInnes, "Speaking as a Listener," broadcast 9 October 1948, 1, CBC Trans-Canada Network, CBC, vol. 193, file 11-18-11-6, pt. 1.

116 Eugene Kash, "Speaking as a Listener," broadcast 16 October 1948, CBC Trans-Canada Network, CBC, vol. 193, file 11-18-11-6. pt. 1.

117 McInnes, "Speaking as a Listener," 2.

118 William E. Goold to Programme Director, Vancouver, 15 October 1948, CBC, vol. 855, file PG1.

119 "Layman's History of Music," *Variety*, 20 October 1948, CBC, vol. 855, file PG1.

120 "The Production of 'A Layman's History of Music,'" CBC *Times*, 21–27 November 1948, 5.

121 Augustin Frigon to Harry Boyle, 15 October 1948, 1–2, CBC, vol. 855, file PG1.

122 "Something New in Music for the Layman," CBC *Times*, 7–13 August 1949, 5. In 1956, *Music and Western Man*, a retrospective of musical history, even netted the CBC a Columbus Award. See "Again CBC Radio Leads the Field," CBC *Times*, 6–12 May 1956, 2–3; W.H. Brodie, "Continuity," 15 November 1945, CBC, vol. 161, file 11-1, pt. 1. "Should Operas Be Translated?" CBC *Times*, 19–25 April 1953, 8; Promotional literature for "The Light Operas of Gilbert and Sullivan," broadcast 3 May – 26 July 1949, CBC, acc. 86-87/031, box 153; "Gilbert and Sullivan," CBC *Times*, 1–7 May 1949, 4;

123 Gladstone Murray, Toronto, to Editor, CBC *Times*, 21–27 August 1949, 5.

124 J.E. Hahn to Murray, 13 December 1937 and 27 December 1937, CBC, vol. 212, file 11-21-1, pt. 1.

125 Murray to W.R. Campbell, 16 December 1937, CBC, vol. 212, file 11-21-1, pt. 1; Hahn to Murray, 12 March 1938, CBC, vol. 212, file 11-21-1, pt. 1. Sponsorships were also secured for the more mainstream programs *The Happy Gang* and *Music for Canadians*, in the case of *The Happy Gang*, after three years sustained by the CBC. See *Happy Gang Fun Book* (1945), CBC, acc. 86-87/031, box 150. See also publicity material from "Music for Canadians," 1944–48, CBC, acc. 86-87/031, box 150.

126 "Ljungh and Surdin," CBC *Times*, 6–14 January 1956, 2, 4.

127 "More Hope Than Charity," *Canadian Broadcaster*, 28 August 1948, 9. An earlier instance of this sense of taste division may be found in David Adams, "Radio Brings Music Home," *Canadian Broadcaster*, 12 January 1946, 14–15; "Jazz? Classics? – Both On 'Musically Yours,'" CBC *Times*, 12–18 June 1949, 5.

128 John Adaskin to H.M. Ball, n.d. [1938], CBC, acc. 86-87/031, box 154.

129 "New Productions by the CBC Opera Company," 1949, CBC, vol. 292, file 14-1-21, pt. 6.

130 "Canadian Music Recorded," CBC *Times*, 2–8 January 1949, 2.

131 "Broadcasting the 'Proms'," CBC *Times*, 1–7 August 1948, 2.

132 "CBC Brings You *British Concert Hall*," 1948, CBC, vol. 292, file 14-1-21, pt. 6; Barkway to T.P. Gale, n.d. [July 1948], BBC, E17/29/4.

133 "Pat Patterson and the Personal Approach," CBC *Times*, 26 August – 1 September 1951, 3; "Records à la Mode," CBC *Times*, 16–22 April 1950, 3.

134 "Meeting with Basic and Affiliated Stations held in Hall 'C,' Royal York Hotel, 10:00 AM, February 18, 1943," CBC, vol. 342, file 15-3, pt. 3.

135 Ira Dilworth, "Report from BC Region," 1945, CBC, vol. 166, file 11-5-1.

136 W.E.S. Briggs to Charles Jennings, 3 December 1951, CBC, vol. 46, file 2-3-2-2, pt. 3; "A New Plan for Evening Radio Listening," CBC Times, 7–13 October 1956, 2.

137 J. Murray Gibbon, "Canada Learns of Its Heritage of Song," n.d. [1941], CBC, acc. 86-87/031, box 153.

138 "Ed McCurdy: Balladeer," CBC Times, 26 December 1948 – 1 January 1949, 4; "Series on Story Ballads Combines Drama and Song," CBC Times, 1–7 May 1949, 5; Ira Dilworth to Director General of Programmes, 20 August 1951, CBC, vol. 162, file 11-1-1.

139 "Legends and Music of Ancient Mexico," promotional poster, 1955; Gordon Winter to Overseas Liaison Officer, 29 April 1955, BBC, E1/500/1, file 1.

140 "'Jazz Unlimited,'" CBC Times, 5–11 September 1948, 2, 11. Quotation from John S. Peach, "Jazz with a Capital 'J,'" CBC Times, 17–23 July 1949, 5; "No Foot-thumping – They're Spell Bound," CBC Times, 26 February – 4 March 1950, 4.

141 "It's Not What You Do, But How You Do It," CBC Times, 6–12 April 1952, 2; "Experiment in Blues," CBC Times, 29 January 1949–4 February 1950, 2; "Experiment in Blues Resumes Weekly Spot," CBC Times, 1–7 May 1949, 5.

142 "Fall Programs," CBC Times, 26 September–4 October 1952, 2–3, 9.

CHAPTER SIX

1 LeMahieu, Culture for Democracy, 4; quotation from Hendy, Life on Air, 2–3.

2 Breen, "What's Happening to the CBC's Skyrocket?" Saturday Night, 26 December 1950, 29.

3 Scannell, "Public Service Broadcasting," 14; G. Hodges to Programme Correspondence, 8 March 1934, British Broadcasting Corporation Written Archives Centre, Caversham, Berkshire (hereafter BBC), R34/281. Reith did not want to create separate minority services for highbrows. The point was to have a stew of everything going at once. See Katz, "Public Patronage."

4 Hendy, "Pop Music Radio," 744.

5 On the hegemonic role of the networks in the United States, see especially pp. 258–62 of Craig, Fireside Politics.

6   Graham McInnes, "Speaking as a Listener," broadcast 30 July 1948, CBC
    Trans Canada Network, 1, Library and Archives Canada, Records of the
    Canadian Broadcasting Corporation, Ottawa (hereafter CBC), vol. 193,
    file 11-18-11-6, pt. 1.

7   "Which System of Broadcasting?"

8   Advisory Council of the National Broadcasting Company, *The President's
    Report and Resume of Programs, Committee Reports, Seventh Meeting,
    1933*, 12–13, National Broadcasting Company Records, Wisconsin
    Historical Society Archives, Madison (hereafter NBC), box 107, fol. 7;
    Bailey, "Rethinking Public Service Broadcasting," 100–1. On the advanta-
    geous position of private stations under the CRBC, see Vipond,
    "Beginnings of Public Broadcasting," 155–7.

9   "Which System of Broadcasting?," 41.

10 Canadian Association of Broadcasters, Statement to the Royal Commission
    on National Development in the Arts, Letters and Sciences, 1950, 4,
    Library and Archives Canada (hereafter LAC), Allard Papers, vol. 5, file 10.

11 Although she discusses television, Jean Seaton offers a succinct explana-
    tion of advertiser involvement in "How the Audience Is Made" in Curran
    and Seaton, *Power without Responsibility*, 179–96.

12 J.E. Mason to Lord and Thomas and Logan, 9 January 1929, NBC, box 4,
    fol. 33. Mason worked for McKim's agency in Toronto.

13 Johnston, "Emergence of Broadcast Advertising."

14 Stallsworthy, "What Price Radio?," 21.

15 "Minutes of Proceedings and Evidence, Radio and Television, 8 September
    1949," 1392, LAC, Royal Commission on National Development in the
    Arts, Letters and Sciences, vol. 34, reel C-2017.

16 Spencer, "We Went to the People," 22.

17 Perry, "What the Public Expect."

18 Quotation from McGuigan, *Cultural Populism*, 3. Cultural pluralism also
    gets referred to as "paternalistic." See also Ferreira, "Cultural
    Conservatism and Mass Culture; Zuidervaart, "Art Is No Fringe," 10.

19 Razlogova, "True Crime Radio," 140.

20 McFadden, "America's Boy Friend," 114.

21 R.W. Ashcroft, "Government vs. Private Ownership of Canadian Radio,"
    1931, 3, LAC, Spry Papers, vol. 97, file 10.

22 Vipond, "British or American?"; Prchal, "He's Going to Sound"; Advisory
    Council of the National Broadcasting Company, the President's Report
    and resume of programs, committee reports, 1932, 1933, 1934, NBC,
    box 107, fols. 6-8. For a later defence of the commercial system as
    audience-controlled, see Seiden, *Who Controls the Mass Media?*, 4–5.

23 Razlogova, *Listener's Voice*.

24 Royal Commission on Radio Broadcasting, "Summary of Public Hearings held at Windsor, 13 May 1929," 15, LAC, Records of the Royal Commission on Radio Broadcasting, vol. 1, file 227-9-6.

25 J.H. Thompson to Sir Noel Ashbridge, 13 February 1936, BBC, E1/490.

26 Messer to Weir, 26 July 1940, CBC, vol. 167, file 11-11, pt. 2.

27 "A Brief Presented by the Association of Canadian Advertisers and the Canadian Association of Broadcasters to the Parliamentary Committee on Radio – 1936," 1936, CBC, vol. 46, file 2-3, pt. 4.

28 Canadian Association of Broadcasters, Statement to the Royal Commission on National Development in the Arts, Letters and Sciences, 1950, 5, LAC, Allard Papers, vol. 5, file 10.

29 Russo, "American Right."

30 Landry, "Wanted," 625.

31 Robert Dunbar, "Ace Radio Impresarios Are Statisticians," *Saturday Night*, 30 November 1946, 23.

32 Brewer, "What's Wrong with Commercial Radio?," 31; Vollmer, "Letter to the Editors," 14–16.

33 "What Is Your Musical Mood?" *CBC Times*, 4–10 February 1951, 4, 8.

34 "Conference Report," 1951, Humanities Research Council of Canada, 2, LAC, Donald Grant Creighton Papers, vol. 10.

35 Reith, "Memorandum of Information on the Scope and Conduct of the Broadcasting Service," 1925, cited in Scannell, "Public Service Broadcasting," 13.

36 Cecil Lamont to Graham Spry, 8 January 1931, LAC, Spry Papers, vol. 94, file 4.

37 W.T. Maxwell, "Broadcast Problems in England," *Saturday Night*, 28 February 1931, 3; John Chabot Smith, "Britain's Bid to Rule the Air Waves," *Saturday Evening Post*, 16 November 1946, 32–3, 58, 61–2.

38 Michael Barkway to Listener Research Director, 15 November 1946, BBC, E12/97/2.

39 Dunham, "Democracy and the Radio," 77; Overstreet and Bonaro, *Town Meeting*.

40 *The Australian Broadcasting Company Year Book 1930*, quoted in Counihan, "Construction of Australian Broadcasting," 225–6 (emphasis in original). Thanks to Simon Potter for this reference.

41 Louis E. Leprohon, Station Manager CKCO, Ottawa, Letter to the Editor (response to: "Our Moronic Radio"), *Ottawa Citizen*, 15 January 1949.

42 Quotations from Canadian Association of Broadcasters, "Report of the Public Relations Committee," n.d. [1943], CBC, vol. 342, file 15-3, pt. 4.

43 "Canadian Association of Broadcasters Statement to Parliamentary Committee of Enquiry into Radio Broadcasting 1946," 37, CBC, vol. 289, file 14-1-12, pt. 5.

44 Raboy, *Missed Opportunities*, 13; McChesney, *Rich Media, Poor Democracy*. See also McChesney, *Telecommunications, Mass Media, and Democracy*.

45 Rothenbuhler, "Commercial Radio as Communication," 125. On organized labour's attempt to enter the conversation, see Fones-Wolf, "Defending Listeners' Rights."

46 Lewis, "For Better or For Worse," 1.

47 "Answering You", n.d. [1943], 6, CBC, vol. 342, file 15-3, pt. 4.

48 Glen Bannerman, "Broadcasting in Canada (a Critique of the System)," 1944, CBC, vol. 342, file 15-3, pt. 5.

49 "Canada's Radio Laws Spell Monopoly," print ad, 1947, CBC, vol. 342, file 15-3, pt. 5.

50 "CBC Drives Listeners to US Stations," *Canadian Broadcaster*, 26 January 1946, 1.

51 "Report to the 1948 Annual Meeting of the Canadian Association of Broadcasters by Director of Public Service," 1948, CBC, vol. 342, file 15-3, pt. 5.

52 Canadian Association of Broadcasters, "Suggested Material for Massey Commission Questions," 1950, 15, LAC, Allard Papers, vol. 5, file 9.

53 CRBC press release, "Distinct Canadian Flavor Permeates Fall Schedule," 16 September 1936, 1-2, CBC, vol. 161, file 11-1, pt. 1.

54 "Memorandum on Policy," 7 April 1942, 2, CBC, vol. 33, file 2-2-3.

55 Royal Commission on Radio Broadcasting, "Summary of Public Hearings held at Fredericton, 13 June 1929," 9–10, LAC, Records of the Royal Commission on Radio Broadcasting, vol. 1, file 227-11-5. See also "Summary of Public Hearings held at London, 14 May 1929," CBC, vol. 1, file 227-9-7.

56 Ernest Bushnell, "What's in the Air?" Address to the Canadian Club, Vancouver, 22 November 1944, LAC, Bushnell Papers, vol. 4.

57 Vipond, "Public Service Broadcasting," 25.

58 Lower, "Question of Private TV," 172.

59 Hutchins, "State of American Radio," 194-5.

60 Arthur Wallace, "On the Air," *Saturday Night*, 7 March 1931, 20.

61 Chamberlain, "So Nobody Listens," 6.

62 H.G. Walker to Weir, 14 December 1945, CBC, vol. 290, file 14-1-12, pt. 9.

63 On the work of such pioneers as Paul Lazarsfeld and his associates, Frank Stanton of CBS and Hadley Cantril at Princeton, see chapter 6 "The Invention of the Audience," in Douglas, *Listening In*.

64 On this same set of questions in the United States, see especially chapter 3 of Slotten, *Radio's Hidden Voice*.

65 Royal Commission on Radio Broadcasting, "Summary of Public Hearings held at Windsor, 13 May 1929," LAC, Records of the Royal Commission on Radio Broadcasting, vol. 1, file 227-9-6.

66 Quotation from Spry, "Case for Nationalized Broadcasting," 156; Graham Spry, "Radio Broadcasting," 1930, LAC, Spry Papers, vol. 97, file 8.

67 Evershed Heron to Graham Spry, 15 March 1931, LAC, Spry Papers, vol. 95, file 1. Letter was in response to an item in *Saturday Night* for 7 March 1931.

68 L.W. Brockington, "Canada Calling," broadcast 4 November 1936, Rare Books and Special Collections, University of British Columbia (hereafter UBC Special Collections), Alan B. Plaunt Papers, box 17, file 4.

69 Atkinson, "European View."

70 "Electrifying Authorship," 3–4.

71 MacMillan, "Problems of Music in Canada," 193.

72 "Private Station Attitude – CBC Sustaining Programmes," 1944, CBC, vol. 342, file 15-3, pt. 4; Gladys Coke Mussen, "Radio Broadcasting in Canada," 23 March 1950, 8–9, LAC, Royal Commission on National Development in the Arts, Letters and Sciences, 1946–51, vol. 48, file 16.02; Charles Jennings to Manson, 13 November 1951, CBC, vol. 46, file 2-3-2-2, pt. 3; Sangster, "On the Air."

73 Tolbridge, "Private Radio Gangs Up," 238.

74 James S. Thomson, "Broadcasting and Civilization," address given at Luncheon Canadian Association of Broadcasters, Toronto, 15 February 1943, 9–10, CBC, vol. 342, file 15-3, pt. 3; "'Listeners, Away!' – Journal's Cue for Good Listening," CBC *Times*, 18-23 December 1949, 3.

75 R.B. Tolbridge, "What the People Wanted in Radio," *Canadian Forum* 25, 302 (1946): 280–2; Tolbridge, "Does Radio Need a Royal Commission?," 157.

76 F.L.J., Ninga, Man., to editors, CBC *Program Schedule*, week of 15 April 1945, 5.

77 A.D. Dunton, "Freedom of the Air," n.d. [1948], BBC, E1/493/3, file 2; Spry, "Radio Broadcasting."

78 CBC brief submitted to the Royal Commission on National Development in the Arts, Letters and Sciences, 1949 14, LAC, Bushnell Papers, vol. 2.

79 Len Peterson, "In Search of Ourselves: The Man behind the Glass," broadcast 3 March 1953, 5, CBC, vol. 204, file 11-18-11-45.

80 Siepmann, *Radio's Second Chance*, xii. Shaw put it more bluntly: "Take care to get what you like or you will be forced to like what you get." See Shaw, *Man and Superman*, 242; "What Australians Hear Most," CBC *Times*, 14–20 September 1952, 11.

81 Fergus Mutrie, "Television – a Challenge to Canadians," address to Fall Meeting of Canadian Radio Council, 21 November 1950, LAC, Canada Foundation, vol. 25, file 4a.

82 Peterson, "Man behind the Glass," 11.

83 Lawren Harris, "Democracy and the Arts," typescript, 1944, 7, LAC, Lawren Harris Papers, file 5-15.

84 "Music," CBC Times, 10–16 February 1952, 3.

85 H.M., Lipton, Sask., to CBC, "Letters," CBC Times, 8–14 April 1951, 9.

86 Gladstone Murray, "Radio's Responsibility for National Culture," address given at Columbus, Ohio, 3 May 1937, 1–2, BBC, E1/555/1; James S. Thomson, "Broadcasting and Civilization," address given at luncheon, Canadian Association of Broadcasters, Toronto, 15 February 1943, 5–6, CBC, vol. 342, file 15–3, pt. 3.

87 Peterson and Kern, "Changing Highbrow Taste"; Emmison, "Social Class and Cultural Mobility."

88 Russell Lynes, "Highbrow, Lowbrow, Middlebrow," Harper's, February 1949, 19–28.

89 Tolbridge, "Dollar Diplomacy."

90 Lambert, "Radio Ideals and Educational Needs"; R.S. Lambert to Gladstone Murray, 14 April 1940, UBC Special Collections, Alan B. Plaunt Papers, box 2, file 18. Later publication plans argued that any print organ must have a popular bent otherwise it would fail, having failed to be democratic. See Report on CBC National Programme Publication, 1943, LAC, E.A. Weir Papers, vol. 13, file 5.

91 In the United States, as Randall Patnode argues, rural listeners were "othered" and encouraged to become modern listeners and consumers. See Patnode, "What These People Need," 287–8; Extracts from the evidence of Mr. L.W. Brockington, Standing Committee on Radio Broadcasting – 1938, CBC, vol. 288, file 14-1-12, pt. 1; Felix Greene to C.D. Howe, 4 January 1936, BBC, E1/52; Andrew Allan to Harry Boyle, 13 May 1948, CBC, vol. 855, file PG 1; Quotation from John Fisher, "Helping Sew the Fabric of Unity," CBC Times, 18–24 December 1949, 2; Hugh M. Palmer to Chairman, 14 November 1951, LAC, Neil Morrison Papers, vol. 6.

92 Kingson and Cowgill, "Domestic Broadcasting in Canada"; Sangster, "On the Air."

93 E.L. Bushnell, "Statement by General Supervisor of Programmes," 1944, LAC, Weir Papers, vol. 2, file 8.

94 Canadian Arts Council, "The Council and the CBC," n.d. [1946], CBC, vol. 289, file 14-1-12, pt. 6.

95 "CBC Music: Outstanding Programs to Be Broadcast on CBC Wednesday Nights during the Fall and Winter Season 1948–1949," CBC, 1948, inside front cover, BBC Written Archives Centre, E1/586/2, Countries: Canada, "Wednesday Night," file 1B, June – December 1948.

96 Simon of Wythenshawe, "Broadcasting in Canada," 3 January 1949, 8, CBC, vol. 988, file 2. Lord Simon's comment echoed that of the BBC's Malcolm Frost, reporting on late CRBC-era broadcasting. See "Report: Empire Broadcasting in Canada," n.d. [1936], BBC, E1/492.

97 Chandler, "Case for Private Broadcasting," 14–15.

98 Gannon, "Commercial Copy," 159, 161.

99 CBC brief submitted to the Royal Commission on National Development in the Arts, Letters and Sciences, 1949, LAC, Bushnell Papers, vol. 2, CBC and the Royal Commission on National Development in the Arts, briefs, corresp. etc. 1949.

100 Charles Jennings, "The National System – Programmes," 24 February 1948, 6, CBC, vol. 161, file 11-1.

101 "Minutes of the National Programme Conference," 7–9 October 1947, 16, CBC, vol. 166, file 11-5-1.

102 Melwyn Breen, "Same Old Faces in the 'Other Audience,'" *Saturday Night*, 12 December 1950, 11.

103 J.R. Finlay, "Talk by Prairie Regional Representative at Monthly Meeting of Winnipeg Ministerial Association," 4 April 1949, 2, CBC, vol. 224, file 11-23-5.

104 Bushnell, commentary on thriller programmes, n.d. [1944], CBC, vol. 861, file 4-2-1, pt. 1; John Kannawin, "Problems of Program Planning," *CBC Times*, 18–24 September 1949, 2, 8, 10-11.

105 L.W. Brockington, "Chatting with the Listener," broadcast 3 February 1938, 10–11, UBC Special Collections, Alan B. Plaunt Papers, box 17, file 5.

106 Minutes of the 1st General Administrative Conference, Ottawa, 2–3 November 1943, app. C, 32, CBC, vol. 466, file 30-16, pt. 1.

107 Miss Burnett (for Mr Davies) to Lindsay Wellington, BBC, 31 July 1944, BBC, E1/493/2, file 1B.

108 Ernest Bushnell, "CBC Programme Standards," address at Queen's University, Kingston, 9 July 1945, LAC, Bushnell Papers, vol. 4.

109 Extracts from the Final Report of the Special Committee on Radio Broadcasting – 1943, CBC, vol. 288, file 14-1-12, pt. 1.

110 Ernest Bushnell, "Trends in Broadcast Programmes," n.d. [1946], LAC, Ernest Bushnell Papers, vol. 3.

111 "Brief Presented by the Canadian Federation of Agriculture and the Canadian Association for Adult Education to the House Select Committee on Radio Broadcasting 1944," CBC, vol. 275, file 11-42-8-1, pt. 1.

112 Andrew Cowan, "Pamphlets and Radio," 1942, LAC, Andrew G. Cowan Papers, vol. 25, file 26.

113 D.W. Buchanan to Gladstone Murray, 31 May 1938, CBC, vol. 165, file 11-2-3, pt. 1; Ernest Bushnell to Programme Staff, "A Statement on Postwar Programme Policy," 26 October 1945, CBC, vol. 164, file 11-2, pt. 1.

114 R.C. Fraser to Captain G.H. Wattsford, 17 March 1949, CBC, vol. 239, file 11-36-15; James Scott, "Critically Speaking," CBC Times, 6–12 March 1949, 4.

115 CBC 1946: A Digest of Statements and Policies, Administration and Programs of the Canadian Broadcasting Corporation, 1946, 10, 37–8, LAC, Ernest Bushnell Papers, vol. 2.

116 Graham McInnes, "Speaking as a Listener," broadcast 4 June 1948, CBC Trans-Canada Network, 1, CBC, vol. 193, file 11-18-11-6, pt. 1; Ernest Bushnell, "We'd Better Get on the Ball," address to the Institute on Religious Broadcasting, n.d. [1949], CBC Trans-Canada Network, 14, CBC, vol. 472, file 31-9, pt. 2.

117 Neil Morrison to Ted Allan, 10 November 1952, LAC, Ted Allan Papers, vol. 20, file 17.

118 Bert B. Jacobs to C.D. Howe, 11 April 1938, CBC, vol. 394, file 21-17, pt. 2.

119 Canadian Association of Broadcasters, "Code of Ethics," 17 February 1943, n.p. LAC, Allard Papers, vol. 25, file 13.

120 "Broadcasters Seek News Freedom," Canadian Broadcaster, 10 March 1945, 12.

121 Goodman, Radio's Civic Ambition, xiv.

122 "Canadian Association of Broadcasters Statement to Parliamentary Committee of Enquiry into Radio Broadcasting 1946," 21–2, CBC, vol. 289, file 14-1-12, pt. 5.

123 "Which Comes First? – The Audience or the Public?" CBC Times, 23–29 November 1952, 3.

124 "CAB Statement to Parliamentary Committee 1946," 22, CBC, vol. 289, file 14-1-12, pt. 5.

125 Minutes of the Programme Advisory Committee, 1945, sec. A, 8, LAC, Weir Papers, vol. 13, file 7.

126 "Remarks made at National Program Planning Conference," September 1951, CBC, vol. 166, file 11-5-1.

127 "Stage '49," *Canadian Broadcaster*, 27 November 1948, 6; Canadian Association of Broadcasters, statement to the Royal Commission on National Development in the Arts, Letters and Sciences, 1950, 5, LAC, Allard Papers, vol. 5, file 10; "What Is a Canadian Program? Private Stations Ask the CBC," *Financial Post*, 18 October 1952, 2.

128 "Note on the Canadian Broadcasting Corporation," November 1948, 5, BBC, E1/489.

129 Eric Nicol, *Province* (Vancouver), 14 October 1952, CBC, vol. 146, file 9-11-1, pt. 5.

130 Raboy, "Making Media."

131 Minutes of Special Committee on Radio Broadcasting, 14 May 1942, 4-5, LAC, Allard Papers, vol. 5, file 15.

132 H.G. Walker, "Report by Manager of Dominion Network," 6 October 1948, CBC, vol. 166, file 11-5-1; "A Second CBC Network," *Saturday Night*, 11 December 1943, 5; "The New CBC Network," *Canadian Forum* 23, 276 (1944): 220; Frigon to Reginald Brophy, 3 February 1944, CBC, vol. 166, file 11-10-1, pt. 1.

133 Ira Dilworth, statement re programme policy, 14 March 1952, CBC, vol. 164, file 11-2, pt. 2.

134 Quotation from Dunton, "Television in Canada," 37-9, 47-8. From an address by A.D. Dunton, Chairman of the Board of Governors of the Canadian Broadcasting Corporation to the Rotary Club of Ottawa, 5 January 1953, E1/493/3, file 2; A.D. Dunton, "CBC and the Nation," n.d. [1948], E1/493/3, file 2; A.D. Dunton, "Freedom of the Air," n.d. [1948], BBC, E1/493/3, file 2.

135 Canadian Association of Broadcasters, "Suggested Material for Massey Commission Questions," 1950, 15, LAC, Allard Papers, vol. 5, file 9.

136 CBC response to Canadian Association of Broadcasters' brief to Royal Commission on National Development in the Arts, Letters and Sciences, 1949, 16, LAC, Bushnell Papers, vol. 2; A.D. Dunton to Lord Beveridge, 26 April 1950, CBC, vol. 988, file 2.

137 Gordon Winter, "BBC in Canada," 4 October 1953, BBC, E1/509/6.

138 "Montreal Listeners Canvassed on CBC's Ballet Broadcast," *CBC Times*, 3-9 April 1949, 2.

139 L.C.C. to *Sentinel* (Kamloops), 27 October 1948, compiled in "Excerpts from Press Comment and Audience Mail on CBC *Wednesday Night* and Other Programs," CBC, vol. 292, file 14-1-21, pt. 3.

140 Arthur L. Phelps, "Good Listening," broadcast 3 December 1947, CBC Trans-Canada Network, 6, BBC, E1/586/1.

141 "To Determine What the CBC Audience Prefers," *CBC Times*, 27 December 1953 – 2 January 1954, 15–16.

142 J.M. Beaudet to Programme Advisory Committee, 22 June 1945, minutes of the Programme Advisory Committee, 1945, sec. D, LAC, Weir Papers, vol. 13, file 7; Moore, "Radio."

143 A. Davidson Dunton, "Freedom for Whom?," convocation address, University of Saskatchewan, 14 May 1954, 3–4, Archives of Ontario, CAAE Papers, ser. E-I-4, box 6.

144 A.D. Dunton, address to the Canadian Club, Toronto, 18 March 1946, LAC, Bushnell Papers, vol. 4.

145 Eaman, *Channels of Influence*, ix-x (emphasis added).

146 Ibid., 9ff.

147 Keane, *Media and Democracy*, 43, 44 (emphasis in original).

148 Scannell, "Public Service Broadcasting," 140.

149 Baillargeon, "CBC and the Cold War Mentality," 18.

150 Oswell, "Early Children's Broadcasting"; Goodman, *Radio's Civic Ambition*.

151 Haugan, "Cultural Democracy."

152 Niergarth, "Missionary for Culture," 4.

153 McClung, "Radio," 5, 7.

154 Roy Dunlop, "Report from Hollywood," September 1938, 17, LAC, Roy Dunlop Papers, vol. 1.

155 "Talks," 1; Denny, Jr, "Radio Builds Democracy."

156 McKenzie, "Radio as Instrument of Democracy"; Shea, "Mass Communications"; Romanow, "Picture of Democracy."

157 D.W. Cameron, "Radio Censorship," letter to the editor, *Toronto Star*, 3 December 1951.

158 A.R.M. Lower, "Brief on the Question of Radio and Television Broadcasting for Submission to the Royal Commission of Inquiry on These Subjects," 22, LAC, Royal Commission on Broadcasting, vol. 34, reel C-7020.

159 Litt, *Muses*, 252–3.

160 House of Commons Special Committee on Radio Broadcasting, "Minutes of Proceedings and Evidence, No. 5," 28–29 May 1942, in *Witness: Gladstone Murray* (Ottawa: King's Printer, 1942).

161 Canadian Radio League, "The Canadian Radio League: Objects, Information, National Support," 1931, 20, LAC, Spry Papers, vol. 158, file 158-1.

162 Gibbon, "Radio as a Fine Art."

163 Cross, "What's Wrong with Canadian Radio." The BBC's Michael Barkway also reported discontent with the opacity of regulatory decisions

made by the CBC. See Barkway to Controller (Overseas Service), BBC, 21 August 1946, BBC, E1/493/2, file 1B.

164 Canadian Association of Broadcasters, "The Case for Freedom of Information," 1953, CBC, vol. 303, file 14-2-2, pt. 15. Submitted to the 84th meeting of the CBC Board of Governors, Ottawa, 22–24 January 1953. This is also one of the core themes in Thomas Allard's memoir. See Allard, *Straight Up*. With television already reaching many Canadian homes in the mid-1950s, commercial broadcasting interests were still arguing along freedom of speech lines as they sought a freer hand in creating networks.

165 Scott Young, "Let's Stop Monopoly Television," *Maclean's*, 1 May 1954, 9, 75-8; Canadian Marconi Company, brief to the Royal Commission on Broadcasting, Montreal, 15 April 1956, esp. 7–10, LAC, Royal Commission on Broadcasting, vol. 34, reel C-7020.

166 Tolbridge, "Does Radio Need a Royal Commission?," 156.

167 Hutchinson, "Is the Air Already Monopolized?"; Hutchinson, "Freedom of the Air"; Thomson, *Radio Is Changing Us*, 21.

168 Spry, "Radio Broadcasting," 123.

169 Raboy, *Missed Opportunities*, 64–5.

170 Jack Scott, "On Monopoly," *Vancouver Sun*, 10 June 1947, CBC, vol. 342, file 15-3, pt. 5.

171 "A Note about Broadcasting and the Individual," *CBC Times*, 22–28 January 1950, 4; Cooke, "Press and Cultural Democracy."

172 J.B. Lamb to editors, "Broadcasting," *Saturday Night*, 6 June 1953, 5; Richard G. Lewis, "'Wednesday Night': Loneliest in Week?" *Saturday Night*, 3 July 1951, 9, 36.

173 "The President's Annual Address", Quebec, 12 February 1945, CBC, vol. 342, file 15-3, pt. 5.

174 Radford to Manson, 6 February 1942, CBC, vol. 433, file 27-1-7, pt. 1.

175 Merrill Denison, "Soap Opera," *Harper's*, April 1940, 505.

176 Gladstone Murray, "Radio's Responsibility for National Culture," address given at Columbus, Ohio, 3 May 1937, BBC, E1/555/1.

177 John Fisher, "Leonard Was Right," *CBC Times*, 13–19 February 1949, 2, 5.

178 Ralph Marven to R.T. Bowman, 27 November 1939, CBC, vol. 251, file 11-39-1.

179 Spry, "Canadian Radio Situation," 85; Spry, "Canadian Broadcasting Issue."

180 A.D. Dunton to the Editor, Ottawa *Citizen*, 1 March 1949, CBC, vol. 239, file 11-36-15; A.D. Dunton, "Let's Look at National Radio: Programs and the Public," n.d. [1949], CBC, vol. 466, file 31-2, pt. 1.

181 Scannell, "For-Anyone-as-Someone Structures," 12.

182 Barlow, "Community Radio in the US"; Lasar, "Hybrid Highbrow."

CONCLUSION

1 Thomson, *Radio Is Changing Us*.
2 Innis differentiated between time-biased modes like parchment, clay, and stone, and the more ephemeral print and broadcast media. See Innis, *Empire and Communications*, 6ff. See also Innis, *Strategy of Culture*.
3 Dahlgren, "Reconfiguring Civic Culture," 151.
4 Attallah, "Public Broadcasting in Canada"; Michael Bérubé, "What's the Matter with Cultural Studies?" *Chronicle of Higher Education*, 14 September 2009.
5 Kammen, *American Culture*, 42ff (emphasis added).

Bibliography

MANUSCRIPT COLLECTIONS

British Broadcasting Corporation Written Archives Centre, Caversham, UK

E1 Canada (especially E1/4xx – E1/5xx)
E2 Foreign
E4 Empire Service
E12 Publicity
E15 Staff Visits Abroad
E17 CBC Transcriptions
L1 Left Staff
R34 Policy

Library and Archives Canada, Ottawa

Records of the Canadian Broadcasting Corporation
Canada Foundation Papers
Andrew Allan Papers
Ted Allan Papers
T.J. Allard Papers
Ernest Bushnell Papers
Andrew G. Cowan Papers
Donald Grant Creighton Papers
Winston Curry Papers
Roy Dunlop Papers
Lawren Harris Papers

Marjorie McEnaney Papers
Jane Mallett Papers
Neil M. Morrison Papers
Gladstone Murray Papers
Gerald Pratley Papers
Records of the Royal Commission on Broadcasting (Fowler Commission)
Records of the Royal Commission on Radio Broadcasting (Aird
    Commission)
Records of the Royal Commission on National Development in the Arts,
    Letters
and Sciences
Frank Shuster Papers
Robert Alexander Sim Papers
Lister Sinclair Papers
Graham Spry Papers
E.A. Weir Papers

Wisconsin Historical Society Archives, Madison, USA

National Broadcasting Company Records (NBC)

PERIODICALS

Individual articles from these publications are not cited here but are fully
    cited in Notes.
Canadian Broadcaster
Canadian Forum
CBC Times
Maclean's
Saturday Night

PRINTED PRIMARY SOURCES

"A Culture for Canada." The Royal Bank of Canada Monthly Letter
    (September 1954): 2.
Adorno, T.W. "A Social Critique of Radio Music." Kenyon Review 7
    (1944): 212.
Allard, T.J. Straight Up: Private Broadcasting in Canada. Ottawa: Heritage
    House, 1979.
Allen, Ralph. Ordeal by Fire: Canada, 1910–1945. Toronto: Doubleday,
    1961.

– *The Chartered Libertine*. Toronto: Macmillan, 1954.

Atkinson, C.F. "A European View of American Radio Programs." *Annals of the American Academy of Political and Social Science* 177 (January 1935): 82–3.

Blackburn, R.H. "Radio in Canada." *Food for Thought* 10, 6 (1950): 23–7.

Brewer, William. "What's Wrong with Commercial Radio?" *Reading* 1, 2 (1946): 31–4.

Brindze, Ruth. *Not to Be Broadcast: The Truth about the Radio*. New York: Vanguard, 1937.

British Broadcasting Corporation. *Broadcast English: Recommendations to Announcers Regarding Certain Words of Doubtful Pronunciation*. London: British Broadcasting Corporation, 1928.

Canadian Association of Broadcasters. *Radio Broadcasting under Private Ownership*, 1929.

Chamberlain, Frank. "So Nobody Listens to Canadian Radio?" *Food for Thought* 3, 6 (1943): 5–7.

Chandler, George C. "The Case for Private Broadcasting." *Public Affairs* (Spring 1952): 6–16.

Charlesworth, Hector. "Broadcasting in Canada." *Annals of the American Academy of Political and Social Science* 177 (January 1935): 42–8.

Columbia Broadcasting System. *Radio's Daytime Serial: The Highlights of Eighteen Months of Intensive Audience and Program Research by the Columbia Broadcasting System*. New York: CBS, 1945.

Cooke, Alistair. "The Press and Cultural Democracy." In *Is the Common Man Too Common? An Informal Survey of our Cultural Resources and What We Are Doing about Them*, ed. Joseph Wood Krutch, 31–44. Norman: University of Oklahoma Press, 1954.

Coulter, John, and Ivor Lewis. *Radio Drama Is Not Theatre*. Toronto: Macmillan, 1937.

Cross, Austin F. "What's Wrong with Canadian Radio." *National Home Monthly* 48, 2 (1947): 6, 18, 20, 43.

Cunningham. R.M. Jr. "Medicine Men of the Air." *New Republic*, 23 October 1944, 515–17.

Damrosch, Walter. "Music and the Radio." *Annals of the American Academy of Political and Social Science* 177 (January 1935): 91–3.

Davis, Ewin L. "Regulation of Radio Advertising." *Annals of the American Academy of Political and Social Science* 177 (January 1935): 154–8.

"Daytime Serials Report Finds Good Points Outweigh Bad." *Radio Daily*, 5 February 1943, 1, 3.

Denison, Merrill. "Radio in Canada." *Annals of the American Academy of Political and Social Science* 177 (January 1935): 49–54.

- "Soap Opera." *Harper's*, April 1940, 505.
- "The Romance of Canada." *Canadian Home Journal* 27, 7 (1930): 18–20.
Denny, George V. Jr. "Radio Builds Democracy." *Journal of Educational Sociology* 14, 6 (1941): 370–7.
"Drama and Features." [No. 8 in the series] *Five Years of Achievement, 1936–1941.* Toronto: Canadian Broadcasting Corporation, 1941.
Dunham, Franklin. "Democracy and the Radio." *Public Opinion Quarterly* 2, 1 (1938): 77–9.
Dunton, A.D. "T.S. Eliot on the Prairie." *BBC Quarterly* 5, 3 (1950), 129–35.
"Electrifying Authorship." *Canadian Author* 14, 3 (1937): 3–4.
Fainmel, Charles, and Henry Eveleigh. "The Proper Function of Advertising." *Canadian Art* 4, 4 (1947): 157–9.
Geiger, Theodor. "A Radio Test of Musical Taste." *Public Opinion Quarterly* 14, 3 (1950): 453–60.
Gibbon, John Murray. "Radio as a Fine Art." *Canadian Forum* 21, 126 (1931): 212–14.
Gruenberg, Sidonie Matsner. "Radio and the Child." *Annals of the American Academy of Political and Social Science* 177 (January 1935): 123–8.
Haugan, W.M. "Cultural Democracy." *Food for Thought* 10, 1 (1949): 13–16, 50.
Hill, V.R. "Broadcasting in Canada – Part II," *Canadian Forum* 22, 242 (1941): 372–4.
House of Commons Special Committee on Radio Broadcasting. *Minutes of Proceedings and Evidence, No. 4, 19 April 1944, Witness: Augustin Frigon* (Ottawa: King's Printer, 1944).
Hutchins, Robert M. "The State of American Radio." *BBC Quarterly* 4, 4 (1949–50), 194–5.
Hutchinson, Paul. "Is The Air Already Monopolized?" *Christian Century*, 1 April 1931, 441–4.
- "The Freedom of the Air." *Christian Century*, 11 March 1931, 340–3.
Innis, Harold A. *Empire and Communications.* Oxford: Oxford University Press, 1950.
- *The Strategy of Culture.* Toronto: University of Toronto Press, 1952.
Jamieson, Don. *The Troubled Air.* Fredericton: Brunswick Press, 1966.
Jennings, Hilda, and Winifred Gill. *Broadcasting in Everyday Life: A Survey of the Social Effects of the Coming of Broadcasting.* London: British Broadcasting Corporation, 1939.
Kingson, Walter, and Rome Cowgill. "Domestic Broadcasting in Canada: Part 2." *Hollywood Quarterly* 5, 2 (1950): 117–26.
Kirstein, Louis E. "Radio and Social Welfare." *Annals of the American Academy of Political and Social Science* 177 (January 1935): 129–34.

Landry, Robert J. *This Fascinating Radio Business* (Indianapolis: Bobbs-Merrill, 1946).

– "Wanted: Radio Critics." *Public Opinion Quarterly* 4, 4 (1940): 620–9.

Lower, A.R.M. "The Question of National Television." *Canadian Forum* 34, 410 (1955): 275.

– "The Question of Private TV." *Queen's Quarterly* 60, 2 (1953): 172.

Lynes, Russell. "Highbrow, Lowbrow, Middlebrow." *Harper's*, February 1949, 19–28.

Marek, George. "The Stuffed-Shirt Presentation of Music." *Good Housekeeping*, May 1948, 4, 171–2.

McClung, Nellie. "Radio – a Stimulus." *Canadian Thinker* 1, 6 (1937): 5–7.

McKenzie, Ruth I. "Radio as Instrument of Democracy." *Dalhousie Review* 26, 2 (1946): 170–7.

– "Radio, Instrument of Democracy." *Hardware and Metal and Electrical Dealer*, 14 June 1947.

MacMillan, Sir Ernest. "Problems of Music in Canada." In *Yearbook of the Arts in Canada*. Toronto: Macmillan, 1936.

Moore, Mavor. "Radio." *Food for Thought* 10, 8 (1950): 20–3.

"Music." [No. 7 in the series] *Five Years of Achievement, 1936–1941*. Toronto: Canadian Broadcasting Corporation, 1941.

Overstreet, Harry A., and Bonaro W. *Town Meeting Comes to Town*. New York: Harper Brothers, 1938.

Parliament of Canada. *Regulations for Broadcasting Stations Made under the Canadian Broadcasting Act, 1936 (as Revised and Amended to 24 March 1941)*. Ottawa: King's Printer, 1941.

Parliament of the Commonwealth of Australia. *Report of the Joint Committee on Wireless Broadcasting*. Canberra: Commonwealth Government Printer, 1942.

Perry, Armstrong. "Weak Spots in the American System of Broadcasting." *Annals of the American Academy of Political and Social Science* 177 (January 1935): 22–8.

Porter, Paul A. "Radio Must Grow Up." *American Magazine*, October 1945, 24–5, 108, 110–11.

Preston, Mary I. "Children's Reactions to Movie Horrors and Radio Crime." *Journal of Pediatrics* 19, 2 (1941): 147–68.

Sangster, Allan. "On the Air." *Canadian Forum* 38, 336 (1949): 230–1.

– "On the Air." *Canadian Forum* 33, 388 (1953): 38–9.

Shaw, George Bernard. *Man and Superman: A Comedy and a Philosophy*. Westminster: Archibald Constable, 1903.

Shea, Albert A. "Mass Communications." *Canadian Forum* 30, 360 (1951): 224–5.

Siepmann, Charles A. *Radio's Second Chance*. Boston: Little, Brown and Co., 1946.

Silvey, R.J.E. *Methods of Listener Research Employed by the British Broadcasting Corporation*. London: BBC, 1944.

Smith, John Chabot. "Britain's Bid to Rule the Air Waves." *Saturday Evening Post*, 16 November 1946, 32–3, 58, 61–2.

"Special Events." [No. 4 in the series] *Five Years of Achievement, 1936–1941*. Toronto: Canadian Broadcasting Corporation, 1941.

Spencer, Philip. "We Went to the People." *Canadian Forum* 21, 243 (1941): 19–24.

Spry, Graham. "Radio Broadcasting and Aspects of Canadian-American Relations." *Canadian-American Affairs* (1935): 106–28.

– "The Canadian Broadcasting Issue." *Canadian Forum* 11, 127 (1931): 246–9.

– "The Canadian Radio Situation." *Education by Radio* 1, 21 (1931): 83–6.

– "The Origins of Public Broadcasting in Canada: A Comment." *Canadian Historical Review* 46, 2 (1965): 134–41.

Stafford, Dorothy Brister. "Educating the Children by Radio." *Canadian National Railways Magazine*, October 1925, 31.

Stallsworthy, H.H. "What Price Radio?" *Canadian Business* 11, 3 (1938): 16–21.

"Talks." [No. 5 in the series] *Five Years of Achievement, 1936–1941*. Toronto: Canadian Broadcasting Corporation, 1941.

Tallents, Stephen. *The Projection of England*. London: Faber and Faber, 1932.

Tausk, Victor. "On the Origin of the Influencing Machine in Schizophrenia." Trans. Dorian Feigenbaum. *Psychoanalytic Quarterly* 2 (1933): 519–56.

Taylor, Deems. "A Share of the Air." In *The Well-Tempered Listener*, 261–8. New York: Simon and Schuster, 1940.

– "Other People's Poison." In *The Well-Tempered Listener*, 269–70. New York: Simon and Schuster, 1940.

Taylor, William A. "Music on the Air in Canada Includes Non-Commercial CBC Wednesday Nights." *Musical Courier*, 1 March 1948.

Thomson, David Cleghorn. *Radio Is Changing Us: A Survey of Radio Development and Its Problems in Our Changing World*. London: Watts and Co., 1937.

Tolbridge, R.B. "Does Radio Need a Royal Commission?" *Canadian Forum* 27, 321 (1947): 156–7.

– "Dollar Diplomacy in the CBC." *Canadian Forum* 22, 263 (1942): 270–4.

– "Private Radio Gangs Up." *Canadian Forum* 22, 262 (1942): 235–8.
– "Sabotaging the CBC." *Canadian Forum* 22, 260 (1942): 175.
– "What the People Wanted in Radio." *Canadian Forum* 25, 302 (1946): 280–2.
Vollmer, Margaret. "Letter to the Editors." *Reading* 1, 3 (1946): 14–16.
Wakeman, Frederic. *The Hucksters*. New York: Rinehart and Co., 1946.
Waller, Judith Cary. *Radio: The Fifth Estate*. Boston: Houghton Mifflin, 1950.
Weir, E.A. "The Prime Purpose of Radio as We See It in Canada." *University of Toronto Monthly* 33, 8 (1933): 255-9.
"What about the CBC?" *Citizenship Items* 8, 5 (1955): 3.
"Which System of Broadcasting?" *RADEX*, n.d. [December 1934 - February 1935], 38–41.
Yorke, Dane. "The Radio Octopus." *American Mercury* 23, 92 (1931): 385–400.

SECONDARY SOURCES

Adams, Mary Louise. "Youth, Corruptibility, and English-Canadian Postwar Campaigns against Indecency, 1948–1955." *Journal of the History of Sexuality* 6(1) July 1995): 89–117.
Adams, Michael. *Fire and Ice: The United States, Canada and the Myth of Converging Values*. Toronto: Penguin Canada, 2003.
Adria, Marco. *Technology and Nationalism*. Montreal and Kingston: McGill-Queen's University Press, 2010.
Ahlkvist, Jarl A. "Programming Philosophies and the Rationalization of Music Radio." *Media, Culture and Society* 23 (2001): 339–58.
Alasuutari, Pertti. "'I'm Ashamed to Admit It, But I Have Watched Dallas': The Moral Hierarchy of Television Programmes." *Media, Culture and Society* 14, 4 (1992): 561–82.
Anderson, Cameron D., and Laura B. Stephenson. "Moving Closer or Drifting Apart? Assessing the State of Public Opinion on the US-Canada Relationship." Research paper, the Canada-US Institute, University of Western Ontario, 2010.
Attallah, Paul. "Public Broadcasting in Canada: Legitimation Crisis and the Loss of Audience." *Gazette* 62, 3–4 (2000): 177–203.
Baade, Christina. *Victory through Harmony: The BBC and Popular Music in World War II*. Oxford: Oxford University Press, 2011.
Babaian, Sharon A. *Radio Communication in Canada: A Historical and Technological Survey*. Ottawa: National Museum of Science and Technology, 1992.

Badenoch, Alexander. "Making Sunday What It Actually Should Be: Sunday Radio Programming and the Re-Invention of Tradition in Occupied Germany, 1945–1949." *Historical Journal of Film, Radio and Television* 25, 4 (2005): 578–9.

Bailey, Michael. "Rethinking Public Service Broadcasting: The Historical Limits to Publicness." In *Media and Public Spheres*, ed. Richard Butsch, 100-1. Basingstoke: Palgrave Macmillan, 2007.

– "The Angel in The Ether: Early Radio and the Constitution of the Household." In *Narrating Media History*, ed. Michael Bailey, 53–65. London: Routledge, 2008.

Balzer, Timothy. "'In Case the Raid Is Unsuccessful …': Selling Dieppe to Canadians." *Canadian Historical Review* 87, 3 (2006): 409–30.

Barlow, William. "Black Music on Radio During the Jazz Age." *African American Review* 29, 2 (1995): 325–8.

– "Community Radio in the US: The Struggle for a Democratic Medium." *Media, Culture and Society* 10 (1988): 81–105.

Barnouw, Erik. *The Golden Web: A History of Broadcasting in the United States 1933–1953*. New York: Oxford University Press, 1968.

Bathrick, David. "Making a National Family with the Radio: The Nazi Wunschkonzert." *Modernism/Modernity* 4, 1 (1997): 115–27.

Bayley, Stephen. *Taste: The Secret Meaning of Things*. New York: Pantheon, 1991.

Beaty, Bart. "High Treason: Canadian Nationalism and Regulation of American Crime Comics." *Essays on Canadian Writing* 62 (Fall 1997): 85–107.

Benjamin, Louise M. "Defining the Public Interest and Protecting the Public Welfare in the 1920s: Parallels between Radio and Movie Regulation." *Historical Journal of Film, Radio and Television* 12, 1 (1992): 87–101.

Berkman, David. "The Not *Quite* So Inevitable Origins of Commercial Broadcasting in America," *Journal of Advertising History* 10, 1 (1987): 34–43.

Berland, Jody. "Marginal Notes on Cultural Studies in Canada." *University of Toronto Quarterly* 64, 4 (1995): 514–15.

– *North of Empire: Essays on the Cultural Technologies of Space*. Durham, NC: Duke University Press, 2009.

– "Radio Space and Industrial Time: Music Formats, Local Narratives and Technological Mediation." *Popular Music* 9, 2 (1990): 179–92.

Bérubé, Michael. "What's the Matter with Cultural Studies?" *Chronicle of Higher Education*, 14 September 2009, 14.

Bingham, Adrian. "'A Stream of Pollution through Every Part of the Country?' Morality, Regulation and the Modern Popular Press." In *Narrating Media History*, ed. Michael Bailey, 113–14. London: Routledge, 2008.

Biocca, Frank. "Media and Perceptual Shifts: Early Radio and the Clash of Musical Cultures." *Journal of Popular Culture* 24, 2 (1990): 1–15.

Bourdieu, Pierre. *Distinction: A Social Critique of the Judgement of Taste*. Trans. Richard Nice. Cambridge: Harvard University Press, 1984.

Briggs, Asa. *Serious Pursuits: Communications and Education*. Vol. 3: *The Collected Essays of Asa Briggs*. Urbana: University of Illinois Press, 1991.

– *The History of Broadcasting in the United Kingdom*. Vol. 1: *The Birth of Broadcasting*. Oxford: Oxford University Press, 1961.

– *The History of Broadcasting in the United Kingdom*. Vol 2: *The Golden Age of Wireless*. Oxford: Oxford University Press, 1965.

– *The History of Broadcasting in the United Kingdom*. Vol. 3: *The War of Words, 1939–1945*. Oxford: Oxford University Press, 1970.

Brison, Jeffrey. *Rockefeller, Carnegie, and Canada: American Philanthropy and the Arts and Letters in Canada*. Montreal and Kingston: McGill-Queen's University Press, 2005.

Brown, James A. "Selling Airtime for Controversy: NAB Self-regulation and Father Coughlin." *Journal of Broadcasting* 24, 2 (1980): 199–224.

Bruce, Jean. "Women in CBC Radio Talks and Public Affairs." *Canadian Oral History Association Journal* 5, 1 (1981-82): 7–18.

Bryson, Bethany. "'Anything But Heavy Metal': Symbolic Exclusion and Musical Dislikes." *American Sociological Review* 61, 5 (1996): 884–99.

Butsch, Richard. "Class and Audience Effects: A History of Research on Movies, Radio, and Television." *Journal of Popular Film and Television* 29, 3 (2001): 112–15.

– "Crystal Sets and Scarf-Pin Radios: Gender and the Construction of American Radio Listening in the 1920s." *Media, Culture and Society* 20 (1998): 557–72.

– *Media and Public Spheres*. Basingstoke: Palgrave Macmillan, 2007.

"Canada's Broadcasting Pioneers: 1918–1932" *Canadian Journal of Communication* 10, 3 (1984): 1–26.

Cardiff, David. "Mass Middlebrow Laughter: The Origins of BBC Comedy." *Media, Culture and Society* 10 (1988): 41–60.

– "The Serious and the Popular: Aspects of the Evolution of Style in the Radio Talk, 1928–1939." *Media, Culture and Society* 2, 1 (1980): 29–47.

– "Time, Money and Culture: BBC Programme Finances, 1927–1939." *Media, Culture and Society* 5 (1983): 373–93.

Castronovo, Russ. *Beautiful Democracy: Aesthetics and Anarchy in a Global Era*. Chicago: University of Chicago Press, 2007.

Champion, C.P. "Mike Pearson at Oxford: War, Varsity, and Canadianism" *Canadian Historical Review* 88, 2 (2007): 263–90.

Chan, Tak Wing, and John Goldthorpe. "Social Stratification and Cultural Consumption: Music in England." *European Sociological Review* 23, 1 (2007): 1–19.

Collins, Richard. *Culture, Communication, and National Identity: The Case of Canadian Television*. Toronto: University of Toronto Press, 1990.

Covert, Catherine. "'We May Hear Too Much': American Sensibility and the Response to Radio, 1919–1924." In *Mass Media between the Wars: Perceptions of Cultural Tension, 1918–1941*, ed. Catherine Covert and John Stevens, 199–220. Syracuse, NY: Syracuse University Press, 1984.

Craig, Douglas B. *Fireside Politics: Radio and Political Culture in the United States, 1920–1940*. Baltimore: Johns Hopkins University Press, 2000.

Craig, Steve. "'The Farmer's Friend': Radio Comes to Rural America, 1920–1927." *Journal of Radio Studies* 8, 2 (2001): 330–46.

– "'The More They Listen, the More They Buy': Radio and the Modernizing of Rural America." *Agricultural History* 80, 1 (2006): 1–16.

Cross, Gary, and Robert Proctor. *Packaged Pleasures: How Technology and Marketing Revolutionized Desire*. Chicago: University of Chicago Press, 2014.

Cull, Nicholas J. "Radio Propaganda and the Art of Understatement: British Broadcasting and American Neutrality, 1939–1941." *Historical Journal of Film, Radio and Television* 13, 4 (1993): 403–4.

Cupido, Robert. "The Medium, the Message and the Modern: The Jubilee Broadcast of 1927." *International Journal of Canadian Studies* 26 (Fall 2002): 101–23.

Curran, James, and Jean Seaton. *Power without Responsibility: The Press, Broadcasting and the Internet in Britain*, 7th ed. London: Routledge, 2010.

Dahlgren, Peter. "Reconfiguring Civic Culture in the New Media Milieu." In *Media and the Restyling of Politics: Consumerism, Celebrity and Cynicism*, ed. John Corner and Dick Pels, 151–70. London: Sage, 2003.

Dahlhaus, Carl. "Trivialmusik." Trans. Uli Sailer. In *Bad Music: The Music We Love to Hate*, ed. Christopher Washburne and Maiken Derno, 335–6. New York: Routledge, 2004.

Davies, Hannah, David Buckingham, and Peter Kelley. "In the Worst Possible Taste: Children, Television and Cultural Value." *European Journal of Cultural Studies* 3, 1 (2000): 5–25.

Day, Patrick. "American Popular Culture and New Zealand Broadcasting: The Reception of Early Radio Serials." *Journal of Popular Culture* 30, 1 (1996): 203–14.

Dennis, Paul M. "Chills and Thrills: Does Radio Harm Our Children? The Controversy over Program Violence during the Age of Radio." *Journal of the History of the Behavioral Sciences* 34, 1 (1998): 33–50.

Doerksen, Cliff. *American Babel: Rogue Radio Broadcasters of the Jazz Age*. Philadelphia: University of Pennsylvania Press, 2005.

Dolan, Josephine. "Aunties and Uncles: The B B C's Children's Hour and Liminal Concerns in the 1920s." *Historical Journal of Film, Radio and Television* 23, 4 (2003): 329–39.

Douglas, Susan. *Inventing American Broadcasting, 1899–1922*. Baltimore: Johns Hopkins University Press, 1987.

– *Listening In: Radio and the American Imagination, from Amos 'n' Andy and Edward R. Murrow to Wolfman Jack and Howard Stern*. New York: Random House, 1999.

Eaman, Ross. *Channels of Influence: C B C Audience Research and the Canadian Public*. Toronto: University of Toronto Press, 1994.

Edwardson, Ryan. *Canadian Content: Culture and the Quest for Nationhood*. Toronto: University of Toronto Press, 2008.

Eichner, Susanne. *Agency and Media Reception: Experiencing Video Games, Film, and Television*. Potsdam: Springer, 2014.

Emmison, Michael. "Social Class and Cultural Mobility: Reconfiguring the Cultural Omnivore Thesis." *Journal of Sociology* 39, 3 (2003): 211–30.

Epp, Michael. "'Good Bad Stuff': Editing, Advertising, and the Transformation of Genteel Literary Production in the 1890s." *American Periodicals* 24, 2 (2014): 186–205.

Evans, William. "Divining the Social Order: Class, Gender, and Magazine Astrology Columns." *Journalism and Mass Communication Quarterly* 73, 2 (1996): 389–400.

Ewen, Elizabeth, and Stuart Ewen. *Typecasting: On the Arts and Sciences of Human Inequality*. New York: Seven Stories Press, 2006.

Fahrni, Magda. "Counting the Costs of Living: Gender, Citizenship, and a Politics of Prices in 1940s Montreal." *Canadian Historical Review* 83, 4 (2002): 484–504.

Ferreira, Jim. "Cultural Conservatism and Mass Culture: The Case against Democracy." *Journal of American Culture* 13 (Spring 1990): 1–10.

Filion, Michel. "Broadcasting and Cultural Identity: The Canadian
Experience." *Media, Culture and Society* 18 (1996): 447–67.
– *Radiodiffusion et société distincte: Des origines de la radio jusqu'à la
Révolution tranquille au Québec*. Laval: Méridien 1994.
Flaherty, David, and Frank Manning. *The Beaver Bites Back? American
Popular Culture in Canada*. Montreal and Kingston: McGill-Queen's
University Press, 1993.
Fones-Wolf, Elizabeth. "Creating a Favorable Business Climate:
Corporations and Radio Broadcasting, 1934 to 1954." *Business History
Review* 73, 2 (1999): 221–55.
– "Defending Listeners' Rights: Labour and Media Reform in Postwar
America." *Canadian Journal of Communication* 31, 3 (2006): 221–55.
Fortner, Robert S. *Radio, Morality, and Culture: Britain, Canada, and the
United States, 1919–1945*. Carbondale: Southern Illinois University
Press, 2005.
Foust, James C. "Technology versus Monopoly: The Clear Channel Group
and the Clear Channel Debate, 1934–1941." *Journal of Radio Studies* 4,
1 (1997): 218–29.
Fowler, Gene, and Bill Crawford. *Border Radio: Quacks, Yodelers,
Pitchmen, Psychics, and Other Amazing Broadcasters of the American
Airwaves*. Austin: University of Texas Press, 2002.
Francesconi, Robert. "Art vs. the Audience: The Paradox of Modern Jazz."
Media, Journal of American Culture 4, 4 (1981): 70–80.
Frick, N. Alice. *Image in the Mind: CBC Radio Drama 1944 to 1954*.
Toronto: Canadian Stage and Arts Publications, 1987.
Friesen, Gerald. *Citizens and Nation: An Essay on History, Communication,
and Canada*. Toronto: University of Toronto Press, 2000.
Frith, Simon. "Music and Everyday Life." *Critical Quarterly* 44, 1 (2002):
35–48.
Gannon, Charles F. "Commercial Copy." *Annals of the American Academy
of Political and Social Science* 177 (January 1935): 159–62.
Gans, Herbert. *Popular Culture and High Culture: An Analysis and
Evaluation of Taste*. New York: Basic Books, 2008.
Garay, Ronald. "Guarding the Airwaves: Government Regulation of World
War II American Radio." *Journal of Radio Studies* 3 (1995–96): 130–48.
Gendron, Bernard. *Between Montmartre and the Mudd Club: Popular
Music and the Avant-garde*. Chicago: University of Chicago Press, 2002.
Gerson, Carole. *A Purer Taste: The Writing and Reading of Fiction in
English in Nineteenth-Century Canada*. Toronto: University of Toronto
Press, 1989.

Gilbert, A.D. "'On the Road to New York': The Protective Impulse and the English-Canadian Cultural Identity, 1896–1914." *Dalhousie Review* 58, 3 (1978): 405–17.

Giles, Judy. "Help for Housewives: Domestic Service and the Reconstruction of Domesticity in Britain, 1940–1950." *Women's History Review* 10, 2 (2001): 299–323.

Gitelman, Lisa. "Unexpected Pleasures: Phonographs and Cultural Identities in America, 1895–1915." In *Appropriating Technology: Vernacular Science and Social Power*, ed. Ron Eglash, Jennifer L. Croissant, Giovanni Di Chiro, and Rayvon Fouché, 331–44. Minneapolis: University of Minnesota Press, 2004.

Given, Jock. "Another Kind of Empire: The Voice of Australia, 1931–1939." *Historical Journal of Film, Radio and Television* 29, 1 (2009): 41.

Glancy, Mark. "Temporary American Citizens? British Audiences, Hollywood Films and the Threat of Americanization in the 1920s." *Historical Journal of Film, Radio and Television* 26, 4 (2006): 461–84.

Glynn, Kevin. *Tabloid Culture: Trash Taste, Popular Power, and the Transformation of American Television*. Durham, NC: Duke University Press, 2000.

Godfrey, Donald G. "Canadian Marconi: CFCF, the Forgotten Case." *Canadian Journal of Communication* 8, 4 (1982): 56–71.

Godfrey, Donald G., and David R. Spencer. "Canadian Marconi: CFCF Television From Signal Hill to the Canadian Television Network." *Journal of Broadcasting and Electronic Media* 44, 3 (2000): 437–55.

Godfried, Nathan. "Identity, Power, and Local Television: African Americans, Organized Labor and UHF-TV in Chicago, 1962–1968." *Historical Journal of Film, Radio and Television* 22, 2 (2002): 117–34.

Goodman, David. "Programming in the Public Interest: America's Town Meeting of the Air." In *NBC: America's Network*, ed. Michele Hilmes, 44–60. Berkeley: University of California Press, 2007.

– *Radio's Civic Ambition: American Broadcasting and Democracy in the 1930s*. Oxford: Oxford University Press, 2011.

Grant, George. *Lament for a Nation: The Defeat of Canadian Nationalism*. Toronto: McClelland and Stewart, 1965.

Griffen-Foley, Bridget. "Australian Commercial Radio, American Influences and the BBC." *Historical Journal of Film, Radio and Television* 30, 3 (2010): 337–55.

Gronow, Jukka. *Caviar with Champagne: Common Luxury and the Ideals of the Good Life in Stalin's Russia*. Oxford: Berg, 2003.

– *The Sociology of Taste*. London: Routledge, 1997.

Grundy, Pamela. "'We Always Tried to Be Good People': Respectability, Crazy Water Crystals, and Hillbilly Music on the Air, 1933–1935." *Journal of American History* 81, 4 (1995): 1591–620.

Gurstein, Rochelle. "Taste and 'the Conversible World' in the Eighteenth Century." *Journal of the History of Ideas* 61, 2 (2000): 203–21.

Hahn, Hazel. "Consumer Culture and Advertising." In *The Fin-de-Siècle World*, ed. Michael Saler, 392–404. New York: Routledge, 2015.

Hajkowski, Thomas. *The BBC and National Identity in Britain, 1922–53*. Manchester: Manchester University Press, 2010.

– "The BBC, the Empire, and the Second World War, 1939–1945." *Historical Journal of Film, Radio and Television* 22, 2 (2002): 135–55.

Han, Shin-Kap. "Unraveling the Brow: What and How of Choice in Musical Preference." *Sociological Perspectives* 46, 4 (2003): 435–59.

Hangen, Tona J. *Redeeming the Dial: Radio, Religion, and Popular Culture in America*. Chapel Hill University of North Carolina Press, 2002.

Haussen, Doris Fagundes. "Radio and Populism in Brazil: The 1930s and 1940s." *Television and New Media* 6, 3 (2005): 251–61.

Hayes, Joy Elizabeth. *Radio Nation: Communication, Popular Culture, and Nationalism in Mexico, 1920–1950*. Tucson: University of Arizona Press, 2000.

Te Heesen, Anke. *The World in a Box: The Story of an Eighteenth-Century Picture Encyclopedia*. Trans. Ann M. Hentschel. Chicago: University of Chicago Press, 2002.

Hendy, David. "Bad Language and BBC Radio Four in the 1960s and 1970s." *Twentieth Century British History* 17, 1 (2006): 74–102.

– *Life on Air: A History of Radio Four*. Oxford: Oxford University Press, 2007.

– "Pop Music Radio in the Public Service: BBC Radio 1 and New Music in the 1990s." *Media, Culture and Society* 22 (2000): 743–61.

Hill, Daniel Delis. *Advertising to the American Woman, 1900–1999*. Columbus: Ohio State University Press, 2002.

Hilmes, Michele. "British Quality, American Chaos: Historical Dualisms and What They Leave Out." *Radio Journal: International Studies in Broadcast and Audio Media* 1, 1 (2003): 13–27.

– "Invisible Men: *Amos 'n' Andy* and the Roots of Broadcast Discourse." *Critical Studies in Mass Communication* 10, 4 (1993): 301–21.

– *NBC: America's Network*. Berkeley: University of California Press, 2007.

– *Network Nations: A Transnational History of British and American Broadcasting*. New York: Routledge, 2012.

– *Radio Voices: American Broadcasting, 1922–1952*. Minneapolis: University of Minnesota Press, 1997.

– "Rethinking Radio." In *Radio Reader: Essays in the Cultural History of Radio,* ed. Michele Hilmes and Jason Loviglio, 1–19. London: Routledge, 2002.

Hilmes, Michele, and Jason Loviglio. *Radio Reader: Essays in the Culture History of Radio.* New York: Routledge, 2002.

Howe, Sondra Wieland. "The NBC Music Appreciation Hour: Radio Broadcasts of Walter Damrosch, 1928–1942." *Journal of Research in Music Education* 51, 1 (2003): 64–77.

Huber, Patrick. "The Interstate Old Fiddlers Contest of 1926: WOS, Rural Radio Audiences, and Music Making in the Missouri State Capitol." *Missouri Historical Review* 100, 1 (2005): 2–18.

Hudson, Heather E. "The Role of Radio in the Canadian North." *Journal of Communication* 27, 4 (1977): 130–9.

Igartua, José. *The Other Quiet Revolution: National Identities in English Canada, 1945–71.* Vancouver: UBC Press, 2006.

Jacobs, Jason. *The Intimate Screen: Early British Television Drama.* Oxford: Oxford University Press, 2000.

Jewell, Richard B. "Hollywood and Radio: Competition and Partnership in the 1930s." *Historical Journal of Film, Radio and Television* 4, 2 (1984): 125–41.

Johnson, Lelsey. "Radio and Everyday Life: The Early Years of Broadcasting in Australia, 1922–1945." *Media, Culture and Society* 3 (1981): 167–78.

– "The Intimate Voice of Australian Radio." *Historical Journal of Film, Radio and Television* 3, 1 (1983): 44–5.

– *The Unseen Voice: A Cultural History of Early Australian Radio.* London: Routledge, 1988.

Johnston, Russell. "The Early Trials of Protestant Radio, 1922–38." *Canadian Historical Review* 75, 3 (1994): 376–402.

– "The Emergence of Broadcast Advertising in Canada, 1919–1932." *Historical Journal of Film Radio and Television* 17, 1 (1997): 29–47.

Kammen, Michael. *American Culture, American Tastes: Social Change and the 20th Century.* New York: Knopf, 2000.

Katz, Richard S. "Public Patronage, Music and the BBC," *Journal of Broadcasting* 24 (1980): 244–6.

Keane, John. *The Media and Democracy.* Cambridge: Polity Press, 1991.

Keightley, Keir. "You Keep Coming Back Like a Song: Adult Audiences, Taste Panics, and the Idea of the Standard." *Journal of Popular Music Studies* 13 (2001): 7–40.

Kinahan, Anne-Marie. "Cultivating the Taste of the Nation: The National Council of Women of Canada and the Campaign against 'Pernicious'

Literature at the Turn of the Twentieth Century." *Canadian Journal of Communication* 32, 2 (2007) 161–79.

Klancher, Jon. *The Making of English Reading Audiences, 1790–1832.* Madison: University of Wisconsin Press, 1987. Cited in Graham Carr, "Literary History: Convergence or Resistance?" *Acadiensis* 23, 1 (1993): 178.

Klee, Marcus. "'Hands-Off Labour Forum': The Making and Unmaking of National Working-Class Radio Broadcasting in Canada, 1935–1944." *Labour/Le Travail* 35 (Spring 1995): 107–32.

Krattenmaker, Thomas G., and Lucas A. Powe, Jr. *Regulating Broadcast Programming.* Cambridge, MA, MIT Press/Washington, DC, AEI Press, 1994.

Kuffert, Len. "'Needful Supervision': Talks and Taste on Canadian Radio." *Canadian Journal of Media Studies* 10, 1 (2012): 1–15.

– "Tempest in the Tea Leaves: Broadcasting the Esoteric Arts and Mystic Sciences, 1937–53." *Canadian Historical Review* 91, 1 (2010): 1–26.

Kuhn, Annette. "Children, 'Horrific' Films, and Censorship in 1930s Britain." *Historical Journal of Film, Radio and Television* 22, 2 (2002): 197–202.

Lacey, Kate. *Feminine Frequencies: Gender, German Radio, and the Public Sphere.* Ann Arbor: University of Michigan Press, 1996.

– *Listening Publics: The Politics and Experience of Listening in the Media Age.* Cambridge, MA: Polity 2012.

Lasar, Matthew. "Hybrid Highbrow: The Pacifica Foundation and KPFA's Reconstruction of Elite Culture, 1946–1963." *Journal of Radio Studies* 5, 1 (1998): 49–67.

Lears, T.J. Jackson. *Fables of Abundance: A Cultural History of Advertising in America.* New York: Basic Books, 1994.

LeMahieu, D.L. *A Culture for Democracy: Mass Communication and the Cultural Mind in Britain between the Wars.* Oxford: Clarendon, 1988.

– "John Reith 1889–1971." In *After the Victorians: Private Conscience and Public Duty in Modern Britain*, ed. Susan Pedersen and Peter Mandler, 193–4. London: Routledge, 1994.

Lambert, R.S. "Radio Ideals and Educational Needs," *Adult Learning* 5, 2 (1939): 2–4.

Lemmings, David, and Claire Walker, eds. *Moral Panics, the Media and the Law in Early Modern England.* Basingstoke: Palgrave Macmillan, 2009.

Lenthall, Bruce. *Radio's America: The Great Depression and the Rise of Modern Mass Culture.* Chicago: University of Chicago Press, 2007.

Levine, Lawrence. *Highbrow/Lowbrow: The Emergence of Cultural Hierarchy in America.* Cambridge, MA: Harvard University Press, 1988.

Lewis, Peter. "Referable Words in Radio Drama." In *Broadcast Talk*, ed. Paddy Scannell, 14–30. London: Sage, 1991.

Lipschultz, Jeremy. *Broadcast and Internet Indecency: Defining Free Speech*. New York: Routledge, 2008.

Lipset, Seymour. *Continental Divide: The Values and Institutions of the United States and Canada*. New York: Routledge, 1990.

Litt, Paul. *The Muses, the Masses, and the Massey Commission*. Toronto: University of Toronto Press, 1992.

Lloyd, Justine. "Intimate Empire: Radio Programming for Women in Postwar Australia and Canada." *Storytelling* 6, 2 (2007): 131–41.

Locke, Ralph P. "Music Lovers, Patrons, and the 'Sacralization' of Culture in America." *19th-Century Music* 17, 2 (1993): 149–73.

Loviglio, Jason. "Eleanor Roosevelt and Radio's Intimate Public." In *Radio in the World: Papers from the 2005 Melbourne Radio Conference*, ed. Sianan Healy, Bruce Berryman and David Goodman, 257–66. Melbourne: RMIT Publishing, 2005.

– *Radio's Intimate Public: Network Broadcasting and Mass-Mediated Democracy*. Minneapolis: University of Minnesota Press, 2005.

Low, Brian. "The New Generation: Mental Hygiene and the Portrayals of Children by the National Film Board of Canada, 1946–1967." *History of Education Quarterly* 43, 4 (2003): 540–70.

Lum, Casey Man Kong. "An Intimate Voice from Afar: A Brief History of New York's Chinese-Language Wireless Radio." *Journal of Radio Studies* 2 (2000): 355–72.

Luneau, Aurélie. "Radio-Canada et la promotion de la culture franco-phone, 1936–1997." *Vingtième Siècle: Revue d'histoire* 55 (July–September 1997): 112–23.

Mackay, Robert. "Being Beastly to the Germans: Music, Censorship and the BBC in World War II." *Historical Journal of Film, Radio and Television* 20, 4 (2000): 514–25.

MacLean, Alyssa. "Canadian Studies and American Studies." In *A Concise Companion to American Studies*, ed. John Carlos Rowe, 387–406. Malden, MA: Wiley-Blackwell, 2010.

MacLennan, Anne. "American Network Broadcasting, the CBC, and Canadian Radio Stations during the 1930s: A Content Analysis." *Journal of Radio and Audio Media* 12, 1 (2005): 89–92.

– "Resistance to Regulation: Early Canadian Broadcasters and Listeners." In *Islands of Resistance: Pirate Radio in Canada*, ed. Andrea Langlois, Ron Sakolsky, and Marian van der Zon, 35–48. Vancouver: New Star, 2010.

- "Women, Radio Broadcasting and the Depression: A 'Captive' Audience from Household Hints to Story Time and Serials." *Women's Studies* 37, 6 (2008): 616–33.

Mahony, Christina Hunt. "Memory and Belonging: Irish Writers, Radio, and the Nation." *New Hibernia Review* 5, 1 (2001): 10–24.

Martin, Lawrence. *The Presidents and the Prime Ministers: Washington and Ottawa Face to Face – The Myth of Bilateral Bliss, 1867–1982*. Toronto: Doubleday Canada, 1982.

Mathews, Robin. *Canadian Identity: Major Forces Shaping the Life of a People*. Ottawa: Steel Rail, 1988.

McChesney, Robert W. "Graham Spry and the Future of Public Broadcasting: The 1997 Spry Memorial Lecture." *Canadian Journal of Communication* 24, 1 (1999): 25–47.

- *Rich Media, Poor Democracy: Communication Politics in Dubious Times*. New York: The New Press, 2000.

- *Telecommunications, Mass Media, and Democracy: The Battle for the Control of US Broadcasting, 1928–1935*. Oxford: Oxford University Press, 1993.

- "The Personal Is Political: The Political Economy of Noncommercial Radio Broadcasting in the United States." In *The Routledge Companion to Global Popular Culture*, ed. Toby Miller, 379–87. New York: Routledge, 2015.

McCracken, Allison. "'God's Gift to Us Girls': Crooning, Gender and the Re-Creation of American Popular Song, 1928–1933." *American Music* 17, 4 (1999): 365–95.

McCusker, Kristine M. "'Dear Radio Friend': Listener Mail and the National Barn Dance, 1931–1941." *American Studies* 39, 2 (1998): 173–95.

McFadden, Margaret T. "'America's Boy Friend Who Can't Get a Date': Gender, Race, and the Cultural Work of the Jack Benny Program, 1932–1946." *Journal of American History* 80, 1 (1993): 113–34.

McGuigan, Jim. *Cultural Populism*. London: Routledge, 1992.

McIntosh, Gillian. *The Force of Culture: Unionist Identities in Twentieth-Century Ireland*. Cork: Cork University Press, 1999.

McKay, Ian. "The Liberal Order Framework: A Prospectus for a Reconnaissance of Canadian History." *Canadian Historical Review* 81, 4 (2000): 617–45.

McLuhan, Marshall. *Understanding Media: The Extensions of Man*. Cambridge, MA: MIT Press, 1994.

Mennell, Steven. "Indigestion in the Long Nineteenth Century: Aspects of English Taste and Anxiety, 1800–1950." In *Food Consumption in*

Global Perspective: Essays in the Anthropology of Food in Honour of Jack Goody, ed. Jakob Klein and Anne Murcott, 135–58. Basingstoke: Palgrave Macmillan, 2014.

Meyers, Cynthia B. "The Problems with Sponsorship in US Broadcasting, 1930s–1950s: Perspectives from the Advertising Industry." *Historical Journal of Film, Radio and Television* 31, 3 (2011): 355–72.

Moores, Shaun. "'The Box on the Dresser': Memories of Early Radio and Everyday Life." *Media, Culture and Society* 10 (1988): 23–40.

Morgan, Eileen. "Question Time: Radio and the Liberalisation of Irish Public Discourse after World War II." *History Ireland* 9, 4 (2001): 38–41.

Moss, Peter, and Christine Higgins. "Radio Voices." *Media, Culture and Society* 6 (1984): 353–75.

Napoli, Philip. "Revisiting 'Mass Communication' and the 'Work' of the Audience in the New Media Environment." *Media, Culture and Society* 32, 3 (2010): 505–16.

Neulander, Joelle. *Programming National Identity: The Culture of Radio in 1930s France*. Baton Rouge: Louisiana State University Press 2009.

Newman, Kathy M. *Radio Active: Advertising and Consumer Activism, 1935–1947*. Berkeley: University of California Press, 2004.

Nicholas, Siân. "'Brushing Up Your Empire': Dominion and Colonial Propaganda on the BBC's Home Services, 1939–45." *Journal of Imperial and Commonwealth History* 31, 2 (2003): 207–30.

Niergarth, Kirk. "'Missionary for Culture': Walter Abell, 'Maritime Art' and Cultural Democracy, 1928–1944." *Acadiensis* 36, 1 (2006): 3–28.

Nolan, Michael. "An Infant Industry: Canadian Private Radio, 1919–36." *Canadian Historical Review* 70, 4 (1989): 496–518.

– "Canadian Election Broadcasting: Political Practices and Radio Regulation 1919–1939." *Journal of Broadcasting and Electronic Media* 29, 2 (1985): 175–88.

– *Foundations: Alan Plaunt and the Early Days of CBC Radio*. Montreal: CBC Enterprises, 1986.

Ohmann, Richard. "The Shaping of a Canon: US Fiction, 1960–1975." *Critical Inquiry* 10 (1983): 199–223.

O'Neill, Patrick B. "The Impact of Copyright Legislation upon the Publication of Sheet Music in Canada Prior to 1924." *Journal of Canadian Studies* 28, 3 (1993): 105–22.

Oswell, David. "Early Children's Broadcasting in Britain: Programming for a Liberal Democracy." *Historical Journal of Film, Radio and Television* 18, 3 (1998): 375–93.

Owen, Bruce. "Regulating Diversity: The Case of Radio Formats." *Journal of Broadcasting* 21 (1977): 305–20.

Parnis, Deborah. "Representation, Regulation and Commercial Radio Broadcasting in Canada." *International Journal of Canadian Studies* 17 (1998): 177–91.

Patnode, Randall. "'What These People Need Is Radio': New Technology, the Press, and Otherness in 1920s America." *Technology and Culture* 44 (April 2003): 285–305.

Peers, Frank W. "The Nationalist Dilemma in Canadian Broadcasting." In *Nationalism in Canada*, ed. Peter Russell, 252–67. Toronto: McGraw-Hill Ryerson, 1966.

– *The Politics of Canadian Broadcasting, 1920–1951*. Toronto: University of Toronto Press, 1969.

Pegg, Mark. *Broadcasting and Society, 1918–1939*. London: Croom Helm, 1983.

Perry, Seth. "'What the Public Expect': Consumer Authority and the Marketing of Bibles." *American Periodicals* 24, 2 (2014): 128–44.

Peters, John Durham. *Speaking into the Air: A History of the Idea of Communication*. Chicago: University of Chicago Press, 1999.

Peterson, Richard A., and Roger M. Kern. "Changing Highbrow Taste: From Snob to Omnivore." *American Sociological Review* 61, 5 (1996): 900–7.

Pickard, Victor. "The Battle over the FCC Blue Book: Determining the Role of Broadcast Media in a Democratic Society, 1945–48." *Media, Culture and Society* 33, 2 (2011): 171–91.

Pickering, Michael. "The BBC's Kentucky Minstrels: Blackface Entertainment on British Radio." *Historical Journal of Film, Radio and Television* 16, 2 (1996): 161–95.

Potolsky, Matthew. *The Decadent Republic of Letters: Taste, Politics, and Cosmopolitan Community from Baudelaire to Beardsley*. Philadelphia: University of Pennsylvania Press, 2013.

Potter, Simon J. "The BBC, the CBC, and the 1939 Royal Tour of Canada." *Cultural and Social History* 3, 4 (2006): 424–44.

– "Britishness, the BBC, and the Birth of Canadian Public Broadcasting, 1928–1936." In *Communicating in Canada's Past: Essays in Media History*, ed. Gene Allen and Daniel J. Robinson, 78–108. Toronto: University of Toronto Press, 2009.

– *Broadcasting Empire: The BBC and the British World, 1922–1970*. Oxford: Oxford University Press, 2012.

– "Strengthening the Bonds of the Commonwealth: The Imperial Relations Trust and Australian, New Zealand and Canadian

Broadcasting Personnel in Britain, 1946–1952." *Media History* 11, 3 (2005): 193–205.

– "Webs, Networks, and Systems: Globalization and the Mass Media in the Nineteenth- and Twentieth-Century British Empire." *Journal of British Studies* 46 (July 2007): 621–46.

– "Who Listened When London Called? Reactions to the BBC Empire Service in Canada, Australia and New Zealand, 1932–1939." *Historical Journal of Film, Radio and Television* 28, 4 (2008): 475–87.

Poulot, Dominique. "The Changing Roles of Art Museums." In *National Museums and Nation-Building in Europe 1750–2010: Mobilization and Legitimacy, Continuity and Change*, ed. Peter Aronsson and Gabriella Elgenius, 89–118. New York: Routledge, 2015.

Powell, Adam Clayton III. "You Are What You Hear." In *Radio: The Forgotten Medium*, ed. Edward C. Pease and Everette E. Dennis, 75–9. New Brunswick, NJ: Transaction, 1995.

Prang, Margaret. "The Origins of Public Broadcasting in Canada." *Canadian Historical Review* 46, 1 (1965): 1–31.

Prieur, Annick, and Mike Savage. "On 'Knowingness,' Cosmopolitanism and Busyness as Emerging Forms of Cultural Capital." In *The Routledge Companion to Bourdieu's "Distinction,"* ed. Phillipe Coulangeon and Julien Duval, 307–17. New York: Routledge, 2015.

Raboy, Marc. "Making Media: Creating Conditions for Communication in the Public Good, The 1997 Spry Memorial Lecture." *Canadian Journal of Communication* 31, 2 (2006): 289–306.

– *Missed Opportunities: The Story of Canada's Broadcasting Policy.* Montreal and Kingston: McGill-Queen's University Press, 1990.

Razlogova, Elena. *The Listener's Voice: Early Radio and the American Public*. Philadelphia: University of Pennsylvania Press, 2011.

– "True Crime Radio and Listener Disenchantment with Network Broadcasting, 1935–1946." *American Quarterly* 58, 1 (2006): 137–58.

Riccio, Barry D. "Popular Culture and High Culture: Dwight Macdonald, His Critics and the Ideal of Cultural Hierarchy in Modern America." *Journal of American Culture* 16, 4 (1993): 7–18.

Richards, Jeffrey. "The British Board of Film Censors and Content Control in the 1930s: Images of Britain." *Historical Journal of Film, Radio and Television* 1, 2 (1981): 95–116.

Robertson, Emma. "'I Get a Real Kick out of Big Ben': BBC Versions of Britishness on the Empire and General Overseas Service, 1932–1948." *Historical Journal of Film, Radio and Television* 28, 4 (2008): 459–73.

Romanow, Paula. "'The Picture of Democracy We Are Seeking': CBC Radio Forums and the Search for a Canadian Identity, 1930–1950." *Journal of Radio Studies* 12, 1 (2005): 104–19.

Rothenbuhler, Eric. "Commercial Radio as Communication." *Journal of Communication* 46, 1 (1996): 125–43.

– "Programming Decision Making in Popular Music Radio." *Communication Research* 12, 2 (1985): 209–32.

Rubin, Joan Shelley. "Information Please!": Culture and Expertise in the Interwar Period." *American Quarterly* 35, 5 (1983): 499–517.

Russo, Alexander. "An American Right to an 'Unannoyed Journey'? Transit Radio as a Contested Site of Public Space and Private Attention, 1949–1952." *Historical Journal of Film, Radio and Television* 29, 1 (2009): 1–25.

– "Defensive Transcriptions: Radio Networks, Sound-On-Disc Recording, and the Meaning of Live Broadcasting." *Velvet Light Trap: A Critical Journal of Film and Television* 54 (2004): 4–17.

Rutherford, Paul. "Made in America: The Problem of Mass Culture in Canada." In *The Beaver Bites Back? American Popular Culture in Canada*, ed. David Flaherty and Frank Manning, 260–80. Montreal and Kingston: McGill-Queen's University Press, 1993.

Savage, Barbara Dianne. *Broadcasting Freedom: Radio, War, and the Politics of Race, 1938–1948*. Chapel Hill: University of North Carolina Press, 1999.

Savran, David. *Highbrow/Lowdown: Theater, Jazz, and the Making of the New Middle Class*. Ann Arbor: University of Michigan Press, 2010.

Scannell, Paddy. "For-Anyone-as-Someone Structures." *Media, Culture and Society* 22, 1 (2000): 5–24.

– "Music for the Multitude? The Dilemmas of the BBC's Music Policy, 1923–1946." *Media, Culture and Society* 3 (1981): 243–60.

– "Public Service Broadcasting and Modern Public Life." *Media, Culture and Society* 11 (1989): 135–66.

– "Public Service Broadcasting: The History of a Concept." In *Understanding Television*, ed. Andrew Goodwin and Garry Whannel, 11-29. London: Routledge, 1990.

– *Radio, Television and Modern Life: A Phenomenological Approach*. Oxford: Blackwell, 1996.

Scannell, Paddy, and David Cardiff. *A Social History of British Broadcasting*. Vol 1: *1922–1939: Serving the Nation*. Oxford: Basil Blackwell, 1991.

Schwartz, Barry. *Vertical Classifications: A Study in Structuralism and the Sociology of Knowledge*. Chicago: University of Chicago Press, 1981.

Sconce, Jeffrey. *Haunted Media: Electronic Presence from Telegraphy to Television*. Durham, NC: Duke University Press, 2000.

Scott, James C. *Seeing Like a State: How Certain Schemes to Improve the Human Condition Have Failed*. New Haven: Yale University Press, 1998.

Scullion, Adrienne. "BBC Radio in Scotland, 1923–1939: Devolution, Regionalism and Centralism." *Northern Scotland* 15 (1995): 64–93.

Seiden, Martin. *Who Controls the Mass Media? Popular Myths and Economic Realities*. New York: Basic Books, 1974.

Shapiro, Stuart. "Places and Spaces: The Historical Interaction of Technology, Home, and Privacy." *Information Society* 14 (1998): 275–84.

Shaw, Colin. *Deciding What We Watch: Taste, Decency, and Media Ethics in the UK and the usa*. Oxford: Clarendon, 1999.

Shrum, Wesley Monroe Jr. *Fringe and Fortune: The Role of Critics in High and Popular Art*. Princeton: Princeton University Press, 1996.

Skinner, David. "Divided Loyalties: The Early Development of Canada's 'Single' Broadcasting System." *Journal of Radio Studies* 12, 1 (2005): 136–55.

Slotten, Hugh. *Radio and Television Regulation: Broadcast Technology in the United States, 1920-1960*. Baltimore: Johns Hopkins University Press, 2000.

– *Radio's Hidden Voice: The Origins of Public Broadcasting in the United States*. Urbana: University of Illinois Press, 2009.

Smethers, J. Steven, and Lee Jolliffe. "Homemaking Programs: The Recipe for Reaching Women Listeners on the Midwest's Local Radio." *Journalism History* 24, 4 (1998–99): 138–47.

Smith, Allan. "Canadian Culture, the Canadian State, and the New Continentalism." *Canadian-American Public Policy* 3 (October 1990): 1–36.

Smith, F. Leslie. "Quelling Radio's Quacks: The FCC's First Public-Interest Programming Campaign." *Journalism Quarterly* 71, 3 (1994): 594–608.

Smith, Philip, and Tim Phillips. "Collective Belonging and Mass Media Consumption: Unraveling How Technological Medium and Cultural Genre Shape the National Imaginings of Australians." *Sociological Review* 54, 4 (2006): 91–116.

Smulyan, Susan. "Live from Waikiki: Colonialism, Race, and Radio in Hawaii, 1934–1963." *Historical Journal of Film, Radio and Television* 27, 1 (2007): 63–75.

– "Radio Advertising to Women in Twenties America: A Latchkey to Every Home." *Historical Journal of Film, Radio and Television* 13, 3 (1993): 299–314.

Smythe, Dallas. *Dependency Road: Communications, Capitalism, Consciousness, and Canada*. Norwood, NJ: Ablex, 1981.

Socolow, Michael J. "Questioning Advertising's Influence over American Radio: The Blue Book Controversy of 1945–1947." *Journal of Radio Studies* 9, 2 (2002): 282–302.

Spencer, David R. "The Social Origins of Broadcasting: Canada, 1919–1945." *American Journalism* 9, 3–4 (1992): 96–110.

Spencer, David R., and Catherine M. Bolan. "Election Broadcasting in Canada: A Brief History." In *Election Broadcasting in Canada*, ed. Frederick J. Fletcher, 3–38. Toronto: Dundurn Press, 1991.

Stamm, Michael. "Questions of Taste: Interest Group Liberalism and the Campaigns to Save Classical Music Radio in Post-World War II Chicago." *Historical Journal of Film, Radio and Television* 25, 2 (2005): 291–309.

Starker, Steven. *Evil Influences: Crusades against the Mass Media*. New Brunswick, NJ: Transaction/Rutgers, 1989.

Steemers, Jeannette. "In Search of a Third Way: Balancing Public Purpose and Commerce in German and British Public Service Broadcasting." *Canadian Journal of Communication* 26 (2001): 69–87.

Street, Seán. "BBC Sunday Policy and Audience Response, 1930–1945." *Journal of Radio Studies* 7, 1 (2000): 161–79.

– *Crossing the Ether: Pre-War Public Service Radio and Commercial Competition in the UK*. Eastleigh: John Libbey, 2006.

Stursberg, Peter. *Mister Broadcasting: The Ernie Bushnell Story*. Toronto: Peter Martin Associates, 1971.

Suisman, David. *Selling Sounds: The Commercial Revolution in American Music*. Cambridge, MA: Harvard University Press, 2012.

Swirski, Peter. *From Lowbrow to Nobrow*. Montreal and Kingston: McGill-Queen's University Press, 2005.

Tausk, Victor. "On the Origin of the Influencing Machine in Schizophrenia." Translated by Dorian Feigenbaum. *Psychoanalytic Quarterly* 2 (1933): 519–56.

Taylor, Timothy D. "Music and the Rise of Radio in 1920s America: Technological Imperialism, Socialization, and the Transformation of Intimacy." *Historical Journal of Film, Radio and Television* 22, 4 (2002): 425–43.

Thompson, John Herd, and Stephen J. Randall. *Canada and the United States: Ambivalent Allies*, 4th ed. Montreal and Kingston: McGill-Queen's University Press, 2008.

Tichi, Cecelia. *Electronic Hearth: Creating an American Television Culture*. New York: Oxford University Press, 1991.

Turvey, Gerry. "'Another of Those Sex Films!': The Transgressive Cinema of Harold Weston, 1914–17." *Early Popular Visual Culture* 9, 1 (2011): 57–73.

Vaillant, Derek. "Sounds of Whiteness: Local Radio, Racial Formation, and Public Culture in Chicago, 1921–1935." *American Quarterly* 54, 1 (2002): 25–66.

– "'Your Voice Came in Last Night ... But I Thought It Sounded a Little Scared': Rural Radio Listening and 'Talking Back' during the Progressive Era in Wisconsin, 1920–1932." In *Radio Reader: Essays in the Cultural History of Radio*, ed. Michele Hilmes and Jason Loviglio, 63–88. London: Routledge, 2002.

VanCour, Shawn. "Popularizing the Classics: Radio's Role in the American Music Appreciation Movement, 1922–34." *Media, Culture and Society* 31, 2 (2009): 289–307.

van Eijck, Koen. "Social Differentiation in Musical Taste Patterns." *Social Forces* 79, 3 (2001): 1163–84.

Vipond, Mary. "'A Living, Moving Pageant': The CBC's Coverage of the Royal Tour of 1939." In *More Than Words: Readings in Transport, Communication and the History of Postal Communication*, ed. John Willis, 335–50. Gatineau, QC: Canadian Museum of Civilization, 2007.

– "British or American?: Canada's 'Mixed' Broadcasting System in the 1930s." *Radio Journal: International Studies in Broadcast and Audio Media* 2, 2 (2004): 89–100.

– "Censorship in a Liberal State: Regulating Talk on Canadian Radio in the Early 1930s." *Historical Journal of Film, Radio and Television* 30, 1 (2010): 75–94.

– "CKY Winnipeg in the 1920s: Canada's Only Experiment in Monopoly Broadcasting." *Manitoba History* 12 (1986): 2–13.

– "Cultural Authority and Canadian Public Broadcasting in the 1930s: Hector Charlesworth and the CRBC." *Journal of Canadian Studies* 42, 1 (2008): 59–82.

– "Desperately Seeking the Audience for Early Canadian Radio." In *Nation, Ideas, Identities: Essays in Honour of Ramsay Cook*, ed. Michael D. Behiels and Marcel Martel, 86–96. Toronto: Oxford University Press, 2000.

– "Going Their Own Way: The Relationship between the Canadian Radio Broadcasting Commission and the BBC, 1933–36." *Media History* 15, 1 (2009): 71–83.

– *Listening In: The First Decade of Canadian Broadcasting, 1922–1932.* Montreal and Kingston: McGill-Queen's University Press, 1992.

- "London Listens: The Popularity of Radio in the Depression." *Ontario History* 88, 1 (1996): 47–50.
- "'Please Stand By for That Report': The Historiography of Early Canadian Radio." *Fréquence/Frequency* 7–8 (1997): 13–32.
- "Public Service Broadcasting and Manitoba Listeners in the 1930s." *Manitoba History* 57 (February 2008): 16–26.
- "The Beginnings of Public Broadcasting in Canada: The CRBC, 1932–1936." *Canadian Journal of Communication* 19, 2 (1994): 151–71.
- "The Canadian Radio Broadcasting Commission in the 1930s: How Canada's First Public Broadcaster Negotiated 'Britishness.'" In *Canada and the British World: Culture, Migration, and Identity*, ed. Philip Buckner and R. Douglas Francis, 270–87. Vancouver: UBC Press, 2006.
- "The Continental Marketplace: Authority, Advertisers, and Audiences in Canadian News Broadcasting, 1932–1936." *Journal of Radio Studies* 6, 1 (1999): 169–84.
- "The Mass Media in Canadian History: The Empire Day Broadcast of 1939." *Canadian Historical Association Journal* 14 (2003): 1–21.
- "The Royal Tour of 1939 as a Media Event." *Canadian Journal of Communication* 35, 1 (2010): 149–72.
Walden, Keith. "Toronto Society's Response to Celebrity Performers, 1887–1914." *Canadian Historical Review* 89, 3 (2008): 373–97.
Waldfogel, Joel. *The Tyranny of the Market: Why You Can't Always Get What You Want*. Cambridge, MA: Harvard University Press, 2007.
Ward, Ian. "The Early Use of Radio for Political Communication in Australia and Canada: John Henry Austral, Mr. Sage and the Man from Mars." *Australian Journal of Politics and History* 45, 3 (1999): 311–29.
Warfield, Patrick. "Amateur and Professional, Permanent and Transient: Orchestras in the District of Columbia, 1877–1905." In *American Orchestras in the Nineteenth Century*, ed. John Spitzer, 194–218. Chicago: University of Chicago Press, 2012.
Webb, Jeff A. "Constructing Community and Consumers: Joseph R. Smallwood's Barrelman Radio Programme." *Journal of the Canadian Historical Association* 8, 1 (1997): 166–86.
- "Cultural Intervention: Helen Creighton's Folksong Broadcasts, 1938–39." *Canadian Folklore* 14, 2 (1992): 159–70.
- *The Voice of Newfoundland: A Social History of the Broadcasting Corporation of Newfoundland, 1939–1949*. Toronto: University of Toronto Press, 2008.
- "Who Speaks for the Public? The Debate over Government or Private Broadcasting in Newfoundland, 1939–1949." *Acadiensis* 35, 1 (2005): 74–93.

Weber, Wiliam. "Mass Culture and the Reshaping of European Musical Taste, 1770–1870." *International Review of the Aesthethics and Sociology of Music* 25, 1/2 (1994): 175–90.

Weir, E. Austin. *The Struggle for National Broadcasting in Canada.* Toronto: McClelland and Stewart, 1965.

Whitehead, Kate. *The Third Programme: A Literary History.* Oxford: Clarendon, 1989.

Williams, Raymond. "A Kind of Gresham's Law." *The Highway* 49 (February 1958): 107–10.

Zuidervaart, Lambert. "Art Is No Fringe: An Introduction," in *The Arts, Community, and Cultural Democracy*, ed. Lambert Zuidervaart and Henry Luttikhuizen, 1–12. Basingstoke, UK: Macmillan, 2000.

THESES, AND DISSERTATIONS

Baillargeon, Philippe J. "The CBC and the Cold War Mentality, 1946–1952." MA thesis, Carleton University, 1987.

Berland, Jody. "Cultural Re/percussions: The Social Production of Music Broadcasting in Canada." PhD diss., York University, 1986.

Counihan, Michael S. "The Construction of Australian Broadcasting: Aspects of Australian Radio in the 1920s." MA thesis, Monash University, 1981.

Graham, Sean. "Radio Revolution, Classic Concerns: The Development Of Canadian Broadcasting, 1927–1936." MA thesis, University of Regina, 2009.

Parnis, Deborah. "'Tuning in': The Political Economy Of Commercial Radio Broadcasting in Canada." PhD diss., Carleton University, 1994.

Rickwood, Roger. "Canadian Broadcasting Policy and the Private Broadcasters: 1936–1968." PhD diss., University of Toronto, 1976.

Rothwell, Carmel Dickson. "Andrew Allan, Nathan Cohen, and Mavor Moore: Cultural Nationalism and the Growth of English-Canadian Drama 1945 to 1960." MA thesis, University of Ottawa, 1993.

Index